Contents

Sparks of Innovation in Human-Computer Interaction,
B. Shneiderman, Ed., Ablex Publ., Norwood, NJ (1993)

Preface

The occasion for this book is the 10th Anniversary of the Human-Computer Interaction Laboratory (HCIL) at the University of Maryland. I have selected two dozen key papers from more than a hundred to represent the work of many participants. My section introductions tell how we do what we do, including some of our failures and background stories that are not appropriate for journal papers. Many papers were trimmed to emphasize the cogent points. They weave together the threads of our work into a unified fabric that reveals the patterns of development. It was difficult to choose the best papers; these exemplify different research methodologies and show the maturation of human-computer interaction research. This book is a tribute to the faculty, staff, visitors, and students who have shared in a decade of work.

Sparks of innovation are the ideas and processes that stimulated these creative and devoted participants. This metaphor emerged as I told potential supporters that our lab felt like a group around a blazing campfire: telling stories, sharing ideas, and enjoying each other's company. Some people (academic and industrial researchers, and commercial developers) enjoyed watching our fire from a distance (we are happy to send technical reports), while others preferred to come and join us for a story or two (we enjoy doing demonstrations and having long-term visitors participate in projects), but we do need some people to throw a log on the fire occasionally (collaborate and support our efforts financially). I thought this told our story well, but an old friend, Fred Hansen, now a researcher affiliated with Carnegie-Mellon University, commented that our lab had something more. He said that we understood the art of fire-making, and that the largest benefit to our visitors and supporters was learning how to spark fires within their own organizations.

We are proud of our role in the emergence of human-computer interaction, a new inter-discipline devoted to researching how people use computers and to improving user interface designs. As in any new venture, we question and are challenged about what we are doing, but there is a growing confidence that comes when there are ten scientific journals in an area that had only one just a decade ago. The confidence stems also from the numerous well-attended and invigorating conferences that are held around the world almost every month, and the stream of national policy documents, corporate business plans, and academic departments declaring their focus on human-computer interaction.

I have gained much by reading earlier work and by frequent contact with colleagues. By learning about our experiences, I hope other academic researchers and advanced commercial developers can speed their efforts and make their own fires.

Acknowledgements

This book was created by the diligent and intense efforts of Lian Arrow, Teresa Casey, Ruth Golembiewski, and Ara Kotchian, who massaged various forms of electronic documents and figures into a consistent and appealing style. Individual authors contributed by writing new sections, redoing figures to put everything in electronic form, revising and trimming published papers, and by commenting on drafts. Robert Jacob, Larry Koved, Charles Kreitzberg, Janis Morariu, and Bob Singers were especially helpful with their constructive and supportive guidance. The staff at Ablex Publishers worked rapidly in making arrangements to publish this book.

Ben Shneiderman
College Park, Maryland
April1993

Sparks of Innovation in Human-Computer Interaction,
B. Shneiderman, Ed., Ablex Publ., Norwood, NJ (1993)

HCIL

Overview: fuel for a new discipline

Increasingly, researchers and designers are conducting experiments on the profound effects that design improvements can have on users: reduced learning times, faster performance on tasks, lower rate of errors, higher subjective satisfaction, and better human retention over time. Theories, taxonomies, and models at differing levels of abstraction are competing for attention. Empirical research has produced breakthroughs in the design of menu selection, form fill-in, pointing devices, and direct manipulation interactions.

Knowledgeable managers are recognizing that excellent user interfaces produce dramatic marketing advantages because they can greatly increase productivity, substantially reduce fatigue and errors, and enable users to be more creative in solving problems. When the user interface is well-designed, users should not only be performing well, but should also experience a sense of accomplishment and a positive regard for the designer of the interface. Usability testing, guidelines documents, and user interface management software tools (UIMS) are the three pillars of successful user interface development. Repeated testing in a usability lab with small numbers (3-12) of typical users performing typical tasks has proven to be very successful in inspiring improved designs and finding flaws. Hundreds of labs have been created in development organizations and a society of usability professionals has sprouted. Guidelines documents are successful in promoting consistency, defining organizational identity, and speeding development. Of course methods for enforcement, enhancement, and exemption must be part of the process. UIMSs dramatically speed development and allow easy modification, thereby supporting the pursuit of quality.

Academic research in human-computer interaction combines the experimental methods and intellectual framework of cognitive psychology with powerful tools from computer science. HCI benefits from related fields such as education where computers are increasingly used in programs ranging from elementary school through professional skills development. The theory and measurement techniques of educational psychology are applicable to studying the learning process in novice computer users. Business system design and management decision making are endeavors which are being increasingly shaped by the nature of the computer facilities. Library and information services are also dramatically influenced by the availability of computer-based systems.

Successful User Interfaces

Usability Lab & Iterative Testing

User Interface Management Systems

Guidelines Documents

Controlled Experimental Research

Theories and Models of Human-Computer Interaction

At the Human-Computer Interaction Laboratory, our goal is to do research on the theory and design of interactive systems that enable users to perform tasks rapidly, learn skills easily, and communicate in an atmosphere of competence, satisfaction, and confidence.

We want to replace arguments about "user friendly systems" with a more scientific approach. We emphasize controlled experiments which yield more objective and reliable results, but also find informal usability studies are helpful in understanding design problems. We specify user communities carefully and identify tasks as thoroughly as possible. Then we turn to measurable criteria such as:

- time to learn specific functions
- speed of task performance
- rate of human errors
- subjective user satisfaction
- human retention of functions over time

These criteria can be established before implementation and measured during an acceptance test. These criteria also serve as dependent variables in experimental research. Our orientation is towards direct manipulation designs that empower users, rather than anthropomorphic agents (e.g. talking bank machines or deceptive teaching machines) and artificially intelligent expert systems (designed to replace rather than support human users). We blend basic research themes and theories with practical projects that can inspire commercial developers.

A typical project team has a senior researcher and one to two graduate students, with help from other faculty, students or staff as needed. There is usually some software development (we try to limit the effort by using powerful tools), which generates comments to spur refinement, and then an empirical evaluation with typical users as subjects. I am devoted to empirical evaluations because they overcome the fog of wishful thinking and produce the clarity that leads to further innovation. Successful experiments can be difficult to conduct, especially in novel domains. We often must re-run experiments till we develop the appropriate training, controls, and tasks that lead to significant results and useful insights.

Administrative organization

The Human-Computer Interaction Laboratory (HCIL) brings together faculty at the University of Maryland who share an interest in these topics. The main participants are the Department of Computer Science, the Department of Psychology, and the College of Library and Information Services, with contributions from the School of Education, College of Business, Computer Science Center, and other units. I've especially appreciated the active and enduring efforts of my respected colleagues Prof. Kent Norman (Department of Psychology), Prof. Gary Marchionini (College of Library and Information Services), and Research Scientist Catherine Plaisant (Center for Automation Research). Valuable contributions over the years have been made by Charles Grantham, Yoram Kochavy, and Richard Chimera. We have conducted joint research projects, interdisciplinary seminars, an annual symposium and open house with presentation of research, cooperation in graduate programs, coordination in developing experimental facilities, work with state and federal agencies, assistance to Maryland corporations, and collaboration with corporate sponsors.

Since May 1983, the Human-Computer Interaction Laboratory has been one of the constituent laboratories in the Center for Automation Research under the direction of Prof. Azriel Rosenfeld. The Center for Automation Research provides assistance in securing supported projects and in administration. This interdisciplinary Center also includes the world-famous Computer Vision Laboratory and a Robotics Laboratory.

We publish in leading journals and present results at major conferences. Our work has led to commercial products such as our hypertext system,Hyperties, which is now disseminated and expanded by Cognetics Corporation, Princeton Jct., NJ, and home automation systems created by Custom Command Systems, College Park, MD. In addition, the University's Office of Technology Liaison licenses several of our software systems and our Questionnaire for User Interface Satisfaction.

We receive external support from the projects that we pursue for corporations (such as Apple, AT&T, General Electric, IBM, Johnson Controls, NCR Corporation, and Sun Microsystems) and government agencies (such as NASA, National Science Foundation, Library of Congress, National Library of Medicine, and the National Center for Health Statistics). The State of Maryland has supported us in working with two large companies (GE Information Services and Hughes Network Systems) and two small companies (Corabi Telemetrics and Custom Command Systems) under the Maryland Industrial Partnerships (MIPS) program. Several Japanese companies (such as NEC, Sony, Panasonic, and Toshiba) have provided support and sent their employees to work on our projects during year-long visits. We've appreciated other support from University of Maryland units such as the Institute for Systems Research, the Departments of Computer Science and Psychology, the College of Library and Information Services, the Institute for Advanced Computer Studies, and the Engineering Research Center.

Sparks of Innovation in Human-Computer Interaction,
B. Shneiderman, Ed., Ablex Publ., Norwood, NJ (1993)

Introduction: supporting the process of innovation

Innovation is a mysterious process. As a community we have been repeatedly, but not consistently, successful in research and practical design, but I still don't know how to predict when and where innovation will appear. Even when I see a bright blaze, I have a hard time predicting how others will perceive our novel ideas, and where they will take them. My fantasy is to have a crystal ball to tell me which of our prototypes or papers will be applied, disseminated, referenced, and extended. This highly social process of innovation within our community and the reception or rejection of novel ideas is fascinating, surprising, sometimes satisfying, and sometimes disturbing.

Over the years I have identified some of the sparks that can help start a research and development fire. No one spark is guaranteed to start a fire, and sometimes even many sparks are not enough. I've tried to report on successful streams of work so as to guide other academic or industrial groups doing basic research and commercial developers building novel systems. My hope is that by reading about our patterns of work, managers of related projects will not only appreciate what we have done, but be able to avoid some mistakes and do even better. Of course, different personalities, organizational goals, or constraints will require variations on our methods.

Our basic approach has been to keep our communities small, personal, flexible, and open. Rather than a rigid hierarchy, I see our organization as a family of cooperating laboratories with commitments to their own university units. Large budgets and bureaucracies are necessary for some projects, especially product development, but innovation seems to be very personal and driven by an individual's passion. We also keep our process open, avoiding proprietary agreements, sharing ideas internally and externally, and avidly learning about the work of others. When there are external stakeholders, we produce our deliverables and meet our deadlines, but the novelty often emerges when individuals pursue an intuition, respond to a hunch, or are provoked by a problem. If someone has an idea they wish to pursue, I encourage it, while making sure that commitments are met. Someone with a good idea will pursue it on their own, late at night and even if they have other papers to write or exams for which they must study. My novel ideas come when I have taken care of the daily requirements and can get away to think big thoughts. Skiing helps loosen my imagination, but beaches or forests with time for reflection are effective too.

When a new idea is raised, community discussion is a helpful reality check: Does it make sense? Has it been done before? Who would benefit? Since we have modest resources, we must work on projects that have high payoffs with realistic effort. I talk about finding projects that reach new destinations rapidly by "tunneling through." At the same time, we try to be practical rather than visionary. We try to build something that really works and then give it an honest empirical evaluation. Once an idea has passed our review, we may seek support to expand, refine, and develop it. In short, our strategy is to open ourselves to innovation, refine through discussion, build to test, and tell the story. Research has a serious side and it requires hard work, but when it is going well it is great fun.

From sparks to fire

The right team of people is vital to turning sparks into fire. Well-trained, brilliant, motivated, diligent, cooperative, and friendly people enhance the chance of success and make the process more enjoyable. You can measure some of these variables by looking at transcripts or standardized test scores (SAT, GRE), but personal judgments are more important. We ask those who want to join our group for reference letters and we conduct personal interviews. Personal judgment of how it would be to work with someone also counts (we envision having lunch with them). Capacity for laughter is a must and visible laugh lines are an asset. These hurdles apply to graduate students and staff, as well as for undergraduate assistants. They make it clear that we are serious about who we choose. New recruits realize that those who participate in the lab have survived similar scrutiny. The process helps us ensure that we are getting good people, and once they begin working, they are motivated to demonstrate that they really are that good.

Our screening methods work well, but imperfectly. On more than one occasion someone who interviewed well did not work out. I start new members on specific short-term tasks and then check in to make sure they deliver. When repeated requests are not satisfied and the excuses mount, I let students or staff know that their work does not match our needs and give them notice that they will not be renewed after the semester ends. This was hard to do the first time, but I discovered that such a clear message, when delivered gently, is appreciated because of its clarity and honesty. What surprised me is the powerful and positive impact of dismissing someone on those who remained. They recognized that the lab management knew the difference between good and poor work, and they took increased pride in their own work. I suppose they were also motivated to produce results to avoid a similar fate.

We begin by choosing excellent and pleasant people. Then the Maryland Way is to foster innovation through seven sparks:

1. Choose a good driving problem
2. Become immersed in related work
3. Clarify short-term and long-term goals
4. Balance individual and group interests
5. Work hard
6. Communicate with internal and external stakeholders
7. Get past failures. Celebrate success!

The Maryland way

Choose a good driving problem

Fred Brooks has commented on the positive influence of choosing a 'good driving problem.' My experience supports his contention. A 'good driving problem' often has a clear goal, for example, build a museum kiosk that patrons can use with zero-trial learning or enable pathologists to operate a microscope remotely. In general, successful projects share these attributes:

- clear and novel challenge: hard enough to be interesting, but modest enough to be attained;
- realistic mechanisms to measure success: specific functionality, human performance goals, or subjective satisfaction;

- well-specified audience: build a system for specific users, clarify a theory for researchers, write a paper for a journal, or deliver reports or products to financial supporters;
- skills required match the researcher's background.

Finding good problems is like antique hunting: you are not quite sure what you want but when you see it, you know it! In the early stages of choosing a problem we brainstorm to come up with divergent possibilities. Then over a period of a few weeks we discard the extreme ideas, refine the remaining possibilities, and focus on one. Constraints can be helpful, such as the student must complete the work by a certain date, or our lab must deliver specified results to a supporter.

A good driving problem has a solution path that is reasonably clear at the beginning, but detours and new routes often appear. The path for our group is typically to identify a realistic need, design an interface, refine the design, build the software, refine the software, test the interface, refine it, and test it again. The need may spawn an application, such as information access by touchscreens for museum patrons, or a basic science quest, such as attempting to build a touchscreen that provides pixel level precision faster than a mouse. Applications lead to observations, field studies, interface critiques, usability studies, or data logging. Basic science leads to controlled experiments, with careful statistical analysis and replications.

Our greatest successes have come from steady commitments to a sequence of related projects over many years. Our quest for high precision pointing and also for hypertext design began in 1983 and continued to 1990. Now our quests include dynamic queries for filtering information from databases, hierarchical information visualization, novel widgets for extending User Interface Management Systems, automated metrics for evaluating screen designs, and methods to enable programming-in-the-user-interface (PITUI). A continuing challenge is the one-in-a-million family of problems. This includes some understanding and guidelines for selecting an item from a menu of 10 items, 100 items, 1000 items, 10,000 items, 100,000 items, and 1,000,000 items. We are often called upon to help design interfaces that include some piece of the one-in-a-million problem, but the constraints vary greatly and we have yet to have a completely specified set of guidelines. Other problems for researchers can be found in my 1986 SIGCHI Keynote Address in Boston: Seven plus or minus two central issues in human-computer interaction (*Proc. CHI '86: Human Factors in Computing Systems*, ACM, 343-350).

Become immersed in related work

I tell my students that I expect them to become the "world's leading expert" on the problem they are investigating. They must become knowledgeable with academic research papers on related studies, commercial products as examples, and personal contact with active researchers. These requirements may seem obvious, but as a journal editor and reader, I am often disturbed to see inadequate knowledge of related and previous work. I expect my students to educate me about related work.

My students must go to the library or the Internet and chase down every reference on their topic. This process has the dual benefits of compelling them to work on something narrow enough that they can become the world's leading expert, and forcing them to clarify what exactly they are working on. It won't be acceptable to say 'I'm working on menu design' or 'virtual reality sounds like fun.'

Trying out commercial products brings a sense of practical reality. The students come to understand the parts in the context of the whole, and see the tradeoffs that designers must make.

Getting in touch with current researchers or developers is a novel and threatening task for many of my students. E-mail helps facilitate the process, but phone calls, letters, and visits are also important. Shy students overcome their awkwardness and are often rewarded by a helpful contact with a respected researcher or an invitation to present their work at a major company.

The diligence required to produce a bibliography of 5-25 items, review and critique commercial products, and contact people helps prepare them for their own creative work. I do not accept the belief that they don't want to be influenced by what others have done -- this is a naive excuse. I also find that contacts with current researchers can lead to unexpected and productive collaborations.

Clarify short-term and long-term goals

When we start a new project we usually spend a few weeks thinking broadly, brainstorming and coming up with diverse alternatives. As we sort out and reject some directions our understanding of what is important sharpens. Then we plan some long-term goals and establish some short-term goals to get started. If the short-term goals are accomplished we can move along; if not, then we can re-direct with only a modest loss of time and energy.

For example, one long-term goal was to develop specification methods for dynamic explorations in a large three-dimensional display space. The short-term goal was to specify something smaller and more specific, such as the window management in a familiar geographic information system. In another case, we contributed to designing a museum exhibit involving a 2500-article electronic encyclopedia. Our initial prototype used 106 articles on a narrower topic, and then we went to 400 articles plus photos and videos. I find scaling up from small prototypes to be the most realistic path, even if you wind up throwing out early prototypes. In fact, throwing out a prototype and starting over is often a shortcut to progress. Similarly, every experiment gets tested out in a pilot study with small numbers of subjects.

The benefit of long-term goals is that they provide a destination, and a shared set of expectations that focuses effort. The benefit of short-term goals is that they provide immediate feedback about progress and a chance to make mid-course corrections with low cost.

Balance individual and group interests

I try to give each student or staff person a role that is clear and one that serves their individual goals (getting a Master's degree within 18 months, doing an independent study summer project, or building a resume to get a desired job). These goals need to be in harmony with the overall goals and directions of the lab. Proposed projects have to fit in with their existing experience, skills, and directions. A student who wants to do a Masters thesis on a topic that is poorly related to our existing work will get a cool reception, and possibly a long lecture about alternate topics.

When visitors tour the lab, students and staff need to know that they will be given a chance to show their work, get feedback, and promote their idea. This works out well, and our visitors usually prefer chatting with the students who are doing the work to a private presentation by senior staff. When visitors are potential funders, direct student and staff involvement in the future of research projects increases motivation, participation, and work quality.

When individual and group goals are in harmony, fortuitous collaborations are likely. One of the ways we have been able to accomplish much with limited resources is that individuals know that they can get help from each other. When one PhD student needed a special routine on an unfamiliar hardware/software environment, another student stepped in and provided a few days of programming help. The favor was repaid by help in reviewing paper drafts and assistance in preparing subjects for an experiment. Since our lab operates with a diverse hardware and software environment, hardly an hour goes by without someone calling out for help on some system.

Work hard

Thomas Edison remarked that innovation requires 1% inspiration and 99% perspiration. An exciting and novel idea is just the starting point. Most ideas have a cascade of smaller ideas behind them and the details do have to be worked out. Special cases, exceptions, and extreme conditions have to be investigated carefully to reveal the limitations of a new idea. Then converting an idea to a piece of functioning software, a set of screen designs in a prototype, or the materials, tasks, and statistics in an experiment takes devoted effort. Polishing, refining, and cleaning up can take ten or a hundred times more effort than the original innovation. This has proven to be the case with:

- developing new interfaces (first designs are mocked up in hours, but prototype testing, full implementation, and revisions can take months)
- creating software (pseudo-code is followed by extensive coding, testing, and refinement)
- conducting experiments (design takes a day, but developing materials, pilot testing, administration, and statistical analysis takes months)
- writing papers (initial draft might be 10 hours, but revisions based on local and external reviews may require 100 hours)

A sustained effort is necessary to achieve excellence, and we encourage realistic expectations. One reason that I have less trouble writing than many colleagues is that I grew up watching my journalist parents revising, cutting and pasting (the old-fashioned way with scissors and glue), and retyping many times. Simply expecting things to take a great deal of effort removes some of the anxiety or expectation of perfection.

There is also a definite improvement in quality when you can revise and improve after reflection or comments from colleagues. The second time through with almost any process or path is smoother and faster, but the second time through means that there is less joyful novelty. Second times are safer but less thrilling.

Communicate with internal and external stakeholders

Our group operates with a high degree of internal communication and external reporting. Internally, we have weekly or less frequent meetings of research teams that work on related topics. We also hold a weekly seminar to discuss a journal or conference paper or to hear a formal presentation of results. However, these traditional business-like meetings tend to be less fun and provocative than the spontaneous demos, informal pre-experiment reviews, participation in pilot studies, pleas for help with statistics, and personal requests for reading of draft papers.

While internal communication helps form and guide our work, the external communications play a vital role by raising the level of importance or anticipation. I am constantly struck by the beneficial influence of preparation for:

- demonstrations to visitors,
- presentations at our annual Open House & Symposium,
- writing term reports, theses, or journal articles,
- production of videotape reports,
- lectures at companies or universities, and
- papers and sessions at conferences.

Preparing something for a friend, staff person, or professor may encourage some diligent effort, but it seems that preparation for a conference talk, a lecture to supporting companies, or important visitors raises the stakes considerably. Telling the story and listening for feedback are often unfamiliar skills for technically oriented people, so we try to practice often and help each other polish our papers, slides, talks, videos, etc.

Get past failures. Celebrate successes!

Some days are exciting, but many days seem filled with hundreds of responsibilities such as reviewing journal papers, showing visitors around, responding to requests for technical reports, writing proposals, or reading a draft of a thesis chapter. Sometimes we are burdened with tedious tasks such as filling out travel vouchers, repairing computers, or preparing budgets. However, when it comes around to writing our annual report or preparing for our Open House & Symposium, I am struck by how much we have accomplished during the previous year. The really good days are when students proudly invite me to see a demonstration of their latest design, improvement, or experiment. As lab members gather around a computer display, we are off and running with cheers, comments, and criticisms. Other memorable days include working intensely to finish a paper, resolving a problem with statistics, brainstorming on designs, rehearsing for a videotape, and fantasizing about future user interfaces.

The intense 'flow' experience that comes with deep engagement in a problem is rewarding in itself. On one occasion I worked closely with a student to revise a journal paper for almost three hours. We sat at adjacent Macintoshes and while I dug out a reference from one file, he added the relevant paragraph. Then while he combined several graphs as requested by a reviewer, I revised the text to refer to the new diagram. We smoothly picked up pieces from each other across the network and came out with a substantially improved paper that wove together the high-level theory with the practical results. Our concentration was intense and as clock-time vanished we were driven by the rhythm of cooperation to complete in a morning what might have taken either of us alone a week.

Other good days are when a student passes a dissertation defense or has a paper accepted for a journal. While we don't have a party for each event, we are well-known for having celebrations in our labs (champagne and strawberries are a

favorite), going out for lunch or dinner, or organizing picnics, ice skating, and theater parties. Occasionally we take a "field trip" to a local museum, company, or government agency that is using computers in a novel way. A more whimsical summer field trip was to a shopping mall to try a virtual reality game, followed by a picnic on the Potomac.

Bad days are very much a part of our life too. Even after 25 years of writing, it is still a great disappointment to get turned down by a conference program committee or journal editorial board. Each new idea seems special and its rejection is felt personally. After the upset, we try to figure out why we failed to convince the reader of the importance of our ideas. Requests from journal editors for major revisions are also painful, but I must admit that some of our most successful papers have had the longest gestation period and endured the most revisions. Rejected grant applications, students who choose to go elsewhere, and funders who decide not to renew are also unpleasant experiences. Even a successful research group must deal with many disappointments.

Once a year, in December, we hold an all day retreat at some "bucolic" (our favorite term) location within an hour's drive. We talk about where we are going in our research, try to see the big picture, have lunch, take pictures of each other, and then hike in the forest before going out to a nice dinner. Since everyone speaks about their plans, there is never enough time, but long lists get carried away for further contemplation. It is a time for making resolutions and visualizing the future in a safe supportive community.

Our annual Open House & Symposium, held in June, is another major celebration in which students, staff, and faculty get to present their work. It is a lot of hard work to prepare but it is an effective way to disseminate our research to several hundred attendees. In the morning we make carefully polished formal presentations and respond to the spirited questions. One memorable exchange followed Richard Potter's talk on a novel graphical programming-by-demonstration technique. The questioner challenged each example as already being available in some exotic software package and was determined to show that Potter's innovation was unnecessary. Potter parried each complaint respectfully, and finally got cheers from the equally annoyed audience when he declared that "If your goal is to go where no one has ever been, you won't be taking a train." Lunch is for informal chatting and birthday cake (decorations have included lab logos, Macintosh windows, pie menus, and treemaps). The afternoon is given over to tours, demonstrations, and personal discussions. At the end of the day, senior staff and faculty go out to dinner with our Advisory Board to reflect on the day and make suggestions for future work.

We discuss authorship expectations of papers early and often. Participants are entitled to know who will receive credit and in which order. We have had disagreements, occasionally serious, but have always found creative ways to resolve such conflicts. We are also devoted to careful acknowledgement of contributors, reviewers, and helpers of all kinds.

Conclusion

Innovation is by its nature different each time. I'm proud of what our group has accomplished and enjoy going to work almost every day. Sometimes we get too busy to sit back and appreciate our good fortune, but sometimes we remember to say kind words to each other. Much credit goes to the faculty and staff who participate in our projects and sit on thesis committees, to the administrative staff who take care of our accounts, travel, and purchase orders, to the secretaries who answer the phones, prepare reports, and copy our papers, and to the systems people who maintain our computers, networks, and software. I hope to learn many more lessons and contribute to making the world a little warmer, wiser, safer, and happier place in the next ten years.

Root is Sys:
Boot>
foo>
memory>
bam>
Bug>
Satellite connection
mico>
unix>
lisp>
Microscope

Sparks of Innovation in Human-Computer Interaction,
B. Shneiderman, Ed., Ablex Publ., Norwood, NJ (1993)

1. Direct manipulation

Introduction

A wise commentator remarked that: "There is nothing so practical as a good theory" and that "Metaphors move mountains." With these in mind, I sought to characterize how to design user interfaces that would be quick to learn, rapid in performance, low in error rates, easy to retain, and high in subjective satisfaction. I chose the term "direct manipulation" carefully to convey that the user is in control and responsible for all actions. I was consciously aware of choosing a provocative term that could be accepted as an alternative to the machine-centered anthropomorphic visions of artificial intelligence. I was also aware of the subtle and possibly subconscious sexual connotation, but haven't wanted to mention it in writing till now. My 1982 description in *Behaviour & Information Technology* (Shneiderman 1982) was the predecessor to the more well-known 1983 *IEEE Computer* paper (see paper 1.1 in this volume, Shneiderman, 1983). Both papers laid out the concepts:

- visual display of objects and actions of interest
- rapid, incremental, and reversible actions

- selection by pointing (instead of typing)
- immediate and continuous feedback of results of actions

These principles were widely referenced and applied in novel systems. While certain repetitious tasks can be accomplished rapidly with compact commands by well-trained frequent users, more creative tasks and intermittent use demand another interaction style. Menus and forms are beneficial in some situations, but the excitement surrounding videogames, flight simulators, and WYSIWYG (What you see is what you get) word processors is stunning. Other influences on my writing were spreadsheets and the novel graphical user interfaces such as the Xerox Star, marketed in 1981, and the Apple Lisa (the Macintosh appeared later in January 1984).

Hutchins, Hollan, and Norman (1986) provided refinements to my characterizations by describing the dual gulfs of execution (the difficulty users have in converting their intentions into multiple actions) and explanation (the difficulty users have in understanding what they are seeing on the display). Later, Donald Norman (1988) promoted the notion of affordances (such as the handles on a door or the drag box on a scroll bar) which fit naturally with the direct manipulation philosophy.

The direct manipulation principles shaped our designs for ten years, and our efforts to refine that understanding led to several experiments. Class projects conducted by undergraduate and graduate student teams have contributed greatly to our research, even though only one in ten were worthy of publication. Many semester-long projects answered important questions and became the basis for further studies. Often they led, with some re-working, to a conference or journal paper. One team studied 30 novices using MS-DOS commands and Macintosh direct manipulation actions for creating, copying renaming, and erasing files. After training and practice, average task times were 5.8 minutes vs. 4.8 minutes and average errors were 2.0 vs. 0.8 (see paper 1.2, Margono & Shneiderman, 1987). Subjective preference also favored the direct manipulation interface. In another study of a command line vs. a direct manipulation database interface, 55 "computer naive but keyboard literate" users made more than twice as many errors with the command line. No significant differences in time were found (Morgan, Morris, and Gibbs, 1991). These users preferred the direct manipulation interface overall and rated it as more stimulating, easier, and as having "more adequate power." Both reports caution about generalizing the results to more experienced users.

A study with novices and experienced users was co-sponsored by Microsoft and Zenith Data Systems (Temple, Barker & Sloane, Inc., 1990). Although details about subjects, interfaces, and tasks were not reported, the results showed improved productivity and reduced fatigue for experienced users with a graphical user interface compared to a character-based user interface.

In a collaboration with Charels 'Skip' MacArthur in the College of Education, we studied 4th to 6th grade remedial reading students learning to use word processors (MacArthur & Shneiderman, 1986). This was especially rewarding because they became proficient and produced cleanly revised essays that we printed up as a newspaper for distribution to their friends. They were really proud of their accomplishment and we learned how beneficial direct manipulation was to these users. Visible control characters at the end of a line and I-shaped insertion points between characters (rather than a blinking box with insertion to the left of the box) were major advantages.

There have been a variety of supportive commentaries on direct manipulation (Ziegler & Fahnrich, 1988; Thimbleby, 1990; Phillips & Apperley, 1991) and other empirical studies (Ulich, Rauterberg, Moll, Greutmann & Strohm, 1991; Rauterberg, 1992; Eberts, 1992, Benbasat & Todd, 1993). Similarly, Te'eni (1990) found that the feedback in direct manipulation designs was effective in reducing logical errors in a task requiring statistical analysis of student grades. The advantage appears to stem from having the data entry and display combined in a single location on the display.

We applied the Maryland Way to study a remotely controlled microscope developed by Corabi Telemetrics for pathologists (see paper 1.3, Plaisant, Keil-Slawik & Shneiderman, 1991). This project, directed by Catherine Plaisant, led to advances in the theory and practice of direct manipulation with application to teleoperation. The key issues are the delay in feedback caused by the network, the slow motion of the physical devices, and the incomplete feedback provided by these systems. We started with the short-term goal of providing a report about how to improve the current interface, then developed a mock-up for a more graphic interface, and conducted a series of basic science studies with varying time delays, input devices, and visual feedback.

Other applications of direct manipulation principles can be found in our work on touchscreens for home automation (see section 4) and especially dynamic queries (see section 6). Some especially bright sparks can travel among several of our projects.

Sparks of Innovation in Human-Computer Interaction,
B. Shneiderman, Ed., Ablex Publ., Norwood, NJ (1993)

1.1 Direct manipulation: a step beyond programming languages

Ben Shneiderman

Direct manipulation systems offer the satisfying experience of operating on visible objects. The computer becomes transparent, and users can concentrate on their tasks.

> Leibniz sought to make the form of a symbol reflect its content. "In signs," he wrote, "one sees an advantage for discovery that is greatest when they express the exact nature of a thing briefly and, as it were, picture it; then, indeed, the labor of thought is wonderfully diminished."
> *Frederick Kreiling, "Leibniz," Scientific American, May 1968*

IEEE Computer '83 , 16, 8, 57-69.
A portion of this article was derived from the author's keynote address at the NYU Symposium on User Interfaces, "*The Future of Interactive Systems and the Emergence of Direct Manipulation,*" published in Human Factors in Interactive Computer Systems, Y. Vassiliou, ed., Ablex Publishing Co., Norwood, N.J., 1983.

Certain interactive systems generate glowing enthusiasm among users in marked contrast with the more common reaction of grudging acceptance or outright hostility. The enthusiastic users' reports are filled with positive feelings regarding:

- mastery of the system,
- competence in the performance of their task,
- ease in learning the system originally and in assimilating advanced features,
- confidence in their capacity to retain mastery over time,
- enjoyment in using the system,
- eagerness to show it off to novices, and
- desire to explore more powerful aspects of the system.

These feelings are not, of course, universal, but the amalgam does convey an image of the truly pleased user. As I talked with these enthusiasts and examined the systems they used, I began to develop a model of the features that produced such delight. The central ideas seemed to be visibility of the object of interest; rapid, reversible, incremental actions; and replacement of complex command language syntax by direct manipulation of the object of interest - hence the term "direct manipulation. "

```
 EDIT --- SPFDEMO.MYLIB.PLI(COINS) - 01.04 ------------------ COLUMNS 001 072
COMMAND INPUT ===>                                               SCROLL ===> HALF
****** ****************************** TOP OF DATA ******************************
000100 COINS:
000200   PROCEDURE OPTIONS (MAIN);
000300     DECLARE
000400       COUNT    FIXED BINARY (31) AUTOMATIC INIT (1),
000500       HALVES   FIXED BINARY (31),
000600       QUARTERS FIXED BINARY (31),
000700       DIMES    FIXED BINARY (31),
I3           NICKELS  FIXED BINARY (31),
000900       SYSPRINT FILE STREAM OUTPUT PRINT;
001000     DO HALVES = 100 TO 0 BY -50;
001100       DO QUARTERS = (100 - HALVES) TO 0 BY -25;
001200         DO DIMES = ((100 - HALVES - QUARTERS)/10)*10 TO 0 BY -10;
001300           NICKELS = 100 - HALVES - QUARTERS - DIMES;
D _              PUT FILE(SYSPRINT) DATA(COUNT,HALVES,QUARTERS,DIMES,NICKELS);
001500           COUNT = COUNT + 1;
001600         END;
001700       END;
001800     END;
001900   END COINS;
****** *************************** BOTTOM OF DATA *****************************
```

Figure 1. This example from the IBM/SPF display editor shows 19 lines of a PL/I program. The commands to insert three lines (I3) and to delete one line (D or D1) are typed on the appropriate lines in the first screen display. Pressing ENTER causes commands to be executed and the cursor to be placed at the beginning of the inserted line. New program statements can be typed directly in their required positions. Control keys move the cursor

Examples of direct manipulation systems

No single system has all the attributes or design features that I admire - that may be impossible - but those described below have enough to win the enthusiastic support of many users.

Display editors. "Once you've used a display editor, you'll never want to go back to a line editor. You'll be spoiled." This reaction is typical of those who use full-page display editors, who are great advocates of their systems over line-oriented text editors. I heard similar comments from users of stand-alone word processors such as the Wang system and from users of display editors such as EMACS on the MIT/Honeywell Multics system or "vi" (for visual editor) on the Unix system. A beaming advocate called EMACS "the one true editor. "

Roberts (Roberts, 1990) found that the overall performance time of display editors is only half that of line-oriented editors, and since display editors also reduce training time, the evidence supports the enthusiasm of display editor devotees. Furthermore, office automation evaluations consistently favor full-page display editors for secretarial and executive use.

The advantages of display editors include:

Display of a full 24 to 66 lines of text. This full display enables viewing each sentence in context and simplifies reading and scanning the document. By contrast,

```
 EDIT --- SPFDEMO.MYLIB.PLI(COINS) - 01.04 ------------------- COLUMNS 001 072
COMMAND INPUT ===>                                             SCROLL ===> HALF
****** ***************************** TOP OF DATA ******************************
000100 COINS:
000200   PROCEDURE OPTIONS (MAIN);
000300     DECLARE
000400       COUNT    FIXED BINARY (31) AUTOMATIC INIT (1),
000500       HALVES   FIXED BINARY (31),
000600       QUARTERS FIXED BINARY (31),
000700       DIMES    FIXED BINARY (31),
000800       NICKELS  FIXED BINARY (31),
''''''       -
''''''
''''''
000900       SYSPRINT FILE STREAM OUTPUT PRINT;
001000     DO HALVES = 100 TO 0 BY -50;
001100       DO QUARTERS = (100 - HALVES) TO 0 BY -25;
001200         DO DIMES = ((100 - HALVES - QUARTERS)/10)*10 TO 0 BY -10;
001300           NICKELS = 100 - HALVES - QUARTERS - DIMES;
001500           COUNT = COUNT + 1;
001600         END;
001700       END;
001800     END;
001900   END COINS;
****** ************************** BOTTOM OF DATA ******************************
```


around the text to positions where changes are made by overstriking. A delete key causes the character under the cursor to be deleted and the text to the left to be shifted over. After pressing an insert key, the user can type text in place. Programmed function keys allow movement of the window forwards, backwards, left and right over the text. (Examples courtesy of IBM.)

the one-line-at-a-time view offered by line editors is like seeing the world through a narrow cardboard tube.

Display of the document in its final form. Eliminating the clutter of formatting commands also simplifies reading and scanning the document. Tables, lists, page breaks, skipped lines, section headings, centered text, and figures can be viewed in the form that will be printed. The annoyance and delay of debugging the format commands is eliminated because the errors are immediately apparent .

Cursor action that is visible to the user. Seeing an arrow, underscore, or blinking box on the screen gives the operator a clear sense of where to focus attention and apply action.

Cursor motion through physically obvious and intuitively natural means. Arrow keys or devices such as a mouse, joystick, or graphics tablet provide natural physical mechanisms for moving the cursor. This is in marked contrast with commands such as UP 6, which require an operator to convert the physical action into correct syntactic form and which may be difficult to learn, hard to recall, and a source of frustrating errors.

Labeled buttons for action. Many display editors have buttons etched with commands such as INSERT, DELETE, CENTER, UNDERLINE, SUPERSCRIPT BOLD, or LOCATE. They act as a permanent menu selection display, reminding the operator of the features and obviating memorization of a complex command-language syntax. Some editors provide basic functionality with only 10 or 15 labeled buttons, and a specially marked button may be the gateway to advanced or infrequently used features offered on the screen in menu form.

Immediate display of the results of an action. When a button is pressed to move the cursor or center the text, the results appear on the screen immediately. Deletions are apparent at once, since the character, word, or line is erased and the remaining text rearranged. Similarly, insertions or text movements are shown after each keystroke or function button press. Line editors, on the other hand, require a print or display command before the results of a change can be seen.

Rapid action and display. Most display editors are designed to operate at high speeds: 120 characters per second (1200 baud), a full page in a second (9600 baud), or even faster. This high display rate coupled with short response time produces a thrilling sense of power and speed. Cursors can be moved quickly, large amounts of text can be scanned rapidly, and the results of commands can be shown almost instantaneously. Rapid action also reduces the need for additional commands, thereby simplifying product design and decreasing learning time. Line editors operating at 30 characters per second with three- to eight second response times seem sluggish in comparison. Speeding up line editors adds to their attractiveness, but they still lack features such as direct overtyping, deletion, and insertion.

Easily reversible commands. Mistakes in entering text can be easily corrected by backspacing and overstriking. Simple changes can be made by moving the cursor to the problem area and overstriking, inserting, or deleting characters, words, or lines. A useful design strategy is to include natural inverse operations for each operation. Carroll (Carroll, 1982) has shown that congruent pairs of operations are

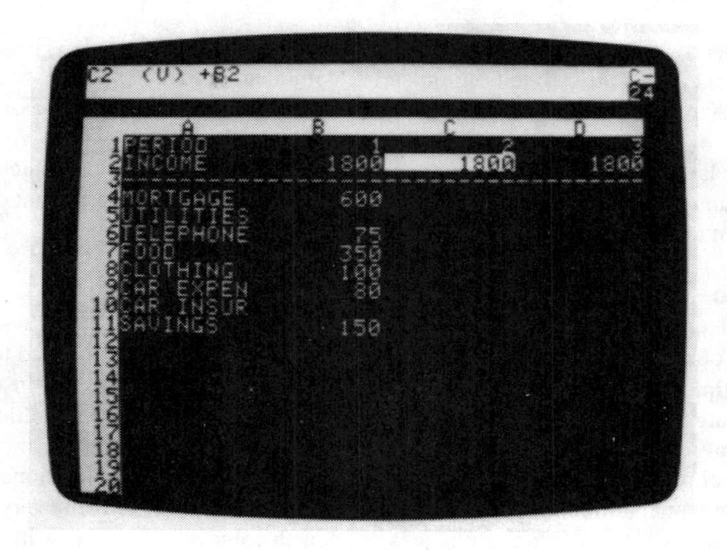

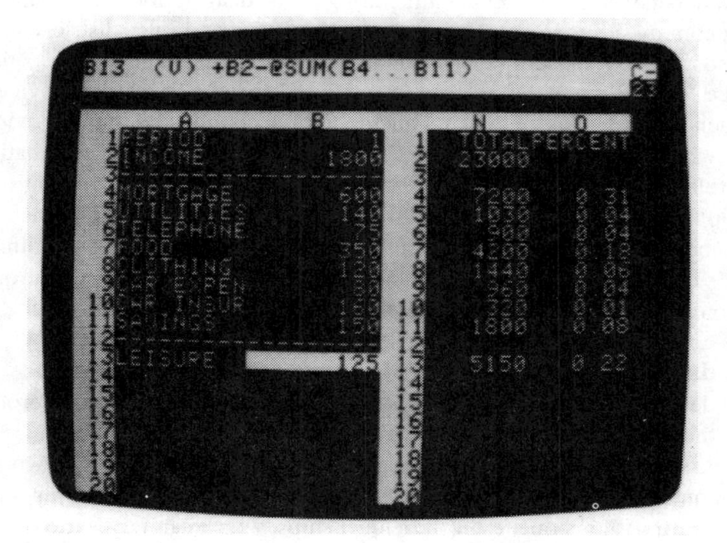

Figure 2. This simple Visicalc program display (top) shows four columns and 20 rows of home budget information. The cursor, an inverse video light bar controlled by key presses, is in position C2. The top command line shows that C2 is a value (as opposed to a text string) that has been set up to have the same value as position B2.

The second display (above) shows two windows over the home budget data with row sums to the right. The last row shows leisure dollar amounts, which are established by the top command line formula as the income minus the sum of expenses. A change to the income or expense values would immediately propagate to all affected values. (Displays reproduced by permission of Visicorp.)

easy to learn. As an alternative, many display editors offer a simple UNDO command that cancels the previous command or command sequence and returns the text to its previous state. This easy reversibility reduces user anxiety about making mistakes or destroying a file.

The large market for display editors generates active competition, which accelerates evolutionary design refinements. Figure 1 illustrates the current capabilities of an IBM display editor.

Visicalc

Visicorp's innovative financial forecasting program, called Visicalc, was the product of a Harvard MBA student, who was frustrated by the time needed to carry out multiple calculations in a graduate business course. Described as an "instantly calculating electronic worksheet" in the user's manual, it permits computation and display of results across 254 rows and 63 columns and is programmed without a traditional procedural control structure. For example, positional declarations can prescribe that column 4 displays the sum of columns 1 through 3; then every time a value in the first three columns changes, the fourth column changes as well. Complex dependencies among manufacturing costs, distribution costs, sales revenue, commissions, and profits can be stored for several sales districts and months so that the impact of changes on profits is immediately apparent.

Since Visicalc simulates an accountant's worksheet, it is easy for novices to comprehend. The display of 20 rows and up to nine columns, with the provision for multiple windows, gives the user sufficient visibility to easily scan information and explore relationships among entries (see Figure 2). The command language for setting up the worksheet can be tricky for novices to learn and for infrequent users to remember, but most users need learn only the basic commands. According to Visicalc's distributor, "It jumps," and the user's delight in watching this propagation of changes cross the screen helps explain its appeal.

Spatial data management

The developers of the prototype spatial data management system (Herot, 1980) attribute the basic idea to Nicholas Negroponte of MIT.

In one scenario, a user seated before a color graphics display of the world zooms in on the Pacific to see markers for military ship convoys. Moving a joystick fills the screen with silhouettes of individual ships, which can be zoomed in on to display structural details or, ultimately, a full-color picture of the captain. (See Figure 3.)

In another scenario, icons representing different aspects of a corporation, such as personnel, organization, travel, production, or schedules, are shown on a screen. Moving the joystick and zooming in on objects takes users through complex information spaces or I spaces to locate the item of interest. For example, when they select a department from a building floor plan, individual offices become visible. Moving the cursor into a room brings the room's details onto the screen. If they

Figure 3. A spatial data management system has been installed on the aircraft carrier USS Carl Vinson. In the photo at top left, the operator has a world map on the left screen and a videodisc map of selected areas on the center screen. After some command selections with the data tablet and puck, the operator can zoom in on specific data such as the set of ships shown in the second photo. With further selections the operator can get detailed information about each ship, such as the length, speed, and fuel. (Photos courtesy of Computer Corporation of America.)

choose the wrong room, they merely back out and try another. The lost effort is minimal, and no stigma is attached to the error.

The success of a spatial data management system depends on the designer's skill in choosing icons, graphical representations, and data layouts that are natural and easily understood. Even anxious users enjoy zooming in and out or gliding over data with a joystick, and they quickly demand additional power and data.

Video games

Perhaps the most exciting, well-engineered certainly, the most successful application of direct manipulation is in the world of video games. An early, but simple and popular, game called Pong required the user to rotate a knob, which moved a white rectangle on the screen. A white spot acted as a Ping Pong ball, which ricocheted off the wall and had to be hit back by the movable white rectangle. The user developed skill involving speed and accuracy in placement of the "paddle" to keep the increasingly speedy ball from getting by, while the speaker emitted a ponging sound when the ball bounced. Watching someone else play for 30 seconds was all the training needed to become a competent novice, but many hours of practice were required to become a skilled expert.

Contemporary games such as Missile Command, Donkey Kong, Pac Man, Tempest, Tron, Centipede, or Space Invaders are far more sophisticated in their rules, color graphics, and sound effects (see sidebar below and on facing page). The designers of these games have provided stimulating entertainment, a challenge for novices and experts, and many intriguing lessons in the human factors of interface design -- somehow they have found a way to get people to put coins into the sides of computers. The strong attraction of these games contrasts markedly with the anxiety and resistance many users experience toward office automation equipment.

Because their fields of action are abstractions of reality, these games are easily understood -- learning is by analogy. A general idea of the game can be gained by watching the on-line automatic demonstration that runs continuously on the screen, and the basic principles can be learned in a few minutes by watching a knowledgeable player. But there are ample complexities to entice many hours and quarters from experts. The range of skill accommodated is admirable.

The commands are physical actions, such as button presses, joystick motions, or knob rotations, whose results appear immediately on the screen. Since there is no syntax, there are no syntax error messages. If users move their spaceships too far left, then they merely use the natural inverse operation of moving back to the right. Error messages are unnecessary because the results of actions are so obvious and easily reversed. These principles can be applied to office automation, personal computing, and other interactive environments.

Every game that I have seen keeps a continuous score so that users can measure their progress and compete with their previous performance, with friends, or with the highest scorers. Typically, the 10 highest scorers get to store their initials in the game for regular display, a form of positive reinforcement that encourages mastery. Malone's (Malone, 1981) and our own studies with elementary school children have shown that continuous display of scores is extremely valuable. Machine-generated value judgments "Very good" or "You're doing great !" are not as effective, since the same score means different things to different people. Users prefer to make their own subjective judgments and may perceive machine-generated messages as an annoyance and a deception.

Carroll and Thomas (Carroll & Thomas, 1982) draw productive analogies between game-playing environments and application systems. However, game players seek entertainment and the challenge of mastery, while application-system users focus on the task and may resent forced learning of system constraints. The random events that occur in most games are meant to challenge the user, but predictable system behavior is preferable in nongame designs. Game players compete with the system, but application system users apparently prefer a strong internal locus of control, which gives them the sense of being in charge.

Computer-aided design/manufacturing

Many computer-aided design systems for automobiles, electronic circuitry, architecture, aircraft, or newspaper layout use direct manipulation principles. The operator may see a schematic on the screen and with the touch of a lightpen can move resistors or capacitors into or out of the proposed circuit. When the design is complete, the computer can provide information about current, voltage drops, fabrication costs, and warnings about inconsistencies or manufacturing problems. Similarly, newspaper layout artists or automobile body designers can try multiple designs in minutes and record promising approaches until a better one is found.

The pleasure in using these systems stems from the capacity to manipulate the object of interest directly and to generate multiple alternatives rapidly. Some systems have complex command languages, but others have moved to cursor action and graphics-oriented commands.

Another related application is in computer-aided manufacturing and process control. Honeywell's process control system provides an oil refinery, paper mill, or power utility plant manager with a colored schematic view of the plant. The schematic may be on eight displays, with red lines indicating a sensor value that is out of normal range. By pressing a single numbered button (there are no commands to learn or remember), the operator can get a more detailed view of the troublesome component and, with a second press, move the tree structure down to examine individual sensors or to reset valves and circuits.

The design's basic strategy precludes the necessity of recalling complex commands in once-a-year emergency conditions. The plant schematic facilitates problem solving by analogy, since the link between real-world high temperatures or low pressures and screen representations is so close.

Further examples

Driving an automobile is my favorite example of direct manipulation. The scene is directly visible through the windshield, and actions such as braking or steering have become common skills in our culture. To turn to the left, simply rotate the steering wheel to the left. The response is immediate, and the changing scene provides feedback to refine the turn. Imagine trying to turn by issuing a LEFT 30 DEGREES command and then issuing another command to check your position, but this is the operational level of many office automation tools today.

The term direct manipulation accurately describes the programming of some industrial robots. Here, the operator holds the robot's "hand" and guides it through a spray painting or welding task while the controlling computer records every action. The control computer then repeats the action to operate the robot automatically.

A large part of the success and appeal of the Query-by-Example (Zloof, 1975) approach to data manipulation is due to its direct representation of relations on the screen. The user moves a cursor through the columns of the relational table and enters examples of what the result should look like. Just a few single-letter keywords supplement this direct manipulation style. Of course, complex Booleans or mathematical operations require knowledge of syntactic forms. Still, the basic ideas and language facilities can be learned within a half hour by many nonprogrammers. Query-by-Example succeeds because novices can begin work with just a little training, yet there is ample power for the expert. Directly manipulating the cursor across the relation skeleton is a simple task, and how to provide an example that shows the linking variable is intuitively clear to someone who understands tabular data. Zloof (Zloof, 1982) recently expanded his ideas into Office-by-Example, which elegantly integrates database search with word processing, electronic mail, business graphics, and menu creation.

Designers of advanced office automation systems have used direct manipulation principles. The Xerox Star (Smith et al., 1982) offers sophisticated text formatting options, graphics, multiple fonts, and a rapid, high-resolution, cursor based user interface. Users can drag a document icon and drop it into a printer icon to generate a hardcopy printout. Apple's recently announced Lisa system elegantly applies many of the principles of direct manipulation.

Researchers at IBM's Yorktown Heights facility have proposed a future office system, called Pictureworld, in which graphic icons represent file cabinets, mailboxes, notebooks, phone messages, etc. The user could compose a memo on a display editor and then indicate distribution and filing operations by selecting from the menu of icons. In another project, Yedwab et al.(Yedwab et al., 1981) have described a generalized office system, which they call the "automated desk. "

Direct manipulation can be applied to replace traditional question-and-answer computer-assisted instruction with more attractive alternatives. Several CDC Plato lessons employ direct manipulation concepts, enabling students to trace inherited characteristics by breeding drosophilla, perform medical procedures to save an emergency room patient, draw and move shapes by finger touches, do chemistry lab projects (see Figure 4), or play games.

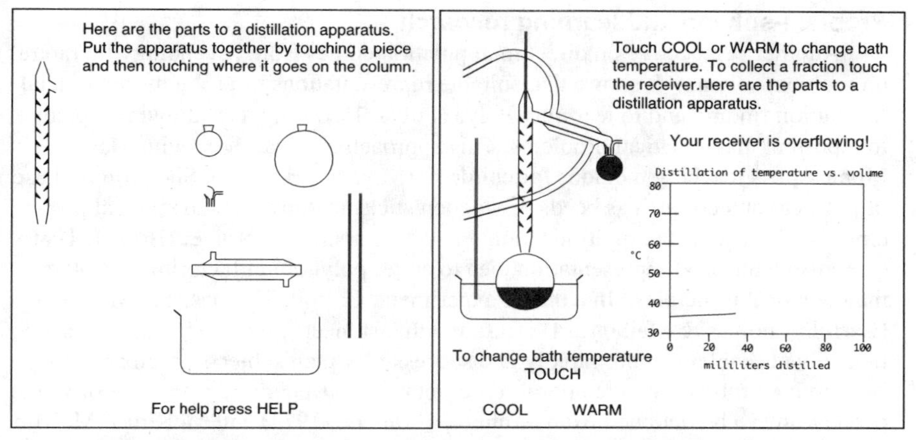

Figure 4. Computer assisted instruction can become more appealing with direct manipulation, rather than simple question and answer scenarios. This CDC Plato lesson written by Stanley Smith of the Department of Chemistry at the University of Illinois allows students to construct a distillation apparatus by proper finger actions on a touch sensitive screen (figure at left). Once the student has assembled the apparatus and begun the experiment, the real-time display gives a realistic view of the process with the graph of distillation temperature vs. volume. The student controls the experiment by touching light buttons. The figure at right shows that the student experimenter has gotten into trouble.

Explanations of direct manipulation

Several people have attempted to describe the component principles of direct manipulation. “What you see is what you get,” is a phrase used by Don Hatfield of IBM and others to describe the general approach. Hatfield is applying many direct manipulation principles in his work on an advanced office automation system. Expanding Hatfield’s premise, Harold Thimbleby of the University of York, England, suggests, “What you see is what you have got.” The display should indicate a complete image of what the current status is, what errors have occurred, and what actions are appropriate, according to Thimbleby.

Another imaginative observer of interactive system designs, Ted Nelson, (Nelson, 1980) has noticed user excitement over interfaces constructed by what he calls the principle of “virtuality,” a representation of reality that can be manipulated. Rutkowski (Rutkowski, 1982) conveys a similar concept in his principle of transparency: "The user is able to apply intellect directly to the task; the tool itself seems to disappear." MacDonald (MacDonald, 1982) proposes “visual programming” as a solution to the shortage of application programmers. He feels that visual programming speeds system construction and allows end users to generate or modify applications systems to suit their needs.

Each of these writers has helped increase awareness of the new form that is emerging for interactive systems. Much credit also goes to individual designers who have created systems exemplifying aspects of direct manipulation.

Problem-solving and learning research

Another perspective on direct manipulation comes from psychology literature on problem solving. It shows that suitable representations of problems are crucial to solution finding and to learning. Polya (Polya, 1957) suggests drawing a picture to represent mathematical problems. This approach is in harmony with Maria Montessori's teaching methods for children. (Montessori, 1964). She proposed use of physical objects such as beads or wooden sticks to convey mathematical principles such as addition, multiplication, or size comparison. Bruner (Bruner, 1966) extends the physical representation idea to cover polynomial factoring and other mathematical principles. In a recent experiment, Carroll, Thomas, and Malhotra (Carroll, Thomas & Malhotra, 1980) found that subjects given a spatial representation solved problems more rapidly and successfully than subjects given an isomorphic problem with temporal representation. (Deeper understanding of visual perception can be obtained from Arnheim (Arnheim, 1972) and McKim.) (McKim, 1972)

Physical, spatial, or visual representations are also easier to retain and manipulate. Wertheimer (Wertheimer, 1959) found that subjects who memorized the formula for the area of a parallelogram, $A = h \times b$, mastered such calculations rapidly. On the other hand, subjects who were given a structural explanation (cut a triangle from one end and place it on the other) retained the knowledge and applied it in similar circumstances more effectively. In plane geometry theorem proving, a spatial representation facilitates discovery of proof procedures more than an axiomatic representation. The diagram provides heuristics that are difficult to extract from the axioms. Similarly, students of algebra are often encouraged to draw a picture to represent a word problem.

Papert's Logo language (Papert, 1980) creates a mathematical microworld in which the principles of geometry are visible. Influenced by the Swiss psychologist Jean Piaget's theory of child development, Logo offers students the opportunity to create line drawings with an electronic turtle displayed on a screen. In this environment, users can receive rapid feedback about their programs, can easily determine what has happened, can quickly spot and repair errors, and can experience creative satisfaction.

Problems with direct manipulation

Some professional programming tasks can be aided by the use of graphic representations such as high-level flowcharts, record structures, or database schema diagrams, but additional effort may be required to absorb the rules of the representation. Graphic representations can be especially helpful when there are multiple relationships among objects and when the representation is more compact than the detailed object. In these cases, selectively screening out detail and presenting a suitable abstraction can facilitate performance.

However, using spatial or graphic representations of the problem does not necessarily improve performance. In a series of studies, subjects given a detailed flowchart did no better in comprehension, debugging, or modification than those

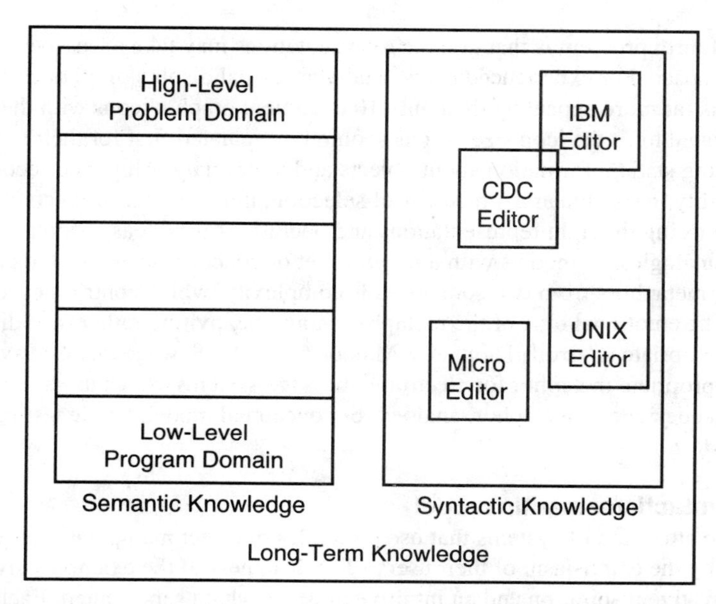

Figure 5. The semantic knowledge in long-term memory goes from high-level problem domain concepts down to numerous low-level program domain details. Semantic knowledge is well-structured, relatively stable, and meaningfully acquired. Syntactic knowledge is arbitrary, relatively volatile unless frequently rehearsed, and acquired by rote memorization. There is usually little overlap between the syntax of different text editors, but they often share semantic concepts about inserting, deleting, and changing lines of text.

given the code only. (Shneiderman, Mayer, McKay & Heller, 1977). In a program comprehension task, subjects given a graphic representation of control flow or data structure did no better than those given a textual description (Shneiderman, 1982). On the other hand, subjects given the data structure documentation consistently did better than subjects given the control flow documentation. This study suggests that the content of graphic representations is a critical determinant of their utility. The wrong information, or a cluttered presentation, can lead to greater confusion.

A second problem is that users must learn the meaning of the components of the graphic representation. A graphic icon, although meaningful to the designer, may require as much or more learning time as a word. Some airports serving multilingual communities use graphic icons extensively, but their meaning may not be obvious. Similarly, some computer terminals designed for international use have icons in place of names, but the meaning is not always clear.

A third problem is that the graphic representation may be misleading. The user may rapidly grasp the analogical representation, but then make incorrect conclusions about permissible operations. Designers must be cautious in selecting the displayed representation and the operations. Ample testing must be carried out to refine the representation and minimize negative side effects.

A fourth problem is that graphic representations may take excessive screen display space. For experienced users, a tabular textual display of 50 document names is far more appealing than only 10 document graphic icons with the names abbreviated to fit the icon size. Icons should be evaluated first for their power in displaying static information about objects and their relationship, and second for their utility in the dynamic processes of selection, movement, and deletion.

Choosing the right representations and operations is not easy. Simple metaphors, analogies, or models with a minimal set of concepts seem most appropriate. Mixing metaphors from two sources adds complexity, which contributes to confusion. The emotional tone of the metaphor should be inviting rather than distasteful or inappropriate (Carroll, Thomas & Malhotra, 1980). Sewage disposal systems are an inappropriate metaphor for electronic message systems. Since users may not share the designer's metaphor, analogy, or conceptual model, ample testing is required.

The syntactic/semantic model

The attraction of systems that use principles of direct manipulation is confirmed by the enthusiasm of their users. The designers of the examples given had an innovative inspiration and an intuitive grasp of what users wanted. Each example has features that could be criticized, but it seems more productive to construct an integrated portrait of direct manipulation:

- Continuous representation of the object of interest.
- Physical actions (movement and selection by mouse, joystick, touch screen, etc.) or labeled button presses instead of complex syntax.
- Rapid, incremental, reversible operations whose impact on the object of interest is immediately visible.
- Layered or spiral approach to learning that permits usage with minimal knowledge. Novices can learn a modest and useful set of commands, which they can exercise till they become an "expert" at level I of the system. After obtaining reinforcing feedback from successful operation, users can gracefully expand their knowledge of features and gain fluency. (Schneider, 1982)

By using these four principles, it is possible to design systems that have these beneficial attributes:

- Novices can learn basic functionality quickly, usually through a demonstration by a more experienced user.
- Experts can work extremely rapidly to carry out a wide range of tasks, even defining new functions and features.
- Knowledgeable intermittent users can retain operational concepts.
- Error messages are rarely needed.
- Users can immediately see if their actions are furthering their goals, and if not, they can simply change the direction of their activity.
- Users experience less anxiety because the system is comprehensible and because actions are so easily reversible .

- Users gain confidence and mastery because they initiate an action, feel in control, and can predict system responses.

My own understanding of direct manipulation was facilitated by considering the syntactic/semantic model of user behavior. The cognitive model was first developed in the context of programming language experimentation (Shneiderman, Mayer, 1979) (Shneiderman, 1980) and has been applied to database query language questions. (Shneiderman, 1981)

The basic idea is that there are two kinds of knowledge in long-term memory: syntactic and semantic (see Figure 5).

Syntactic knowledge

In a text editor, syntactic knowledge of the details of command syntax include permissible item delimiters (space, comma, slash or colon), insertion of a new line after the third line (I3,I3, or 3I), or the keystroke necessary for erasing a character (delete key, CONTROL-H, or ESCAPE). This knowledge is arbitrary and therefore acquired by rote memorization. Syntactic knowledge is volatile in memory and easily forgotten unless frequently used. (Ausubel, 1968) This knowledge is system dependent with some possible overlap among systems.

Semantic knowledge

The concepts or functionality of semantic knowledge are hierarchically structured from low-level functions to higher level concepts. In text editors, lower level functions might be cursor movement, insertion, deletion, changes, text copying, centering, and indentation. These lower level concepts are close to the syntax of the command language. A middle-level semantic concept for text editing might be the process for correcting a misspelling: produce a display of the misspelled word, move the cursor to the appropriate spot, and issue the change command or key in the correct characters. A higher level concept might be the process for moving a sentence from one paragraph to another: move the cursor to the beginning of the sentence, mark this position, move the cursor to the end of the sentence, mark this second position, copy the sentence to a buffer area, clean up the source paragraph, move the cursor to the target location, copy from the buffer, check that the target paragraph is satisfactory, and clear the buffer area.

The higher level concepts in the problem domain (moving a sentence) are decomposed, by the expert user, top-down into multiple, lower level concepts (move cursor, copy from buffer, etc.) closer to the program or syntax domain. Semantic knowledge is largely system independent; text editing functions (inserting/deleting lines, moving sentences, centering, indenting, etc.) are generally available in text editors, although the syntax varies. Semantic knowledge, which is acquired through general explanation, analogy, and example, is easily anchored to familiar concepts and is therefore stable in memory.

The command formulation process in the syntactic/semantic model proceeds from the user's perception of the task in the high-level problem domain to the decomposition into multiple, lower level semantic operations and the conversion into a set of commands. The syntax of text editors may vary, but the decomposition from problem domain into low-level semantics is largely the same. At the syntax level the user must recall whether spaces are permitted, whether program function keys are available, or whether command abbreviations are permitted .

As a user of a half-dozen text editors during a week, I am very aware of the commonality of my thought processes in problem solving and the diversity of syntactic forms with which I must cope. Especially annoying are syntactic clashes such as the different placement of special characters on keyboards, the multiple approaches to backspacing (backspace key, cursor control key, or a mouse), and the fact that one text editor uses "K" for keeping a file while another uses "K" for killing a file.

Implications of the syntactic/semantic model

Novices begin with a close link between syntax and semantics; their attention focuses on the command syntax as they seek to remember the command functions and syntax. In fact, for novice users, the syntax of a precise, concise command language provides the cues for recalling the semantics. Novices review the command names, in their memory or in a manual, which act as the stimuli for recalling the related semantics. Each command is then evaluated for its applicability to the problem. Novices may have a hard time figuring out how to move a sentence of text, even if they understand each of the commands. Novices using editors that have a "CHANGE/old string/new string/" command must still be taught how to use this command to delete a word or insert a word into a line.

As users gain experience, they increasingly think in higher level semantic terms, which are freer from the syntactic detail and more system independent. In addition to facilitating learning, direct manipulation of a visual representation may aid retention.

The syntactic/semantic model suggests that training manuals should be written from the more familiar, high-level, problem domain viewpoint. The titles of sections should describe problem domain operations that the user deals with regularly. Then the details of the commands used to accomplish the task can be presented, and finally, the actual syntax can be shown. Manuals that have alphabetically arranged sections devoted to each command are very difficult for the novice to learn from, because it is difficult to anchor the material to familiar concepts .

The success of direct manipulation is understandable in the context of the syntactic/semantic model. The object of interest is displayed so that actions are directly in the high-level problem domain. There is little need for decomposition into multiple commands with a complex syntactic form. On the contrary, each command produces a comprehensible action in the problem domain that is immediately visible. The closeness of the problem domain to the command action reduces operator problem-solving load and stress.

Dealing with representations of objects may be more "natural" and closer to innate human capabilities: action and visual skills emerged well before language in human evolution. Psychologists have long known that spatial relationships and

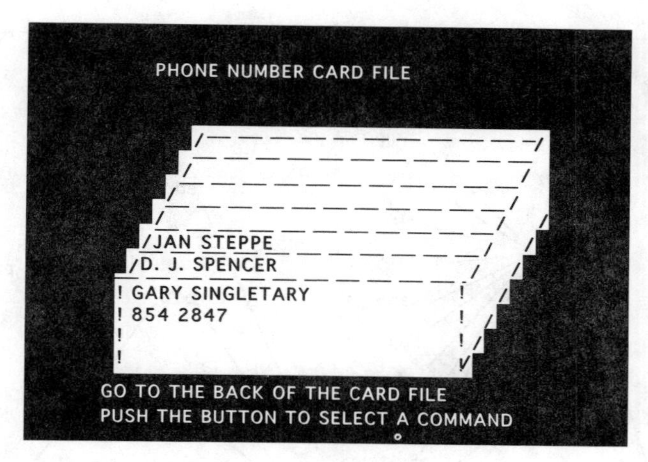

Figure 6. This electronic Rolodex or phone-number card file gives users rapid control over the card motion by a forward or backward joystick press. Different commands can be displayed by moving the joystick left or right. The lively motion of the cards and the natural commands appeal to many users. Implemented by Gary Patterson in Basic on an Apple II, this system was part of a course project at the University of Maryland.

---

actions are more quickly grasped with visual rather than linguistic representations. Furthermore, intuition and discovery are often promoted by suitable visual representations of formal mathematical systems.

Piaget described four stages of growth: sensorimotor (from birth to approximately 2 years), preoperational (2 to 7 years), concrete operational (7 to 11 years), and formal operations (beginning at approximately 11 years) (Copeland, 1979). Physical actions on an object are comprehensible during the concrete operational stage, and children acquire the concept of conservation or invariance. At around age 11, children enter the formal operations stage of symbol manipulation to represent actions on objects. Since mathematics and programming require abstract thinking, they are difficult for children, and a greater effort must be made to link the symbolic representation to the actual object. Direct manipulation is an attempt to bring activity to the concrete operational stage or even to the preoperational stage, thus making some tasks easier for children and adults.

It is easy to envision direct manipulation in cases where the physical action is confined to a small number of objects and simple commands, but the approach may be unsuitable for some complex applications. On the other hand, display editors provide impressive functionality in a natural way. The limits of direct manipulation will be determined by the imagination and skill of the designer. With more examples and experience, researchers should be able to test competing theories about the most effective metaphors or analogies. Familiar visual analogies may be more appealing in the early stages of learning the system, while more specific abstract models may be more useful during regular use.

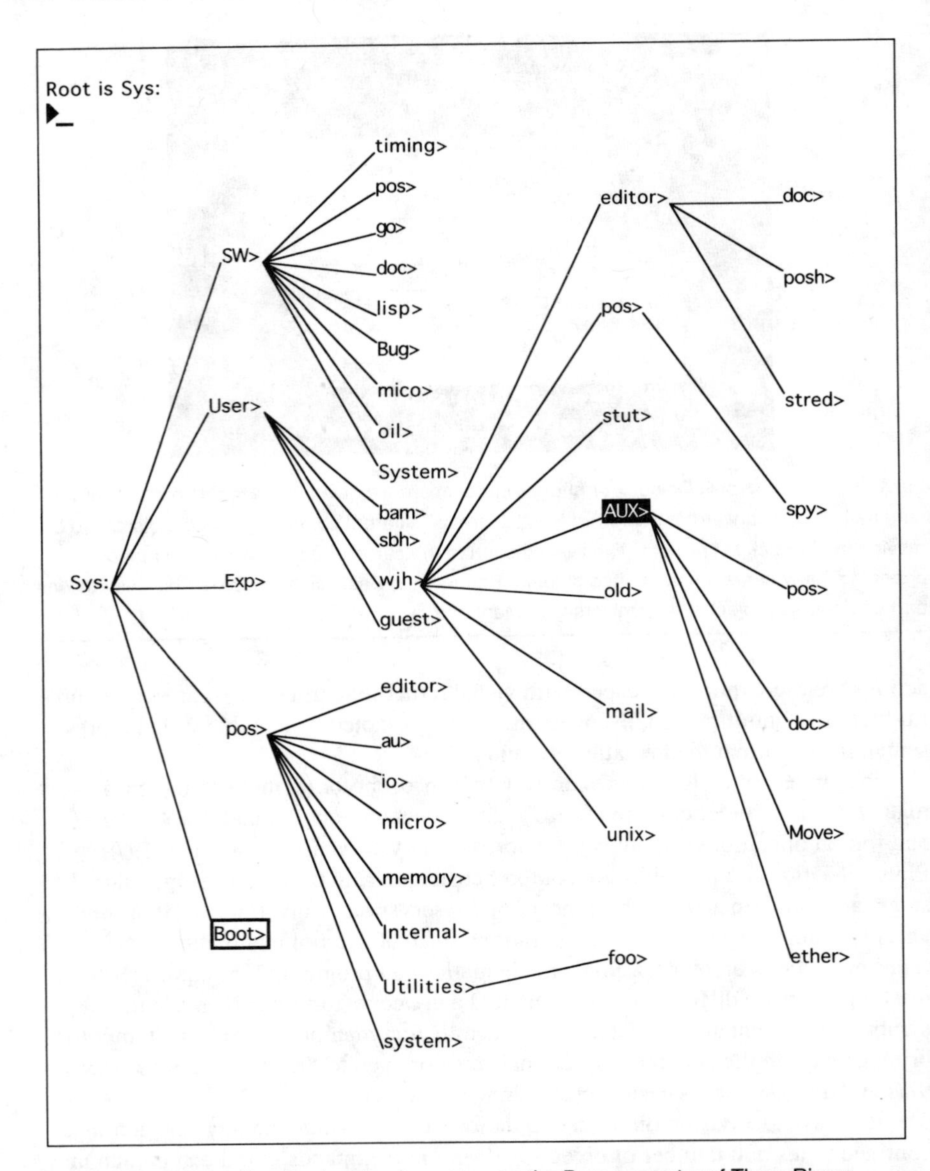

Figure 7. The Dirtree (for directory tree) program on the Perq computer of Three Rivers Computer Corporation is built from left to right by puck selections. The details of lower level directories appear, and the items can then be selected by moving a cursor onto the item. In this figure, the current item is AU, shown in inverse video, but the user has moved the cursor to Boot, which is shown with a box around it. If the button on the puck is pressed, Boot would become the current item. (Figure courtesy of Three Rivers Computer Corporation)

The syntactic/semantic model provides a simple model of human cognitive activity. It must be refined and extended to enhance its explanatory and predictive power. Empirical tests and careful measurements of human performance with a variety of systems are needed to validate the improved model. Cognitive models of user behavior and mental models or system images of computer-supplied functions are rapidly expanding areas of research in computer science and psychology.

Potential applications of direct manipulation

The trick in creating a direct manipulation system is to come up with an appropriate representation or model of reality. I found it difficult to think about information problems in a visual form, but with practice it became more natural. With many applications, the jump to a visual language was initially a struggle, but later I could hardly imagine why anyone would want to use a complex syntactic notation to describe an essentially visual process .

One application that we explored was a personal address list program that displays a Rolodex-like device (see Figure 6). The most recently retrieved address card appears on the screen, and the top line of the next two appear behind, followed by the image of a pack of remaining cards. As the joystick is pushed forward, the Rolodex appears to rotate and successive cards appear in front. As the joystick is pushed further, the cards pass by more quickly; as the joystick is reversed, the direction of movement reverses. To change an entry, users merely move the cursor over the field to be updated and type the correction. To delete an entry, users merely blank out the fields. Blank cards might be left at the top of the file, but when the fields are filled in, proper alphabetic placement is provided. To find all entries with a specific zip code, users merely type the zip code in the proper field and enter a question mark.

Checkbook maintenance and searching might be done in a similar fashion, by displaying a checkbook register with labeled columns for check number, date, payee, and amount. The joystick might be used to scan earlier entries. Changes could be made in place, new entries could be made at the first blank line, and a check mark could be made to indicate verification against a monthly report. Searches for a particular payee could be made by filling in a blank payee field and then typing a question mark.

Bibliographic searching has more elaborate requirements, but a basic system could be built by first showing the user a wall of labeled catalog index drawers. A cursor in the shape of a human hand might be moved over to the section labeled "Author Index" and to the drawer labeled "F-L." Depressing the button on the joystick or mouse would cause the drawer to open up and reveal an array of index cards with tabs offering a finer index. .Moving the cursor-finger and depressing the selection button would cause the actual index cards to appear. Depressing the button while holding a card would cause copying of the card into the user's note-book, also represented on the screen. Entries in the notebook might be edited to create a printed bibliography or combined with other entries to perform set intersec-tions or unions. Copies of entries could be stored on user files or transmitted to colleagues by electronic mail. It is easy to visualize many alternate approaches, so careful design and experimental testing will be necessary to sort out the successful, comprehensible approaches from the idiosyncratic ones.

It is possible to apply direct manipulation to environments for which there is no obvious physical parallel. Imagine a job control language that shows the file directory continuously, along with representations of computer components. A new file is created by typing its name into the first free spot in the directory listing. A file name is deleted by blanking it out. Copies are made by locking a cursor onto a file name and dragging it to a picture of a tape drive or a printer. For a hierarchical directory, the roots are displayed until a zoom command causes the next level of the tree to appear. With several presses of the button labeled ZOOM a user should be able to find the right item in the directory, but if he goes down the wrong path, the UNZOOM button will return to the previous level. (See Figure 7 for a different approach to hierarchical directories.)

Why not make airline reservations by showing the user a map and prompting for cursor motion to the departing and arriving cities? Then use a calendar to select the date, a clock to indicate the time, and the plane's seating plan (with diagonal lines across already reserved seats) to select a seat.

Why not take inventory by showing the aisles of the warehouse with the appropriate number of boxes on each shelf? McDonald (McDonald, 1983) has combined videodisc and computer graphics technology in a medical supply inventory with a visual warehouse display.

Why not teach students about polynomial equations by letting them bend the curves and watch how the coefficients change, where the x-axis intersects, and how the derivative equation reacts? (Shneiderman, 1974)

These ideas are sketches for real systems. Competent designers and implementers must complete the sketches and fill in the details. Direct manipulation has the power to attract users because it is comprehensible, natural, rapid, and even enjoyable. If actions are simple, reversibility ensured, and retention easy, then anxiety recedes and satisfaction flows in.

The tremendous growth of interest in interactive system design issues in the research community is encouraging. Similarly, the increased concern for improved human engineering in commercial products is a promising sign. Academic and industrial researchers are applying controlled, psychologically oriented experimentation (Shneiderman, 1980) to develop a finer understanding of human performance and to generate a set of practical guidelines. Commercial designers and implementers are eagerly awaiting improved guidelines and increasingly using pilot studies and acceptance tests to refine their designs.

Interactive systems that display a representation of the object of interest and permit rapid, incremental, reversible operations through physical actions rather than command syntax are attracting enthusiastic users. Immediate visibility of the results of operations and a layered or spiral approach to learning contribute to the attraction. Each of these features needs research to refine our understanding of its contributions and limitations. But even while such research is in progress, astute designers can explore this approach.

The future of direct manipulation is promising. Tasks that could have been performed only with tedious command or programming languages may soon be accessible through lively, enjoyable interactive systems that reduce learning time, speed performance, and increase satisfaction.

Acknowledgments

I am grateful to the Control Data Corporation for partial support (grant 80M 15) of my work and to the University of Maryland Computer Science Center for computer resources to prepare this report. I thank Gordon Braudaway, Jim Foley, John Gannon, Roger Knights, John Lovgren, Harlan Mills, Phyllis Reisner, Sherry Weinberg, and Mark Weiser for their constructive and supportive comments on draft versions. Gio Wiederhold, Stephen Yau, and the reviewers provided useful guidance in shaping the final article.

Sparks of Innovation in Human-Computer Interaction,
B. Shneiderman, Ed., Ablex Publ., Norwood, NJ (1993)

1.2 A study of file manipulation by novices using commands vs. direct manipulation

Sepeedeh Margono
Ben Shneiderman

Abstract

There are three basic interactive styles of control in human interfaces with computers: command, menu, and direct manipulation. In the past few years, these three styles have become the subject of many studies. However, few comparisons have been done between interfaces that use direct manipulation and command styles. This experiment compares file manipulation operations on the Apple Macintosh, which has a direct manipulation interface, with the IBM PC with MS-DOS, which has the command interface. After a brief training period, novices accomplished file manipulation tasks more rapidly, with fewer errors and greater satisfaction with the Apple Macintosh. Problems arising for both versions are discussed and suggestions for improvements are made.

26th Annual Technical Symposium, Washington, DC Chapter of the ACM, 154-159.

Command interfaces (textual)

Command interfaces require the user to communicate with the computer by typing a formal language with specific syntax. The user is required to learn and memorize the commands and the sequences needed for an operation.

Command interfaces create a feeling of indirectness, because the interface is an implied intermediary between the user and the world of action, i.e., the user is constantly describing the actions. As a result, the user may make mistakes due to:

1. the confusion of the syntax of the language with English;
2. inconsistency in the language;
3. arbitrary syntax (commands made of punctuations);
4. errors made when typing the commands; and;
5. mismatch between the user's intention in the task domain with the computer concepts or syntax.*26th Annual Technical Symposium, Washington, DC Chapter of the ACM, 154-159.*

Therefore, a possible route to increasing a user's understanding of the computer is to make the relationship between the command and action more immediate and direct.

Direct manipulation

Many people form pictures or patterns of tasks in their mind. These people may more easily understand, learn, and memorize when they can visualize objects and actions. In direct manipulation the visual representation should match the way people think about the problem. Direct manipulation interfaces have these characteristics [Shneiderman, 1987, 1983]:

1. continuous representation of the objects and actions of interest;
2. physical actions (movement and selection by mouse, joystick, touch screen, etc.) or labeled button presses instead of complex syntax;
3. rapid, incremental, reversible actions whose impact on the objects of interest is immediately visible; and
4. layered or spiral approach to learning that permits usage with minimal knowledge.

A central goal of the direct manipulation designs is to give the user a sense of directness, that is, an impression or a feeling of close contact with the objects and actions of interest. There are two aspects of directness. One of the aspects is the distance between what the user intends to do and what the system can do. The shorter the distance the stronger the feeling of directness. By short distance, we mean that the translation of the user's thoughts into the actions, required by the system, is straightforward and the system output is easily translated in terms of the user's goals. Therefore, distance emphasizes that directness is not a characteristic of just the interface, but rather a characteristic of the linkage between what the user intends to do and the way in which his/her goal is achieved through the interface [Norman, 1984].

The other aspect of directness, engagement, involves the feeling that the user is acting directly on the objects. Engagement gives the user a feeling of control over the objects in the task domain. Here, the user performs actions on the objects of interest, and the system shows the actions that are performed on the objects. When these aspects are included in an interface, they may make the user's learning process easier, since little effort is needed to get from intention to action and from output to interpretation. Hence, the goal is that the user should learn the task domain instead of the computer system. Thus, a good direct manipulation interface eliminates the visibility of the computer system and its interface from the user, i.e., it should appear to the user that the task domain is manipulated directly.

Systems that have applied direct manipulation include the Xerox Star, the Apple Macintosh, and many application software products such as spread sheets, desk top managers, drawing tools and so forth.

Comparisons between the features of the Macintosh and the IBM PC

Our intention was to determine the ease of use for novices of the Macintosh file commands and the IBM PC with MS-DOS. The Macintosh uses several direct manipulation concepts:

1. files and commands on the Macintosh are visible on the screen in forms of icons and menus;
2. selections of objects and actions on those objects on the Macintosh are generally performed via a mouse mechanism as opposed to the conventional keyboard approach;
3. it is easier to learn Macintosh commands because it taps analogical reasoning on the part of the user.

Most conventional computers are made to serve people with good knowledge of computers, preferably programmers. Macintosh was designed for people with no computer background and for a group identified as "knowledge workers" — anyone who creates reports, budgets, or memos. IBM PC with MS-DOS can be most effectively operated by people with a good knowledge of computers. It is widely available and a reliable computer for accounting, moderate sized data-base management, and many other tasks.

"Macintosh is often viewed as friendly and IBM PC as intimidating by the first-time computer users," (Burns & Veint, 1985). The "user-friendliness" aspect of a system centers on the kind of help the system provides and the ease with which the user can cause the effects they wish to cause. The system should be able to help the user find out what went right or wrong and what can be done next.

Design issues of interactive interfaces

The screen of a Macintosh is a 9-inch black and white, 512 x 342 pixel resolution video display. The number of lines and the number of characters per line depend on the different fonts and font sizes. Along the top of the screen is a menu bar which contains several pull-down menus. These menus include the commands for file-handling, text-editing, desk accessories, etc. The Macintosh screen is an icon-oriented display (i.e., every object (disk or file representation) is depicted by an icon) which continuously displays users' objects of interest.

Actions on an object (e.g., opening a file) are generally performed by selecting an object and then choosing a command from the pull-down menus. Selecting an object is done by pointing and clicking on the object via a mouse. The results of performing an action on an object are immediately visible to the users (i.e., the user does not have to explicitly issue another command to see the results of an action).

The Macintosh screen also incorporates a windowing mechanism allowing users to "open" one or more windows; however, only one of these opened windows may be active at any given time. The design tries to simulate a real-world working environment. For instance, the "desktop" of a Macintosh is supposed to resemble a typical office with a clock, clipboard, trash can, folders, and files (inside a folder).

The IBM PC screen is an 11-inch green on black, 640 x 200 resolution pixel video display. The display features a 25 x 80 character screen. File manipulations are performed by typing MS-DOS commands. This approach has several disadvantages:

1. most commands are difficult to memorize (thus very error prone);
2. uncertainty of whether or not a certain command did what the user expected (this usually requires the user to display a directory after performing a certain command to see if a file has been deleted, copied, etc.); and
3. inability to scroll the directories backward and forward (which can be found in many graphic oriented screens such as the Macintosh, Xerox Star, etc.).

A mouse gives a user a much higher degree of freedom of movement on the screen than cursor keys. A mouse also replaces special function keys present on the IBM PC keyboard. Its movements are smooth, not jumpy. To operate the mouse, a user rolls it along the desktop in any direction, while the cursor represents these movements on the screen. This interaction allows a user to manipulate texts, documents, etc. For example, a user can dispose of a document by using the mouse pointer to drag the document icon to the graphic representation of a waste basket.

The Macintosh design features have a good reputation for being easy to learn and use. But many experienced users find it annoying to move off the keyboard to use the mouse and tedious to locate menu items in the pull-down menus. The graphic interface and mouse selection provide users with direct manipulation interaction and allow users to operate intuitively, while conventional user interfaces require that a user learn commands and procedures before typing them into the computer.

Review of the previous studies

The July 1985 issue of the *PC Magazine* described an experimental comparison of the Macintosh and the IBM PC. The study compared the features of IBM PC with Macintosh which were similarly implemented on the two machines, in order to avoid comparing widely different aspects of the programs. For example, two 512K machines were used, a Microsoft mouse was added to the IBM PC to compare with the Macintosh mouse, and a color monitor and graphic card were also added to the

IBM PC to run the graphics programs. The standard test simply timed the execution of three common operations: 1) loading a file, 2) saving a file, and 3) opening a saved file. The time for performing the above task was approximated to the tenth of a second. In addition, they selected two or more common operations for each application. For instance, a search and replace operation using a word processor and a recalculation using a spreadsheet were timed. Keystrokes on the keyboard and mouse strokes or double clicking on the mouse were counted. Only the computer's execution time was measured, since a variation in operator speed and the time taken to enter a keystroke often made no significant difference.

In the final wrap-up, no conclusion was made as to which machine was more user-friendly. However, they mentioned that even though more software manufacturers began to make the IBM PC more Macintosh-like, the Macintosh still has an advantage over the IBM PC in that its screen designs are built from the inside out, whereas the PC's software packages are a face-lift until a high-resolution screen with built-in processing can be made for the IBM PC. The keyboard of the IBM PC was preferred, since it displayed typed characters far more quickly on the screen, whereas Macintosh's smaller keyboard has an advantage of being portable. The mouse movement was smooth on the Macintosh but did not match all of the advantages of the IBM PC function keys. Macintosh's smaller screen was preferred to that of the IBM PC's, because of its high resolution as opposed to a larger screen with low resolution. One subjective comment was that Macintosh's black and white image was less tiring to read than the darker images of the IBM PC's color monitor. The experimenters also concluded that menu driven software appeared to be slower than the command languages with keyboard macros software. The slowness of menu commands is often a subjective experience, possibly because we don't experience the time passing when actively inputting commands, while menu operations force us to be idle.

Others reviewed the Macintosh and the IBM PC:

1. *Consumer Reports* (January 1985) recommended: "Macintosh is far and away the easiest computer to learn and use that we have yet seen," (Consumer Reports, 1985).
2. *Data Decisions* (June 1985) claimed that: "There is little question that Macintosh is extremely easy to learn and use. The graphic interface and the mouse selection device provide the user with a very direct method of interaction with the computer which allows a user to operate intuitively," (Data Decisions, June 1985).
3. "The IBM PC is relatively easy to use and a powerful computer that enjoys unprecedented hardware and software support from the microcomputer industry" (Sargent& Shoemaker, 1984).

Experiment

Introduction and hypothesis

This experiment compared the user interfaces of an IBM PC with MS-DOS and an Apple Macintosh. Due to a variety of operations that both systems can handle, we chose to limit our comparisons to the file manipulation "commands" on both systems.

Our hypothesis is that Macintosh has a more "user-friendly" interface than IBM PC for novices due to the following:

1. files and commands on a Macintosh are visible on the screen in forms of icons and menus;
2. on a Macintosh, selection of objects and operations are generally performed via a "mouse" mechanism as opposed to the conventional keyboard approach;
3. it is easier to learn Macintosh commands because it requires minimal knowledge on the part of the user;
4. it takes less time to perform a task on a Macintosh than on an IBM PC; and
5. users will make fewer errors in performing commands.

Independent Variables (Computer Type for File Manipulation Commands):

1. IBM PC with MS-DOS
2. Macintosh

Dependent Variables:

1. Time taken to perform a specific task
2. Number of errors made
3. Subjective satisfaction

Subjects

Since this experiment was to test for the "user-friendliness" of the interfaces of both systems, we decided to choose people with limited computer background. We sought thirty people with no previous experience in using either the IBM PC or the Macintosh. Eighteen of the subjects were students obtained from the psychology subject pool, and had no computer experience. Twelve subjects were acquired by personal contact. Among the thirty subjects who participated in our experiment, five had used a computer other than the IBM PC and the Macintosh for less than one month. Four subjects had moderate computer experience but no prior exposure to the IBM PC or the Macintosh.

Materials

Experimental materials included:

1. a Macintosh (main unit, keyboard, mouse, disk drives, and diskettes);
2. an IBM PC (main unit, keyboard, disk drives, and floppy disks);
3. consent forms;
4. instruction sheets; and
5. questionnaires.

Subjects were provided with two instruction sheets, one for the IBM PC, the other for the Macintosh. Both instruction sheets showed how to perform file commands such as creating, copying, renaming, and erasing. For the IBM PC, the subjects were instructed step by step on what to do, (for example, looking for the right prompt, typing in the right command and pressing the ENTER key after each command). The following is an example of an instruction for the IBM PC.

Copying a file (IBM PC)

To make a duplicate of a file, we have to issue a copy command to the PC.

1. You should see the prompt B> on the screen. Type copy first.txt second.txt and then press the ENTER key.
2. The PC should return the message:
1 file(s) copied
If it does not return the message, then you need to repeat steps 1 and 2.

For the Macintosh, the subjects were also instructed step by step as to what to do. For example, how to use the mouse, how to select an icon, and how to choose commands from the menu bar. The following is an example from the Macintosh instruction sheet:

Copying a file (Macintosh)

1. Now on the screen you can see 2 icons: Edit and First.
Position the pointer on the icon First, and click on it.
2. Place the pointer on the word File in the menu bar.
3. Press the mouse button and hold it down while you drag the pointer to the word Duplicate, then release the mouse button.
4. To the right of First, you will see a copy of it called Copy of First.

The questionnaire consisted of three pages, of which the first page inquired about the subject's background. The rest of the pages contained questions about the different features of both systems. For example :

i. What do you think of IBM' s display? Please explain.
ii. Please explain what you think of the Macintosh's:
    a. iconic feature
    b. display
iii. If you got error messages, were they helpful in explaining what you did wrong?
    IBM PC : Helpful <- 1 2 3 4 5 6 -> Not helpful
    Macintosh : Helpful <- 1 2 3 4 5 6 -> Not helpful

User's satisfaction questions included:

i. Which machine do you find simpler to use?
    IBM PC : Hardest <- 1 2 3 4 5 6 -> Easiest
    Macintosh : Hardest <- 1 2 3 4 5 6 -> Easiest
ii. Which machine are you more satisfied with?

Procedures

To make good use of our time, we tried to have two subjects in each one hour session. While one subject worked on the IBM PC and then the Macintosh, the other subject worked on the Macintosh and later on the IBM PC. A typical session consisted of the phases:

1. Introduction: Subjects were informed of the purposes and procedures of the experiment. They were then asked to sign a consent form. Subjects were then given a demo of each computer. For the Macintosh, the experimenters talked about the display (screen appearance and color, icons and pull down menus, windows), the mouse and its usage, and the keyboard. The demo of the IBM PC provided information on the display (screen appearance and color, cursor, prompts) and the keyboard.
2. Practice: The subjects were allowed to read and practice the tasks in the instruction sheets twice. The first practice was to familiarize the subjects with both systems and the second practice was to make the subjects memorize the steps. The maximum time permitted for this phase was twenty minutes for each machine. The time taken for each practice was measured.
3. Test: The subjects were asked to perform four tasks without referring to the instruction sheets. These four tasks — creating a file, copying a file, renaming a file, and erasing a file — were chosen by the experimenters. The maximum time permitted for this phase was twenty minutes. The time taken by each subject to perform the four tasks was measured.
4. Evaluation: The subjects were given a questionnaire after they had tried both systems. The questionnaire asked about the subject's views on the tasks described in the instruction sheets and the interfaces of both machines.

Whenever subjects took less time to complete a phase, they would start the next phase. During the practice and test phases, they were assisted whenever they had trouble. We took notes on the subjects' behaviors, their performance in using the Macintosh mouse, the commands on both systems, and their comprehension of the commands. We also took notes on the number of errors they made. These errors were 1) not performing the requested tasks (e.g., requested task was to copy a file while the performed task was renaming a file), 2) typing the wrong syntax for the commands on the IBM PC, and 3) confusing the steps on the Macintosh (e.g., instead of dragging the mouse, the subject clicked it).

Administration

A pilot study of eight subjects was conducted over a period of one week. The subjects had no previous experience with computers. Each experiment lasted about an hour. After the pilot study, the instruction sheets and the questionnaire were revised. We also made some changes to the practice and test phases of the experiment.

A series of one-hour experiments were conducted over a period of three weeks with thirty subjects. The subjects signed a consent form and were asked to sit in front of the computers after the computers were set up. The subjects were advised to relax and enjoy the experiment. During the experiment, the experimenter sat beside the subject and assisted him or her whenever they had difficulties. We recorded the time for each practice and the time for the test phase. We also recorded the number of errors made by the subjects.

Grading

In order to measure the satisfaction level, we created an ad hoc scale. First, we added the results of questions 1 and 2 in the questionnaire. Question 1 asks the subjects to indicate, on a scale from 1 to 6, which machine they found simpler to use. Question 2 asks the subjects to indicate, on a scale from 1 to 6, which machine gave them a better understanding of what they did. Next, a score of 1 was added to the average if the subject preferred the IBM PC or the Macintosh. In some cases, where the subject was equally satisfied with both machines or could not make a decision, a score of 0 was added to the average.

Results

The mean time for the first practice on the IBM PC was 9.37 minutes, and the mean time for the first practice on the Macintosh was 8.2 minutes. However, the mean time for the second practice of the IBM PC decreased to 5.1 and for the Macintosh the mean time dropped to 4.8. These new values indicated the subjects became familiar with both the typing commands in the IBM PC and in moving the mouse in the Macintosh.

The mean time for the test phases of the IBM PC and the Macintosh were 5.77 minutes and 4.80 minutes respectively, statistically significant by t-test at the $p < 0.10$ level. The mean for the number of errors made on the IBM PC was 2.03, and that of the Macintosh was 0.80 ($p < 0.01$). The mean for the satisfaction levels of the IBM PC and the Macintosh were 3.80 and 5.37 respectively, out of a 7 point scale ($p < 0.01$).

The following tables represent the mean values for the time taken to complete the tasks in the test phase, number of errors made during the test phase, and the satisfaction level on both machines.

Out of thirty subjects, eighteen of them preferred the Macintosh, ten preferred the IBM PC, one was undecided, and one liked both machines equally.

Discussion

Observations made during the experiment indicated that almost all of the subjects had a difficult time in using the mouse for the first few minutes. More than twenty of them learned how to use the mouse correctly after nine to ten minutes. Five subjects did have a very difficult time with the mouse the entire time they worked on the Macintosh. Similarly, nine subjects were not familiar with the keyboard and could not type easily.

Half of the subjects had problems in remembering when and how to select, open, or drag a document using the mouse. Another common problem was with renaming a document, somehow the subjects always wanted to do more, rather than simply typing in a word. Forgetting the punctuation, adding unnecessary spaces, and omitting the parameters in such commands as copy and rename were among the

		Test Time (minutes)	Error	Satisfaction
IBM PC	Mean N = 30	5.77	2.03	3.80
	S.D. N = 30	2.37	1.54	1.78
Macintosh	Mean N = 30	4.80	0.80	5.37
	S.D. N = 30	1.61	0.76	1.41

Table 1. Mean and Standard Deviation Values for Test Time (in minutes), Number of Errors, and Satisfaction Level for IBM PC and Macintosh.

common problems the subjects had on the IBM PC. More than half of the subjects had difficulty recalling the steps involved in creating a file on the IBM PC.

The following results were gathered from the subjects' responses to the questionnaire:

1. Four subjects were not happy with the display of the IBM PC, because it was hard for them to know what was happening. The rest of the subjects found the display easy to read and to use and the size of screen and letters appropriate.
2. More than half of the subjects thought the commands on the IBM PC were easy to remember, although it seemed confusing to some of them for the first few times. A number of them found the commands hard to remember and to use.
3. Few subjects voted for typing in the commands. Most of them preferred the use of the mouse because they found it to be easier to use, more fun, and faster.
4. The majority of the subjects claimed that the iconic feature of the Macintosh gave them a better understanding of what was happening, since they could see the results of actions immediately. Some subjects thought that the icons were fun, amusing, and even silly.
5. The display on the Macintosh was considered to be clear, easy on the eyes, have an appropriate size of screen and letters, and have a good resolution by a majority of the subjects. A few commented that a larger screen and larger letters would be better. A couple of subjects did not like the display.
6. Many of the subjects rated the pull-down menus as being fast and easy to use because no command memorization and typing was required. A few of the subjects did not like this feature since it looked silly and awkward to them.

7. More than half of the subjects preferred the black characters on the white background of the Macintosh to the green characters on the black background of the IBM PC. The former was considered to be easier to look at, relaxing to the eyes, and clear. The latter was criticized for being harsh on the eyes, a little fuzzy, and hard to look at. Nevertheless, a few subjects did prefer the latter and believed it made reading easier.
8. The following commands on the IBM PC chosen by a majority of the subjects in descending order of difficulty were creating a file, renaming a file, copying a file, listing a file, and erasing a file. A few claimed that none of the commands were difficult.
9. The following commands on the Macintosh chosen by a majority of the subjects in descending order of difficulty were copying a file, renaming a file, creating a file, removing a file, and erasing a file. A few claimed that none of the commands were difficult.
10. Half of the subjects who made errors on the IBM PC found the error messages helpful; the other half claimed that the error messages did not help them find out what they did wrong.
11. A majority of the subjects who made errors on the Macintosh found the error messages helpful in finding what they did wrong. A few did not find these messages helpful.
12. All but three of the subjects thought that the file recovering feature of the Macintosh is a novel idea and it should be implemented in all computers. Most of them commented that discarding something important by mistake is very frustrating and a recovery feature can help a great deal.

Conclusion

This study provided some support for the conjecture that Macintosh has a more "user-friendly" interface than the IBM PC with MS-DOS for novices doing file manipulation commands, because:

1. it is easier to learn and use the commands and procedures, as it requires only modest memorization on the part of the users, and,
2. it takes less time for the users to perform tasks on the Macintosh, due to the presence of the mouse and the pull-down menus, which increase the speed of performance and eliminate typing of the commands.

The reason for this may be that Macintosh uses more familiar concepts, whereas IBM PC with MS-DOS uses a language based on computer terminology, which is difficult for most of the users to learn and to retain. For instance, the TRASH icon on the desktop of the Macintosh looks familiar to most users. The users know that a trash can is for throwing things away. As a result, users can make a connection between the computer display and objects they are familiar with. Also, the combination of words and illustrations (icons) requires less memorization by the users.

Using the mouse can be easier than typing because working with the mouse is very similar to the way people do things. For instance, to turn on a light we must first touch the switch before pushing it (i.e., point to or select the object of interest before performing an action on it). Working with the mouse may decrease the number of errors, since less typing is involved and thus, fewer typographical errors can be made.

From the subjective responses in the questionnaire, eighteen of the subjects preferred the Macintosh while ten preferred the IBM PC. Overall, Macintosh created a sense of directness, that is, the users felt that they were in control of the system since they were directly manipulating the objects of interest and the actions.

These results should not be used as the sole guide in making purchasing decisions about hardware and software. Many other factors influence such decisions. Rather, these results should serve as a guide to designers in developing future applications and for researchers who are seeking to understand direct manipulation. Furthermore, this experiment dealt only with novices in a learning situation. Additional experiments are necessary to study frequent and expert users, who often prefer and may work more rapidly with command language strategies.

Acknowledgments

We thank Wai-Yee Wong for her contribution to conducting the experiment, to our subjects for their participation, and to the reviewers for their comments.

Sparks of Innovation in Human-Computer Interaction,
B. Shneiderman, Ed., Ablex Publ., Norwood, NJ (1993)

1.3 Remote direct manipulation: a case study of a telemedicine workstation

Richard Keil-Slawik
Catherine Plaisant
Ben Shneiderman

Abstract

This paper describes our experience with the design of a remote pathologist's workstation. We illustrate how our effort to apply direct manipulation principles led us to explore remote direct manipulation designs. The use of computer and communication systems to operate devices remotely introduces new challenges for users and designers. In addition to the usual concerns, the activation delays, reduced feedback, and increased potential for breakdowns mean that designers must be especially careful and creative. The user interface design is closely linked to the total system design.

Human Aspects in Computing: Design and Use of Interactive Systems and Information Management, Bullinger H.-J., Ed., Elsevier, Amsterdam *(Proc. of the 4th Int. Conf. On HCI,* Stuttgart, Sept. 91) 1006-1011.

Introduction

Direct manipulation has been described as a visual representation of the world of action with rapid, incremental and reversible actions (Shneiderman 1983). The objects and actions of interest are shown continuously, users generally point, click, or drag rather than type, and feedback, indicating change, is immediate. However, when the devices being operated are remote, these goals may not be realizable and designers must spend additional effort to cope with slower response, incomplete feedback, increased likelihood of breakdowns, and error recovery. The problems are strongly connected to the hardware, physical environment, network design, and the task domain.

We studied these problems in the context of a remotely controlled microscope system used by pathologists to make diagnoses based on seeing microscope slides of tissues, blood, or other specimens. Our task was to redesign an existing system (developed by Corabi International Telemetrics, Inc.) to enhance its usability and provide for future extensions. This paper presents our solutions to some of the problems and discusses the extension of direct manipulation principles to an environment that includes remote control. We describe the Corabi Project and show examples of user interface design issues and then outline principles of remote direct manipulation.

The Corabi telepathology workstation

Telemedicine is the practice of medicine over communication links. The physician being consulted and the patient are in two different locations. Corabi International Telemetrics developed the first telepathology system (Weinstein, Bloom & Rozek, 1987 and 1989) that allows a pathologist to render a diagnosis by examining tissue samples or body fluids under a remotely located microscope. The transmitting workstation consists of a high resolution camera mounted on a motorized light microscope. The image from the camera is transmitted via broadband satellite, microwave or cable. The consulting pathologist sits at the receiving

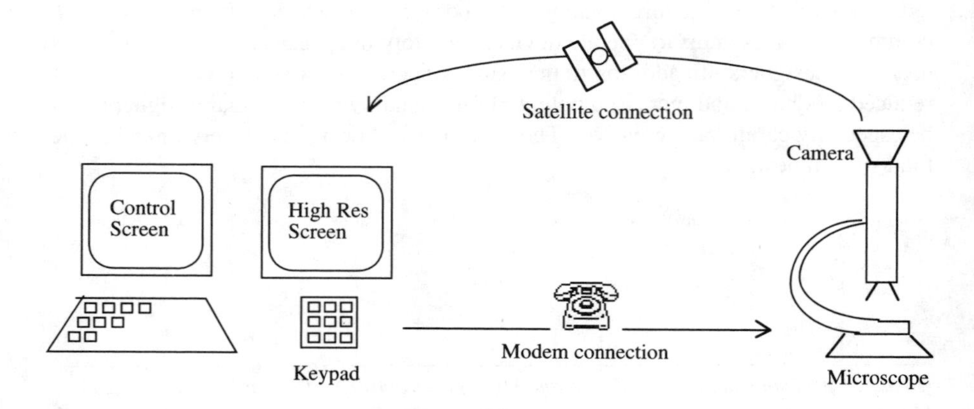

Figure 1. Simplified diagram of a telepathology system.

workstation where she/he can manipulate the microscope using a keypad and look at the high resolution image of the magnified sample. Both physicians talk by telephone to coordinate control of the system and to request slides that have to be manually placed under the microscope.

The system also allows the pathologist to store the results, recall the case at a later time, ask for second advice and manage the patient's records. During a work session the pathologist alternates between selecting cases to work on and performing a diagnosis. To conduct the diagnosis the pathologist goes back and forth between reading the patient record, choosing the slide to be viewed and entering the diagnosis.

Practically, the pathologist sees a high resolution screen displaying the analog image from the microscope, and a control screen (a PC display). The control screen only displays alphanumeric data and is used for database management tasks on the patient records, as well as to establish connections with the remote site and display status data during the connection. In the original system a third monochrome screen was used to display a small scanned global image of the whole specimen. To control the microscope the pathologist uses a keypad (with arrow keys and function keys) as well as a large number of buttons and toggles mounted on the rack holding the circuitry. The microscope controls include:

- magnification (three or six objectives),
- focus (coarse and fine bidirectional control),
- illumination (bidirectional adjustment continuous or by step), and
- position (2-dimensional placement of the slide under the microscope objective).

Our overall task was to redesign the database access, navigation among the tasks, and remote control of the microscope during the diagnosis. According to the principles of direct manipulation, our first step was to group related displays and controls that were originally dissociated such that all alphanumeric displays (all displays except the high resolution one) and controls are found on the control screen and can be manipulated with a pointing device. The control screen becomes the central part of the user interface.

Typical problems of remote direct manipulation

The architecture of a remote environment such as the one described above introduces several complicating factors that rarely occur in direct manipulation environments:

Time delays. The network hardware and software cause delays in sending user actions and receiving feedback: transmission delays, i.e., the time it takes for the command to reach the microscope (in our case, transmitting the command through the modem), and operation delays, i.e., the microscope itself does not respond right away. These delays in the system prevent the operator from knowing the current status of the system. For example, if a positioning command has been issued it may require several seconds for the slide to start moving. As the feedback appears showing the motion, the users may recognize that they are going to overshoot their destination, but it will also take a few seconds to have the stopping command take effect.

Incomplete feedback. Devices originally designed for direct control may not have adequate sensors or status indicators. For instance, our microscope can report its current position but it is so slow to provide it that it cannot be used continuously. Thus, it is not possible to indicate on the control screen the exact current position relative to the start and desired positions.

Feedback from multiple sources. Incomplete feedback does not imply that there is no feedback at all. The image received on the high resolution screen is the main feedback to evaluate the result of an action. In addition, the microscope can occasionally report its exact position allowing recalibration of the status display. It is also possible to indicate the estimated stage position during the execution of a movement. This estimated feedback can be used as a progress indicator whose accuracy depends on the variability of the time delays. To comply with the physical incompatibility between the high resolution feedback (analog image) and the rest of the system (digital), the multiple feedbacks are spread over several screens. Thus, the pathologists are forced to switch back and forth between multiple sources of feedback, increasing their cognitive load.

Unanticipated interferences. Since the devices operated are remote, and may be also operated by other persons in this or another remote location, unanticipated interferences are more likely to occur than in traditional direct manipulation environments. For instance, the slide under the microscope may be moved (accidentally) by a local operator. As a result, the positions indicated may not be correct. A breakdown may also occur during the execution of a remote operation, without indicating this event properly to the remote site. Such break-downs require additional information and actions that allow for the cancellation of actions to prevent their completion.

Our proposed solution to these problems is to make explicit the network delays as part of the system, without compromising the overall system usability. The user needs to see a model of the:

- starting state of the system,
- action that has been issued, and
- current state of the system as it carries out the action.

In addition, we believe that it is preferable to provide spatially parametrized positioning actions (i.e., move of a distance +x, +y or to a fixed point (x, y) in a two dimensional space), rather than providing temporal commands (i.e., start moving right at a 36° angle from the horizontal). In other words, the users specify a destination (rather than a motion) and wait until the action is completed before readjusting the destination if necessary. In general, we try to turn the remote environment as much as possible into a direct manipulation environment by applying the same basic principles.

However, there may be obstacles to implementing these principles. We will highlight the problems involved by discussing the redesign of the slide position control, because it illustrates the additional challenges of dealing with remotely operated devices.

Slide movement control - a design example

To provide a visual representation of the world of action it is certainly helpful to present a global view of the slide to the pathologist on the control screen. Since the specimen itself only occupies a small part of the slide, the global view lets the pathologist know what parts of the slide need to be observed and if the specimen under the slide is made of one or several separate parts. A red rectangle shown on the slide indicates the position of the microscope objective and tells what portion of the slide (the stage) is being viewed on the high resolution screen. Markers can be also placed on the map to indicate points saved. The rectangle can be selected with a pointing device and used to move the stage to another position on the slide. Similarly, a saved point can be selected to be retrieved. These actions are handled with direct manipulation principles, making them easy to learn and to remember. Unfortunately, several problems blocked the extension of these principles to the control of all movements of the slide.

The first problem is that the microscope movements require very precise and smooth moves when using a high magnification. This makes it very difficult to use direct manipulation of the rectangle (then very small) on the global slide view. Of course, we envisioned using zoomed images of the global view of the slide. Despite the fact that this technique would require the user to zoom and pan the

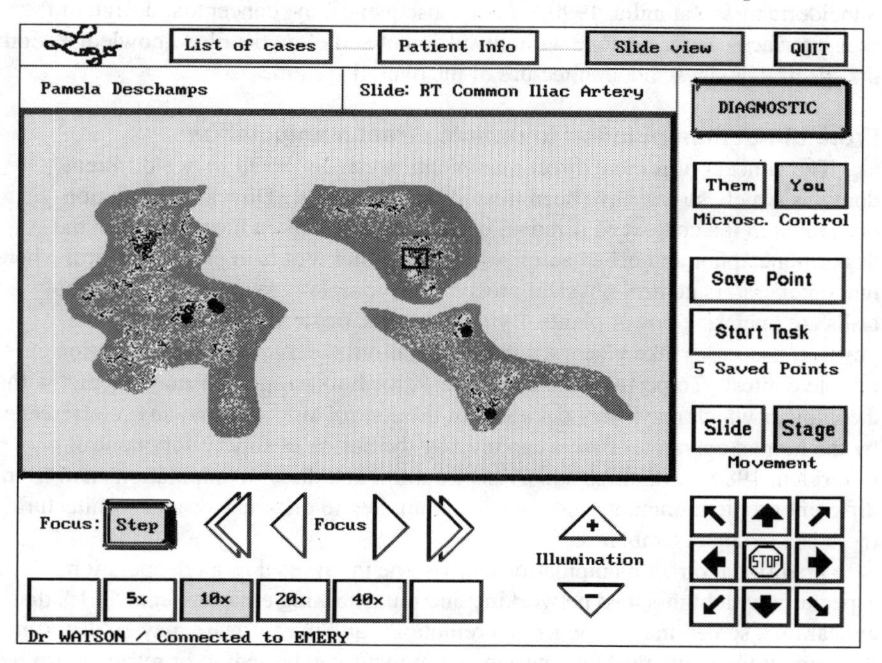

Figure 2: the control screen, showing the global view of the slide and the stage position mark.

global view before actually controlling the slide movement, we were faced with the problem that there was no practical way to obtain a useful zoomed image. The microscope was too slow to scan a full slide, it could not guarantee a precise and consistent placement of the slide to have the scanning done in advance by a technician, and the stored image was space expensive.

What we could provide, however, was the fine control of the slide relative to its current position (i.e., specify a direction and distance) rather than in an absolute manner (i.e., specify a position). The global view of the slide is used only to give feedback about the position of the stage. Thus, it cannot be used as an object that can be manipulated (moved) directly with respect to all levels of magnification. But the spatial representation provides more control for the pathologists because it indicates where the part visible on the high resolution screen is located with respect to the whole specimen. Since the saved points are displayed as well, this may provide additional, implicit feedback, for instance, about regions that have been scanned already. This information is only implicitly given because it can only be derived by connecting the displayed data with the specific activities performed by the pathologists, e.g., when they choose a systematic strategy for scanning a slide.

The example shows that the device characteristics were of paramount importance in the user interface design. This is a very common problem: remotely controlled devices often fail to provide any usable feedback at all. For example, current home automation user interfaces are constrained by the fact that home devices do not return status information to the central control [Plaisant, Shneiderman & Battaglia, 1990]. As a consequence, the conceptual design of the user interface cannot be done without sufficient and often detailed knowledge about the specific devices and architecture of the overall system.

From direct manipulation to remote direct manipulation

The concept of remote direct manipulation can be rooted in two different domains which, so far, have been treated independently. Direct manipulation originated in the context of personal computers and is often identified with the desktop metaphor and office automation. The other root is in process control where human operators control physical processes in complex environments. Typical tasks are operating power plants, flying airplanes, or steering vehicles. If the physical processes take place in a remote location, we talk about teleoperation or remote control. To perform the control task, the human operator may interact with a computer which may carry out some of the control tasks without any interference by the human operator. This is captured by the notion of supervisory control (Sheridan, 1988). Although supervisory control and direct manipulation stem from different problem domains and are usually applied to different system architectures, there is a strong resemblance.

Traditional direct manipulation can also be interpreted as a teleoperation, especially with high-speed networking and multi-tasking environments. Files that appear on a screen may come from a remote PC and the software may be distributed throughout the network. Messages and documents can be sent to or retrieved from remote machines, printers, or file servers. Even the letters on a display may be composed of font descriptions stored in a remote location from where the keystrokes are issued. Thus, the essential components of a teleoperation environment such as sensors, displays, controls, remote effectors or tools, and communication links are involved.

Remote direct manipulation (as well as supervisory control) cannot be taken as a design criterion which is either fulfilled or not. One interface can be slightly more direct than another. Similarly, the control can be felt to be more or less remote. Thus, remote direct manipulation denotes a range of possible solutions rather than a binary variable. Direct manipulation is still an imprecise and subjective concept, although it has proved eminently useful in stimulating designers, revising existing systems, training designers, and in comparing systems. The connection between direct manipulation and supervisory control seems promising.

Conclusions

We believe that there are great opportunities for the remote control of devices if proper remote direct manipulation interfaces can be constructed. The notion of user control seems to play a key role. It requires designers to provide adequate feedback in sufficient time to permit effective decision making and operation. A thorough task analysis as well as detailed knowledge about the technical environment are indispensable means to come up with creative solutions that put the user into control. The designers have to understand the system architecture, its strengths and weaknesses and the users' needs to achieve a good conceptual design.

In domains such as office automation and process control, as well as in many others, the design of human-computer interfaces and the development of general models of human computer interaction, rather than the improvement of devices, are regarded as the major challenge for researchers. However, devices are not yet sufficiently well designed to allow for their smooth integration in a remote environment according to the principles of remote direct manipulation:

- shorten time delays,
- provide extensive feedback of status,
- coordinate available feedback, and
- reduce possible interferences.

The development of these new integrated and remotely controlled environments also provides a stimulus for new applications. Remote controlled environments in medicine could enable specialists to provide consultations more rapidly. Home automation applications are being developed to allow more than remote operation of telephone answering machines by including security and access systems, energy control, and operation of appliances. Scientific applications in space, underwater, or in hostile environments can enable new research projects to be conducted economically and safely.

Acknowledgments

We appreciate the support of the Maryland Industrial Partnerships program and Corabi International Telemetrics, Inc. in providing partial funding for this research. We would like to thank Beth Newberger, Tom Throop, and Ann Regan-Jean fromm Corabi International Telemetrics, Inc. for their helpful suggestions.

Note: There is a 10 minute segment in the HCIL Open House '92 video. This segment is also published in the ACM INTERCHI '93 technical video.

References

Arnheim, R. (1972) *Visual Thinking*, University of California Press, Berkeley, CA.

"Apple Macintosh", Data Decisions (June 1985). 1-4.

Ausubel, D.P. (1968) *Educational Psychology: A Cognitive Approach*, Holt, Rinehart and Winston, New York.

Benbasat, I, Todd, P. (March 1993),An experimental investigation of interface design alternatives: icon bvs. text and direct manipulation vs. menus, *International Journal of Man-Machine Studies*, Vol. 38, No. 3, 369-402.

Bruner, J. (1966) *Toward a Theory of Instruction,* Harvard University Press, Cambridge, MA.

Burns, D., Veint, S. (July 1985) "IBM PC vs. MAC", *PC Magazine*, 112-131.

Carroll, J. M., Thomas, J.C., Malhotra, A. (1980) "Presentation and Representation in Design Problem-Solving," *British J. Psych.*, Vol. 71,143-153.

Carroll, J. M. (1982) Learning, Using and Designing Command Paradigms, *Human Learning*, Vol. I, No. I, 31-62.

Carroll, J. M., Thomas, J. C. (Mar./Apr. 1982) Metaphor and the Cognitive Representation of Computing Systems, *IEEE Trans. Systems, Man, and Cybernetics*, Vol. SMC-12, No. 2, 107-116.

"Computers: Apple Macintosh" (Jan. 1985) *Consumer Reports*, 31.

Copeland, R. W. (1979) *How Children Learn Mathematics*, third ed., MacMillan, New York.

Herot, C. F. (Dec. 1980) Spatial Management of Data, *ACM Trans. Database Systems*, Vol. 5, No. 4, 493 -513.

Hutchins, E.L., Hollan, J.D., Norman, D.A. (1986) Direct Manipulation Interfaces., *User Centered System Design. New Perspectives on Human-Computer Interaction,* Norman, D.A., Draper, S.W., Eds., Hillsdale: Lawrence Earlbaum, 87-124.

Hutchins, E. L., Hollan, J. D., Norman, D. A (1986) *User Centered System Design*, Lawrence Erlbaum Associates, Hillsdale, NJ.

"IBM Personal Computer" (Sept. 1985) *Datapro Research Corporation*, 101-107.

Keil-Slawik, R., Plaisant, C., Shneiderman, B. (April 1991) Remote direct manipulation: a case study of a telemedicine workstation, *Human Aspects in Computing: Design and Use of Interactive Systems and Information Management*, Bullinger H.-J. Ed., *Proc. of the 4th Int. Conf. on HCI,* Stuttgart (Sept. 91). Elsevier, Amsterdam, 1006-1011.

MacArthur, C., Shneiderman, B. (Jan. 1986) Remedial-reading students' difficulties in learning to use a word processor: Implications for design, *ACM SIGCHI Bulletin* 17, 3 41-

46.
MacDonald, A. (Oct. 1982) Visual Programming,"*Datamation*, Vol. 28, No. 11 132-140.
Malone, T. W. (Dec. 1981) What Makes Computer Games Fun?"*Byte*, Vol. 6, No. 12 258-277.
Margono, S., Shneiderman, B. (June 1987) A study of file manipulation by novices using commands vs. direct manipulation, *26th Annual Technical Symposium*, Washington, DC Chapter of the ACM, 154-159.
McDonald, N., Multi-media Approach to User Interface, *Human Factors in Interactive Computer Systems*, Vassiliou, Y., Ed., Ablex Publishing Co., Norwood, N.J.
McKim, R. H. (1972) *Experiences in Visual Thinking*, Brooks/Cole Publishing Co., Monterey, Calif.
Montessori, M. (1964) *The Montessori Method*, Schocken, New York.
Morgan, K., Morris, R. L., Gibbs, S. (1991) When does a mouse become a rat? or.. Comparing performance and preferences in direct manipulation and command line environments, *The Computer Journal* 34, 3, 265-271.
Nelson, T. (Nov. 1980) Interactive Systems and the Design of Virtuality, *Creative Computing*, Vol. 6, No. 11, 56 ff., and Vol. 6, No. 12, (Dec. 1980), 94 ff.
Norman, D. A. (1984) Stages and levels in human-machine interaction, *International Journal of Man-Machine Studies*, Vol. 21, 365-375.
Norman, D. (1988) *The Psychology of Everyday Things*, Basic Books, New York.
Norman, K., Weldon, L., Shneiderman, B. (1986) Cognitive layouts of windows and multiple screens for user interfaces, *International Journal of Man-Machine Studies*, Vol. 25, 229-248.
Papert, S.(1980) *Mindstorms: Children, Computers, and Powerful Ideas*, Basic Books, Inc., New York.
Plaisant, C., Shneiderman, B., Battaglia, J. (Dec. 1990) Scheduling home-control devices: a case study of the transition from the research project to a product, *Human-Factors in Practice* , Santa-Monica, CA: Computer Systems Technical Group, Human-Factors Society, 7-12.
Polya, G. (1957) *How to Solve It*, Doubleday, New York,
Rasmussen, J., Goodstein, L.P. (1988) Information Technology and Work, *Handbook of Human-Computer Interaction*, Helander, M., Ed., Amsterdam: North-Holland 175-201.
Rauterberg, M., (1992) An empirical comparison of menu-selection (CUI) and desktop (GUI) computer programs carried out by beginners and experts, *Behaviour & Information Technology*, Vol. 11, No. 4, 227-236.
Roberts, T. L. (1980) Evaluation of Computer Text Editors, Ph.D. dissertation, Stanford University. Available from University Microfilms, Ann Arbor, Michigan, order # AAD 80-11699.
Rubenstein, R., Hersh, H. (1984) *The Human Factor/Designing Computer Systems For People*, Digital Press, Hudson, MA.
Rutkowski, C. (Oct. 1982) An Introduction to the Human Applications Standard Computer Interface, Part 1: Theory and Principles, *Byte*, Vol. 7, No. 11 291-310.
Sargent, M., Shoemaker, R. L. (1984) *The IBM Personal Computer from the inside out*, Addison-Wesley Publishing Co., Reading, MA.
Schneider, M. L. (1982) Models for the Design of Static Software User Assistance, *Directions in Human-Computer Interaction*, Badre, A., Shneiderman, B. Eds., Ablex Publishing Co., Norwood, N.J.
Sheridan, T.B. (1987) Teleoperation, Telepresence, and Telerobotics: Research Needs for Space, *Human Factors in Automated and Robotic Space Systems Proc.,* Sheridan, T.B.,

Kruser, D.S., Deutsch, S., Eds., National Research Council, Washington, DC, 279-291.

Sheridan, T.B. (1988) *Task Allocation and Supervisory Control*, Helander, M., Ed.

Shneiderman, B. (Feb. 1974) A Computer Graphics System for Polynomials, *The Mathematics Teacher*, Vol. 67, No. 2, 111-113.

Shneiderman, B., Mayer, R., McKay, D., Heller, P. (June 1977) Experimental Investigations of the Utility of Detailed Flowcharts in Programming, *Communications of the ACM*, Vol. 20, No. 6, 373-381.

Shneiderman, B., Mayer, R. (1979) Syntactic/Semantic Interactions in Programmer Behavior: A Model and Experimental Results, *International Journal of Computer and Information Sciences*, Vol. 8, No. 3, 219-239.

Shneiderman, B. (1980) *Software Psychology: Human Factors in Computer and Information Systems*, Little, Brown & Co., Boston, MA.

Shneiderman, B. (Feb. 1981) A Note on Human Factors Issues of Natural Language Interaction with Database Systems, *Information Systems*, Vol. 6, No. 2, 125-129.

Shneiderman, B. (Jan 1982) Control Flow and Data Structure Documentation: Two Experiments, *Communications of the ACM*, Vol. 25, No. 1, 55-63.

Shneiderman, B. (Aug. 1983) Direct Manipulation: A step beyond programming languages, *IEEE Computer* 16, 8, 57-69.

Shneiderman, B. (1987) *Designing the User Interface: Strategies for Effective Human-Computer Interactions*, Addison-Wesley Publishing Co., Reading, MA.

Smith, C. et al. (Apr. 1982) Designing the Star User Interface, *Byte*, Vol. 7, No. 4, 242-282.

Te'Eni, D. (1990) Direct manipulation as a source of cognitive feedback: A human-computer experiment with a judgment task, *International Journal of Man-Machine Studies,* Vol. 33, 453-466.

Temple, Barker, and Sloane, Inc. (Winter 1990) The benefits of the graphical user interface, *Multimedia Review*, 10-17.

Thimbleby, H. (1990) *User Interface Design*, ACM Press, New York, NY.

Ulich, E., Rauterberg, M., Moll, T., Greutmann, T., Strohm, O. (1991) Task orientation and user-oriented dialog design, *International Journal of Human-Computer Interaction* 3, 2 117-144.

Weinstein, R., Bloom, K., Rozek, S. (1987) Telepathology and the networking of pathology diagnostic services, Archive of Pathology and Laboratory Medicine, Vol. 111, 646-652.

Weinstein, R., Bloom, K., Rozek, S. (1989) Telepathology: Long distance diagnosis, American Journal of Clinical Pathology, Vol. 91, S39-S42.

Wertheimer, M. (1959) Productive Thinking, Harper and Row, New York.

Yedwab, L., Herot, C. F., Rosenberg, R. L. (Oct. 1981) The Automated Desk, *Sigsmall Newsletter*, Vol. 7, No. 2, 102-108.

Ziegler, J. E., Fähnrich, K.-P. (1988) Direct manipulation, *Handbook of Human-Computer Interaction,* Helander, M., Ed., Elsevier Science Publishers, Amsterdam, The Netherlands, 123-133.

Zloof, M. M. (1975) Query-by-Example, *AFIPS Conf. Proc.*, Vol. 44, 1975 NCC, AFIPS Press, Montvale, N.J.

Zloof, M. M. (1982) Office-by-Example: A Business Language that Unifies Data and Word Processing and Electronic Mail, *IBM Sys. J.*, Vol. 21, No. 3, 272-304.

Save
Close
victorious Allies
Enter the number of the item of interest:
1 - New Books
2 - All Books
3 - New Periodicals
4 - All Periodicals
5 - Other Library Services
Enter the first letter of the
a selection:
Compile Edit Run
Save Options Quit
Login
Logout
Open
Close
Hardcopy
Shrink
Shape
Move
elevated
elevator
Right
Right
evaluate
elevate
elevated
elevator
Locate
File
Save
Tie
Insert
Paste
Cut
File
Save
Tie
Insert
Paste
Cut

Sparks of Innovation in Human-Computer Interaction,
B. Shneiderman, Ed., Ablex, Publ., Norwood, NJ (1993)

2. Menu selection

Introduction

Menu selection was a great step forward from the batch-oriented command languages of the 1960s. As interactive systems became widespread, menus became identified with modern 'user friendly' designs, but skeptics were convinced that menus were only for novices. Devoted hackers felt that menus slowed them down and consumed valuable screen real estate. These complaints were legitimate in the days of long response times, slow display rates, small screens, and no shortcuts. These impediments have generally been overcome and modern graphic user interfaces depend heavily on rapid pull-down or pop-up menus with ample keyboard shortcuts for frequent users. Even for expert users, there will be many applications and task domains for which their knowledge is lacking and then a menu approach becomes desirable.

The good news is that the days of name calling have passed and menus are an important and respected interface style. The transition is nicely exemplified by the improvement from the command characters of VISICALC to the clever and rapid menus of Lotus 1-2-3. I believe that this user interface improvement was central to 1-2-3 displacing VISICALC within two years. New applications for novel menu strategies are enabling new communities of users to apply computers to their problems. The issues now are how to design more effective menu structures, item descriptions, pointing devices, feedback, and shortcuts. Prof. Kent Norman, in the Department of Psychology, reviewed the extensive menu research at the University of Maryland and elsewhere in a comprehensive and thoughtful book, *The Psychology of Menu Selection: Designing Cognitive Control at the Human-Computer Interface* (Norman, 1990).

Our research with menus dealt with novel applications. We developed the idea of embedded menus to represent hypertext (see paper 2.1, Koved and Shneiderman, 1986) and went on to create effective hypertext authoring tools to deal with large databases and multiple authors (see section 3). The idea of embedded menus came to me while working on a photographic retrieval prototype for the US Holocaust Memorial and Education Center. On one screen there was a brief caption mentioning four Polish poets, and then a menu offering further information on each of the four poets. The names were duplicated in the caption and menu accounting for a 40% redundancy and a distraction. The inverse video highlighting was moved from the menu to the caption and the menu was eliminated, leading to a much cleaner screen and a clear visual focus of attention. The notion was generalized to free text and we set about developing software tools to support authoring of documents with this novel form of embedded menus.

Another innovation was the circular menus that Don Hopkins called pie menus (see paper 2.2, Callahan, Hopkins, Weiser & Shneiderman, 1988). Don is one of the truly great hackers and he came up with the idea based on a sound analysis of the selection times for linear vs. circular pop-up menus. He understood that if the cursor popped up in the center of a circle of menu items, then just a short mouse motion in any direction would be needed to make a choice (Figure 1). He implemented his idea in Sun's NeWS system, refined it, and explored many interesting variations. Then another student, Jack Callahan, conducted an empirical study to document the benefits. The University encouraged Don to pursue some form of legal protection, but he was devoted to the spirit of sharing and disseminated his software freely. Pie menus are a clever innovation and most people who see them are convinced of their benefits, but change comes slowly and after seven years pie menus are still not widely applied. Don succeeded in getting a paper published in the popular magazine, *Dr. Dobbs Journal* (Hopkins, 1991), and recently Rollo (1992) had an article in the same publication, offering a Windows version of pie menus. A British group conducted another empirical study, and even though their implementation of pie menus was clumsy, the pies were faster than all the linear menu strategies that they studied (Mills & Prime, 1990). Momenta implemented a pen-based system using a variant of pie menus and the Japanese implementation of Habitat, a multi-user virtual reality environment, uses pie menus. Don has now implemented an X-Windows version that he used for his version of SimCity (commercial product from DUX Software), so this idea is still unfolding.

Training methods for large menu structures were studied and the benefits of a menu map that provides a global overview were clearly demonstrated (Parton, Huffman, Pridgen, Norman & Shneiderman, 1984). Several student projects replicated earlier menu selection studies that found that mnemonic letters, as compared to numbered menus, were selected more rapidly and they also facilitated type-ahead that doubled productivity. We explored shortcut strategies and determined that users learned meaningful names of destinations (jump-ahead by typing WEATHER) more easily than the sequences of menu choices to get there (type-ahead by typing 3, 1, 5) (Laverson, Norman & Shneiderman, 1987).

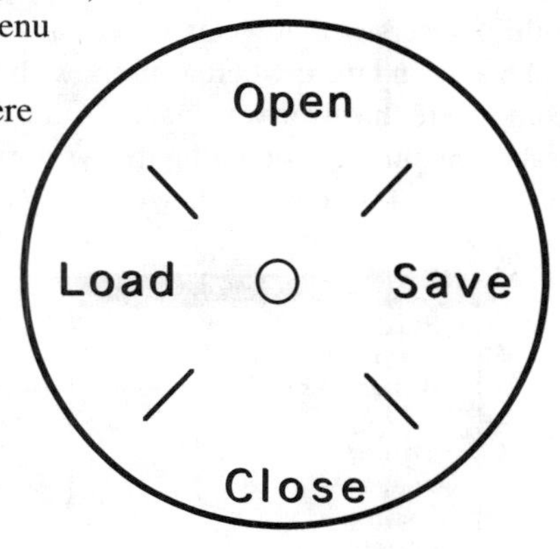

Figure 1. A four-way pie menu

A popular issue on which we shed light is the Breadth vs. Depth controversy in menu tree design. Some early guidelines documents had suggested limiting the number of menu items to 5 or 7 even if the depth was greater, but this guideline is not appropriate with rapid display rates and larger screens. While several other studies had also shown the benefits of broader shallower trees, our study had a further surprising result (II.3, Wallace, Anderson & Shneiderman, 1987). We found that time stress led to far worse performance; simply telling the users to work rapidly led to more errors and slower performance.

Dynamic or adaptive menus have been proposed occasionally to deal with menus having highly varying and skewed selection frequencies. After each selection the menu order is changed to put the most selected items at the top of the list. Unfortunately, frequent changes to the menu order have a very unsettling effect on users as was demonstrated in a study conducted by Jeff Mitchell (Mitchell & Shneiderman, 1989). I had spoken out against adaptive systems and in favor of predictable user-controlled designs. Jeff set out to prove me wrong and chose conditions that he thought would be favorable to the adaptive menus. The results support stability in menu order. However, it certainly seems appropriate to capture usage frequencies and enable users of system administrators to make an occasional shift in some of the menu items. It took several years for these embers to catch fire, but the failed concept of automatically adapting menus gave the inspiration to a new possibility. The idea of bringing just a few (2-5) frequently selected items to the top and keeping the remaining items in their original order was recently explored by Andrew Sears (Sears & Shneiderman, 1992) (Figure 2). These split menus have proven to be beneficial in two field trials and a controlled experiment.

Kent Norman and his students dealt with cognitive issues such as the importance of menu item distinctiveness on performance (Schwartz & Norman, 1986). A later series of studies demonstrated the importance of individual differences and spatial visualization abilities (Norman, 1990). Users with above average spatial visualization ability performed at nearly twice the rate of those with below average ability. Users with low spatial visualization tend to restart the whole search if they make a wrong turn; whereas users with high spatial visualization tend to back up from where the error was made. A map of the menu structure significantly aids usage. Menus are becoming the write rats for a new generation of cognitive and experimental psychologists who study human-computer interaction.

Figure 2. The standard menu appears on the left and the split menu with the three high frequency items brought to the top appears on the right.

Sparks of Innovation in Human-Computer Interaction,
B. Shneiderman, Ed., Ablex, Publ., Norwood, NJ (1993)

2.1 Embedded menus: selecting items in context

Larry Koved
Ben Shneiderman

In many situations, embedded menus represent an attractive alternative to the more traditional explicit menus, particularly in touchtext, spelling checkers, language-based program editors, and graphics-based systems.

When compared to command driven systems, computer menu systems are appealing because they reduce memorization of commands, reduce training, and structure the user's decision making. Menus can be categorized as either embedded or explicit (Koved, 1984), the difference being the context in which the menu items are presented.

Communications of the ACM, Vol. 29, No. 4, 312-318. Edgar H. Sibley, Panel Editor. Also appeared as (August 13, 1985), IBM Research Report RC 11310. Reprinted in Hebrew in Maaseh-Hoshev.

Explicit menus (Figure 1) usually supply an explicitly enumerated list of items from which the user selects by typing a number or letter; a variant to this theme highlights or capitalizes the first letter of the selectable item. The use of icons, where all selectable icons are displayed on the screen, is a kind of enumeration and therefore also a form of explicit menu. Instead of entering numbers, letters, or icons, some systems permit the user to point to an item in the menu by physically touching the screen (if a touch screen is used), or by using arrow keys or a mouse. The item to be selected is highlighted (e.g., intensified, underlined, or put in reverse video), and pressing another key or button selects the item.

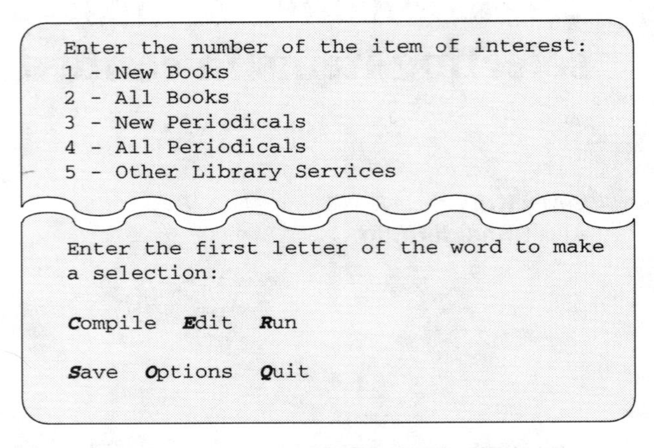

Figure 1. Explicit Menu. The menu items are explicitly enumerated.

While explicit enumeration of menu items poses certain obvious advantages over command-driven systems, in some situations explicit menus can themselves be inefficient. Listing items wastes viewing space on the computer display, and extracting information from the original context to construct menu items may mean the items have to be excessively verbose to be meaningful.

Embedded menus, where menu items are embedded within the information being displayed on the screen, in some respects represent an improvement on the more traditional explicit menu. In embedded menus (Figure 2), highlighted or underlined words or phrases within the text become the menu items, and are selectable using the commonly used touchscreen, cursor, and mouse methods cited above.

Our own experience with embedded menus began in the interest of providing adequate man-machine interfaces for two textual databases: The Interactive Encyclopedia Systems (TIES), a European history database functioning in a museum environment [Shneiderman, 1985], and the OnLine Maintenance Manual (OLMM) system, an on-line maintenance manual for electrical and mechanical equipment repair (Koved, 1984; Weldon, Mills, Koved & Shneiderman, 1985). In this article, we review the use of embedded menus in these two specific systems and

```
The options for the NESW intercom system
are controlled by a set of switches on the
controller card. Locate the controller card
and remove it from the system unit.
Find the serial number.
 Set the switches based on the serial number.
Once the switches are set,
insert the controller card.
```

Figure 2. Embedded Menu. The menu items are the underlined phrases: To make a selection, the user moves the cursor to the desired phrase and presses the select key.

examine the more general application of embedded menus in interactive spelling checkers, language-based program editors, and interactive graphics systems. In so doing, we address the relative advantages and disadvantages of embedded menus in different contexts, highlighting areas of equivocation where more research is warranted.

The Interactive Encyclopedia System

TIES was designed for a museum environment where visitors walk up to a TIES machine and explore a database on European history [Shneiderman 1985]. Since most TIES users were expected to be novices (i.e., people who had never used TIES or even, perhaps, a computer), the simplicity of the user interface was considered paramount. To this end, instead of extracting menu items and displaying them as an explicit menu, selectable items were highlighted directly in the text (Figure 3), a method of displaying text with embedded items that has since become known as touchtext.

In TIES, there are three active keys—move cursor left, move cursor right, and select menu item—each of which is activated by a single key stroke. The initial screen presents an article with highlighted phrases—the selectable menu items—and the user positions the cursor on the phrase for which more detail is desired, and selects the item; a new article is retrieved, and the process is repeated, if desired.

The top line of the screen shows the article title and page number. At the bottom of the screen are additional page-turning commands listed in the form of an explicit menu: "Next Page," "Previous Page," and "Return to (previous article)." Menu items not applicable are omitted (e.g., the "Previous Page" option when the first page of an article is being displayed).

All in all, TIES provides a very simple strategy for accessing information. To the user, the database is a network of related articles that can be retrieved by starting with an introductory article and then making menu selections. At every node in the network (except the introduction), the user can request a return to a previous article.

Online Maintenance Manual

In many respects, the OLMM system is similar to TIES: It also uses touchtext, and the syntax and semantics of the two systems are almost the same (Koved, 1985; Weldon, Mills, Koved & Shneiderman, 1985). The OLMM is designed to be used with databases containing training, diagnostic, and repair manuals: Its objective is

```
EVENTS:  ANSCHLUSS                    Page 2 of 7
The victorious Allies disapproved of such
a union and specifically forbade it in both
the Treaty of Versailles and the Treaty of
St. Germain-en-Laye.  Austrian nationalism
remained weak throughout the interwar
period (1918-1939).  During these years,
Austria, like Germany, gave rise to a number
of right-wing and fascist political movements.
Indeed, Adolph Hitler's own Nazi Party had a
sizable Austrian branch.  In 1934, Engelbert
Dollfuss, a member of the Christian Social Party,
destroyed the First Republic's fragile
parliamentary democracy and established a
right-wing dictatorship.
______________________________________________
Next Page    Previous Page    Return to FREUD, SIGMUND
```

Figure 3. TIES Menu. The above example is an embedded menu from a TIES database. The menu items are shown in bold type, and the cursor is an inverse video bar.

to replace paper manuals with on-line versions through the use of alternate modes of presentation and database structuring.

Replacing paper manuals with on-line versions, however, is fraught with problems. First of all, the process of flipping through the pages of a book to find a section of interest is a familiar one to most people: Place markers are commonly inserted, and even notations made in margins—possibilities not frequently available with on-line systems. Also, the informational content per page in a book is greater than on a 24-line screen. Furthermore, in most cases, manuals are stored on-line as they would be printed on paper, and typically suffer from overly complex retrieval methods, limited display space, and poor screen readability (Gould & Grischowsky, 1984 ; Hansen, Doring & Whitlock, 1978 ; Mills & Weldon, 1987 ; Wright & Lickorish, 1983).

To deal with the diagrams and pictures commonly found in maintenance manuals, graphical data in the OLMM are associated with each database node so that each time a new section of the manual is retrieved from the database, an illustration is also retrieved and displayed on an accompanying graphics screen. In the initial implementation of the OLMM, only simple line drawings were included, although more complex graphics are possible—even animation or videodiscs. The types of output possible are limited only by the capabilities of the graphics hardware and software, and the writer's imagination.

Spelling checking and correcting programs

Touchtext is only one example of an embedded menu. Another familiar example is the use of embedded menus in interactive spelling programs, where the document is displayed to the user as it was given to the spelling program, but words detected as possibly misspelled are highlighted or underlined; the user points to a highlighted misspelled word and requests that the spelling program display an explicit menu of the possible correct spellings (Figure 4). Once the user selects a correct spelling from the menu, the spelling program substitutes the correct for the incorrect spelling. If the user determines that a highlighted word is in fact spelled correctly, he or she can simply skip past the word, avoiding an unnecessary search in the dictionary. Typically a command, possibly a single keystroke, moves the cursor to the next misspelled word in the document.

The style checker—a variant of the spelling program—goes one step further and detects possible misuses of a word in a given context, highlighting the possibly incorrect word. In a document containing the word "than" when the correct word should probably be "then," the program will highlight the word "than" to indicate that it may be incorrectly used.

The use of embedded menus in spelling programs is a natural one as the possibly misspelled words are presented within the original context of their usage. The alternative, taking words out of context, greatly increases the difficulty of determining whether a particular word is actually misspelled or simply not in the program's dictionary. If a spelling program were to extract all supposedly misspelled words from the document and simply display them as an explicit menu without showing where in the document the misspelled words were located

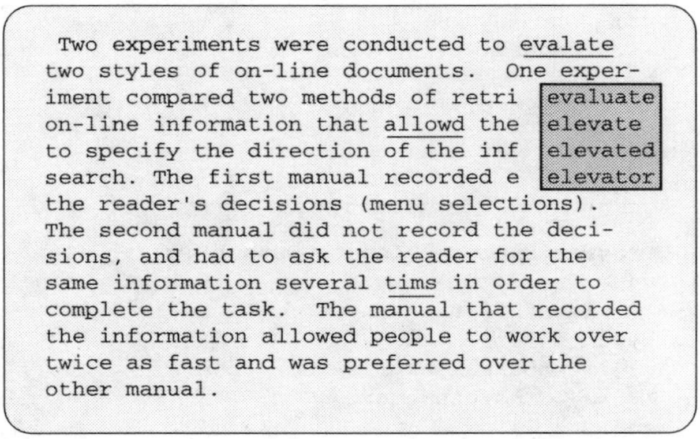

```
 Two experiments were conducted to evalate
two styles of on-line documents.  One exper-
iment compared two methods of retri  evaluate
on-line information that allowd the  elevate
to specify the direction of the inf  elevated
search. The first manual recorded e  elevator
the reader's decisions (menu selections).
The second manual did not record the deci-
sions, and had to ask the reader for the
same information several tims in order to
complete the task.  The manual that recorded
the information allowed people to work over
twice as fast and was preferred over the
other manual.
```

Figure 4. Spelling Checker with Embedded Menu and Possible Correct Choices. The misspelled words are highlighted in the embedded menu. Sine the word "evaluate" is considered to be the most likely correct spelling, it is at the top of the list of words in the explicit menu.

(Bentley, 1985), it would be difficult to decide if the word "Martian" was the adjective to describe an inhabitant of the planet Mars, or whether the word should be "Martial." In a situation like this, the user simply guesses whether or not the word is correct. Moreover, it is possible that a word may be correctly spelled in one place in the document and incorrectly in another.

Language-based program editors

In recent years, there has been increased interest in language-based editors like the Cornell Program Synthesizer (Teitelbaum & Reps 1981). Language-based editors differ from text editors in that they incorporate the syntax of the programming language to help create syntactically correct programs by only permitting the entry of information that maintains a syntactically correct program. One beneficial by-product of these editors is the automatic pretty printing of programs.

In a language-based editor, the program is maintained as a syntax tree. The user creates a new program in a top-down fashion, generating program constructs and filling in the details. In many respects, it is akin to a fill-in-the-blanks style of editing. The user moves the cursor to the desired part of the program, for example, the (statement) nonterminal in the derivation tree. The (if) command then causes the editor to expand the (statement) nonterminal into a new subtree containing the derivation subtree for an IF-THEN statement, with nonterminals (boolean-expression) and (statement) (see Figure 5). Each of these nonterminals may be expanded or filled in with appropriate terminal and nonterminal symbols, or modified, or deleted.

Because the program is represented as a syntax tree, it is possible to hide the details of a program subtree — for example, the details of a procedure body or a

```
Program Example (Input, Output);
var
   <identifier> : <type>;
begin
   <STATEMENT>
end.
   (a)
```

```
Program Example (Input, Output);
var
   <identifier> : <type>;
begin
   if <boolean-expression> then
         <statement>;
end.
   (b)
```

Figure 5. Language-Based Editor. Part (a) is a basic program template. By pointing to (statement) and selecting the (if) function, the nonterminal was expanded, resulting in part (b).

while loop (Figure 6). This procedure is known as holophrasting (Hansen, 1971). In this way, the user is able to manipulate the display of the subtrees so that only certain portions of the syntax trees are displayed, and the details of other portions are hidden from view. By pointing to the appropriate subtree, the user is able to expand (zoom) or contract (unzoom) the view of these hidden subtrees.

Language-based editors also make it possible to easily locate and display the declarations of an identifier. If a user points to a variable in a program, the editor can search through the syntax tree, using the language's scoping rules, to locate the

```
Program Example (Intput, Output);
var
   <identifier> : <type>;
Procedure Hidden;
   . . .
begin
   while Condition1 do
   . . .
   while Condition2 do
   . . .
   <statement>
end.
```

Figure 6. Holophrasting. The body and declarations of the procedure Hidden are suppressed, indicated by the ellipses; and the body of the program contains two while loops, the bodies of which are also suppressed. This suppression of details allows more of the high-level structure of the program to be displayed on the screen.

declaration of the variable in the current context. The same is true of procedure and function declarations.

An explicit menu system that would perform a comparable function for language-based editors would be extremely cumbersome or seem very unnatural. With an explicit menu, the editor would ask the user which subtree should be manipulated based on its location within the program (see Figure 7,), and by entering a number between 1 and 4, the user would designate the assignment statement to be modified or deleted. The explicit enumeration of menu items, however, would consume a large portion of the available display space, thereby reducing the amount available for program text; it would also remove the statements from context, making the user's decision more difficult as several items may be syntactically identical.

Further examples

Spatial Data Management Systems (SDMS) (Herot, 1984) uses a technique of displaying general database information by using graphics. Presented with a map of the United States, a user wishing to see all counties with a population greater than

```
Program Example (Input, Output);
      . . .
Function Compute (Arg : Integer);
begin
      . . .
   a:=a+1;
   b:=Compute(a);
   a:=a+b;
   c:Compute(a);
   a:a+b;
   b:=Compute(a);
   a:=a+b;
      . . .
end.
_____________________________________

Enter the number of the statement to be
deleted:

(1) a:=a+1;
(2) a:=a+b;
(3) a:=a+b;
(4) a:=a+b;
```

Figure 7. Using an Explicit Menu to Modify a Program. Since the assignment statements are removed from their context, it is more difficult to determine which of the four assignment statements should be deleted.

1,000,000 would be shown those locations satisfying the criterion on the graphics display. The user may then use a pointing device to select a particular region of the map and thereby retrieve a more detailed map from the database. By entering more selection criteria (e.g., manufacturing or industry), the user may continue the database search process. The leaves of the database are represented as icons displayed on the screen and may be selected by the user. At any time, the user can undo the effects of the selection process by returning to the less detailed maps.

Embedded menus are also found in graphics-based systems. For example, when designing a VLSI chip, the user interacts with the system through direct manipulation of the graphical objects [Newcomer, 1980; Shneiderman, 1983]. The objects displayed on the screen form an embedded menu from which the user may make selections. A selection is made by pointing to a desired object and then requesting that it be moved, copied, deleted, etc.

Discussion

Despite the many obvious benefits of embedded menus, more research is needed. In the case of touchtext, for example, it is not clear what kind of negative effects may arise from the use of highlighted or underlined menu items. It is possible that the highlighting of phrases is disruptive, causing reduced reading speed and comprehension. Also, since embedded menu items can be selected in any order, the novice or inexperienced user may get lost by jumping around in the material rather than traversing the database in an in-order or sequential fashion. The touchtext systems do not enforce a search order. On the other hand, for experts, or searches initiated to locate very specific information, the ability to skip material or peruse the material in a different order may be enormously beneficial and may dramatically reduce search time (Koved, 1985).

Another possible drawback, particularly for touchtext systems, is that the mixing of information with menu selection items may be disruptive to the learning process in the sense that the user may be inclined to examine a particular subject or subjects in detail without first getting an appreciation of the overall context. By traversing down through several levels of the database, the user may forget the original context in which the material was retrieved.

For the frequent or sophisticated user, embedded menus that require frequent traversals of familiar paths to access details of the system may become cumbersome: An alternative may be offering shortcuts or command languages as a means of bypassing certain menus.

Finally, more research is needed in the area of computerized books and documents, which are not well understood from the cognitive point of view and for which improved man-machine interfaces are necessary. We do know that reading material from most currently used computer screens is slower than from paper, although the specific reasons are not completely understood [Gould & Grischkowsky, 1984]. To compensate, we can try to use the technology and capabilities of the computer to provide new means of storing, locating, retrieving, and displaying information. This new technology, however, presents the users with an environment that is quite different and not particularly well understood: the syntax and semantics of computerized books and documents being quite distinct from that of their paper counterparts. Special training will be needed, although the use of embedded menus may help reduce the amount of time needed.

Experimental results

Several experiments conducted with embedded menus seem to indicate that, all things considered, embedded menus may represent an attractive alternative to traditional menus and command syntax.

One of the first experiments performed to compare embedded and explicit menus used TIES with a database describing the Student Union of the University of Maryland at College Park (Powell, 1985). A within-subject experimental design required that subjects search the TIES database for answers to 20 questions about the Student Union, all in a 15-minute period. The number of correctly answered questions was recorded for each experimental condition—embedded versus explicit menu. The results showed that many more questions were answered correctly using embedded menus than with explicit menus ($p < 0.001$); in addition, fewer screens were viewed when using embedded menus ($p < 0.001$), and the subjects actually preferred the embedded over the explicit menu ($p < 0.001$).

A second between-subjects experiment was conducted with the OLMM system to compare embedded menus versus page-turning commands for online manuals (Koved, 1985; Weldon, Mills, Koved & Shneiderman 1985). In the page-turning mode, the text on the screens was augmented with the page number for each embedded menu item. However, instead of allowing embedded menu selection, page turning mechanisms were provided—forward and backward and "first-page" keys, and page-number entry for direct access to specific pages. Results gathered from a post-test questionnaire revealed that embedded menus were preferred to the page-turning method ($p < 0.03$), even though the design of the material in the embedded menu condition prevented subjects from solving problems as fast as with the page-turning technique ($p < 0.01$). This slowness was due to the fact that the design forced subjects to view more pages to solve each problem ($p < 0.04$), which suggests a need to investigate alternative rapid access strategies, particularly for frequent users.

A third experiment involving the OLMM system was conducted to study the performance of people using a novel textual database searching technique known as pruning(Koved, 1985). In this within-subject experiment using embedded menus, a pruning technique was used to trim text not relevant to the task at hand. This reduced both the amount of text that had to be read, and the complexity of the questions that had to be answered to complete each problem. Using embedded menus and the pruning technique, problems were solved in less than half the time ($p < 0.001$) and required the viewing of fewer pages ($p < 0.001$); in addition, less time was spent viewing each page ($p < 0.001$). These results are considered important because, for many applications, reading from 2 manuals printed on paper is faster than from computer displays (Gould & Grischkowsky, 1984; Hansen, Doring & Whitlock 1978; Mills & Weldon; 1984, Wright & Lickorish, 1983). The results also suggest that embedded menus, together with the pruning technique, may make on-line manuals an effective alternative to printed manuals.

Conclusion

Using embedded menus makes it easier to avoid computer-related syntax and semantics issues when referring directly to the object being manipulated. The embedded menu can be much simpler than a comparable explicit menu since only a simple cursor movement is required to find an object of interest. In the case of textual information, the cursor control may be as simple as a single cursor movement key; for graphics-based systems, the cursor may be cross hairs pointing to the object of interest. Of course, the newer pointing devices—the mouse, track ball, and touch screen—can also be used to point to either textual or graphical information. The selection mechanism in this case is either a single keystroke or the click of a mouse button.

In an explicit menu approach, the viewing becomes divorced from the selection process, and may become unwieldy if the selection command must include operation type as well as operands to specify the target of the operation. When this happens, the association between displayed information and menu items may become less clear.

One of the most appealing aspects of embedded menus is the direct manipulation approach to controlling the application. It allows the user to point directly to an object of interest, with the underlying system performing the desired operation. Embedded menus in some respects resemble WYSIWYG (what-you-see-is-what-you-get) text editors. There is no arbitrary syntax associated with the menu selection process. Instead, the syntax consists of simply moving the cursor, or rectangular window in graphics systems, to a desired location on the display, and requesting that an operation be performed on the currently referenced object.

With the emergence of very small portable computers and a space limitation of 24 or 25 lines by 80 columns for many of today's screens, space saving techniques will remain important. Although in the future we expect larger computer displays to become more common and the conserving of screen space less critical for some applications, we believe that embedded menus will remain an important human-computer interaction technique.

Sparks of Innovation in Human-Computer Interaction,
B. Shneiderman, Ed., Ablex, Publ., Norwood, NJ (1993)

2.2 An empirical comparison of pie vs. linear menus

Jack Callahan
Don Hopkins
Mark Weiser
Ben Shneiderman

Abstract

Menus are largely formatted in a linear fashion listing items from the top to bottom of the screen or window. Pull down menus are a common example of this format. Bitmapped computer displays, however, allow greater freedom in the placement, font, and general presentation of menus. A pie menu is a format where the items are placed along the circumference of a circle at equal radial distances from the center. Pie menus gain over traditional linear menus by reducing target seek time, lowering error rates by fixing the distance factor and increasing the target size in Fitts's Law, minimizing the drift distance after target selection, and are, in general, subjectively equivalent to the linear style.

ACM CHI '88 Conference, Human Factors in Computing Systems, ACM, New York, 95-100.

Introduction

In presenting a list of choices to the user, most computer system designers have been limited, largely by the available hardware and software, to a linear format. The items are listed from top to bottom, sometimes with an index number for each item. Occasionally the lists are multi-columned, have multiple items per line, or are even hierarchical (i.e. indented sub-choices), but for the most part lie in a strictly one-dimensional structure. Many of these menus are static on the display screen or activated from mouse actions in two formats: pull-down (menu appears at a fixed label on screen when mouse directed) or pop-up (menu appears anywhere within a fixed area, occasionally the whole screen) (Shneiderman 1987). Some systems have used the two dimensional nature of the computer display to the advantage of certain menu applications. Many flight simulation programs, for example, lay out directional headings in a typical compass format.

Item placement in menus has been an important research topic for many years. Menu organization is typically divided into three types (Dray, Ogden, & Vestewig, 1981): alpha/numeric, categorical (functional), and random ordering. It is generally agreed that the performance of subjects (i.e., time to seek a target) with different placement styles converges with practice (Card, 1982; Perlman, 1984). Further studies (McDonald, Stone & Liebelt 1983) revealed that a functional placement of items is superior when the task domain is unambiguous to the user, whereas an alphabetic organization can be useful in uncertain task descriptions. All of these studies have concentrated on the linear display format.

Login
Logout
Open
Close
Hardcopy
Shrink
Shape
Move

Figure 1. A typical linear menu

Has defaulting to a linear format (Figure 1) made some menus easier to use? Harder? By changing the menu format, can users find the item they seek faster? Is a particular menu format faster than other formats even with practice? What type of formats should be tested?

These are important questions for the designers of many systems. Software libraries of menu display routines are widely used as a default by programmers of many window systems and applications. Would it be worthwhile to present items in variable formats or perhaps in another fixed general format like the compass?

A pie menu (Hopkins, Callahan, Weiser, 1988) is a system

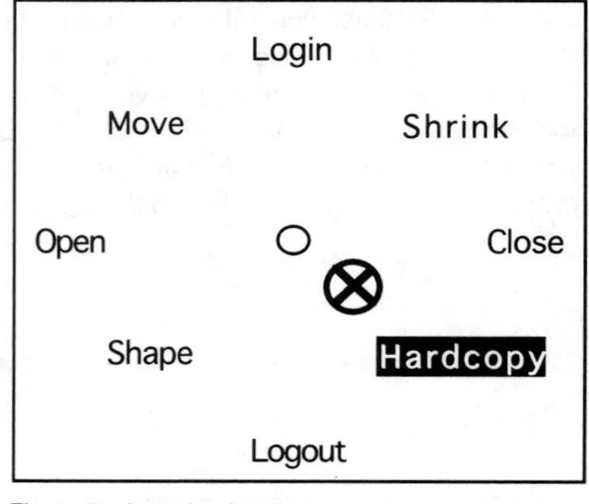

Figure 2. A crude pie menu

facility for pop-up menus built into MIT's X windows (Gettys & Newman, 1985]) window management system, and Sun Microsystem's NeWS window system (Gosling, 1986) and SunView window system. The pie menu interface supplies a standard library of functions that can be used by programmers to format and display menus in a circular format. The system is written in C and Forth and currently runs on a Sun Microsystems workstation. Items in the menu are placed at equal radial distances along the circumference of a circle (Figure 2). The starting cursor position is at the center of the menu as opposed to being at the menu title or first item as in traditional pull-down menus. The cursor is under the control of a three button optical mouse on a fixed-size moveable pad.

Imaginative menu formats are an inevitable future with the latest advances in window management systems. Window imaging systems using technology from laser printing protocol standards such as PostScript (Adobe 1985) and Interpress (Xerox, 1984) will make it possible to display a large variety of non-rectangular shaped windows effectively on a bitmapped display. There are some obvious advantages to this organization for particular applications: compass directions, time, angular degrees, and diametrically opposed or orthogonal function names are some groupings of items that seem to fit well into the mold of the pie menu design. Alternatively, items with a sequential nature may not benefit and may in fact suffer from such a format. In addition, pie menus consume greater screen area and become polynomially larger than linear menus in both height and width with increased item size and number of items.

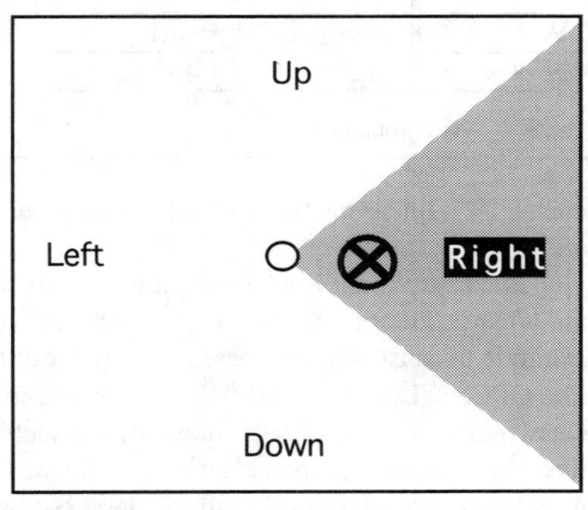

Figure 3. Pie menu activation region

Distance to and size of the target are important factors that give pie menus the advantage over traditional linear menus. Even with linear menu initial cursor placement schemes where the cursor may initially be in the middle or at the last item selected, there remain target items at relatively great distances from the cursor location. Pie menus enjoy a two fold advantage because of their unique design: items are placed at equal radial distances from the center of the menu and the user need only move the cursor by a small amount in some direction for the system to recognize the intended selection. The advantages of decreased distance and increased target size can be seen as an effect on positioning time as parameters to Fitts's Law (Card, Moran & Newell 1983).

The distance to an item in any menu style can be defined as the minimum distance needed to highlight the item as selected. In both menu styles, this is defined by a region rather than a point. This region is typically of greater area than the actual target (Figure 3). Once the cursor has entered the region, the item is highlighted as feedback to the user.

Pie	*Linear*	*Unclassified*
North	First	Center
NE	Second	Bold
East	Third	Italic
SE	Fourth	Font
South	Fifth	Move
SW	Sixth	Copy
West	Seventh	Find
NW	Eighth	Undo

Table 1. Task groupings

Experiment

Introduction and hypothesis

This paper describes a controlled experiment to test two hypotheses: that pie menus decrease the seek time and error rates for menu items and that pie menus are especially useful in menu applications suited for a circular format, diametrically opposed item sets (e.g. open/close), directions (e.g. up/down) or even linear sets of items, and conversely, linear menus are useful for sets of linear items (e.g., one, two, three etc.).

The experiment is a 2x3 randomized block design. Each cell is an element of the cross product of menu and task type. A typical pie task would be the compass example because it seems best suited functionally for pie menus. List of elements, like OPEN/CLOSE and UP/DOWN, whose meanings are antonyms, are also classified as pie tasks. Lists, like numbers, letters and ordinals, are best suited for linear menus and are thus classified as linear tasks. Groups of menu items that have no relation to each other fall in the unclassified category. Table 1 shows an example of the groupings.

There are a total of 15 menus, a group of 5 for each task type. Subjects perform the experiment for all cells in the experiment matrix in random order in accordance with a randomized block design (Kirk, 1968). The subjects see each of the 15 menus four times, a total of twice in each menu format. Each cell in the experiment consists of 10 menus. Each subject therefore sees a total of 60 menus. Targets are uniformly distributed over the eight possible items.

Pilot study results

A pilot study of 16 subjects showed that users were approximately 15% faster with the pie menus and that errors were less frequent with pie menus. Statistically significant differences were found for item seek time but not task type. Subjects were split on their subjective preference of pie and linear menus. Some commented that they were able to visually isolate an item easier with linear menus and that it was hard to control the selection in pie menus because of the sensitivity of the pie menu selection mechanism. These subjects tended to be the most mouse naive of all, whereas those who had heard of or seen a mouse/cursor controlled system but had not used one extensively tended to prefer pie menus. The most mouse naive users, while finding linear menus easier, tended to be better at pie menus and commented that with practice, they would probably be superior and in fact prefer the pie menus because of their speed and minimization of hand movement with the mouse. Not surprisingly, therefore, most of those preferring linear menus did not have a strong preference on the scaled subjective questionnaire.

Subjects

Subjects were volunteers from the University of Maryland Psychology Department Subject Pool. All 33 subjects were undergraduate students with little or no mouse experience. They were rewarded with 1 extra credit point for participating.

Materials

As stated, pie menus run on a Sun Microsystems Workstation as part of an enhanced version of MIT's X windows system. The screen is a 19-inch bitmapped high resolution black and white display. Cursor location is controlled by a three button optical mouse on a moveable mousepad made of a specially formatted reflective material.

Procedures and problems

Some changes were made from the pilot design of the experiment: a better distribution of menu targets and doubled number of menu trials, though the total number of menus remained constant.

The process of selecting items from a pop-up menu, regardless of format, can be characterized in three stages: invocation, browsing, and confirmation. To make a selection, the user invokes the menu by pressing a mouse button (invocation), continues to hold the mouse button down and moves to an item which is then highlighted (browsing) and releases the mouse button confirming the selection (confirmation).

The typical sequence of events for a subject is as follows:

- The target is displayed to the user in a fixed-text window at the top of the screen. The cursor associated with the mouse is marked by a small hash mark "x" on the display screen.
- The user invokes the menu by pressing and holding any one of three mouse buttons. The menu appears with the cursor location unchanged (except near screen boundaries where the cursor must "jump away" to accommodate the menu). The cursor is located in the center or menu title region of pie and linear menus respectively
- With the mouse button still depressed, the user moves the cursor with the mouse towards the textual target as indicated. Selections highlight as the cursor moves into distinct activation regions. As noted, the activation regions for pie menus are "pie" shaped sections that extend to the screen boundaries and are rectangular sections extending horizontally towards the screen boundaries for linear menus.

- Once selection is made, the user releases the mouse button to confirm the selection. The menu disappears from the display screen. The cursor remains at the screen position relative to the selection location. If the selection is correct, the process begins again with a new target and possibly a new menu style. Otherwise, if the selection is not the requested target, an audible "beep" tone is heard and the user attempts the task again.

Basically, the computer posts the target name at the top of the screen, the user invokes the current menu, moves to the target item, and confirms the selection by releasing the mouse button. This sequence, called a task, is repeated 60 times by each subject. Each subject saw 6 sequences of 10 menus each. In each ten-menu sequence, the menu type was the same, either pie or linear, and since there are only 5 menus per task type, each menu appears twice in the sequence.

The 10 menu sequences correspond to the cells in the experiment table design. Each subject performed a sequence for all 6 cells in random order. 60 data points

	Task Type			
	Pie	Linear	Unclass	$Mean_{menu}$
Using pie menus	2.20	2.18	2.40	2.26
Using linear menus	2.68	2.30	2.94	2.64
$Mean_{task}$	2.44	2.24	2.67	

Table 2. Target seek time (sec) means per cell, menu type, and task type

	F	*PR > F*
Menu type	16.23	0.0003
Task type	6.93	0.0030
Menu type *X* TaskType	2.82	0.0750

Table 3. Repeated measures analysis of variance results for target seek time

are collected per subject. A total of 33 subjects performed the experiment for a total of 1980 data points.

For each task, the time from the first mouse button down to the correct target selection is the seek time for the item. If the user selected the wrong item, the time is included in this interval. The number of errors made, as well as the sub-interval times when errors are made, is recorded during the experiment by the system. All subjects performed the test adequately and no person failed to finish the assignment.

Results and discussion

A repeated measures analysis of variance was performed on the data. Table 2 shows the means per cell, per row, and per column. Table 3 displays the repeated measures ANOVA results. A Tukey analysis reveals that there is a statistical significant difference ($P < 0.01$) between overall menu type performance and task type performance in target seek times. Pie tasks and linear tasks did not significantly differ from each other, but both organizations are an improvement over the unclassified menu tasks. Slight statistically significant difference ($P = 0.05$) between cells in the experiment design is also observed. No other interaction was observed to be significant.

The statistically significant difference between menu type performance is the central result of this study. The task type difference reiterates earlier study results (Card, 1982; McDonald, Stone, & Liebelt, 1983) that showed that some organization is helpful. Furthermore, the slight interaction between menu types and task types tends to confirm the hypothesis that certain task groupings perform well with particular menu formats. The reason for a lack of strong correlation is evident in the lower mean for pie menus even on linearly grouped tasks.

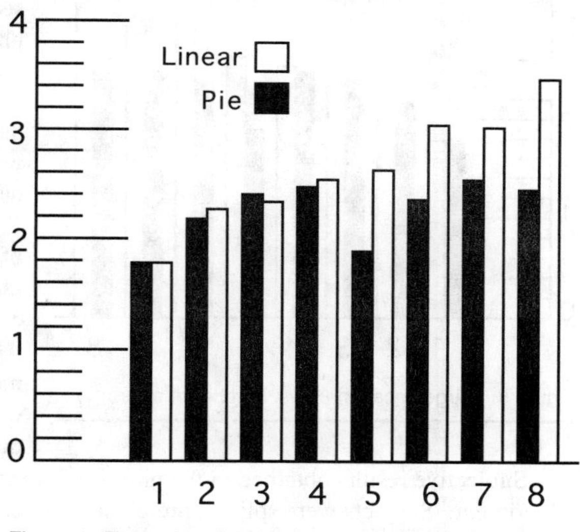

Figure 4. Target location (x) vs. seek time (y) seconds

Figure 4 displays the target location by item plotted against the mean seek time. The mean seek time across target location for pie menus is fairly constant. As expected for linear menus, the mean seek time increases proportionally to the distance of the target from the initial cursor location. Analysis of seek time vs. number of menus seen shows that no strict convergence occurs between the two menu styles, though mean seek times did decrease for both pie and linear menus with practice.

With error times removed from the results (measuring time from menu invocation to first correct choice), the menu styles compared relatively the same as the comparison which includes error times because of the error rates.

An analysis of seek time based on Fitts's Law $T = K0 + K\log 2 \ (D/S + 0.5)$ where T = time to position cursor using mouse (seek time), $K0$ = constant time to adjust grasp on mouse, K = constant normalization factor (positioning device dependent), S = size of target in pixels 2, D = distance in screen pixels, helps explain our results because the ratio of the distance (D) to target size (S) is smaller for pie menus. The fixed target distance and increased size of targets for pie menus decreases the mean positioning time as compared with linear menus. In our experiment, the activation region for an item constitutes the target. All subjects were informed of the fact that their target was not necessarily the text, but the region containing the text target item. This was clearly understood by all participants. The font size for text items in both menu styles was the same, yet the target region size for pie menus (3500—6000 pixels) was on the order of 2-3 times the size of linear menu activation region sizes (1000—2000 pixels). The distance from the center of a pie menu to an activation region is 10 pixels while the distance in linear menus varied from 13-200 pixels.

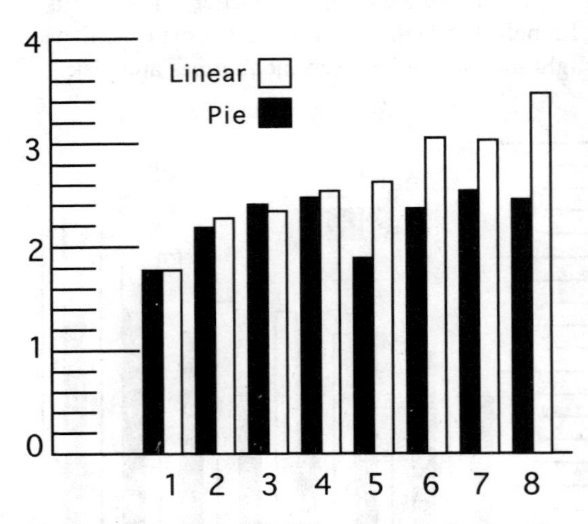

Figure 5. Target location (x) vs. number of errors (y)

Figure 5 displays the target location plotted against the total number of errors across all subjects. Pie and linear menus seem to suffer from a similar phenomenon - errors are made more often on items in the central region of the menu display. These are the items with the most interaction with neighboring items (Card, 1982)

Repeated measure analysis of variance results on the error rates show marginally statistically significant differences (P = 0.087) between pie and linear menus (Tables 4 and 5). No other statistically significant differences were observed.

Subjective results obtained in the pilot study repeated themselves in the experiment. Subjects were split on preferring one menu type over another but those who preferred linear menus had no strong conviction in this direction and most agreed that with further practice they might prefer the pie menu structure. Those who preferred pie menus generally felt fairly confident in their assessment and this is reflected in the questionnaire.

One subject complained of having a problem with menu drift, which is the phenomenon which occurs as the result of the cursor relocating to the relative screen location of the last selected target. With linear menus, this tends to "drift" the cursor towards the bottom of the screen. This may explain the higher error rate for linear menus, but the same problem occurs to a lesser degree with pie menus. This, in fact, we believe to be another positive feature of pie menus: the cursor drift distance is minimized. Most subjects had no problems coping with drift in either

	Task Type			
	Pie	Linear	Unclass	$Mean_{menu}$
Using pie menus	0.45	0.60	0.60	0.55
Using linear menus	0.88	0.73	1.24	0.95
$Mean_{task}$	0.66	0.66	0.92	

Table 4. Number of errors means per cell, menu type, and task type (all observations including no errors)

	F	*PR > F*
Menu type	3.12	0.0869
Task type	0.93	0.4066
Menu type X TaskType	1.34	0.2773

Table 5. Repeated measures analysis of variance results for number of errors

menu style. One area of further research is measuring the extent and effect of this problem.

Conclusions

What does this mean? Should we program pie menus into our bitmapped window systems tomorrow and expect a 15-20% increase in productivity, since users can select items slightly faster with pie menus? Pie menus seem promising, but more experiments are needed before issuing a strong recommendation.

First, this experiment only addresses fixed length menus, in particular, menus consisting of 8 items - no more, no less. Secondly, there remains the problem of increased screen real estate usage. In one trial a subject complained because the pie menu obscured his view of the target prompt message. Finally, the questionnaire showed that the subjects were almost evenly divided between pie and linear menus in subjective satisfaction. Many found it difficult to "home in on" a particular item because of the unusual activation region characteristics of the pie menu.

One assumption of this study concerns the use of a mouse/cursor control device and the use of pop-up style menus (as opposed to menus invoked from a fixed screen location or permanent menus). Certainly, pie menus can and in fact have been incorporated to use keyed input (Hopkins, Callahan, Weiser, 1988) and fixed "pull-down" style presentation (the pie menu becomes a semicircle menu). These variations are areas for further research.

One continuing issue with pie menus is the limit on the number of items that can be placed in a circular format before the size of the menu window is impractical. Perhaps, like the limiting factors in linear menus concerning their lengths, pie menus reach a similar "breaking point" beyond which other menu styles would be more useful. Hierarchical organization, arbitrarily shaped windows (Figure 6), numeric item assignment and other menu refinements as well as further analysis is contained in Hopkins, Callahan & Weiser (1988). Pie menus offer a novel alternative worthy of further exploration.

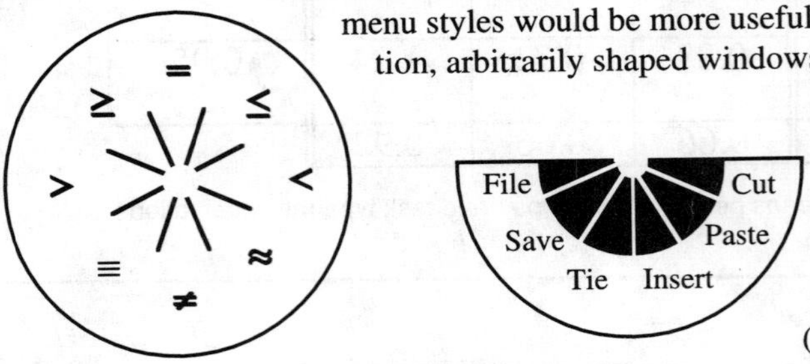

Figure 6. Advanced "pie" menus

Acknowledgments

The authors wish to thank the following people for their invaluable help in the preparation of the experiments, analysis of results and statistics, and this paper: Jim Purtilo, Nancy Anderson, Kent Norman, John Chin, Linda Weldon, Mark Feldman, Mike Gallaher, Mitch Bradley, and Glenn Pearson.

Sparks of Innovation in Human-Computer Interaction,
B. Shneiderman, Ed., Ablex, Publ., Norwood, NJ (1993)

2.3 Time stress effects on two menu selection systems

Daniel F. Wallace
Nancy S. Anderson
Ben Shneiderman

Abstract

The optimal number of menu items per display screen has been the topic of considerable debate and study. On the one hand, some designers have packed many items into each menu to conserve space and reduce the number of menus, whereas on the other hand there are designers who prefer a sparse display for menu structures and other videotex information. This study evaluated the effects of a broad/shallow menu compared to a narrow/deep menu structure under two conditions of time stress for inexperienced users. Results indicated that time stress both slowed performance and increased errors. In addition, it was demonstrated that the broad/shallow menu was faster and resulted in fewer errors. Implications for menu design are discussed.

Proc. 31st Annual Meeting - Human Factors Society, (1987), 727-731
Reprinted with permission from *Proc. of the Human Factors Society 31st annual Meeting*, 1987.

Introduction

As computers become more common in the home and workplace, the need for an efficient means of user selection of actions and objects becomes an important aspect of the user-computer interface. Many designers have sought out effective means whereby the user's intent can be communicated to the system rapidly, with low error rates and with minimal user training.

Although several interaction strategies have been employed by designers, one of the more common interfaces used to provide the less experienced computer user with choices about the possible actions in using word processors or spreadsheets is menu selection (Parton et al., 1985). Hierarchical decomposition of the user's selection of action is often necessary because there is insufficient screen space to display all possible courses of action to the user, and because the novice user lacks sufficient memory capacity to learn and recall all of the commands necessary to execute the desired actions. The challenge, therefore, is to enable the user to select the desired course of action using a clear, well defined sequence of steps to complete a given task. A menu selection system is well suited for this type of task, provided that it is designed thoughtfully and carefully.

The advantages provided novice users by menu selection makes it a very attractive interface to many programmers and software marketers, since novice users not only seem to perform better on menu systems, but they prefer them as well (Shneiderman, 1987).

The issue of breadth vs. depth

Since menu selection systems have been so popular, a number of research studies have focused on the depth/breadth tradeoff in the design of hierarchical menus (Miller, 1981; and Landauer & Nachbar, 1985). Miller set the stage in 1981 for menu research in his study of the depth/breadth tradeoff in hierarchical menus, finding that eight (8) items per frame resulted in the fastest goal acquisition time (task completion). Snowberry, Parkinson & Sisson (1983) have shown that for practiced users the optimal number of choices per screen is about four to eight items. Lee & MacGregor (1985) also found the optimum to be in the range of four to sixteen items. While these studies point toward a favoring of menus with four items or more per screen, Paap & Roske-Hofstrand (1986) indicated that the factor of "funneling" shows potential advantages in situations where the processing time per option is long or where there is ambiguity between the alternatives presented. Most of the research has compared the time it takes to search through menu selection systems which are constructed in a hierarchical or tree like fashion, and the majority of these studies indicate that menus that provide a larger number of alternatives per screen enjoy an advantage in performance speed (Paap & Roske-Hofstrand, 1986).

Breadth advantages

Possible advantages for broad menu systems include decreased memory load upon the user, recognition of actions for the user to select rather than recall of those commands. Another factor favoring breadth is that hierarchical menu trees with greater depth may be more subject to navigation problems — such as getting lost, or using an inefficient pathway to the goal (Paap & Roske-Hofstrand, 1986). Similarly, Snowberry, Parkinson & Sisson (1993) found error rate increases from 4% for a single level menu to 34% for six levels. It makes sense that the misstriking of keys may also be less likely to occur in a broad, shallow menu since there are fewer keystrokes to be made.

Depth advantages

Since greater depth implies fewer items per screen, then there is less "clutter" on the screen, and more room to give an adequate description of the menu choices in question. Greater depth also provides for a fewer total number of items to be read and processed for the total task, thus "insulating" against unlikely or illegal responses which may lead to errors. This effect, referred to as "funneling" by Pap and Roske-Hofstrand (1986), is noteworthy in the event that there is a great cost incurred with the processing of each individual menu item in a frame. In such a case, restricted breadth and greater depth is desirable since fewer items require processing. It appears, therefore, that funneling is of greatest value in settings in which categories are more complex, ad hoc, ambiguous, or unstructured.

The issue of "time-stress"

The other factor of interest in the present study is "time pressure" or time-stress. Time-stress is defined as "an externally induced urgency (exerted upon the user) to complete an assigned task within a specified or limited amount of time." Stress of this sort is known to have an adverse effect on human performance in many cases, but of greater interest to the present research is the interaction between the factor of time-stress, and that of menu structure (breadth/depth).

In general, designers should seek to minimize any harmful effects of excessive stress, but that is not always possible in the many situations where demands for completion require time limits. For example, the airline reservationist, the stock broker, and the bank teller are all under a great deal of pressure to perform, and to perform quickly. The effects of time-stress have not been adequately studied in the area of human-computer interfaces.

Time-stress is thought to have at least two components, one positive, and the other negative. The positive effects of stress may be evidenced in the enhanced arousal it provides in helping the user to perform quickly, but the "anxiety" introduced may lead to greater dissatisfaction and an increased error rate. In addressing any issue in human-computer interaction, one must realize that there is no "best" system, only better or inferior ones for a particular job at hand. As a result, the interaction between time-stress and menu tree structure is a relevant one, since it may add new information to assist the designer in tailoring an interface to the task at hand, depending upon the degree of time pressure associated with that task.

The current study extends some of the prior results on optimal number of choices in menu interfaces. Also, a factor of time-stress was introduced to see how inexperienced users would allocate processing resources to complete a relatively simple menu search task in a given time period in which few errors would be expected. It was assumed that the time-stress factor would induce some sort of speed - accuracy tradeoff which would be differentially influenced by the type of menu structure.

Method

Subjects

Five male and seventeen female undergraduate students from a large east-coast state university participated in this study as subjects. All subjects (N=22) were 'novices' in that they all stated that they had one month or less experience on any computer system. Ages ranged from 17 to 25 years of age, and all had normal or corrected to normal vision. Two subjects were dropped from the study due to excessive variability in their performance.

Design

A two way between subjects design was utilized to evaluate 1) the effects of the presence or absence of time-stress and 2) the effect of menu structure. The task employed required searching for an item (household or personal product) in an hierarchical menu tree with 64 terminal nodes in each of the tree structures. The first independent variable, time-stress, was manipulated by verbal request upon the subjects. The manipulation of menu structure employed a broad/ shallow menu having three levels with four items each, and a narrow/deep form having six levels with two items each. The same 64 terminal objective items were used with each form. Figure 1 demonstrates the 2x2 design used.

Menu Structure

	Narrow/Deep	Broad/Shallow
No Time-stress	N = 5	N = 5
Time-Stress	N = 5	N = 5

Figure 1. Experimental design.

Materials and apparatus

System

A Kaypro II micro-computer was employed to display the menus in addition to recording subject responses and errors. Subject selections were made by entering a one digit number corresponding to a menu item on a numeric keypad, and the system would then send to the subject the appropriate menu frame. Subjects were also allowed to go back to the previous frame if they determined that an error had occurred.

Stimuli

Menu items were presented in the center of the terminal screen. Each target item was a consumer product that might be purchased at a department store. The menus themselves were constructed in such a way that the target item could be selected by means of a set of hierarchically-ordered choices, and the arrangements were pretested to reduce choice ambiguities.

Procedure

Prior to entering the lab and receiving verbal instructions, the subjects were given a printed instruction sheet outlining what the task would involve, including a sample run of the task, and the general purposes of the study. Once finished, further instructions were given by the experimenter delineating the precise task in which the particular subject would be participating. The lab was a quiet, well-lighted room of about 5 x 5 meters.

In the time-stress conditions the subjects were told, "It is imperative that you finish the task just as quickly as possible," whereas the other subjects were instructed, "Take your time, there is no rush." It is assumed that these statements successfully manipulated the amount of time-stress. The manipulation for the other factor — menu structure — was controlled by the program. Once all instructions were given, the subjects were given an opportunity to ask questions before giving informed consent.

Subjects searched for each target item presented on the screen at the start of each trial. When that item was found, the screen would display a message that the user was successful and then another target was shown. On erroneous trials, the subject was informed that he or she would have to try again until the item was found. Twenty-five targets were chosen per subject. The subject's overall performance was timed, and errors made by the subject were recorded by the system. Following completion, the subjects were given the opportunity to ask any questions, were debriefed as to the specific purposes and other conditions in the study, and were given a subjective evaluation questionnaire to express their impressions of the menu that they used.

During the experiment, two of the subjects could not finish the task without the assistance of the experimenter, and even with his help, their scores were on the order of six standard deviations from the mean of their respective groups. As a result, two additional subjects were run to replace them.

Results

The results indicated that it took 622.6 seconds on the average to complete the task under the time-stress instructions, but only 538.2 seconds under the no time-stress condition. Thus, the presence of a time-stressor actually slowed performance

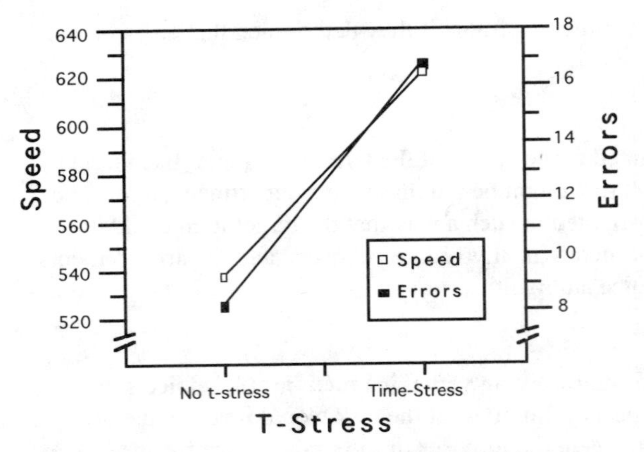

Figure 2. The effect of Time-stress on Speed and Errors.

on this task by 84.4 seconds for these subjects. Also, the results showed that the broad/shallow menu structure required an average of 449.0 seconds compared to the narrow/deep menu structure with 711. 8 seconds on the average.

A two-way analysis of variance demonstrated both of these main effects to be significant: for time-stress, $F(1,16)=5.14$ and for menu structure, $F(1,16)=49.97$, (both effects having $p<.05$).

The average number of errors was 16.7 under time-stress, and only 8.5 under no time-stress. Furthermore, the average number of errors was only 3.6 for the broad/shallow structure, but 21.6 for the narrow/deep menu. These results of error differences were also significant: for time-stress, $F(1,16)=7.1$ and for menu structure, $F(1,16)=34.2$, (again, both effects having $p<.05$).

No significant interaction was found between the two main effects. The main effects of time-stress, and menu structure are shown in Figures 2 & 3 respectively.

Discussion

As found in previous studies, the results support the superiority of a broad/shallow menu structure for faster performance, and indicated that fewer errors were made. These results may be explained in part by the cognitive processing requirements for broad/shallow menu structures that require less memory load while searching. Or, that items in the categories or the categories themselves may be more ad hoc and hence less ambiguous. In addition, a user's subjective probabilities for choices between only two items in the narrow/deep structure may be too similar, and result in erroneous choices.

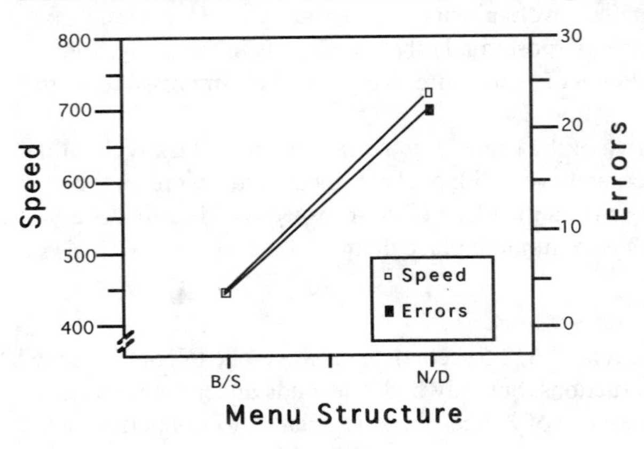

Figure 3. The effect of Menu Structure on Speed and Errors.

One additional finding of this study was

that the presence of time-stress not only inflated the number of errors, but resulted in a decrement in speed of performance as well, thus indicating that there was no speed-accuracy tradeoff, but only an overall reduction in performance. Why this resulted may be explained in part by the manipulation used to induce time-stress on this particular population of subjects. Since subjects were novices in this task and in the use of computers, no facilitation effects of time-stress may have occurred. On the other hand, the presence of the experimenter may have caused the subjects to become nervous, and the request of the experimenter to finish as quickly as possible may have increased the amount of time taken. Although no interaction between time-stress condition and presence of the experimenter is hypothesized, it is nevertheless a strong possibility.

The subjective evaluation questionnaire revealed no significant differences in reported satisfaction, although there were a few more comments expressing dissatisfaction from subjects using the narrow/deep menu. This was due mostly to the small number of subjects used.

The concordance of the two performance measures for “time to completion” and “errors” (see Figure 2 & Figure 3) implies that the longer time taken to complete a narrow/deep structure may reflect a greater number of errors made under that condition. Thus, subjects who make errors have to track back in a tree, and subsequently take longer to complete the task. Whether speed and errors are confounded in this particular design is currently under investigation. Further research into the issues of time-pressured and forced-paced menu performance has great potential value. User performance varies greatly under different conditions of time-pressure, and greater understanding of the dynamics that influence these differences will be useful in settings where a menu structure can be tailored to an unavoidable requirement of time-pressure on the task.

References

Adobe Systems, Inc, (1985) *Postscript Reference Manual*, Palo Alto, CA.

Bentley, J. (May 1985) Programming pearls: A spelling checker. *Communications of the ACM* Vol. 28, No. 5 456 462.

Callahan, J., Hopkins, D., Weiser, M., Shneiderman, B. (May 1988) An empirical study of pie vs. linear menus, *Proc. ACM CHI '88, Human Factors in Computing Systems,* 95-100.

Card, S. K. (1982) User perceptual mechanisms in the search of computer command menus, *Proc. Human Factors in Computer Systems*, Washington, DC ACM, 190-196.

Card, Stuart, Moran, Thomas, Newell, Allen, (1983) The Psychology of Human-Computer Interaction, Lawrence Erlbaum Assoc., Hillsdale, NJ.

Dray, S. M., Ogden, W. G., Vestewig, R. E. (1981) Measuring performance with a menu-selection human-computer interface, *Proc. Human Factors Society, 25th Annual Meeting*, Santa Monica, CA, 746-748.

Gettys, J., Newman, R. (1985) X Windows, MIT, Cambridge, MA.

Gosling, J., (1986) NeWS: A Definitive Approach to Window Systems, Sun Microsystems, Mountain View, CA.

Gould, J.D., Grischkowsky, N. (June 1984) Doing the same work with hard copy and with cathode-ray tube (CRT) computer terminals, *Human Factors* Vol. 26, No. 3 323-337.

Hansen, W.J. (1971) User engineering principles for interactive systems, *Proc. of the Fall Joint Computer Conference*, vol. 39 (Las Vegas, NV., Nov. 16-18). AFIPS Press, Montvale, N.J., 523-532.

Hansen, W.J., Doring, R., Whitlock, L.R. (Sept. 1978) Why an examination was slower on-line than on paper, *International Journal of Man-Machine Studies* Vol. 10, No. 5, 507-519.

Herot, C.F. (1984) Graphical user interfaces, *Human Factors and Interactive Computer Systems*, Y. Vassiliou, Ed. Ablex, Norwood, N.J., 83-103.

Hopkins, D., (December 1991) The design and implementation of pie menus, *Dr. Dobbs Journal.*

Kirk, R., (1968) *Experimental Design: Procedures for the Behavioral Sciences*, Brooks-Cole, Belmont, CA.

Koved, L. (1984) *Implicit versus Explicit Menus,* IBM Thomas J. Watson Research Center, Yorktown Heights, N.Y.

Koved, L. (July 1985) Restructuring textual information for online retrieval, Master's thesis, TR-1529, Dept. of Computer Science, Univ. of Maryland, College Park, (Also, IBM Res. Div. Rep. RC 11278, IBM Thomas Watson Research Center, Yorktown Heights, N.Y.)

Koved, L., Shneiderman, B. (April 1986) Embedded menus: selecting items in context, *Communications of the ACM* Vol. 29, No. 4, 312-318.

Laverson, A., Norman, K., Shneiderman, B. (1987) An evaluation of jump-ahead techniques in menu selection, *Behaviour &Information Technology* Vol. 6, No. 2, 97-108.

Lee, E., MacGregor, J. (1985) Minimizing user search time in menu retrieval systems, *Human Factors* Vol. 27, 157-162.

McDonald, James E., Stone, Jim D., Liebelt, Linda S. (1983) Searching for items in menus: The effects of organization and type of target, *Proc. of the Human Factors Society 27th Annual Meeting,* Santa Monica, CA, 834-837.

Miller, D. P. (1981) The depth/breadth tradeoff in hierarchical computer menus, *Proc. of the Human Factors Society 25th Annual Meeting,* (Santa Monica, CA: HFS) 296-300.

Mills, C.B., Weldon, L.l. (Dec. 1987) Reading text from computer screens, *ACM Computing Surveys* Vol. 19, No. 4, 329-358.

Mitchell, J., Shneiderman, B. (1989) Dynamic vs. static menus: an experimental comparison, *ACM SIGCHI Bulletin* Vol. 20, No. 4, 33-36.

Newcomer, l.M. Ed. (1980) *SUDS Users' Manual.* Carnegie-Mellon Univ., Pittsburgh, PA.

Norman, K. L. (1990) *The Psychology of Menu Selection: Designing Cognitive Control at the Human-Computer Interface* , Ablex Publishing Co., Norwood, NJ.

Paap, K. R., Roske-Hofstrand, R. J. (1986) The optimal number of menu items per panel, *Human Factors* Vol. 28, 377-386.

Parton, D., Huffman, K., Pridgen, P., Norman, K., Shneiderman, B. (1985) Learning a menu selection tree: training methods compared, *Behaviour & Information Technology*, Vol.4, 81-91.

Perlman, Gary (1984) Making the right choices with menus, *INTERACT '84*, North-Holland, Amsterdam, 291-295.

Powell, D. (1985) Experimental evaluation of two menu designs for information retrieval, Unpublished report, Dept. of Computer Science, Univ. of Maryland, College Park.

Rollo, C. (Nov. 1992) Pie menus for windows, *Dr. Dobbs Journal.*

Schwartz, J. P. Norman, K. L. (1986) The importance of item distinctiveness on performance using a menu selection system, *Behaviour & Information Technology* Vol. 5, No. 2, 173-182.

Shneiderman, B. (Aug. 1983) Direct manipulation: A step beyond programming languages. *IEEE Computer* Vol. 16, No. 8 , 57-69.

Shneiderman, B. Designing menu selection systems. *Journal of the American Society for Information Science* Vol. 37, No. 2, 57-70.

Shneiderman, B., Ostroff, D. (Dec. 1985) TIES authoring system. Univ. of Maryland, College Park.

Shneiderman, B. (1987) *Designing the User Interface, Strategies for Effective Human-Computer Interaction*, Reading, MA: Addison-Wesley.

Snowberry, K., Parkinson, S. R., Sisson, N. (1983) Computer display menus, *Ergonomics* Vol. 26, 699-712.

Teitelbaum, T., Reps, T. (Sept. 1981) The Cornell Program Synthesizer: A syntax-directed programming environment, *Communications of the ACM* Vol. 24, No. 9, 563-573.

Wallace, D., Anderson, N., Shneiderman, B. (1987) Time stress effects on two menu selection systems, *Proc. 31st Annual Meeting - Human Factors Society*, 727-731.

Weldon, L.l., Mills, C.B., Koved, L., Shneiderman, B. (1985) The structure of information in online and paper technical manuals, *Proc. of the Human Factors Society Conference* , (Baltimore, MD, Sept. 29-Oct. 3), Human Factors Society, Santa Monica, Calif., 1110-1113.

Wright, P., Lickorish , A. (July-Sept. 1983) Proof-reading texts on screen and paper, *Behaviour & Information Technology* Vol. 2, No. 3, 227-235.

F3 LOOKUP WORDS
F1 ABOUT KEYS
Students
Instructors
F2 SEARCH WORDS
F4 SHOW TITLES
Hypertextbook
Excercises
Chapters
Illustrations
Definitions
F6 RELATN OPTION
F7 NEW QUERY

Sparks of Innovation in Human-Computer Interaction,
B. Shneiderman, Ed., Ablex Publ., Norwood, NJ (1993)

3. Hypertext

Introduction

Our lab's greatest success in terms of direct commercial impact is in the creation of Hyperties, a hypertext authoring and browsing package for the IBM family of computers (Shneiderman 1989). The idea of hypertext is usually traced back to 1945 when President Roosevelt's Science Adviser, Vannevar Bush, described a desk-sized system he called memex, for memory extender. However, it took until the 1970s for the creation of interactive systems such as the medical system PROMIS at the University of Vermont (a menu structured approach to medical care), ZOG at Carnegie-Mellon University (an early information system built for the USS Vinson to show maps, naval information, etc.), and the Spatial Data Management System at MIT (spatial presentation of information with maps, organization charts, and rapid selection).

We were pioneers in hypertext starting in 1983 when we created a system for museum patrons: The Interactive Encyclopedia System (TIES). The beauty of our system is that it allowed easy and rapid authoring facilities for text databases. Users who were skilled with a word processor could learn to make links in a half hour and could produce something interesting in a day. Our software provided the management tools to coordinate the work of several people and to maintain large hypertext databases with numerous links.

Graduate student Dan Ostroff was instrumental in the early design and did the first implementation in APL on an early IBM PC with a green monochrome display. Then TIES was rewritten in DeSmet C and Lattice C with help from Kobi Lifshitz and low resolution color images plus videodisk photos enlivened our displays. The College of Library and Information Services provided space for our project - even their windowless fourth floor room was a step up from the dingy basement of the Computer Science Building. Prof. Janis Morariu applied her knowledge of educational software and took a major role in developing the concepts and software design. Prof. Gary Marchionini became a strong partner and helped tell the story in the context of his emerging theory of information-seeking behavior (see paper 3.1, Marchionini & Shneiderman, 1988).

We spawned many small hypertexts, but our major effort was a collaboration with Prof. Marsha Rozenblit of the Department of History to create a small encyclopedia of 106 articles on "Austria and Holocaust" (sponsored by the Washington-based US Holocaust Memorial and Education Center). She and her graduate students grasped the idea of writing for hypertext and their efforts were later expanded to 400 articles as a prototype for a larger (2500 articles, plus images, maps, and videos) "Encyclopedia of Jewish Heritage" (sponsored by the New York-based Museum of Jewish Heritage). It was an honor to be able to inspire both of these groups by our new technology. While there were skeptics who felt technology had no place in dealing with such difficult emotional issues, our cause was promoted when the elder statesman of the museum design team declared that "this technology is the best way for young people to learn about the Holocaust."

By 1987, our authoring tools and browsing software were rewritten for the third time and were ready for commercial distribution. Since TIES turned out to be a trademarked name, we had to choose a new name. Our choice was Hyperties to reflect the current interest in hypertext. The University licensed Hyperties to Cognetics Corporation of Princeton, NJ, and our work was now in the hands of a trusted colleague and friend, Charles Kreitzberg. Charlie was a partner in many projects and we eventually sat down to write about what we had learned about this new style of writing and reading (see paper 3.2, Kreitzberg & Shneiderman 1988). The commercial path was not easy, well-financed competition made us cringe, and our software needed a lot of further work. The story is not yet finished, but six years later Cognetics is still selling and improving Hyperties, with innovative applications in government agencies such as the FAA, Library of Congress, and Environmental Protection Agency and commercial success stories from Union Carbide, AT&T, and Hewlett-Packard, among others.

Meanwhile our efforts with several museums led to participation in an exciting archaeology exhibit, "King Herod's Dream," at the Smithsonian Institution's National Museum of Natural History. Our partner in this project was Prof. Ken Holum of the Department of History, and by no small coincidence the husband of Marsha Rozenblit. In one month, Ken and a graduate student were able to prepare more than 200 descriptions of archaeological dig sites that would accept volunteers, plus dozens of articles describing volunteer archaeology, geographic regions, and historical periods (Plaisant 1991). These were carefully linked together and our software to support touchscreen selection of colored map regions was rapidly cleaned up. By March 1988, we were ready for the exhibit opening with two sturdy stand-up kiosks that lasted very well for 18 months and 6 cities for this traveling exhibit. In the first few weeks, we observed and interviewed patrons, learning many lessons beyond what we found from usability testing in our lab (see paper in section 5.2, Shneiderman, Brethauer, Plaisant & Potter, 1989). Catherine Plaisant, who led this effort, also put her French skills to use in making a version for Ottawa. Having museum patrons as users was an especially potent challenge that kept our group working intensely for many weeks.

In the spring of 1988, we began discussions with the Association for Computing Machinery (ACM) to explore ways that they might use hypertext to publish their scientific journals. At that time, the editors of *Communications of the ACM* were preparing eight papers from the 1987 conference on hypertext for a special issue in July 1988. We proposed making a hypertext version and it caught on. While we rapidly converted the eight files and the many figures on the IBM PC, colleagues at Brown University were creating a Macintosh HyperCard version, and others were preparing a Sun version. The Hypertext on Hypertext project was done in a month, with Andrew Sears and Yoram Kochavy working about half- time each. Once again, the clear deadline, focussed audience, and specific goal evoked a vigorous effort and intense devotion.

By 1989, we were more ambitious and produced the world's first commercial hyperbook, *Hypertext Hands-On!* , with Greg Kearsley as my co-author. This was a more complex project because of the additional concerns inherent in commercial distribution. Almost a dozen reviewers provided comments in three stages over a 14 month period. Peter Gordon, our editor at Addison-Wesley, became deeply involved in this book and pioneered many changes in marketing, promotion, and distribution to make this project a success. For example, when bookstore owners saw the disks, many immediately rejected the book because they thought of it as software. Peter had to convey that this was really a book, guaranteeing that bookstore owners could return damaged copies of the book. If they accepted the book, their decision was often to shelve it with books on wordprocessors or spreadsheets - no one had ever seen a book like this one. I thought we could convey the story by saying "Please buy this book, then throw away the paper and read the disks," but the marketing people had trouble with the idea of recommending that a book be thrown away. We had some controversial reactions, but I'll always remember S. L. Fowler's comments in *ACM's Computing Reviews* (March 1990, p. 140): "This book is exactly the one to get if you need or must recommend a hypertext primer. It is simple, easy to read, and best yet, includes two diskettes containing hypertext samples."

We continued to refine our understanding of what makes for a good or bad hyperdocument by conducting two dozen empirical studies (Shneiderman, 1987;

Jones and Shneiderman, 1991). We developed automated strategies for loading and linking textual databases (Furuta, Plaisant & Shneiderman, 1989a; Furuta, Plaisant & Shneiderman, 1989b), that laid the basis for the commercial tools developed by Cognetics. We developed novel string searching algorithms and interfaces (Faloutsos, Lee, Plaisant & Shneiderman, 1990).

A separate chapter was our development of an advanced version of Hyperties on the Sun workstation under NASA support. The large screen Sun version using the NeWS environment had a 3-D eye-catching technique called pop-out (developed by William Weiland and applied by Don Hopkins) for highlighting selected items in a diagram. For example, the irregularly-shaped components of the Hubble Space Telescope would appear to pop-out of the screen when selected by a mouse placement, due to their being shifted a few millimeters with a dark drop shadow beneath. We also included pie menus for rapid control, a simple multiple window management strategy, conditional hypertext links, and a powerful macro facility (Shneiderman, Plaisant, Botafogo, Hopkins & Weiland, 1991). This version of Hyperties, developed under the leadership of Catherine Plaisant, was a successful demonstration to visitors and we had several groups who were eager to use it in their projects (we continue to receive inquiries to this day), but we were unsuccessful in finding the funding to clean up and support the software. It was one of my great frustrations that I could not find a supporter or a commercial company to take on our workstation version. Since then we've carefully focused on innovative interface design and allowed others to take on the large software development effort necessary for commercial distribution.

As our software development ended, we spent time building novel applications such as a touchscreen kiosk describing our Department of Computer Science, including courses and faculty resumes. Another project was to develop and test a hypertext authoring course using Hyperties (Jones & Shneiderman, 1991). As the requests for us to help in constructing hypertexts grew, we steered them to Cognetics Corporation, preferring to devote ourselves to more research oriented projects.

Rodrigo Botafogo developed several provocative methods for evaluating, understanding, and reorganizing hypertexts (Botafogo and Shneiderman, 1991, Botafogo, Rivlin, and Shneiderman, 1992). Prof. Kent Norman in the Department of Psychology has expanded the definition and application of hypertext to HyperCourseware, his continuing effort to provide online tools within the AT&T Teaching Theater (20 student workstations networked with an instructor's workstation and two large screen projectors). Prof. Gary Marchionini applied his skills to a multiple-year evaluation of Harvard University's Perseus Project, HyperCard stacks with ancient Greek manuscripts, plus English translations, dictionaries, maps, photos, etc. The latest project is an evaluation of the use of Perseus at the nearby National Gallery of Art in connection with the "Greek Miracle" sculpture exhibit.

Hypertext is still just getting launched as a viable technology. The hype is fading and the useful applications are emerging, but this new idea has taken much longer than I expected to become widespread.

Sparks of Innovation in Human-Computer Interaction,
B. Shneiderman, Ed., Ablex Publ., Norwood, NJ (1993)

3.1 Finding facts vs. browsing knowledge in hypertext systems

Gary Marchionini
Ben Shneiderman

For hypertext and electronic information systems to be effective, designers must understand how users find specific facts, locate fragments of text that satisfy information queries, or just browse. Users' information retrieval depends on the cognitive representation (mental model) of a system's features, which is largely determined by the conceptual model designers provide through the human-computer interface. Other determinants of successful retrieval include the users' knowledge of the task domain, information-seeking experience, and physical setting.

In this article we present a user-centered framework for information-seeking that has been used in evaluating two hypertext systems. We then apply the framework to key design issues related to information retrieval in hypertext systems.

IEEE Computer, 21, #1, 70-80, Reprinted, with permission, from IEEE 1988

Hypertext

Hypertext and other electronic information systems overcome human limitations by providing mechanisms for compact storage and rapid retrieval of enormous volumes of textual, numeric, and visual data. The importance of these systems lies in their potential capacity to augment and amplify human intellect. We need t his capacity because of the exponential growth, increasing complexity, and multidisciplinary nature of scientific, economic, medical, and other knowledge.

Early information retrieval systems searched large databases of records (library card catalogs, legal citations, scientific journal abstracts, etc.) to retrieve items that satisfied a Boolean, keyword-oriented query. A second strategy made information resources available in videotex systems through menu selection hierarchies. Large full-text databases were explored with string search strategies to locate lines or paragraphs with desired patterns. A fourth familiar strategy—database management systems—retrieved structured records of accounting, scientific, or other data according to the search logic of a procedural program or a precise query language.

The applicability of these strategies overlap, but the differences reveal the diverse approaches and tools that exist. A physician trying to find every clinical study of Parkinson's disease is very different from a high school student needing information for a term paper.

A new approach—hypertext—has recently joined electronic information systems. The term, coined by Ted Nelson (1981), describes a vast network of text fragments linked together, an electronic writing and reading system that uses the power of the computer for more than editing and display. Nelson's followers worked on a prototype and Douglas Engelbart (1963) created a variant approach during the 1960s. But only in the past few years have practical, commercially viable systems and provocative research implementations appeared. (For a review, see Conklin (1987). For discussions of particular systems, see Yankelovich, Meyrowitz, and van Dam, (1985), Halasz, Moran, and Trigg (1987), and Goodman (1987).)

Hypermedia and hypertext systems allow users to traverse complex networks of information quickly. Authors can easily link passages and references and collapse or expand outlines; readers can freely move among text fragments to find sources of quotations, journal article references, definitions, and related passages.

From the writer's point of view, hypertext systems are the next generation of word processing. In addition to word processing features like block moves, search and replace, and spell or style checking, hypertext writing tools may support and extend the writing process with telescoping outlines, posted notes that do not affect the main text, electronic bookmarks, and browsing modes.

From the reader's point of view, hypertext systems are a new generation of database management. Full text is accessible from multiple perspectives, for various purposes, and through different search strategies. Thus, hypertext databases are more malleable to the user than print or early electronic text formats.

In this article we focus on hypertext from the reader's perspective, in particular, how users find information in such systems.

Hypertext usage depends on what mental models users have for the system. These mental models in turn depend on the conceptual models used by designers to create and present the system. Therefore, effective use depends on better understanding of how information-seeking processes are learned and applied.

Since hypertext systems have a brief history of application, we have sparse evidence for their effectiveness, let alone proven principles to guide design. Advocates enthusiastically point out the similarity between human associative memory and the network of text fragments that allows freedom in linking ideas. While there are undoubtedly information search tasks that hypertext suits, promoters may fail to realize that the very same freedom of linkage they admire can complicate some search or learning tasks.

Present systems may support browsing strategies attractive to end users but inefficient for fact retrieval. To compensate, cumbersome analytical strategies that take advantage of indexing to improve retrieval may be supported; however, the overall design may become complex. Analytical strategies include consulting thesauri before search, using Boolean connectives, and systematically iterating queries.

Determining criteria for optimal mixes of browse and analytical support is critical to development. Balancing the power for retrieval with the ease of understanding is a central problem for designers of future systems. We believe that the solution is to provide flexible, powerful human-computer interfaces to maximize benefits for every community of users.

Three pillars of hypertext research

The maturation of software and hardware and the widespread availability of personal and mainframe computers have stimulated great interest in the design of electronic information systems and made possible search strategies impractical in manual systems. Research related to human performance with hypertext and other electronic information systems integrates methods and ideas from information retrieval, interface design, and cognitive science.

Information retrieval

Research related to on-line searching has focused on systems that aid professional intermediaries in finding a small number of "hits" in a large collection of records (library card catalogs, scientific journal abstracts, UPI reports, etc.). The emphasis has been on designing systems that aid or replace professional intermediaries (see Marcus [1983] for an example of an actual system).

Professional on-line searchers primarily clarify information requests and retrieve relevant information for end users. They carefully plan in advance, consult thesauri, and combine terms in systematic and precise steps by applying logical connectives (AND, OR, NOT) and by adjusting proximity limits (the range of words within which query terms must co-occur) and scoping limits (the range of documents over which search takes place). Unless they are themselves a part of a research team effort, they act as communication channels, locating and transferring information to end users who interpret and apply it.

The primary goal of on-line searchers is to retrieve and communicate information efficiently—their analysis usually focuses on the facets of a request for information, not on the problem that motivated the question or the possible application of the answer. Search intermediaries rarely browse informally, because focusing on the goal yields efficient and cost-effective performance. Their analytical strategies include much preplanning, application of Boolean connectives, and systematic iterations of the querying and refinement process.

End users, on the other hand, often browse despite accruing costs because they have long-term commitments to an area of research and may later benefit from extraneous information in that area. In other words, end users rationalize inefficient information-seeking strategies by hoping that incidental learning will have a beneficial cumulative effect. Browsing is an exploratory, information-seeking strategy that depends on serendipity. It is especially appropriate for ill-defined problems and for exploring new task domains.

Today's electronic retrieval systems were designed for use by professional intermediaries, or to emulate their performance. These systems focus on coding, indexing, and cross-referencing (organization for retrieval) rather than on meaning, readability, and assimilation (organization for understanding). Systems meant for end users must take into account these differences and support appropriate information-seeking strategies.

Hypertext systems differ from existing on-line retrieval systems in that they encourage informal, personalized, content-oriented information-seeking strategies. Hypertext system users can actually apply information during the retrieval process by noting context, and during browsing by saving, linking, or transferring text or images. Of particular interest in our research is the support of end users through flexible and powerful human-computer interfaces that balance end-user browsing strategies with efficient analytical strategies like those used by professional intermediaries.

Interface design

Improvements in human-computer interface design have come rapidly in the last decade. Hardware advances offer designers a range of input devices (such as mouse or touch panel) and output devices (such as high-resolution screens). Likewise, software advances allow designers to choose from a variety of selection mechanisms in addition to traditional command languages. (See Shneiderman (1987) for a set of interface design principles and references to the growing body of literature.) Although command languages offer expressive power to expert users, a variety of menu selection styles (pull-down, icons, embedded) offer novice and casual users ease of use. Powerful personal computers have now made visually oriented direct manipulation styles possible. Instead of remembering commands or traversing menus, the user sees a representation of the "world of action". Because the user points (with mouse, touchscreen, etc.) at given objects and actions, the impact of actions is immediately visible, thereby reducing errors and speeding performance. Actions should be rapid, incremental, and reversible to promote a sense of mastery, control, and confidence. Examples include display editors, the Macintosh or Star desktop, most video games, and many CAD/CAM systems.

Direct manipulation interfaces may consume more system resources, may be more difficult to implement, and may not always be as efficient to use as other interfaces, but in general they lead to less cognitive load in using computers, thus enabling users to apply severely limited human working memory to the task domain. As with information retrieval, a key design problem is balancing the ease of learning afforded by direct manipulation and access to powerful features for experts.

Cognitive science

The linchpin of an information-seeking theory is the human user. A first step to understanding information-seeking in electronic environments is to develop an understanding of the basic cognitive processes that guide information-seeking. We lack a clear definition, much less understanding, of the interactions among an information seeker's knowledge about a problem, past experience in searching for information, and knowledge of possible sources for information. Furthermore, since any system that supports information-seeking must structure knowledge to make it accessible, the systems themselves affect how users think when using them. The emerging interactive systems that encourage dialog and progressive query formulation instead of requiring direct commands can serve as environments for testing cognitive augmentation.

Cognitive scientists have proposed dynamic internal representations—mental models—that can serve as the focal point for building and testing a theory of information-seeking. (See Gentner & Stevens (1983) for a set of examples, and Borgman (1986) for an example applied to information-seeking.) A mental model is a cognitive representation of a problem situation or system that is active in the sense that it can take inputs from the external world and return predictions of effects for those inputs. It can thus be "run" internally and the results used to make decisions about actions. Mental models allow us to both understand problem situations and predict consequences of actions contemplated for solving problems. Users develop mental models for systems through reading documentation, training, experience with systems, and comparing them with previously encountered systems.

The rules for navigating a database as well as the mechanisms for interaction (input and output) affect the user's scope of application—determine what the user thinks is possible with the system. Designers must not only consider how to structure knowledge from a system performance vantage, but also consider what views and corresponding navigational tools are provided for the user. The views and navigational tools will be easily assimilated into a mental model for a system if they are familiar. This reasoning lies behind the desktop and other metaphors. However, a tension exists between the learnability and applicability of a system; a too-rigid metaphor may limit the development of users' mental models for new systems. Designers must know how users seek information in traditional print systems and existing electronic systems if they are to produce effective interfaces for new systems. An understanding of how users learn and apply existing systems will allow designers to build interfaces that accentuate the familiar and serve as bridges to the new features and functions of hypertext systems.

A framework for information-seeking

The following framework for information-seeking is meant to guide designers of hypertext systems and users who apply them to write and read hypertext documents. Figure 1 presents an overview of these components and their relationships. The interactions of these components determine the overall performance of an information-seeking system.

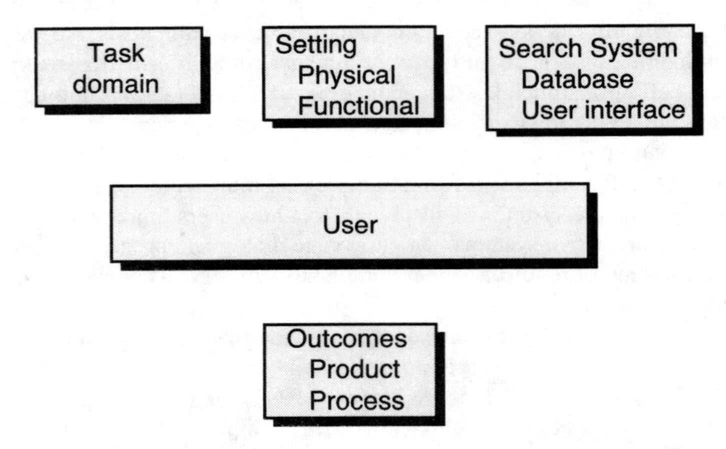

Figure 1. This information-seeking framework helps to identify the determinants of success. Issues include the complexity of the task domain, the physical and functional setting, the search system structure and user interface, and the user's knowledge of each. The outcomes of a search are specific information and the sequence of steps to generate the product.

Setting

The setting within which information-seeking takes place constrains the search process. The physical setting (in a user's private office versus in a public place with a line of impatient would-be users nearby) determines physical constraints such as the amount of time allocated, physical accessibility, and cost. These act as external control mechanisms for the search process.

The setting also determines functional constraints such as the motivation and purpose for conducting the search, whether pleasure, job assignment, or ongoing research interest. The setting actually enables the search task. Thus, the setting helps delimit the task domain and motivate the user, and affects the selection and application of the search system.

Task domain

A task domain is a body of knowledge, whether hematology or bridge design, composed of entities and relationships. Task domains vary in complexity (number of entities and relationships), specificity (similarity of the entities and relationships), and evolutionary status (clarity of definition of the entities and relationships, and their rate of growth and change). These characteristics determine the amount of information and level of organization for a task domain.

The amount of information and level of organization vary immensely across task domains. The task domain is critical because it affects the strategies and search systems available. A task domain like hematology offers substantial on-line information from various vendors in various forms, from abstracts to full texts. On the other hand, a task domain like contemporary music offers little on-line information and limited access through such common entry points as subject headings. Furthermore, the type of search system available depends on the task domain. For example, in the humanities the primary vehicle of information is the book, whereas in the physical sciences technical reports and journal articles dominate.

Search system

The search system consists of a database and a human-computer interface that allows access and manipulation of the database through a set of search rules. A print encyclopedia consists of words on pages and alphabetical ordering rules for using the index or finding articles by titles. In the case of electronic search systems, some of the rules and structures are embodied in software.

The user's first concern about the database is content—whether it is primary or secondary (pointer) information, full-text or symbolic, and how it matches the task domain and the information problem at hand. Once the user has selected the right database for the task, the organizational structure of the database becomes the primary determinant of information-seeking performance.

The database may be a simple sequence of full-text passages, a set of fixed-length records related through hash coding or b-trees, or a loose web of graphics and text linked through pointers. The organizational scheme chosen by the designer is critical to performance and will influence the interface as well. In turn, physical database organization is influenced by hardware and media. (See Zoellick (1986) for a discussion of how CD-ROM characteristics affect design.)

The human-computer interface is a communication channel with hardware and software components. The physical input/output devices, selection and feedback mechanisms, and search features determine the power and flexibility of a search system. The search system works because the designer has a view of the typical user when creating the interface. Primitive systems have static internal representations for users; they are controlled by the user and a set of default conditions that reflect the system designer's conceptual view of typical users and their information problems. Information systems that have some adaptive capability enable users to change aspects of the internal representations or the user interface.

The search system is critical because it structures knowledge and defines how it is accessed. The way knowledge is organized and made available affects the strategies used to access this knowledge and thus information-seeking performance.

User

Each user is unique, possessing mental representations for task domains. A generic knowledge base of information-seeking experiences includes mental models for various search strategies, dynamic mental models for search systems, and a control mechanism for relating these internal representations to one another and to external entities. Of particular interest for designers is how users develop mental models for new systems and how they apply these mental models when using systems.

A user's mental model for a search system is critical to the search process because it determines expectations for outcomes and the search strategies used. A mental model is active—it "runs" internally before action takes place. A user's mental model includes both the entities and relationships represented (how knowledge is structured) in the search system and rules for controlling the system.

Users can be classified along three continua: frequency of use, complexity of application, and general range of computer experience. The position of users in a space defined by these dimensions determines how quickly and accurately they will develop a mental model for a system and how effectively they can apply it.

Low-frequency users may develop accurate mental models for what the system can do, but forget the details of system use. These users need menus and on-line reference aides. Frequent users, on the other hand, may prefer commands to expedite their use of the system.

Users who perform only straightforward tasks do not need all the features a system supports and thus need only abbreviated menus. On the other hand, users who push the limits of a system access the complete hierarchy of menus, invoking every system feature.

Users with little computer experience have more to learn and fewer mental models of related systems from which to draw analogies. These users depend more heavily on experience with the system to develop their mental models. Their initial experiences must be simple enough to allow success and continued learning. On the other hand, just as first impressions are socially critical for future interaction among people, initial experiences with a computer system play a critical role in framing a person's emerging mental model for a system. If the initial experiences lead to ambiguous or inaccurate mental models, users will have difficulty extending their use of the system.

Because users vary so much in their individual abilities, experiences, and purposes, designers must struggle with providing an interface that does not frustrate or confuse yet is rich enough to support the eventual appendage of a full set of system features.

Outcomes

Outcomes for information-seeking include both products and a process. Products of search, from individual facts to complete documents that are interpreted to satisfy the problem condition, provide one basis for evaluating search effectiveness. Typical measures of search products include assessment of relevance or utility by users during or after search, structured or informal subjective evaluations, and examination of the resultant products or artifacts (for example, documents or abstracts).

The behavioral moves made by users and systems during a search—the search process—also help in evaluating performance. Evaluators assume that user behaviors are manifestations of internal information-seeking strategies, which are themselves "runs" of the user's mental model for the search system.

Although information units retrieved by the system are easily collected for analysis, the analysis of the search process causes more problems. Examination of paths taken and decisions made in jumping to other nodes allow us to make inferences about users' cognitive activity and provide evaluative data on system effectiveness.

Another important aspect of the search process is that the experience itself becomes part of the user's knowledge for dealing with future information problems. Therefore, consistency in design can help support incremental development of users' mental models.

Hypertext systems research

Since the information-seeking components described above are multifaceted variables, research efforts that attend to their interaction must be longitudinal and cumulative. We have studied two hypertext systems extensively and describe some of our results to encourage related empirical work and raise design issues.

Both these systems are what Conklin (1987) calls structured browsing systems. The databases used were static, in that users could not change them.* Both systems were designed for casual or novice users and thus the research efforts reported here focus on interface issues and users' mental models. In most of the work reported, the researchers controlled setting and task domain to focus on the user and system components of information-seeking. This research is further limited to information retrieval; the results and design issues discussed are thus directed to the reading aspects of hypertext systems.

Hyperties

Hyperties (hypertext based on the Interactive Encyclopedia System) enables users to easily traverse a database of articles and pictures by merely pointing at highlighted words or images in context (see Figure 2). Highlighted or colored words or phrases within the text become the menu items, selectable using a pointing

---

*Hyperties allows both writing and reading, but in separate modes, called Author and Browser.

WASHINGTON, DC: THE NATION'S CAPITAL PAGE 2 OF 3

Located between **Maryland** and **Virginia,** Washington, DC embraces the **White House** and the **Capitol**, a host of **government offices** as well as **Smithsonian mus**
Designed by **Pierre L'Enfant**, Washington, DC is a graceful city of broad boulevards, **national monuments**, the rustic **Rock Creek Park**, and the **National Zoo**.

First-time visitors should begin at the **mall** by walking from the **Capitol** towards the **Smithsonian museums** and on

---

SMITHSONIAN MUSEUMS: In addition to the familiar castle and popular Air & Space Museum there are 14 other major sites.
SEE ARTICLE ON "SMITHSONIAN MUSEUMS"

NEXT PAGE BACK PAGE RETURN TO "NEW YORK CITY" INDEX

Figure 2. This Hyperties display on an IBM Personal Computer shows the highlighted embedded menu items available for selection by touchscreen or arrow keys. The user can follow a topic of interest, turn pages (NEXT or BACK), RETURN to the previous article, or select the INDEX.

device. Rather than isolated and explicit menu items, the context of embedded menu items provides information and cues for the selection of further information.

This embedded-menus approach and the simple user interface enable users to explore large databases easily. Hyperties has been used to create a guide to the Student Union, an on-line help service for a bibliographic search system, training materials about software, a supplement for a museum exhibit about photographer David Seymour, an encyclopedia about the Holocaust, an introduction to the computer science department, and so forth.

Hyperties users merely touch or use a cursor to specify topics of interest; a brief definition appears at the bottom of the screen. Users may continue reading or ask for details about the selected topic. An article about a topic may be one or more screens long and contain several pictures. As users traverse articles, Hyperties traces the path and allows them to return to previous articles, all the way back to the introductory article. Users can also select articles and pictures from an index.

Hyperties has been under development since 1983 at the Human-Computer Interaction Laboratory at the University of Maryland.** In addition to the standard IBM PC version, there is a Sun workstation Hyperties browser that provides two windows with 34 lines in each and graphics with embedded menus (see Figure 3).

**Hyperties was first implementated in APL by Dan Ostroff, and has been rewritten in C twice. It is distributed by Cognetics Corporation of Princeton Junction, N.J.

Embedded menus are good examples of specialized indexing for systems that emphasize understanding rather than retrieval. As local indexes they highlight semantic relationships rather than physical relationships. Questions about how deep embedded menus should be, whether they should be available in definitions as well as articles, whether networks are superior to hierarchical structures, whether string searching should be supported, and how alphabetical indexes and embedded menus complement or interfere with one another are under investigation.

It is clear from the information-seeking framework that the type of database, user, and task affect the use of embedded menus. Results of an experiment comparing versions of Hyperties with and without embedded menus demonstrate the critical role of tasks and users' existing mental models for search tasks. When subjects were asked to perform efficiently in searching for specific factual information in a Hyperties database, the predominant strategy (14 of 16 subjects) was to use the alphabetical index. These subjects, experts at searching in manual indexes, used the familiar strategy rather than a strategy the new system was designed to promote.

In contrast, a log of usage in two museums over eight months showed that more than two-thirds of all selections were through the embedded menus, thereby demonstrating the orientation toward browsing in a museum setting.

Another study required subjects to use embedded menus or the index to search for specific facts in the same database.

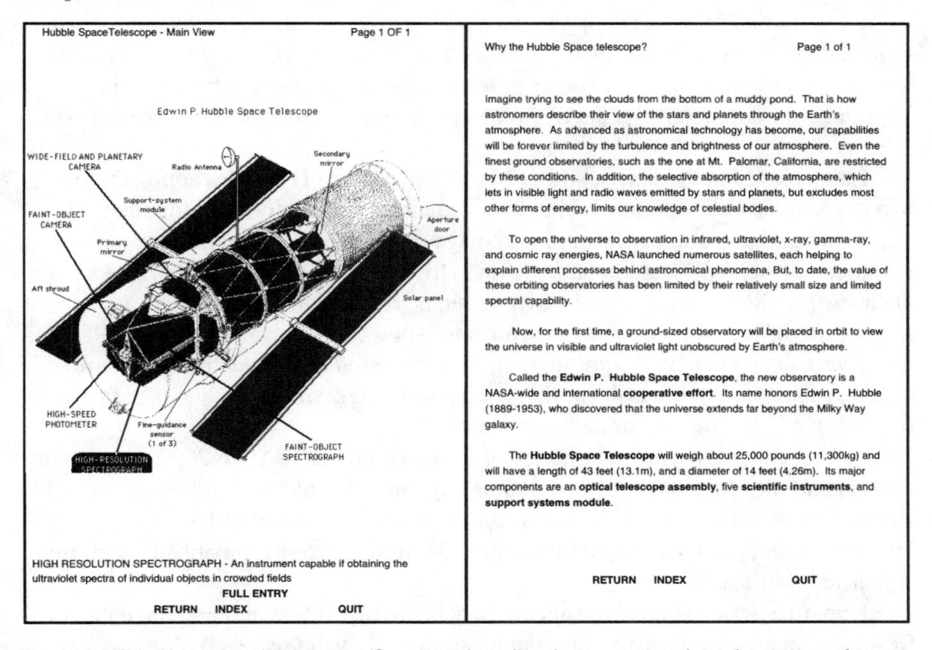

Figure 3. This Hyperties display on a Sun 3 workstation demonstrates the advantages of a larger screen, two windows, and touchable graphics. With the mouse users can select highlighted phrases in text or point at components of the space telescope to retrieve more information. The components pop out and the user can elect to see a diagram of the contents.

All tasks could be accomplished with either search strategy, but index users located facts more quickly than embedded menu users. The differences in performance between the groups became progressively smaller as more searches were conducted. This result suggests a learning effect as subjects become more familiar with the conceptual aspects of embedded menus. By systematically varying task and user variables we expect to build guidelines for future implementations that support a range of information-seeking activities ranging from fact retrieval to general browsing.

Another research study with Hyperties demonstrated the advantage of embedded menus versus explicit menus in speed of fact retrieval and subjective preference. Two experiments explored several pointing devices and demonstrated the speed advantage of the jump-arrow method over the mouse, probably because of novice users overshooting or undershooting the highlighted word or phrase with the mouse. The arrow keys forced easily controlled discrete moves. A touchscreen proved still faster and yielded higher satisfaction, although the touchscreen used produced high error rates. We have now developed touchscreen strategies that are fast and also accurate enough to point at single characters. In one implementation, the user touches the surface to produce a cursor (above the finger) that can be moved rapidly onto the desired target. When satisfied that the selection is correct, the user removes the finger to initiate action.

Of particular interest are our studies of Hyperties versus paper versions of the same database. Previous studies have shown a 30-percent penalty in reading speed for typical computer displays versus typewritten text, and up to a twofold disadvantage for computer users performing certain fact retrieval tasks (Shneiderman, 1987).

Larry Koved at the University of Maryland used the Hyperties approach for two experiments with on-line maintenance manuals for electronic equipment. A tree-structured and a linear form of a 52-page maintenance manual were prepared for screen presentation and in paper form. Differences in the time taken to accomplish 12 tasks showed use of the paper versions to be significantly faster. No significant differences for speed or error rates showed up between the tree and linear versions. However, a pruning algorithm applied to the electronic version to trim text unrelated to the task cut the time in half, suggesting an advantage in the flexibility of electronic information systems.

In a recent study using a larger database (106 articles of 50 to 2000 words) on Austria and the Holocaust, paper versions with an index had a speed advantage with simple fact retrieval questions. But as the query complexity increased, the Hyperties users performed equally rapidly. Moreover, users dramatically preferred Hyperties over paper.

Hyperties was designed to support easy browsing of text and graphic databases. Results of many evaluative studies demonstrate that even novices find it easy and effective to use.

Electronic Encyclopedia

Another system we examined is the full text of Grolier's Electronic Encyclopedia on CD-ROM (see Figure 4). The print version of the encyclopedia occupies 20 volumes. The hypertext version consists of 60 megabytes of text and 50 megabytes of indexes that contain pointers to each occurrence of every word in the encyclopedia, all occupying less than one-fifth of a single CD-ROM disc. The powerful search software for this system provides rapid access to all occurrences of any word or phrase entered by the user. The Boolean connectives AND, OR, and NOT are supported as well as right truncation, character masking, proximity limitations from one to 999 words, and scope limitations for various sections of articles.

One study (Marchionini 1989) examined the information-seeking strategies used by elementary school students. Results demonstrated the tendency of novices to use low cognitive load browsing strategies. The children used the system successfully even though their application of Boolean connectives was weak or incorrect. Their success came from the system itself; results of queries were displayed as alphabetical lists of titles with frequency of term occurrence. A single keystroke would then retrieve a full article with the query terms highlighted. This interface facilitated a scan and select strategy. Searchers simply entered a query; scanned the resulting list of articles for titles that were semantically relevant or had high frequency of term occurrence; and then selected the full text of the article and scanned for term occurrences (highlighted in the text) to locate relevant sections. Thus, the hypertext features of the search system compensated for some of the formal search inadequacies of these children.

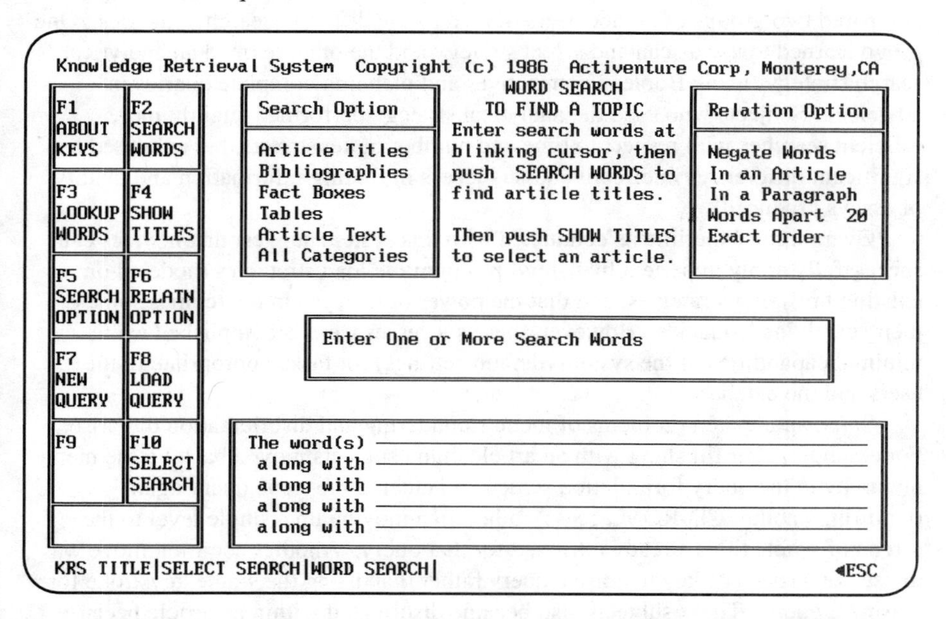

Figure 4. This main menu from Grolier's Electronic Encyclopedia offers users several search options and information about function key usage.

Follow-up studies (available from the authors) were conducted with high school students to compare print and electronic searches and examine the development of mental models for this system. One study examined the default conditions provided by the search software. The results indicate that setting proximity defaults to a paragraph seem optimal for a generic encyclopedia. The default scope condition on searching all categories of the article also proved optimal for this database. These results may not extend to other databases, since the theoretical framework predicts that strategy depends partly on task domain, and some domains may require special default settings. For example, technical documents—typically terse and specific—may require proximity settings that span more than a paragraph.

Another study simulated the effects of adding a controlled vocabulary to the search system. Many novices cannot articulate morphological variations or synonyms for search terms. Three levels of vocabulary control were tested: morphological (using variant forms and endings for terms); synonymic (using synonyms for terms); and semantic (using a hierarchical thesaurus that included broader, narrower, and related terms). Subject searches were reconstructed with these controls applied and analyzed for recall (ratio of relevant items retrieved to total relevant items in the database) and precision (ratio of relevant items retrieved to total number of items retrieved). All levels of control improved recall, but only semantic control improved precision, albeit only slightly. Designers of hypertext systems must decide whether to support vocabulary control of any sort, and then at what levels.

The power of this search system was demonstrated in another study that compared two groups of novice users trained to use different search strategies. One group learned to use a scan and select strategy and the other learned an analytical search strategy (using Boolean connectives and planning complete queries in advance). Subjects who used the analytical strategy performed slightly more efficient searches with respect to time and number of keystrokes, but exhibited no significant differences in effectiveness (success in finding information and quality of essays produced).

Overall, the experiments conducted with this system suggest that novices can successfully apply hypertext by using low cognitive load strategies modeled on existing browsing strategies, and that the power of the system overcomes some of their search inadequacies. However, these successes were accomplished using minimal capabilities of the system (default settings) for tasks appropriate to the users and the database.

Some anticipated problems of menu floundering and disorientation did arise. For example, after finishing with an article many subjects moved back up the menu hierarchy to the query formulation screen and entered the same query again (requiring another CD-ROM access) rather than moving up a single level to the screen of article titles already retrieved for that query. Another common move was to use the backspace key to erase a query rather than using the single keystroke for erasing a query. These subjects also became disoriented within an article because of the way the system put sections of text on the screen. When a user selects an article from the title list, the text of the article is displayed beginning with the first paragraph that contains the query term(s). Many students did not notice that they were in the middle of an article rather than at the beginning.

A similar problem came up with subjects who could not distinguish when they had the beginning or end of an article on the screen. Since the system provided no explicit positional cues, they erroneously continued to page up or down when at the beginning or end, respectively.

In general, the interface actually provided no feedback for queries that yielded no results. It also presented complex and dense screen displays (see Figure 4). We can easily overcome these problems with closer attention to the results from human-machine interface research. This system is currently under revision.

Inaccurate or incorrect mental models of how the system worked were apparent at the general level as well. For example, very young subjects entered queries in sentence or phrase form—they tried to conduct a natural language dialog with the system. The present system clearly cannot compensate for user's mental models that ascribe intelligence to it. Having little experience with encyclopedias of any kind, these young children modeled use of the computer system on their most common strategy for information-seeking-asking an "expert". Older children modeled the electronic encyclopedia on the familiar print versions.

Another common problem was subjects' poor mental models for searching in general. For example, some subjects added terms to queries that yielded no hits and contained ANDed terms. The system could trap such logical errors by pointing out that adding additional terms actually narrows a query (more terms yield fewer hits). Such forms of automatic help and remediation promote accurate mental model development, but if applied too often they may deter beginners from accomplishing immediate tasks and thus discourage continued use.

Perhaps an incremental approach is possible with systems that themselves record histories of use for users, but for hypertext systems like public access encyclopedias, we must find a balance between support for Boolean connectives and automatic adjustment of default conditions. For such systems, we believe that we can achieve significant cognitive advantage by amplifying low cognitive load browsing strategies and making the high cognitive load strategies that require Boolean manipulations and default adjustments transparent to the novice user.

The Electronic Encyclopedia is much more controlled than other hypertext systems in that jumps from article to article depend on a list of articles retrieved by a query. A user who wants to see an article not on the retrieved list must pose another query or enter a separate mode that allows lookup of single articles by title. On the other hand, the full-text search feature is totally under the control of the user. Problems of information overload did occur, but were minimized by the combined effects of the database (a set of generic, highly organized encyclopedia articles) and search rules (easy modification of queries and easy use of the scan and select browsing strategy). Complex, highly specific, or loosely organized databases may require distinct designs.

Design issues

Designers of hypertext systems or databases should consider the information-seeking framework (Figure 1). The overall design must attend to the physical system, the conceptual model the system presents (the user interface), and the mental model the user is expected to develop for the system. Design decisions that affect information-seeking in hypertext systems are related to defining access points, creating the user interface, and providing search strategy features. These decisions interact in unexpected ways, but thoughtful designs can preserve power and flexibility while reducing complexity of use.

Defining access points

In traditional electronic databases, access points for retrieval include characters, fields, records, and tables or files. Access points may be restricted to selected points, organized in alphabetical or hierarchical sequence, or multiply indexed. Consider the access points typically available in printed books: table of contents, indexes (author, subject, permuted, etc.), glossary, chapter, article (section), physical page, paragraph, footnotes, reference notes, lists, and appendices. Pagination is critical to access in books, since page number is the primary pointer to a field location.

Hypertext databases can support all these access points except physical page. A screenful of text cannot be used as an analog of the physical page in systems that permit control of text window size, scrolling, and stacking or juxtaposing windows. However, since the machine can assist in maintaining pointer information, hypertext systems can link field locations in many other ways, including electronic bookmarks, temporary notepads, graphic maps, backward citation pointers, and pattern matches on characters or words.

Hypertext systems also allow other access points that books do not, such as cumulative record of path, string search, animation, sound, video, or immediate link to related software. (For example, access software for Microsoft's Bookshelf on CD-ROM can be memory resident for immediate use from within another program.) Whether users can take advantage of these features remains to be determined.

A key decision for designers or authors is what access points to define and how to link these points. Users will likely expect access points at least as rich as those available in books. Designers must decide how much more to offer and how much unrestrained jumping from point to point to allow. Links at every word to every word are clearly not desirable from the perspective of user or system performance. The trade-offs in machine overhead and user cognitive load (in the form of overchoice) must be weighed carefully. Designers should consider the targeted task domains and typical user population in deciding how fine the access points should be and what links among access points should be visible to users.

Creating the user interface

An interface enables users to perform their tasks by providing selection mechanisms, feedback mechanisms, and input/output devices. In a book the default sequence is top-down due to the linear nature of the text. The interactive and flexible characteristics of hypertext require users to make more choices (selections) in searching for information. Furthermore, each selection requires appropriate and understandable feedback to maintain a fruitful interaction. Since the organization of the information in hypertext is not linear, mechanisms for selection and feedback are critical to good design.

Results from menu design research offer some guidance, but there are trade-offs to consider. The key issue is one of user control. The extreme cases range from allowing the user to jump anywhere from anywhere (hyperchaos) to forcing the user through a linear sequence of screens with no deviation possible (drill and practice). The degree of user control provided will depend on the user, his or her purpose, and the task domain. Expert users who are specialists in the task domain will welcome great power and control, but novices to the system and the task domain will likely benefit from limited menus and less control.

The direct manipulation approach with embedded menus seems very effective for hypertext applications, but there are many variations on the theme. We believe that embedded menus provide meaningful task domain (as opposed to computer domain) terms and concepts, thereby reducing disorientation. However, we need more research to help guide designers in choosing highlighting techniques to indicate selectable text or graphic items without distracting too much from the content.

Similarly, feedback can range from cryptic codes to pseudo-intelligent context-sensitive help. Experts will quickly seek ways to avoid lengthy feedback because it slows down the dialog and impedes progress toward their goals. On the other hand, too little feedback will frustrate and confuse novices, yet too much can distract them. One approach for hypertext systems in public access settings permits users to specify their level of knowledge of the database content, information-seeking experience and purpose, and previous experience with this and other systems. Feedback settings can then be adjusted accordingly, with the user able to change settings at any point in a session.

Input/output devices affect user information-seeking performance at the behavioral level. Good choices on the part of the system designer can facilitate ease and efficiency of use, but poor choices can lead to user frustration or fatigue. Pointing devices such as touchscreen, mouse, jump-arrow keys, or keyboards need to be refined and evaluated. Improvements in screen readability through proper font design, text/background color pairs, or higher resolution would benefit users. Increased screen size and multiple window strategies also require investigation. Mapping the proper input/output devices to the system requires consideration of user, setting, and task domain characteristics.

Setting default conditions for these and other issues will depend on how the designer views the typical user. A range of alternative selection mechanisms can then be provided for use by atypical users. Mixed strategies are also possible. For example, a linear "tour" could be threaded through a complex network to offer new users a guided introduction.

Providing search strategy features

Search features like Boolean connectives, string search, proximity limits, scope limits, and truncation facilitate rapid access to information, but cause additional cognitive load on the part of the user and substantial preprocessing of the database itself. Systems that provide only browsing features allow casual, low cognitive load exploration, but are typically inefficient for directed search tasks or fact retrieval. Defining a hybrid system that guides discovery seems an appropriate compromise, but involves a number of trade-off decisions. How deeply the database is indexed, whether some automatic controlled vocabulary is included, and how feedback is summarized and even formatted on the screen affect the strategies users will apply. If every word is indexed, the possibility of information overload increases. Therefore, features for filtering such as frequency of occurrence per node or support for NOT operators must be enhanced. If a controlled vocabulary is included, automatic thresholds must be established, or the user must be prompted to apply the controlled vocabulary or be alerted to its effects. For example, in an encyclopedia, a query that retrieved more than 50 articles could automatically trigger a narrowing function.

Secondary databases (containing pointer information) such as on-line catalogs or bibliographic databases and highly structured primary databases require analytical strategy support. Text or graphic databases seem to invite scan and select browsing strategies, although the size and complexity may warrant some additional indexing to improve user search efficiency. In general, each feature added to a system demands additional machine overhead. Many also add user cognitive load. These effects must be considered in all design decisions.

The flexibility/complexity trade-off

Systems transparent to one user may frustrate and impede others. Flexibility inevitably leads to complexity. Just as printed indexes and directories are organized to facilitate retrieval (nobody reads the phone book), so electronic information systems must be organized to suit the typical purposes of anticipated users. All designers must grapple with the issue of when to stop adding features — they face a law of diminishing returns. Empirical results and the marketplace will determine what the next version of a system should include and how much complexity users can tolerate.

A similar design issue is the tension between the learnability and applicability of a system. A system that is easy to learn may not be easy to apply in full. Results from cognitive science demonstrate that users' mental models will depend on initial training or experience with a system. An incomplete and simple conceptual model used to present the system to new users may limit their understanding of the system and their ability to apply it to future problems.

One approach to this problem, used in systems like HyperCard, is to choose a familiar metaphor (stacks of cards) and provide several levels of application (user preferences), examples, and help. The metaphor of the familiar flat index card will surely facilitate initial learnability, but may limit applicability of the multidimensional electronic card. As information systems continue to increase in complexity and power, they will likely become more difficult to learn and apply.

Some designers believe in adaptive systems, in which the computer is programmed to recognize user skills or information needs and then modify the interface or guide the user to the desired destination. Another school concentrates on adaptable systems in which the user is given the power to alter the user interface or is offered a rich variety of traversal methods. Adaptive systems represent an attractive but unproven idea, while adaptable systems place a greater burden on the user even as they provide increased control.

Hypertext systems offer the potential for highly personalized information-seeking if designers can apply principles from traditional information systems and the results of empirical studies.

Inevitably, the application of computers as cognitive augmenting agents will improve cognitive performance and change the way we think. An empirical base of evidence is coalescing around research and development on how to create hypertext systems, how to write using hypertext systems, how to read using hypertext systems, and how to find information in hypertext systems.

Our experience suggests that a general information-seeking framework that includes setting, task domain, user, search system, and outcomes aids the design and study of hypertext. Key design issues include:

- finding the correct information unit granularity for particular task domains and users;
- presenting interfaces with low cognitive load for selection and feedback mechanisms, and reasonable default conditions; and
- striking a balance between analytical and browsing search strategies.

The general problem of maximizing power and flexibility while minimizing complexity of use must always be attacked.

Although much remains to be learned about how users apply hypertext for information-seeking, clearly these systems offer distinct advantages for finding facts, browsing knowledge, and—we hope—acquiring wisdom.

Sparks of Innovation in Human-Computer Interaction,
B. Shneiderman, Ed., Ablex Publ., Norwood, NJ (1993)

3.2 Restructuring knowledge for an electronic encyclopedia

Charles B. Kreitzberg
Ben Shneiderman

Introduction to Hyperties™

Hyperties is a powerful, yet simple, new software tool for organizing and presenting information. It has been developed over the past five years at the University of Maryland's Human-Computer Interaction Laboratory and has been used for more than 50 projects (Shneiderman 1987a, 1987b). Hyperties authors can create databases consisting of articles that contain text and illustrations. Without the need for programming, authors can link these articles together so readers can easily browse through them.

Proc. International Ergonomics Association 10th Congress (Sydney, Austrialia, Aug. 1988) 615-620

Hyperties can be used for a wide variety of applications, including:

- On-line encyclopedias
- Instruction and dynamic glossaries
- Summaries of products and services
- Regulations and procedures
- On-line help
- Corporate policy manuals
- Newsletters
- Reference manuals
- Employee orientation
- Museum exhibits
- Biographies

The strategies for gaining the benefits of paper texts are well understood, but there is a great need for study of how knowledge must be restructured to take advantage of hypertext environments (Yankelovich, Meyrowitz & Van Dam, 1985; Conklin, 1987; Marchionini & Shneiderman, 1988). This paper provides some guidance for designing Hyperties databases and reports on an exploratory study of comprehension tasks when article length was varied.

Authoring and browsing

Hyperties consists of two programs: The Authoring System and The Browser. The Authoring System is used to create a database of articles and illustrations. Using theAuthoring System is simple — like using a familiar word processor. The author types in the text of the articles and specifies the links or cross references to other articles and illustrations. Hyperties automatically ties the articles and illustrations together into a unified database and constructs an index to the entire database (See Figure 2 of Finding facts vs. browsing (p 108)).

The Browser enables readers to access the Hyperties database of articles and illustrations. Using the browser is extremely easy and requires virtually no training. Readers can access complete articles, definitions of important terms, illustrations and cross references by using only three keys: the left arrow key <—, the right arrow key —>, and the enter key. If the computer is equipped with a touchscreen, readers can browse without the use of a keyboard at all.

Links

The power of Hyperties comes from the links that tie articles and illustrations together. A link is a cross reference, an indication that more information on a particular word or phrase is available. For example, suppose you were writing an article on the joys of owning pet fish. In a Hyperties article, you might write a sentence such as:

> Among the most interesting fish are ~guppies~ and ~goldfish~.

The tildes (~) that surround the words guppies and goldfish inform Hyperties that these words are links to additional information. The additional information may be simply a definition or footnote. Or it may be a complete article, with links of its own. When the Hyperties browser displays text, the tildes are removed and the links are highlighted on the computer screen:

Among the most interesting fish are **guppies** and **goldfish**.

On a monochrome monitor (IBM PC or compatible, or SUN 3 workstation), the links are displayed in boldface, like the example above. On a color monitor the links are displayed in a different color from the rest of the text. The highlighted text signals the reader that more information is available. Figure 2 of Finding facts vs. browsing (p 108) shows highlighted embedded menu items that can be selected by touchscreen or arrow keys. The user can follow a topic of interest, turn pages (NEXT or BACK), RETURN to the previous article, or view the INDEX.

The reader may choose to explore the database by using the links to travel among articles and illustrations. Hyperties automatically keeps track of the path so readers can return to previously seen articles.

Illustrations

Illustrations for Hyperties databases are prepared using a standard graphics editor. A scanner can be used to capture photographs and drawings. Prototype versions of Hyperties also support video disc.

Index

Sometimes readers will be looking for a specific article and will not want to browse the database starting with the introductory article. Hyperties automatically creates an index which lists all the articles in the database. Readers may go to the index at any time and access any article in the database directly.

Synonym

Authors may wish to refer to the same article using different words or phrases as links. This is often a matter of style. For example, suppose you were creating a Hyperties database about the presidents of the United States and included an article on George Washington. Here are three sentences you might write (in the same or different articles) that link to the same article on George Washington:

George Washington was the first president of the United States.

A well-known anecdote about **Washington** involves a hatchet, a cherry tree, and his father's wrath.

In understanding the political motivation of **the president**, it is important to consider his roots.

Hyperties can treat **George Washington**, **Washington**, and **the president** as synonyms which all link to the same article. The author need not plan this in advance; as Hyperties builds its index it will ask if certain terms are to be considered synonyms or not.

Highlighting is selective

Just because a word or phrase can be used as a link to an article or illustration does not mean that it must be used that way every time it appears. Authors decide when a word or phrase is a link by enclosing it in tildes. This keeps articles from becoming cluttered with gratuitous highlighted terms. For example, you could write:

> ~George Washington~ was a military leader and as such commanded political respect. It was said that George Washington was autocratic and it was said that George Washington was a democrat.

When Hyperties displays this text, only the first reference would be highlighted as a link:

> **George Washington** was a military leader and as such commanded political respect. It was said that George Washington was autocratic and it was said that George Washington was a democrat.

Introductory article

In each Hyperties database the author specifies an article as the lead or introductory article. Since many encyclopedia readers will browse the introductory article first, this article should be composed so that it references as many key articles as possible. There are several strategies for composing the introductory article.

One strategy is to fill the introductory article with many references making it a summary of the entire database. By scanning it, the reader can select one of many places to begin browsing.

A second strategy for the introductory article is to confine it to only a few key references. In this strategy, the idea would be to minimize the number of details which the reader must deal with and start him or her down an appropriate path. For example, suppose you were building a policy manual which had many detailed articles on specific policies. Rather than referencing many policies in the introductory article you could develop a more general approach such as the following:

> This database contains policies relating to:
> **permanent employees**, **temporary staff**, and **consultants**. In addition you will find policies which apply to all staff relating to **security**, **non-disclosure**, and **dealing with the press**.

A third strategy for the introductory article is to design it as a high level index. Here is an example:

CORPORATE POLICIES

Permanent Staff

Hiring Permanent Staff
Termination Procedures
Benefits and Vacation Policies

Temporary Staff

Approval Policy for Hiring Temps
Approval Policy for Retaining Consultants

This technique of using the introductory article as an index can be extended to other articles. For example, **Approval Policy for Hiring Temps** could link to a new article that provided a detailed "index" to relevant policies, for example:

APPROVAL POLICIES FOR HIRING TEMPS

Hiring Short-term Temporaries from Agencies
Establishing Qualifications of Temporary Staff
Hiring Independent Contractors

This technique can yield an extensive network of indexes. A particular article could appear in several indexes, so readers can access it from many points. For example, an article on *Vacation Policies for Permanent Staff* could be highlighted under *vacations*, *benefits*, *permanent staff*, or any other relevant area.

Planning for expansion

The Hyperties browser will not highlight a reference to an article or picture unless the article or picture exists. If you are writing an article and are discussing a topic which may eventually be the subject of its own article, you can put tildes around a link to a word or phrase. Because the referenced article does not exist, Hyperties will not highlight the link. Later, when the article is written, Hyperties will automatically highlight the reference.

Writing style

In general, it is best to keep articles short, and keep a sharp focus. Instead of discussing a subsidiary topic which is not the main subject of an article, you can merely mention it, delimiting the key word or phrase with tildes. Then you can make that topic the subject of its own article, or at least give the topic a definition which can be called up by the reader.

The same technique can be applied to details. Rather than including detailed information in an article, you can simply reference it and create separate articles for it. This shields the reader from unnecessary details, but provides a path to them when the reader deems it relevant. This technique can be especially useful when the material contains case studies, experiments or many examples.

Creating instructional material

Hyperties can be used as a tool to reduce the difficulty of creating educational software and allow authors to focus on content and instructional design, rather than on technical factors. In Hyperties, concepts and information can be entered and linked together. Developing courseware in such an environment is more like writing a book than writing a computer program. With Hyperties, the development of courseware should become an instructional, rather than technical, endeavor.

For example, an introductory psychology module might contain the following text:

> The basic process in **behavioral psychology** was presumed to be **conditioning**. Two types of conditioning were extensively studied: **operant conditioning**, the more powerful form is most associated with **John Watson**; the less powerful paradigm of **respondent conditioning** is most frequently associated with the studies of **Ivan Pavlov**.

The highlighted words and phrases in boldface indicate to the student that additional information is available on the topics: **behavioral psychology**, **conditioning**, **operant conditioning**, **John Watson**, **respondent conditioning**, and **Ivan Pavlov**. This additional information might be: a definition (for example, a definition of behavioral psychology), a new article (for example, an article on operant conditioning), an illustration (for example, a graph of conditioning and extinction), or a videodisc sequence (a brief biography of Ivan Pavlov).

Implicit within Hyperties is a cognitive model based on associative relationships. Articles in Hyperties explain concepts and tie articles, illustrations, and videodisc sequences together to create relationships among concepts. A Hyperties database may therefore be viewed as an associative network of concepts and examples at various levels. The power of this simple structure is attractive. Instructors can express the relationships among ideas by the manner in which articles are linked. Concepts can be expressed at multiple levels, with high level concepts linked to more specific concepts and specific concepts linked to examples.

Because a Hyperties database is organized according to the relationships inherent in the instructional material, it may help students learn the material in an integrated, holistic fashion. One of the most difficult instructional tasks in any content area is conveying the systems and interrelationships which underlie the facts. Memorization of isolated facts leads to rote learning; integration of concepts and their relationship into the learner's cognitive structure should lead to meaningful, useful learning.

Hyperties also creates materials that are learner-controlled. Much computer-based instruction is based on a dialogue model in which the computer constantly prompts the student to respond to questions. This can be a powerful instructional model but is often implemented in a fashion which forces the student to accommodate to the pace and presentation units of the software. It is this factor which makes so much computer-based education unappealing to the student. In Hyperties, the student has greater control. Learning proceeds according to the pace and paths selected by the student. Students need not waste time on material they already know and they can pursue a topic of interest to any depth desired.

We do not suggest that Hyperties is ideal for all forms of instruction; rather, we suggest that it is excellent for certain types of instruction. In particular, Hyperties, we believe, will be extremely effective in the following areas:

- familiarization - situations in which a person is introduced to a new content area and needs to become familiar with the key concepts which underlie it and their relationships.
- annotation - situations in such areas as literature, poetry, art, law, and politics in which student read source material which may be heavily annotated. The annotations remain "hidden" behind the links and so do not interrupt the flow of primary material but are instantly available for reference
- dynamic glossaries - glossaries prepared in Hyperties not only define terms but provide links to related concepts. This enables the reader to more fully understand the key terms.
- diagnosis and review - coupled with objective test items, Hyperties becomes a powerful diagnostic and review technique for any achievement test. Students answer questions. If they are correct, the software moves on to the next item. If the student answers incorrectly, Hyperties presents an explanation which serves as an entry to the database. Students can browse the database until they feel confident they understand the area and then return to the diagnostic test.
- diagnostic problem-solving- maintenance problems fit the Hyperties structure conveniently. The reader can select model numbers, problem features, symptoms, or other conditions and receive further information about how to proceed. This strategy has potential for machine repair, business procedures, medical diagnosis, etc.
- organizational information - when there is a need to teach organizational relationships (for example, the structure of government) Hyperties can represent the relationships by linking informational articles together. Hyperties is also useful in presenting the facilities and services of an organization. For example, it can be used to create orientation courses for new college students.

Newsletters

Hyperties can be used to create efficient newsletters. The essence of a newsletter is that the reader wants to obtain up-to-date information efficiently. In Hyperties, you can create a series of "headlines" or short abstracts which let the reader know what information is available. If the information is of interest, the reader can then select the article for more information. For example, the first page of a newsletter for personnel departments might be structured as follows:

NEW COURT RULING ON MATERNITY LEAVE. A federal court recently ruled that corporations must provide maternity leave to long term temporary employees. See **Higgens vs Retco**.

LIABILITY ON ALCOHOL-RELATED ACCIDENTS. An employee, who became drunk at a company sponsored party and later was injured in an auto accident, sued the company. For details of this case see **Carnevale vs. Rapido Trucking**. For a review of the legal issues see **Alcohol and Corporate Liability**.

Creating reading sequences

A final authoring strategy is the development of reading sequences in Hyperties. By its nature, the articles in a Hyperties database can be randomly accessed. However, sometimes it is desirable to provide readers with a path to read the articles in sequential order.

For example, suppose a set of materials was organized into five key articles. These articles contain the main ideas that your readers should encounter. In addition, there are a number of more detailed articles, that expand upon the key articles. What you want the reader to do is:

(1) read all five key articles in sequence
(2) within a key article, use the browser to explore the details of any concepts for which (s)he wants more information.

You can accomplish this in at least two ways. The first way would be to use the introductory article to list the five key articles:

Please read the following key articles, in sequence:

Article 1: Buying Your Fishtank
Article 2: Selecting Your Fish
Article 3: Setting Up Your Tank
Article 4: Feeding Your Fish
Article 5: Care of Fish Babies

The reader would select each article in turn. Within each article, the reader could browse related articles of interest, and ultimately return to the introductory article to select the next article.

The second technique is to create a link at the end of each article to the next article which you want the reader to see. For example, the first article, Buying Your Fishtank, might end as follows:

Congratulations! Having followed the instructions in this article, you are now the proud owner of a fishtank. But what is a fishtank without fish? To move on to this exciting step, please read Selecting Your Fish, next.

This technique can be expanded to create several paths through the material, if you desire.

Article length: an exploratory experiment

One design issue about this environment is the appropriate size of articles. Since following a reference by turning to another article is more rapid than on paper, smaller fragments of text may be more suitable. Also, considering the small size of many computer screens, slow page turning, and possibly poor readability, some designers suggest that hypertext articles should be brief. To test this conjecture an exploratory study was run by Dana Miller and Anna Williams under the direction of the second author.

Thirty-two psychology student volunteers were given brief instructions and ten minutes of practice with a Hyperties database dealing with personality types. Then the subjects were given 30 minutes to answer as many multiple-choice questions as they could. A typical question was: What are introverts interested in at their work? A) the procedures. B) the results. C) the idea behind the job.

The major independent variable was article size. The short database had 46 articles from 4 to 83 lines, while the long database had 5 articles of 104 to 150 lines. A second independent variable was personality type of the subjects, but the measurement instrument was ad hoc and this variable failed to produce statistically significant results. Therefore the remainder of the discussion focuses on the article length variable and performance time data.

The 16 subjects working with the short articles answered an average of 10.1 questions correctly while the 16 subjects working with the long articles answered an average of only 7.2 questions correctly ($F(3,30)=4.73$, $p < .01$). The average time per correct answer was 125 seconds with the short articles and rose to 178 seconds for the long articles ($F(3,30)=9.22$, $p < .001$).

While these results support the conjecture that short articles facilitate fact finding in a hypertext environment, they need replication with other databases, questions, subjects, and screen environments (e.g. larger or multiple windows). Longer practice sessions, an effective subjective satisfaction questionnaire, and within-subjects design would be useful improvements in a new study.

Conclusion

The new opportunities offered by hypertext systems call for a re-thinking of the presentation of knowledge. Hyper-chaos is a serious danger and effective guidelines will be necessary to assist authors in creating useful materials. Empirical studies can be a great aid in sharpening thinking, developing appropriate guidelines, and formulating new theories of how people seek and acquire knowledge.

Sparks of Innovation in Human-Computer Interaction,
B. Shneiderman, Ed., Ablex Publ., Norwood, NJ (1993)

3.3 The Electronic Teaching Theater: interactive hypermedia & mental models of the classroom

Kent L. Norman

Abstract

The introduction of hypermedia into the classroom presents both an opportunity to expand the power of teaching through electronic facilitation of the media and a challenge to redesign the classroom and instructional environment to exploit the enhanced features of hypermedia. This paper briefly surveys the current state of computers in the classroom and then argues that a more integrated approach is required. To this end the concept of an electronic teaching theater is proposed which takes advantage of hypermedia and collaborative work environments. The aim of the electronic teaching theater is not to totally redesign the classroom and instructional interaction, but rather to facilitate it using well understood metaphors to lay out the dynamics of classroom interaction on the electronic media and to use the results from research in human/computer interaction to design the interface. To facilitate the application of hypermedia, a model of instructional interaction among

Current Psychology, 1990, *Research & Review*, 9 (2), 141-161 the students, the instructors, the course material, and the products of instruction is presented. A number of component models pertaining to course preparation, lectures, note taking, and other instructional activities are then discussed that should prove useful in designing the electronic classroom. The origin of these models is the mental representation of the interaction as perceived by the teacher and the student. The idea is to start with such models as a base metaphor, to instantiate the metaphors in the electronic classroom, and then to explore innovations in the technology that go beyond the strict application of the metaphor.

Introduction

The use of computers in classroom instruction has been growing over the years in the midst of much enthusiasm, controversy, and numerous problems. The early advocates of computers in the classroom argued that computers would revolutionize education and free students and instructors from the drudgery of learning. On the other hand, a survey of current applications reveals numerous problems and a serious skepticism with the idea that computers are the solution to education. Moreover, there have been numerous problems with the misapplication of the technology, the lack of the funding, and the lack of training.

Over the years computers have been used in many different facets of instruction. From the onset they have been used for administrative purposes, managing grades, and basic record keeping. They have been used to present programmed learning materials, to automate drill and test exercises, and to provide the full range of computer assisted instruction. In addition, computers have been used to present games, simulations, and demonstrations that would otherwise not be possible in the class room. Moreover, they have been used as intelligent tutors and exploratory aids in an attempt to meet the individual needs of the students and the requirements of the subject matter.

Quite apart from the success of any particular application, computers have for the most part been applied to the classroom as supplements and alternatives rather than as an integrating medium of instruction. In essence, computers have been applied in a piecemeal approach to education. In the classroom the computer has often been viewed as an excursion in the instructional process rather than as a unifying medium. While each application of the computer in education has had its merits, the lack of connectivity across the various activities of instruction has severely limited its impact. Indeed, one can claim that despite the emphasis on computers in the classroom, computers have yet to change, in any real way, the day-to-day instructional activities of the classroom.

Consequently, the purpose of this paper is to explore ways of using computers as an integrating medium in the classroom to facilitate instructional interaction and the collaborative learning process. Consequently, the question changes from "How will this particular application improve the instructional process?" to, "What is the instructional process and how can it be facilitated in a computer environment?" The shift in emphasis from application to environment is motivated by the concept of the "electronic teaching theater" and by a project supported by AT&T to develop an environment for collaborative learning and research. The focus of this project is to create an environment capable of hosting instructional activities rather than on writing particular educational packages. The context for this discussion is the university classroom outfitted with high resolution video displays, workstations at each desk, and shared computing facilities. Although this may be perceived as a limited application, a number of the issues generalize to a wide range of educational contexts.

In developing an environment for collaborative learning and inquiry, we will first consider the objectives and physical design of the electronic classroom to support the environment. Next we will consider ways in which the human/computer interface may be designed. In doing so, we will use the concept of mental models to elucidate the representations and expectations that teachers and students have about the instructional process. We will then ask how these models may be supported and facilitated in the electronic media. Finally, we will consider the design space for creating the electronic teaching theater and evaluate the prospects for success. A basic component of this space will be the use of hypermedia and collaborative work environments.

Objectives of the Electronic Teaching Theater

Rather than concentrating on pedagogical methods or on theories of instruction, the goals of the electronic teaching theater focus on the development of a computer environment to support a wide range of instructional and classroom activities. The environment is a product of both the software and hardware hosting it. An environment in the present context is a medium within which users can perform the functions required in the process of learning and instruction. Specifically, the goals of the electronic teaching theater are:

1. to provide a more interactive learning experience than is generally possible in traditional lecture and seminar courses at the college level.
2. to provide interactive and hypermedia technologies during lectures and seminars.
3. to increase student-to-student and student-to-faculty collaboration and group problem solving.
4. to provide students with an integrated learning environment with access to hypermedia databases, communications, and simulations.

These technological objectives, however, should in no way obscure or take precedence over higher educational objectives. A good lecture devoid of technology many be necessary to engage the students in a theme. Face-to-face unmediated interaction may be necessary to drive a point home. Only when it proves beneficial should the instruction turn to electronic assistance.

In addition to the aforementioned objectives, a number of functional capabilities have been outlined that might be supported by the environment:

1. Group Collaboration: Groups of students should be able to work together on complex problems. Classes as a whole should be able to explore problems together.

2. Interactivity: Feedback and communication facilities should be available during lectures and discussion. This includes student polling and course evaluation both during class time and after.
3. Multi-media Tools: The environment should provide high resolution video and electronic blackboards and other drawing and digitizing devices.
4. Real-Time Classroom Computing: The environment should provide interactive simulations that either the instructor may run as a demonstration for the class or that students may run individually or in groups.
5. Student Help: Students should be able to receive online help from teaching assistants or from the system with respect to both class materials and the operation of the electronic teaching theater.
6. Richer Note-Taking Facility: The environment should assist in note taking and provide student scratchpads and workspaces.
7. Improved Class Communications: The environment should provide a multi-media file exchange system so that course materials can be cut and pasted by the instructor during course preparation and by the student during note taking and study time.

In order to explore such an environment, a prototype electronic classroom is currently being constructed with approximately 20 student workstations at the University of Maryland. The workstations are UNIX-based and multi-windowed (Ed: the final decision was to use Windows 3.1). Each workstation will have several megabytes of memory and 80 megabytes of local storage. High resolution mega-pixel color monitors will be provided with a real-time video window. Input devices will include a keyboard and a mouse.

The system will be supported by a high-speed local area network that will provide network configuration tools, collaborative work tools, and multi-window scratchpads. Software packages will provide utilities for word processing, drawing, analysis, file manipulation, games, and simulations. However, the basic aim of the software is to build a hypermedia environment in which the data and utilities reside as objects. The multi-media environment will provide an electronic blackboard that can be copied into electronic documents, a video system including VCRs, a video disk, a high resolution projector, and a digitizing camera.

Finally, the room will be configured as shown in Figure 1. Seating will allow for up to two students per workstation. The desks will have a low profile so as not to obstruct visual contact, and the monitors will be recessed in the desks at approximately a 40 degree angle.

Interface design

An essential feature of the electronic teaching theater is hypermedia. Both instructors and students must have access to text, graphics, audio, and video in a way that will allow instructors to guide the students through course material with excursions to exercises and simulations, and allow the students to navigate a course through the material to support the completion of projects and study for exams.

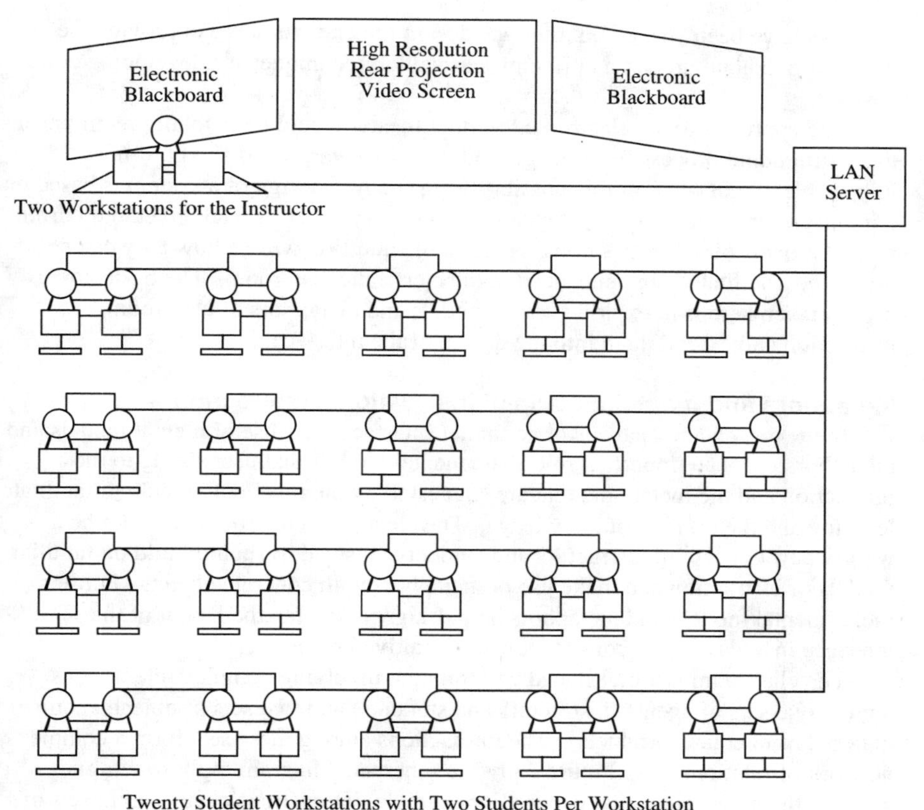

Figure 1. A schematic of the basic layout of the AT&T Electronic Teaching Teacher

Specifically, the design challenge is to create a hypermedia environment with tools that:

1. are easy to learn, operate in an obvious way, and are easy to use.
2. are integrated, appear seamless, and require a minimum number of steps to perform desired functions.
3. reduce the cognitive load of students and instructors rather than increase it.
4. reduce the difficulty of instructors generating materials to bring to the course and of students copying materials to take from the course.
5. promote active interaction with course materials and collaboration among the students and the instructor.

Given the feasibility of technology to support the electronic teaching theater and the extensive list of objectives and capabilities, the question then is how it should be designed. Research in hypertext and hypermedia suggests that these goals are achievable in the emerging hypermedia environment and provides guidance as to how to design the environment. Moreover, in recent years a number of books have been written on interface design. Such texts serve to provide the basis for good human factors principles as well as techniques for developing good design.

One approach to the electronic teaching theater would be to totally re-engineer the instructional process from the ground up. However, it is difficult, if not impossible, to conceive of this possibility since any redesign of a system is based on our current understanding and conception of that system. Instead, given our current mental models of the instructional process, the question will be how they can be preserved, facilitated, and enhanced in the electronic classroom. The basic approach taken here is to exploit current models and metaphors of classroom instruction and extend them into the design of the interface.

Metaphors and mental models of instructional interaction

In the design and analysis of computer interfaces, the use of mental models and metaphors plays an important role. The mental models that users bring to the interaction and the metaphors that are suggested by the media often help to facilitate learning and the transfer of knowledge. The electronic classroom need not be a wholly new concept to instructors and students. Instead, it should build on familiar models of instruction and make use of metaphors with concrete objects. Furthermore, mental models and metaphors help designers to plan the layout of the interface in a way that is consistent with cognitive processes.

The classroom is a multifaced environment involving complex interactions among two sets of agents (instructors and students) and two sets of objects (course materials and course products). The interactions among these sets form a complex network of relationships. Figure 2 gives a schematic diagram of these sets and some of the interactions that occur. For example, interactions occur within sets of agents. Instructors interact among themselves by way of formal printed media (e.g., books and journals) and by way of informal methods (e.g., conversation and exchange of notes). Student interaction is generally limited to informal methods of communication such as in-class discussion and out-of-class study groups.

The instructional process basically involves interactions across sets of agents. Instructors convey information to the students and students convey information back often in the form of questions, answers, and reports. In general, however, the interactions are conveyed by means of the two sets objects, the course materials and the course products. Furthermore, the source of the information is from the sets of objects and is conveyed by means of the instructor.

In the electronic teaching theater, the course materials and course products will be contained in hypermedia databases. Interaction with these databases will be by way of the human/computer interface. Following the model of Norman et. al. (1980), the interface is represented as the intersection of areas covered by the domains. There are in this case six intersecting areas as shown in Figure 2. The Instructor-Material Area A pertains to the instructors' access to course material outside of their direct interaction with students. Course preparation would be a major activity in this area. Similarly, the Student-Material Area B pertains to

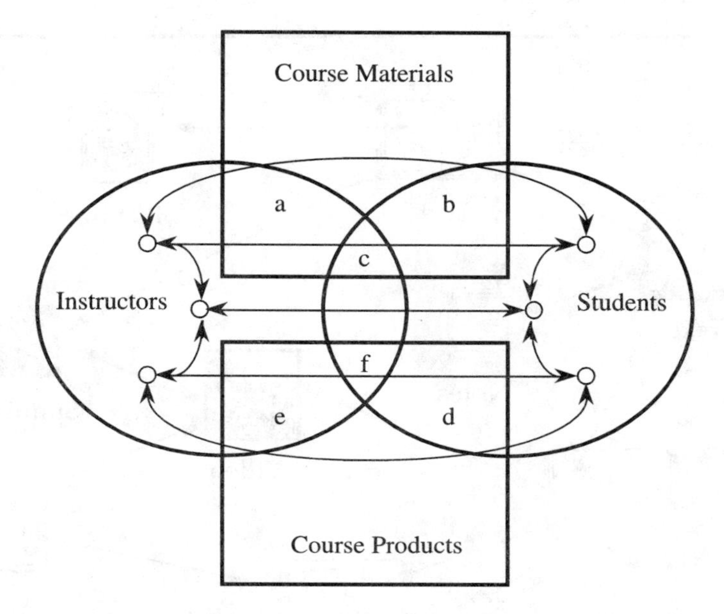

Figure 2. A schematic of the sets of agents and objects in the instructional process. Arrows represent some of the many possible interactions among the agents though the instructional media of course materials and course products. Overlapping areas indicate interfaces between agents and objects.

student access to course material outside of direct interaction with the instructors. This would include the activities of reading and studying. The Instructor-Material-Student Area C is a three-way interface of the instructors and the students together interacting with the course material. This area basically represents the activities of delivering lectures and classroom interaction with course material. The Student-Product Area D pertains to student authoring of papers, completion of assignments, and taking of exams. Since students may also be grouped, this area may also contain collaborative work. The Instructor-Product Area E pertains to instructor access to course products for evaluation and grading. Finally, and central to this project, is the Instructor-Products-Students Area F, a three-way interface of instructors and students with the products. Instructors and students may work together on collaborative class projects.

The generalized concepts of interaction and interfaces must take on concrete form in actual practice. In this paper, we consider a college seminar or lecture course as the scenario. Our current methods of instruction result in a set of mental models that help to define the characteristics of the agents, the objects, and the interfaces shown in Figure 2. To help translate these concepts into a working interface, the following section outlines the specific objects in the set of materials and products, and sets forth a prototypic screen layout to allow instructors and students access to the hypermedia database.

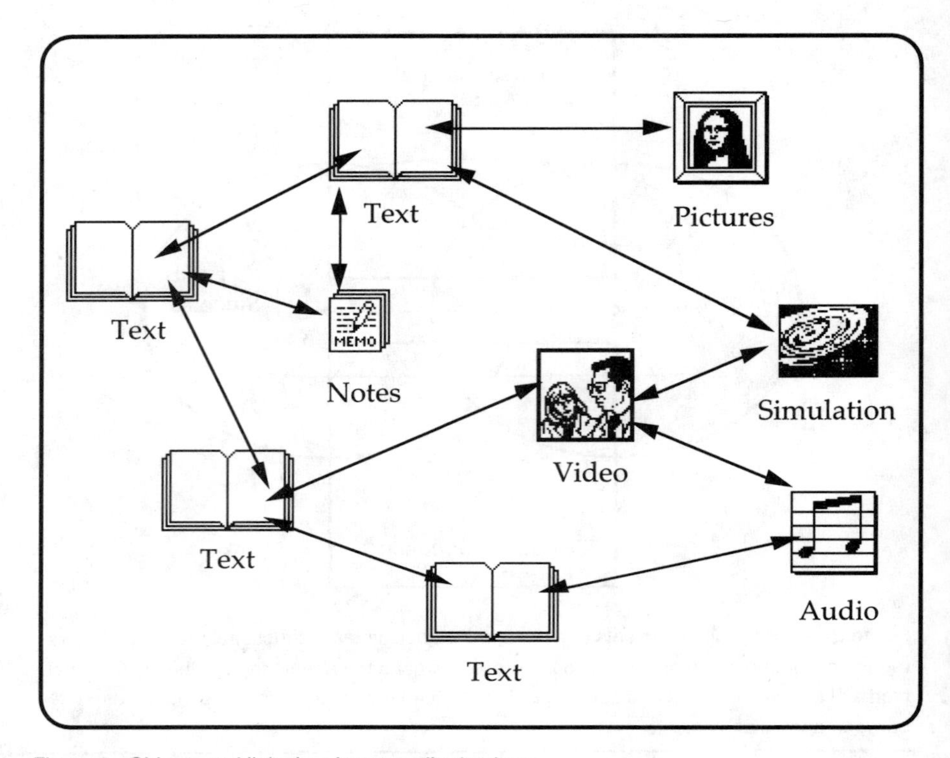

Figure 3. Objects and links in a hypermedia database.

Hypermedia layout of course materials

Although the precise definition of what constitutes a hypermedia system may not be clear, in the present discussion we will consider it to be a collection of electronic documents represented as objects with links tying them together in a network. A hypermedia system provides a facility to go from one object to another and effectively browse through the material following any number of paths. Hypermedia includes both print and non-print media. Figure 3 shows a general network of the types of documents that may constitute a hypermedia database.

In the electronic teaching theater, the hypermedia database will be composed of two basic sets of objects, course materials and course products. Table 1 lists some of the major objects composing the sets of course materials and course products.

Each of these objects will be thought of as a node in the hypermedia environment which leads into a hypertext or hypermedia document. For example, the syllabus might be laid out in typical manner. However, using the concept of embedded menus, the student would have a facility to select the lecture topic for a particular date and open up a window showing the lecture notes for that day, select the supplementary reading and go directly to page one of that reading, or select the assignment for that date and open up a window showing the assignment. Although

Course Materials	Course Interaction	Course Products
Syllabus	Blackboard	Student's Notebook:
Textbook	Simulations	Class Notes
Supplementary Readings	Games	Projects/Reports
Lecture Notes/Outlines	Instructor Questions	Exams
Handouts	Student Questions	Instructor's File:
Audio/Visual Aids	Discussion	Projects/Reports
	Feedback	Exam Results
		Gradebook
		Course Evaluations

Table 1. Objects Composing the Set of Course Materials, Classroom Interaction, and Course Products.

the textbook and readings may initially be linear documents, they could include links from the table of contents and index to the text, from the text to figures and references, and to and from other objects in the set of course materials. Eventually the textbook and the readings may be replaced by true hypertext documents that provide a rich network of links through the information.

In addition, lectures would be hypermedia nodes authored by the instructors. They would be composed of lecture outlines and links to other course material such as references to the textbook, graphics, simulations, class exercises, and so on. Similarly, class notes would be hypermedia nodes authored by students. They would contain text as well as links to lecture notes, textbooks, and other course materials.

In addition, Table 1 lists a set of objects which originate primarily in the overlapping areas of interaction among instructors and students with the materials. These include things written on the blackboard; the results of demonstrations, simulations, and games; and questions, discussions, and feedback. These objects would also constitute nodes in the hypermedia database, but in contrast to other objects, they would be the focal points for interactions and collaboration among the instructors and the students.

To support the hypermedia environment and to provide access to the media by the instructors and students, a windowing environment is provided. In one conceptualization of the hypermedia environment, each workstation would display a desktop with icons representing the instructional objects, a workspace for browsing, authoring, and linking, and a set of tools represented as icons. Figure 4 shows one such layout.

In this prototype, the course materials are represented as icons listed down the left side of the screen, course products are listed down the right side of the screen, and hypermedia tools for interaction are listed along the bottom of the screen. The center of the screen provides a workspace in which various windows can be opened for browsing, authoring, and viewing simulations or videos. Each of these windows

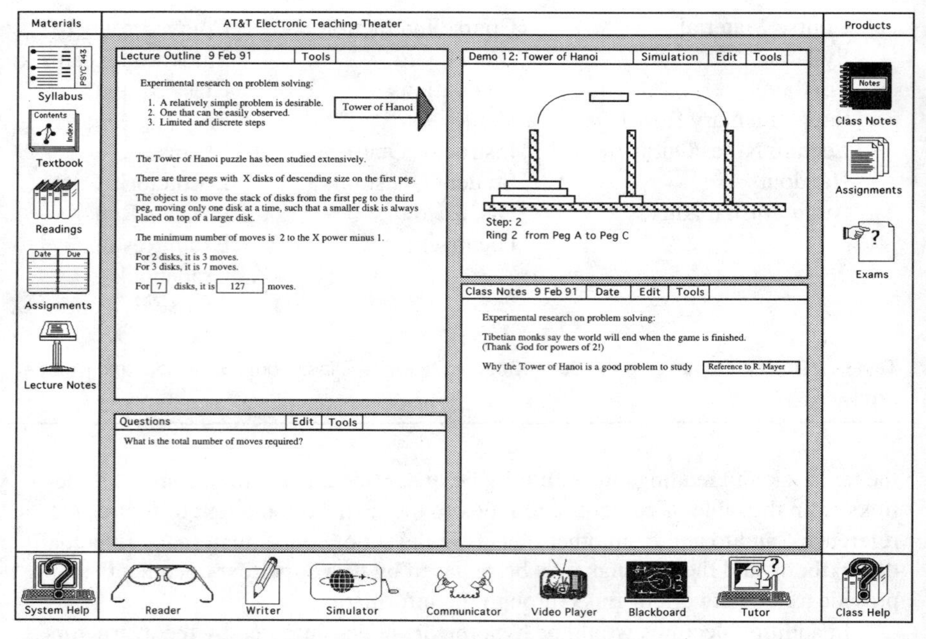

Figure 4. Possible layout of the desktop screen for an electronic classroom.

would have pull-down menus associated with them for operations specific to that window. In the following section we will consider how such an instructional desktop would be used in various models of classroom activities.

Hypermedia models of instructional interfaces

The hypermedia database and collaborative environment must support a number of models of instructional activities in the electronic teaching theater. In this section we will survey a number of these activities and consider how they might be modeled. The approach taken here is similar to that taken by Johansen in describing the models of interaction in computer support for collaborative work and decision making. A scenario of group interaction is considered. It is then transferred to the electronic medium and evaluated.

Course preparation

Instructors vary greatly in how they prepare for teaching a course. At one end of the continuum, an instructor may only generate an outline of the contents of the course. In this case, lectures are fairly impromptu discourses on the topic. At the other end, an instructor may have detailed notes, an extensive set of examples, and a number of presentation aids for each lecture. In either case, the information conveyed originates from the instructor's study of the course material.

In an electronic environment, we may imagine ways in which course preparation will be facilitated. Access to information, examples, and demonstrations should be faster. Furthermore, in an electronic media the instructor should be able to easily copy and paste material into the course. However, we can also see the challenge of preparing for such a course in an electronic medium the first time. One important consideration of an instructor using an electronic classroom will be added time to prepare materials for presentation.

However, in this treatment we will assume a complete hypermedia database. All course materials, class outlines, assignments, lecture notes, textbooks, readings, illustrations, exams, laboratory exercises, and so on are available in a hypermedia database. All course products, exam results, student notes, reports, project results, results of class exercises, homework, and so on are generated in a hypermedia database. In fairness, this is no small assumption. The conversion and authoring of such a hypermedia database is a difficult task which deserves attention.

Course preparation involves Area A in Figure 2 and may proceed as follows: The instructor surveys the hypermedia database of course materials to generate a syllabus for the course or modify a preexisting one. The syllabus is coordinated with a calendar and will eventually be filled in with lesson plans, lecture notes, reading assignments, and homework. One metaphor that proves useful is to think of each class meeting or each lecture as a node in the hypermedia. As instructors survey the course material, they may create links between objects in the hypermedia database to lecture nodes thereby making that information directly accessible during

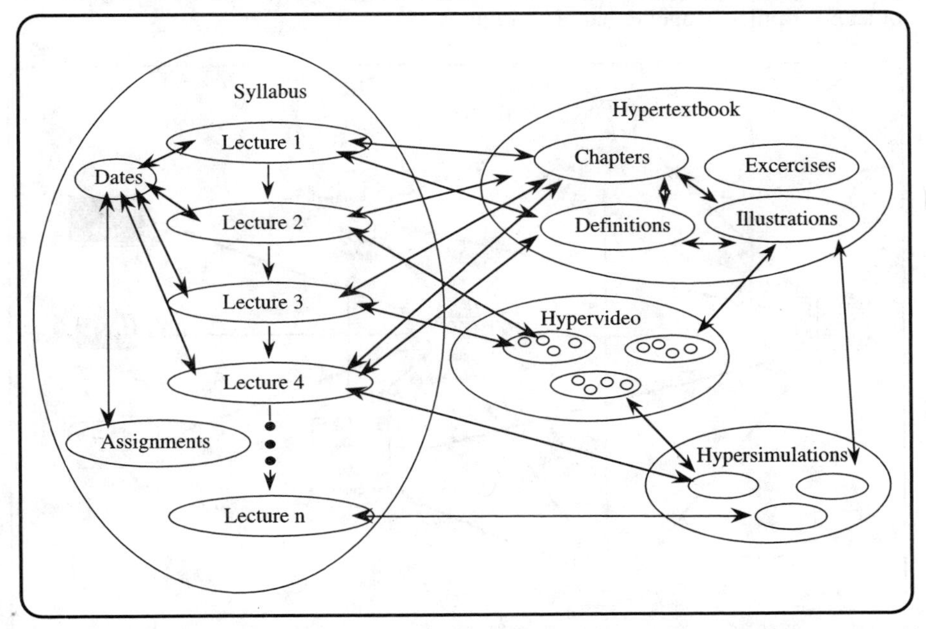

Figure 5. A model of course preparation in which course material is organized around the model of class lectures represented as nodes in the hypermedia database.

the lecture. Figure 5 shows a diagram of this model imposed upon the hypermedia database.

Lectures

Given the lecture notes and links shown in Figure 6, the delivery of a lecture would proceed as a browsing of the hypermedia database with the instructor acting as the guide through Area C of Figure 2. The instructor would probably start with his or her lecture notes. Selected portions of these notes would be available to the students and would appear on the student's desktop. The instructor's personal cues and notes would appear only on his or her own desktop. In addition, the instructor's desktop would display links to video segments, simulations, and other documents as shown in Figure 4. The instructor would select these as appropriate during the presentation.

During the lectures the students may ask questions either directly or via an interaction window. Questions in the interaction window may be fielded by teaching assistants or addressed by the instructor. During a lecture these questions may open up other topics and lead to further excursions through the hypermedia database. Furthermore, it is conceivable that the class could be broken into groups depending on need or interest to pursue different directions through the information. Whether it is feasible to address questions online and how to handle a queue of questions in a non-disruptive way will be a topic of concern and investigation. Furthermore, there are serious social and psychological questions regarding the use of an electronic channel to handle problems.

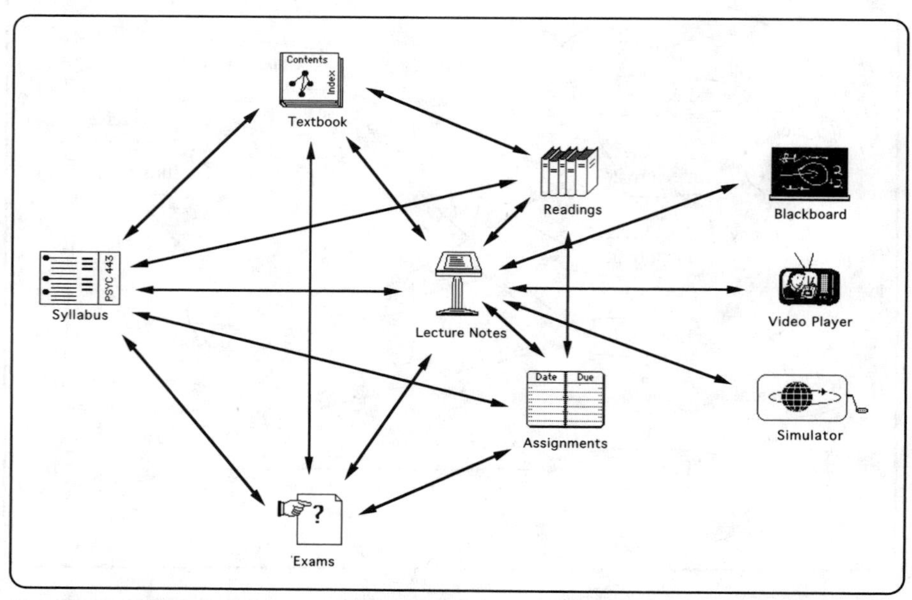

Figure 6. A hypermedia database for the electronic teaching theater with links created by the instructor.

At the other extreme, lectures may be entirely unstructured and the class may as a whole engage in a sort of collaborative exploration of lecture materials. The selection of paths through the hypermedia would be a group decision and could be displayed on the large projection screen or in a common window shown on each workstation.

Help

One of the greatest difficulties in teaching is dealing with the diverse needs of students for help. In the electronic teaching theater students may need either help in the use of the interface or on the course material itself. Figure 4 displays an icon on the left for access to system help. This help would provide information about the use of particular tools. It would provide access to software manuals as well as context dependent help. The system help itself would be an access point into a hypermedia database.

Help on the course material would be accessed via the icon on the right of the desktop shown in Figure 4. Help on the course material may provide access to a tutorial, a glossary of terms, an index to the material, or a facility to ask more or less open-ended questions.

In contrast to lectures originating with the instructor and passing through Area C of Figure 2, help may be thought of as originating from the student and passing through Area C to the instructor and back. The instructor and/or the teaching assistant could respond to these questions after class during what might be called "electronic office hours." If a number of accesses to course help reveal a fundamental lack of understanding in some area, the instructor may address it in the next lecture or special help sessions could be arranged. These sessions would essentially be nodes in the hypermedia database that point to specific information in the textbook, provide special examples or demonstrations, or present practice problems.

Access to course help may be structured such that the student is presented with a list of topics and may request help on a particular one. The student may then be asked about what type of help is needed or what aspect is not understood. This interaction may then serve as a point of entry into an intelligent tutoring system on that topic.

One of the major of goals of the help function would be to allow students to ask questions in a non-threatening environment and to help them ask questions that may otherwise be ill-defined. Furthermore, the system could help the instructor record and manage questions from the students. However, it is important in the area of help not to circumvent or inhibit the direct interaction between students and instructors. The question rather is how interactive help systems can be used to break down the barriers and facilitate communication and transmission of knowledge.

Note taking

Note taking is, in a sense, the inverse of lecture delivery. It is the attempt of the student to process and record the contents of the lecture. On the one side however, it is generally a less than perfect transformation of information; and on the other side, it may add to the content with idiosyncratic embellishment. In terms of Figure 2, the process originates in Area C and ends up in Area F. However, the model of what constitutes note taking by the student is highly variable. Furthermore, the type of notes taken will depend on the style and content of the lecture. At one extreme, notes may be a more or less verbatim record of the lecture. If so, students in the electronic teaching theater need only copy the lecture notes from the course materials into the course products or alternatively, create a pointer between the two. Alternatively, notes may be entirely new products authored by the students. They may record students' perceptions, opinions, ideas, and asides, as well as markings as to the importance and priority of materials (e.g., "This will be on the exam.").

The electronic teaching theater may provide a note-taking tool that is totally unstructured, much like the traditional pencil and notebook but with enhanced editing capabilities. For example, it may be a generic document processor that allows the student to enter, copy, paste, and edit text and graphics. Or it may be much more structured and start with the lecture outline and require the student to fill in the details. Alternatively, it could start with the complete lecture notes as a base document and provide a facility for attaching different types of notes, annotations, and links to other hypertext documents.

In a collaborative environment, notes may also be shared or passed among the students. Students may be able to compare their notes and to combine them to produce a richer and more accurate recording and comprehension of the information.

Class discussion

In the general model of a class discussion the instructor acts as a facilitator to prompt questions, stimulate ideas, limit digression, and summarize the points addressed. Students are expected to generate ideas, provide examples and illustrations, and voice and defend opinions. Traditional class discussion is limited by the fact that only one person may talk at a time. Consequently, instructors often divide the class into smaller groups which may report back at the end to the group as a whole.

In the electronic teaching theater, the same model of class discussion would be assumed; however, the collaborative network would be used to enhance several aspects of the discussion process. First, the network could allow a number of students to enter ideas simultaneously that could be viewed on all of the student workstations. Second, the instructor could organize the points expressed by an outlining or graphic tool. Third, small groups could be created by networking together students that share a common viewpoint rather than sit next to one another. Finally, the results of the discussion could be summarized by the instructor by cutting and pasting the information generated by the groups. Furthermore, in a hypermedia context, the final product of a class discussion could be a hypermedia document expressing the views taken by different individuals or groups with links supporting arguments and examples.

Course assignments

Typically, course assignments are either listed in the syllabus or announced in class. They may refer to problems in the textbook, to readings, or to sets of data. They are linked to a start date and a due date. In a hypermedia and collaborative work environment, new possibilities may be exploited. The assignment may be directly linked to problems, readings, or databases. In addition, the start date and due dates may be used to remind the student of the time factor involved. The assignment would be completed in the hypermedia environment in the sense that the student authors new objects and links in the database.

Finally, collaborative networks may be established between students who are working on an assignment together. Links would tie together the various parts that have been authored by each student. For example, three students may be designing a space station, one working on the structural details, another on the life support system, and a third on the power systems. The progress of each system might be linked together via planning software and finally presented as an integrated project at the time of completion.

Study and individual exploration and inquiry

The electronic teaching theater also opens up the possibility of individual browsing of the material during non-class periods. The student may access the materials before class (e.g., complete reading assignments) or review materials after class (e.g., study for exams). The hypermedia database, however, can provide a much richer context. For example, the student could replay the events of a lecture complete with demonstrations and group discussion. Paths through the hypermedia database could be recorded and replayed for review.

During study and exploration the student could record the path or create new links to facilitate navigation through the media. For example, the student may create new links among objects to organize them according to some new theme. A path may be recorded that serves as a study guide through material for an upcoming exam. Creating new links in the database may itself serve as a learning experience. Figure 7 illustrates the potential links that the student could create and browse during study sessions.

Exams

The presentation of exams on computer is nothing new. However, in the context of a hypermedia database, several new possibilities open up. First, a hypermedia database expands the idea of an open book exam. The student may browse the database in the course of working problems or writing essays. Second, the product of the exam may itself be the location of the objects in the database or the pathways through the information. Thus, the hypermedia database may itself be a topic of examination as well as the medium of examination. As such, the environ-

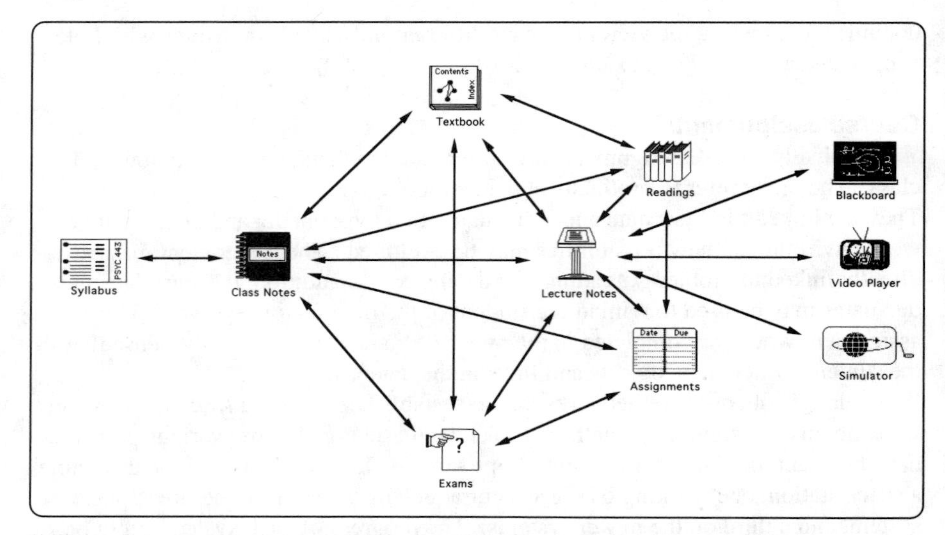

Figure 7. A hypermedia database for the electronic teaching theater with links created by the students.

ment provides a means for directly testing student's exploratory ability and creativity in browsing and authoring. These abilities will be indicators of both the procedural knowledge about the environment and the semantic knowledge about the content of the course.

The student's notebook

The ultimate product of a course is ideally not merely a good grade, but an individual armed with new information and skills. All too often in the traditional classroom, however, the student leaves with little to show for it of a tangible nature. The basic product that the student retains is his or her notebook containing class notes, completed assignments, and exams. In addition the student may retain the textbook. These materials may be accessed at a future date to review the material or in order to answer a question to solve a problem in one's subsequent work. In hypermedia, the students may take with them the hypermedia database, both the course materials and the course products in the form of their personal notebooks or have continued access to it via a network. This database would be immeasurably richer than that resulting from a traditional classroom. Future access to the hypermedia materials would continue to be facilitated by the computer medium and even enriched by additional products and links and updated over time.

The instructor's file

Similarly, the instructors will leave the classroom with a file of completed assignments and exams, a record of grades and course evaluations, a record of the access to help information and questions of students, a record of the interactions in the electronic blackboard, collaborative browsing, and so on. This wealth of information should in principle be the input to improving the course for the next go around. In the traditional classroom, however, such information too often goes into a file cabinet never to be seen again. If the access to such information can be facilitated in the electronic teaching theater and if tools are provided to analyze and incorporate the results of one class into the next, it may be possible to make productive use of this information.

Additional considerations

While the concepts of hypermedia and collaborative environments suggest revolutionary changes in the instructional process, one must proceed with caution and healthy skepticism. During the introduction of a new technology the pitfalls may very well outnumber the advantages. Consequently, a number of considerations are in order.

1. Level of Complexity. Hypermedia databases add an additional level of complexity to the material. It may be difficult enough to manage the content material of a course. To manage both the course material and the media may overload both instructors and students. To avoid this, the hypermedia interface must convey the organization and structure of the course, not its own. That is, in navigating the database, one should learn something about the organization and content of the course material rather than navigating hypermedia itself. Prior knowledge about the material should facilitate the use of the interface, and conversely, use of the interface should facilitate learning of the material.
2. Information Granularity. Although the instructor should be knowledgeable about the vast information underlying the course content, only a small portion of that information may be appropriate for presentation in a lecture. Consequently, the instructor summarizes and distills the information for presentation as a lecture. Often the point is to provide a look at the forest and not the trees. Consequently, the instructor must gauge the proper granularity of information and not allow the hypermedia to shift to another level at inappropriate times. During a lecture, for example, the instructor may wish to convey high level generalities and not get bogged down in specifics. However, during a laboratory section or study session, fine detail may be appropriate.
3. Information Rate. One can travel through hypermedia databases faster than one can process the information. It may be tempting for instructors to browse through information at a rate faster than the students can follow. Furthermore, some students may at times move through the information in a collaborative session faster than others can follow. It is important, therefore, that the instructor act as a guide and set a reasonable rate of information flow. Even students at their own workstations may exceed their limits and race through material too fast and come out remembering little if anything except the impression that things whizzed by.

4. Extensiveness of the Network. The classroom provides the primary hypermedia database. However, it could be connected to the university network and in turn to other networks and databases. In principle, the classroom could be extended to all electronic information. Here again, it may be important for the instructor to set limits on the domain of information accessible during the course. Search through extensive databases and networks may lead the students to not focus on the course but rather to digress through endless passageways of information.
5. Hypermedia and Collaborative Tools. It is one thing to speculate on the possibilities, and another to create the tools to bring them about. Success of the electronic classroom will depend on the interface tools that instructors and students have for browsing, authoring, and analyzing the hypermedia database. Research on what tools are necessary and how they should be designed is only beginning.
6. Price Considerations. Initial implementations are always extremely expensive. Funds are often over spent on some facilities that may not be used and fall short on others that are under great demand. It is conceivable that the electronic classroom of the future will not be so expensive and, in fact, will be a natural outgrowth of the prevalence of hypermedia databases, local area networks, university networks, and personal computers. Another scenario for the electronic classroom in contrast to Figure 1 would be for the students to plug their own laptop computers into a classroom network provided by the university. When the class is over they leave with their laptop computers but may at any time during the week access the university network with all of the hypermedia information still available to them.

Conclusions

Hypermedia and collaborative work environments may provide a unifying medium for classroom instruction. As such, they may be used to bridge the gap between the numerous applications of computers to education and the overall instructional process. Furthermore, they may add new possibilities for exploration and collaboration that have previously not been possible in the classroom.

This paper reviewed a number of models describing how instructors and students might interact with hypermedia and collaborative environments in the context of an electronic teaching theater, a facility providing high performance workstations and a high-speed local area network in the classroom. Although many possibilities exist, it remains to be seen what aspects of instruction will indeed be facilitated, enhanced, or changed in some other manner. Considerable research and evaluation of the use of the electronic teaching theater is required, but most certainly, the exploration of this medium will help to expand our understanding of the underlying models of instruction and the human/computer interface.

Acknowledgments

This work was supported in part by a grant from AT&T to the University of Maryland during the author's visit to the Medical Research Council - Applied Psychological Unit, Cambridge England. Appreciation is expressed to Patricia Wright and Richard M. Young for their helpful comments on this paper.
Requests for reprints should be addressed to Kent L. Norman, Department of Psychology, University of Maryland, College Park, MD 20742.

References

Anderson, J. R. (1980) *Cognitive psychology and its implications.* San Francisco: W. H. Freeman.

Borgman, C.L. (1986) The User's Mental Model of an Information Retrieval System: An Experiment on a Prototype On-line Catalog, *International Journal of Man-Machine Studies*, Vol. 24, 47-64.

Botafogo, R., Rivlin, E., Shneiderman, B. (April 1992) Structural analysis of hypertexts: identifying hierarchies and useful metrics, *ACM Transactions on Information Systems* Vol. 10, No. 2, 142-180.

Botafogo, R., Shneiderman, B. (April 1991) Identifying aggregates in hypertext structures, *ACM Proc. of Hypertext '91*, (San Antonio, TX) 63-74.

Campagnoni, F. R., Ehrlich, K. (1988) Information retrieval using a hypertext-based help system. Report, Sun Microsystem, Inc., Billerica, MA.

Carroll, J. M., Mack, R. L. (1985) Metaphor, computing systems, and active learning, *International Journal of Man-Machine Studies* Vol. 22, 39-57.

Chin, J. P. (Oct. 1989) Fixed vs. dynamic user adaptable menus: Menu structure, search performance and subjective satisfaction, Human Factors Society, Denver, Colorado.

Clabaugh, S., Destler, W. W., Falk, D. S., Gilbert, W., McDaniel, C. K., Power, D. J., Ricart, G. Shneiderman, B. (1988) The AT&T teaching theater: An environment for collaborative learning and research. University of Maryland, College Park, MD.

Conklin, J. (1987) Hypertext: a survey and introduction. *IEEE Computer* Vol. 20, 17-41.

D'Arcy, J. (1986) Computers, education, and behavioral research: A signifcant interaction, *Current Psychological Research and Reviews*, 5, 175-188.

Engelbart, D. (1963) A Conceptual Framework for Augmentation of Man's Intellect, *Vistas in Information Handling,* Vol. 1 Spartan Books, Washington, D.C., 1-29.

Faloutsos, C., Lee, R., Plaisant, C., Shneiderman, B. (1990) Incorporating string search in a hypertext system: User interface and signature file design issues, *Hypermedia*, 183-200.

Furuta, R., Plaisant, C., Shneiderman, B. (1989a) A spectrum of automatic hypertext constructions, *Hypermedia* Vol. 1, No. 2, 179-195.

Furuta, R., Plaisant, C., Shneiderman, B. (1989b) Automatically transforming regularly structured liner documents into hypertext, *Electronic Publishing* Vol. 2, No. 4, 211-229.

Gentner, D. Stevens, A.,Eds. (1983) *Mental Models*, Lawrence Erlbaum Associates, Hillsdale, N.J.

Goodman, D. (Oct. 1987) The Two Faces of HyperCard, *Macworld*, 122-129

Halasz, F., Moran, T., Trigg, R. (1987) Notecards in a Nutshell, *CHI+GIConf. Proc.*: Human Factors in Computing Systems and Graphics Interfaces, 45-52.

Holden, C. (1989) Computers make slow progress in class, *Science*, 244, 906-909.

Johansen, R. (1989) User approaches to computer-supported teams, *Technological support for work group collaboration*, M. Olson, Ed., New York: Lawrence Erlbaum, 1-31.

Jones, T., Shneiderman, B. (Nov. 1990) Evaluating usability for a training-oriented hypertext: Can hyper-activity be good?, *ELECTRONIC PUBLISHING* Vol. 3, No. 4, 207-225.

Kearsley, G., Seidel, R. J. (1985) Automation in training and education, *Human Factors* Vol. 27, 61-74.

Koved, L., Shneiderman, B. (1986) Embedded menus: selecting items in context, *Communications of the ACM* Vol. 29, 312-318.

Kreitzberg, C., Shneiderman, B. (Aug. 1988) Restructuring knowledge for an electronic encyclopedia, *Proc. International Ergonomics Association* 10th Congress Sydney, Australia.

Marchionini G., Information-Seeking Strategies of Novices Using a Full-Text Electronic Encyclopedia,"*Journal of the American Society for Information Science* , Vol. 29 (3) 1989, 165-176.

Marchionini, G., Shneiderman, B. (Jan. 1988) Finding facts vs. browsing knowledge in hypertext systems, *IEEE Computer* Vol. 21, No. 1, 70-80.

Marcus, R. (1983) An Experimental Comparison of the Effectiveness of Computers and Humans as Search Intermediaries, *Journal of the American Society for Information Science* Vol. 34, 381- 404.

McAleese, R., Ed., (1989) *Hypertext: theory into practice*, Osney Mead, Oxford: Blackwell Scientific Publications.

McKnight, C., Richardson, J., Dillon, A. (1989) The authoring of hypertext documents, *Hypertext: theory into practice*, R. McAleese Ed., Osney Mead, Oxford: Blackwell Scientific Publications, 138-147.

Monk, A. Ed., (1985) *Fundamentals of Human-Computer Interaction*, New York: Academic Press.

Nelson, T.H. (1981) *Literary Machines*, Swarthmore, Penn., Available from Nelson.

Norman, K. L., (1990) *The Psychology of Menu Selection: Designing Cognitive Control at the Human/Computer Interface* , Ablex, Norwood, NJ.

Norman, K. L., Weldon, L. J., Shneiderman, B. (1986) Cognitive layouts of windows and multiple screens for user interfaces, *International Journal of Man-Machine Studies* Vol. 25, 229-248.

Norman, K. L., Anderson, N. S., Schwartz, J. P., Singer, M. J., Shneiderman, B., Bartol, K., Weiser, M. (1980) Computer aided decision making and problem solving: A program of research, (CLC No. 19), College Park, Maryland: University of Maryland, Center for Language and Cognition.

Olson, M.,Ed. (1989) *Technical Support for Work Group Collaboration*, New York: Lawrence Erlbaum.

Ostroff, D. Shneiderman, B. (1988) Selection devices for users of an electronic encyclopedia: An empirical comparison of four possibilities, *Information Processing and Management* Vol. 24, No. 6, 665-680.

Posner, M. I. (1980) Computers in the training of inquiry, *Behavior Research Methods and Instrumentation* Vol. 12, 87-95.

Potter, R., Berman, M., Shneiderman, B. (Oct. 1989) An experimental evaluation of three touch screen strategies within a hypertext database, *International Journal of Human-*

Computer Interaction Vol. 1, No. 1, 41-52.

Rada, R., Keith, B., Burgoine, M., George, S., Reid, D. (1989) Collaborative writing of text and hypertext, *Hypermedia* Vol. 1, 93-110.

Seabrook, R. Shneiderman, B. (1989) The user interface in a hypertext, multi-window browser, *interacting with Computers* Vol. 1, No. 3, 299-337.

Shneiderman, B. (1989) Reflections on authoring, editing, and managing hypertext, *The Society of Text*, Barrett, Ed., MIT Press, Cambridge, MA, 115-131.

Shneiderman, B. (1987) *Designing the User Interface: Strategies for Effective Human Computer Interaction*, Addison-Wesley, Reading, MA.

Shneiderman, B. (1987) User Interface Design and Evaluation for an Electronic Encyclopedia, *Cognitive Engineering in the Design of Human-Computer Interaction and Expert Systems*, G. Salvendy, Ed., Elsevier, Amsterdam, 207-223.

Shneiderman, B. (1987a) User interface design for the Hyperties electronic encyclopedia, *Proc. Hypertext '87 Workshop,* University of North Carolina, Raleigh, NC, 199-204.

Shneiderman, B., Kearsley, G. (1989) *Hypertext Hands-On!*, Reading, MA: Addison-Wesley.

Sleeman, D., Brown, J. S. Ed. (1985) *Intelligent tutoring system,*. New York: Academic Press.

Smith, P. E. (1987) Simulating the classroom with media and computers: Past efforts, future possibilities, *Simulation and Games* Vol. 18, 395-413.

Smith, S. L., Mosier, J. N. (1986) Guidelines for designing user interface software, (ESD-TR-86-278) Electronic System Division, AFSC, United States Air Force, Hanscom Air Force Base, MA.

Trigg, R. H., Suchman, L. A. (1989) Collaborative writing in notecards, *Hypertext: theory into practice*, R. McAleese, Ed., Osney Mead, Oxford: Blackwell Scientific Publiciations, 45-61.

Wright, P. (1989) Interface alternatives for hypertexts, *Hypermedia* Vol. 1, 146-467.

Yankelovich, N., Meyrowitz, N., van Dam, A. (Oct. 1985) Reading and Writing the Electronic Book, *IEEE Computer*, 15-30.

Zoellick, W. (1986) CD-ROM Software Development, *Byte*, Vol. 11, 177-188.

Advanced Features
ENVIRONMENTAL CONTROL
04 : 12 am
ON ON ON
OFF OFF OFF
DONE
ON
OFF

Sparks of Innovation in Human-Computer Interaction,
B. Shneiderman, Ed., Ablex Publ., Norwood, NJ (1993)

4. Touchscreens

Introduction

We started working with crude touchscreens in 1983, and by 1988 had found ways to make pixel precision pointing with dragging a reality, and then we began to apply touchscreens to novel areas such as home automation, museums, and finger painting. The early touchscreens had such poor precision that to point at a single word in our hypertext systems, we had to get special boards to produce large fonts that had only 16 lines of 52 characters. We recognized the power of touchscreens for our museum applications: touchscreens were the most durable technology for public access situations, and the simplicity of pointing to highlighted terms or areas was very much in harmony with the direct manipulation philosophy.

As we learned more about touchscreen technology our goals became more refined and precise. By 1987 we had found a touchscreen that enabled us to write software to point to a single character. Our solution was to place a large blinking cursor about a quarter inch above the user's finger, and allow the user to drag the cursor around the screen. The selection was made only when the user lifted-off the screen surface, hence the term lift-off. This simple and comprehensible approach worked like a charm and the experiment showed dramatic benefits in a task that required pointing at a two-letter state abbreviation in a compact display of five columns by ten rows with all fifty states (see paper 4.1, Potter, Weldon, & Shneiderman, 1988). We won the University of Maryland's award for Outstanding Innovation in 1988 for this work. This strategy was employed in our Smithsonian Institution kiosk (see Introduction to Section 3) by March 1988.

By September 1988 I proposed a more difficult goal to Andrew Sears: enable pointing to a single pixel. I thought this was a clear goal and I had some ideas about how to get started, but I was not sure it was attainable. The stimulus of a clear goal led to rapid progress and in a month the necessary smoothing software was working. The empirical study (see paper 4.2, Sears & Shneiderman, 1991) that showed that a bare finger on a touchscreen could be used effectively to point at a single pixel met resistance from journal reviewers who felt we must have left out secrets of our technology. The path to publication took almost three years - a frustrating delay when you are excited about a breakthrough. While Andrew Sears gets much of the credit for developing pixel level precision, the Maryland Way helped lead him to his goal.

The technology now enabled us to build novel applications in home automation, public access, point of sale terminals, pocket devices, and games (IV.3, Shneiderman, 1991). One of the most appealing products was a fingerpainting software tool called PenPlay, which Andrew Sears wrote in a few weeks during the summer of 1989. It allowed simple finger tracking built on top of our software toolkit, plus some cute ideas like concentric circles that became known as raindrops, smaller patterns that became known as finger prints, varying color patterns, and sound effects. Its success with us and our visitors was immediate. By the summer of 1990 Andy put in another week or two of programming and PenPlay II emerged with about 20 drawing tools whose behavior varied depending on the speed, direction, and origin of the gesture (see paper 4.3, Figure 4). Children, elderly users, computer science visitors, and professional artists have all spent hours doodling and drawing. An important feature was the capacity to record sequences of actions and then replay them.

The high precision also enabled us to put many buttons closely packed on the screen and develop virtual keyboards (sometimes called projected keyboards) using the touchscreen (see paper 4.4, Plaisant & Sears, 1992). We could even shrink a full QWERTY keyboard down to three inches wide and still get 20 words per minute with practice. We don't recommend widespread use of such a small keyboard, but we demonstrated that it was possible. Several reviewers doubted that what we did was possible, but eventually our papers were published.

Our work on home automation grew from the touchscreen technology which was appreciated by the principals of Custom Command Systems (Jim Battaglia, Hank Levine, and Reuel Launey) (Figure 1). They had built technology to accomplish basic functions such as turning off all the lights with a single touchscreen button or with voice controls. But they also understood that entertainment devices (elaborate home theaters, distributed audio and video, scheduling VCR recording, or CD jukeboxes selectable from anywhere in the home), security control (simple control over a hundred sensors, video cameras at entrances, and controlled access), and luxury items (automatic whirlpool filling or heaters to melt ice on walkways) could all be simply controlled with touchscreens scattered throughout the house. Our lift-off method made precise pointing on floorplans possible. For three years we worked with them to develop these methods and polish the VCR recording strategy that is still being pursued as a patent (see paper 5.5, Plaisant, Battaglia & Shneiderman, 1990). The future of home automation is bright, but it will take a decade for the price to come down and for the desired functions to be understood. Still, there are unsettling questions about whether computer control will make life at home safer and more enjoyable, or whether the intrusion of technology will be confusing and disrupting. The benefits to handicapped and older users are potentially great but many of the early implementations are for the healthy and wealthy. We believe that, like other initially expensive technologies (refrigeration, air-conditioning, etc.), home automation systems will become inexpensive and widespread.

There is currently great interest in pen-based computers using character and voice recognition. While these technologies will find some application, I predict that handheld touchscreen devices with selection from menu items and buttons will prove to be the more widespread technology. We hope for cheaper touchscreens, built in to the monitor by manufacturers, and small, cheap touchscreens on liquid crystal displays that could be carried around, mounted on walls and doors, or embedded in refrigerator doors or car dashboards. Another improvement that we want is multiple-touch touchscreens that allow touching several points at once. This would facilitate innovative drawing devices, novel musical instruments, and better three-dimensional manipulation.

Figure 1. Six toggles studied as part of the home automation research by Plaisant and Wallace (Touchscreen toggle switches: push or slide? Design issues and usability study.)

Sparks of Innovation in Human-Computer Interaction,
B. Shneiderman, Ed., Ablex Publ., Norwood, NJ (1993)

4.1 Improving the accuracy of touchscreens: an experimental evaluation of three strategies

Richard L. Potter
Linda J. Weldon
Ben Shneiderman

Abstract

A study comparing the speed, accuracy, and user satisfaction of three different touchscreen strategies was performed. The purpose of the experiment was to evaluate the merits of the more intricate touch strategies that are possible on touchscreens that return a continuous stream of touch data. The results showed that a touch strategy providing continuous feedback until a selection was confirmed had fewer errors than other touch strategies. The implications of the results for touchscreens containing small, densely-packed targets are discussed.

Proc. of the Conference on Human Factors in Computing Systems (CHI '88) (Washington, DC, 1988) 27-32.

Introduction

Reaching up and placing a finger on a touchscreen at a selectable region seems simple and direct enough. However, peculiarities in both touchscreen technology and human dexterity leave room for improvements in this simple touchscreen strategy for some applications. For example, parallax between the touchscreen surface and the display surface can cause users to misinterpret where their fingers are actually touching by a significant amount.

Touchscreens are attractive because they enable quick learning and rapid performance, do not consume desk or other workspace, have no moving parts, and evoke high user satisfaction (Muratore, 1987; Pickering, 1986; Shneiderman, 1987; Stone, 1987). However, widespread use of touchscreens has been limited by the high error rates shown in many studies, lack of precision, fatigue in arm motion, and concern for screen smudging (Ostroff & Shneiderman, Pickering, 1986).

Common touchscreen applications include information kiosks at airports or shopping malls, educational games, and exhibits at museums and amusement parks. The simplicity of touchscreen usage is attractive for novices and the durability of touchscreens is favored by designers. Current touchscreens have found little use for more frequent knowledgeable users, such as air traffic controllers or medical equipment operators, probably because of the annoyance of high error rates. However, we believe that it is possible to overcome this problem.

We believed that we could preserve the benefits of touchscreens and reduce the disadvantages by providing continuous feedback of pointing position and enabling users to drag a cursor on the screen with their fingers, thus creating a "finger mouse." Users can adjust their initial touch until they arrive at the precise position desired. Selection is completed when the users lift their fingers from the screen or alternatively when the first valid target is encountered.

There are many possible strategies that can allow a user to select one of a set of displayed predefined areas. The user's intentions can be expressed in an infinite number of ways by changing the articulation of the touch. For example, the user could select an area in the center of the screen by pressing in the center. Alternatively, the selection could be made by tapping the center twice, followed by a circular motion around the center. Certainly most of the possible strategies will be impractical. Still, we are left with a multitude of imaginative practical strategies from which to choose.

The type of touch technology used can limit or expand the range of expression possible by the user. Some touchscreens only register the initial impact with the screen so dragging the finger cannot be interpreted as part of the interaction. Other touchscreens can detect two different touch points, while some average multiple simultaneous touches to derive only one point. Some touchscreens can even report the pressure the user is applying during different moments of the interaction.

The touchscreen used for the present experiment was a MicroTouch screen which returns a succession of data records. Each record contains whether a finger is touching the screen, and whether the finger was lifted at that position. For the MicroTouch screen our range of interaction can be summarized by the location of the final touch, and the path taken in between. Only one touch can be tracked at one time. From this array of possibilities we designed and implemented three touch strategies: land-on, first-contact, and take-off.

The simplest strategy, land-on, uses only the initial touching of the touchscreen for selection. If a selectable item is under the initial touch then it is selected, otherwise nothing is selected. All further contact with the touchscreen is ignored until the finger is removed. Thus dragging the finger has no effect. The land-on strategy was meant to simulate technologies, such as piezo-electric, that do not provide continuous touch data.

The second strategy, first-contact, was designed to work basically the same as land-on but take advantage of the continuous stream of touch data provided by technologies such as those used in some capacitive touchscreens. Users make selections by dragging their fingers to the desired item. The human-computer interaction is not limited to the initial impact with the touchscreen. In this strategy it is not what position the user lands on that becomes selected, rather it is whatever selectable item the user first contacts. Of course if the user makes first-contact with some undesired item before reaching the desired item, the undesired item will be selected.

The third strategy, take-off, was designed to utilize the continuous stream of touch data and give more user feedback. Whenever users make contact with the touchscreen, a cursor (in the form of a plus sign < + >) appears slightly above their fingers so that the specific position of selection is known. As long as users keep their fingers in contact with the screen, no selection will be made. After dragging the cursor, when the users are satisfied with its placement, they confirm the selection by removing their finger from the touchscreen.

We tried to make each strategy perform at its best. For the land-on strategy and to a lesser extent first-contact strategy, the accuracy of the initial touch was deemed important. The cursor was placed directly below the finger so that the users would not have to judge some arbitrary biasing. However, for the take-off strategy a slight bias, placing the cursor about 1/2 inch above the finger, was employed. In this case the users need a clear view of the cursor. Users can easily adjust the position of the cursor with the take-off strategy so any inaccuracies of the initial contact caused by the bias can be easily corrected. In all three strategies if the finger is removed and no item has been selected, the cursor remains visible at the point on the screen where the finger last positioned it.

In addition to the cursor considerations, take-off received other minor enhancements to take advantage of its unique qualities. Since the cursor traveled within character boundaries, there existed positions where minute shifts of the finger would cause the cursor to jump back and forth by an entire character. Cursor stabilization was added so that users could better keep the cursor in one place while deciding if its placement was desirable. There also existed an interval from the time the user placed the cursor on the desired item to the time the user's finger was released. This introduced the ability to highlight the entire item by inverse video during this time. This highlighting gave the user even more feedback as to what would be selected should the finger be removed from the touchscreen.

A related experiment used an infra-red touchscreen that could register multiple touches (Murphy, 1986). Seven touch strategies were tested in the experiment. The subjects were to select from 60 targets which were 3/4 inch square and displayed in a grid that was six high by ten wide. One of the strategies tested was similar to the take-off strategy and another was similar to the first-contact strategy in the present experiment. There were no significant differences between these two particular strategies in task completion time or number of errors. We also have recently become aware of other attempts to create a take-off strategy (Eller, 1987).

The characteristics of the touch strategies we used in this experiment are:

1.Land-On:
- cursor is directly under the finger
- only the position of the first impact with the screen is used
- a selection is made upon first impact if a target exists at that location

2. First-Contact:
- cursor is directly under the finger
- all position data is used until the first contact with any target
- a selection is made upon first contact with any target

3. Take-Off:
- cursor is about 1/2 inch above the finger
- all position data is used throughout selection
- a selection is made upon release if a target exists at that cursor location
- jitter stabilization of cursor for when finger is on character boundaries
- entire item is highlighted when cursor appears on top of it

The characteristics of the cursor are:
- a plus sign < + >
- moves on character boundaries in discrete jumps
- flashes so that both the cursor, and the character it appears on, alternate to remain visible.

Our experiment investigated how well people use and accept these more intricate touch strategies. Performance was measured in terms of speed and number of incorrect selections. The task the subjects had to complete required searching for two letter state abbreviations from a group of 50 on the screen. Thus the subjects experienced some cognitive load in making each selection; the task was easy but required concentration.

Method

Subjects. Twenty-four people volunteered to participate in the study. Subjects were informed of the measures that would be taken. Each subject was run individually, in an experimental session that typically lasted for approximately 20 minutes. A post-experiment questionnaire about the subjects' computer experience revealed a range from no experience to over nine years of experience, with a median of four years of experience. Because of the location of the experiment, most of the subjects who volunteered were computer science students.

Equipment. In all cases, the touchscreen strategies were implemented using a MicroTouch screen mounted on an IBM PC-AT with an Enhanced Graphics Adapter and color display. This touchscreen uses conductive glass technology that provides continuous touch information to the computer. Software was written to create the three different touch strategies for use in selecting items from the array on the display.

Design and Procedure. Touch strategy was a within-subjects variable. Each subject was tested on all three of the strategies that were implemented. Each subject had 5 practice trials followed by 15 test trials for each condition. The experimental conditions were counter-balanced across subjects. In each trial, the subject pressed the spacebar on the keyboard which controlled the presentation of the message informing the subject of the target for the trial. The subject would then touch the target on the screen and receive feedback on the item touched. If an error was made, the subject was directed to try again. The response time for each selection was recorded automatically. Following the experiment, subjects received a post-experiment questionnaire that asked for background information, their subjective evaluation of the touch strategies, and additional comments.

Materials. The experimental array on the selection screen consisted of the two-letter postal abbreviations for 50 states arranged in the middle of the screen. The abbreviations were listed in alphabetical order in 10 rows of 5 columns with two blank spaces between each column. The targets were approximately 1/4 square inch in area. A prompt line at the top of the selection screen displayed an abbrevia-

```
Select CT from the items below.




                    AK  HI  ME  NJ  SD
                    AL  IA  MI  NM  TN
                    AR  ID  MN  NV  TX
                    AZ  IL  MO  NY  UT
                    CA  IN  MS  OH  VA
                    CO  KS  MT  OK  VT
                    CT  KY  NC  OR  WA
                    DE  LA  ND  PA  WI
                    FL  MA  NE  RI  WV
                    GA  MD  NH  SC  WY
```

Figure 1. The screen format, showing the experimental array and the target being requested.

tion for the user to touch in the experimental array. Figure 1 shows the format of the screen. If the user touched the wrong item, an error message appeared in the prompt line. A message line appeared at the bottom of the selection screen showing the state name corresponding to the item selected.

Results

Analyses were conducted for the performance measures that were collected during the experiment and for the ratings made by the subjects on the subjective evaluation questionnaire that was given at the conclusion of the experiment. Analyses of variance with repeated measures were used in the evaluation of the performance and subjective evaluation data that were collected.

Performance. The two performance measures were the time from the presentation of the target item until the correct target was selected and the errors that were made by the subjects.

Time. The item selection times for the 15 trials were divided into 3 blocks of 5 trials. The blocks represented the beginning trials, the middle trials, and the final trials. The analysis was a 3 (strategy) x 3 (block) x 6 (order) analysis of variance with repeated measures on the first two factors. There was a significant main effect for strategy, $F(2,36) = 10.41$, $p < .001$. A post hoc analysis showed that the overall mean time for the first-contact strategy (16.93 sec) was significantly faster than the take-off strategy (20.92 sec). The mean performance time for the land-on strategy (17.73 sec) did not differ significantly from the other two strategies.

There was also a significant main effect for block, $F(2,36) = 23.82$, $p<.001$, which reflected a significant difference between the beginning block of trials (20.20 sec) and the middle and final trials. The performance times decreased significantly after the first block of trials. The times for the middle and final blocks did not differ from each other (18.03 and 17.35 sec, respectively).

There was no significant interaction between strategies and blocks of trials. Although there was a main effect for order, $F(2,18) = 2.84$, $p<.05$ attributable to the difference between the fastest and slowest counterbalancing orders, there were no interactions between order and the other factors.

Errors. Two types of errors were identified. One type of error occurred when a subject selected a wrong target. A second type of error occurred when the subject touched a blank part of the screen. The analysis showed a significant main effect for strategy, $F(2,36) = 7.64$, $p < .002$. A post hoc comparison of the means showed that there were significantly fewer errors with the take-off strategy (mean = 2.25) than with either the land-on strategy (mean = 5.08) or the first-contact strategy (mean = 4.08).

There was a significant main effect for type of error, $F(1,18) = 19.89$, $p < .001$, attributable to the greater number of wrong target errors (mean = 2.49) than blank space errors (mean = 1.32).

There was also a significant interaction between strategy and type of error, $F(2,36) = 6.40$, $p < .004$. Figure 2 shows the mean error rates for the three strategies for each type of error. The take-off strategy had significantly fewer wrong target errors (mean = 1.08) than the first-contact and land-on strategies (with means for wrong targets of 3.29 and 3.08, respectively). The land-on and first-contact strategies did not differ significantly from each other in terms of number of wrong target errors. Within the first-contact strategy, there were significantly more wrong target errors than blank errors. The post hoc analysis showed that the first-contact and land-on wrong target errors were also significantly greater than the mean number of blank space errors for both first-contact and take-off strategies (0.79 and 1.17, respectively).

There were no order effects.

Subjective Evaluation. After the timed trials on the three strategies, the subjects were asked to rate the strategies on the dimensions of ease of learning, awkwardness, and satisfaction. The analysis showed a significant interaction between strategies and rating dimension, $F(4,72) = 4.71$, $p<.002$. A post hoc analysis of the interaction showed that the take-off strategy had a significantly higher rating of satisfaction (mean = 6.75) than the land-on strategy (mean = 5.63), but not the first-contact strategy (mean = 5.96). The remaining meaningful comparisons reflected the overall ratings of the ease of learning the touchscreen for all three strategies.

Discussion

We were pleased to find that we could develop a touchscreen strategy that produced statistically significant lower error rates than commonly applied strategies. Our enthusiasm for the take-off approach was tempered by the recognition that this

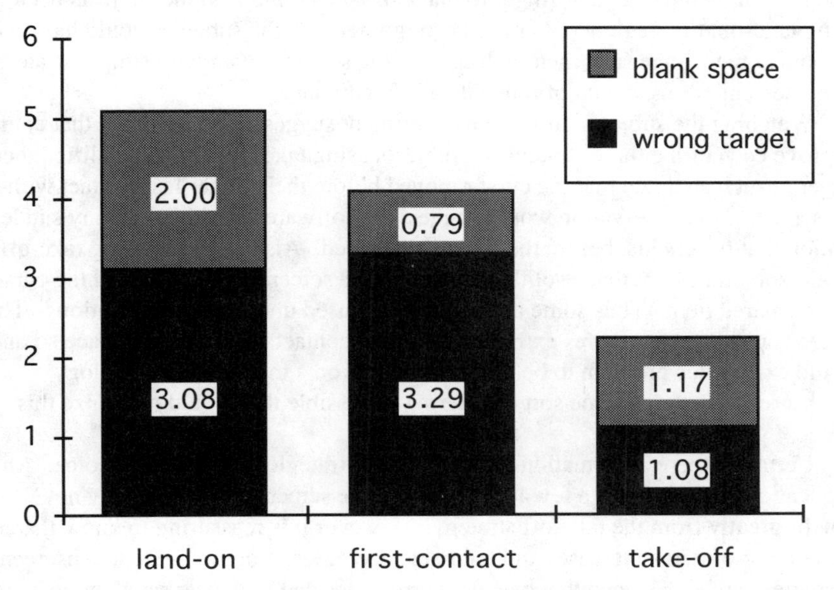

Figure 2. Mean error rates for selecting wrong targets and blank spaces for three touch strategies.

more intricate strategy did indeed take significantly longer. We were encouraged by the learning curve for take-off and would like to see if with more than 15 trials the time differences with other strategies would continue to decrease. The take-off strategy produced significantly fewer errors thereby reducing one of the severe problems with touchscreens. We believe that ideas gained from this experiment will lead to refinements that will have still fewer errors.

The subjective reactions confirmed the impression that more intricate strategies with continuous feedback and confirmation are acceptable to users. Comments and our observations reminded us that there are still many design issues that strongly affect performance and satisfaction, such as the placement of the cursor (plus sign) or the stability of the feedback.

Subjects sometimes took great exception to the location of the cursor when using the take-off strategy. They believed that the cursor should be directly under the finger. The drag feature of take-off was used by subjects differently. Some subjects waited until they located the target on the screen and then placed their finger close to the target and made slight adjustments. Other subjects placed their finger on the screen immediately and then proceeded to drag, sometimes letting their finger help in the search. This flexibility probably helped take-off obtain its favorable user satisfaction rating.

Since in this experiment the items were small and densely spaced, there was little difference between the way the subjects used land-on and first-contact. The users noted this in their written comments and verbally during the performance of the experiment. It was common to see subjects using first-contact miss a target slightly and then jiggle their finger to make the selection. Had the subjects been using land-on, the jiggle would have been ignored and the subjects would have had to remove their finger and then replace it on the screen. Even with simple strategies, the continuous stream of touch data is beneficial .

Watching the subjects during the experiment suggested possibilities that could improve each of the three strategies. Subjects using take-off sometimes lifted their finger at such an angle that the cursor moved before their finger lost contact with the screen. This observation would suggest the software should ignore any sudden motion that occurs just before the finger is released. Also, subjects using take-off would sometimes not make solid contact with the screen as they dragged the cursor to the desired item. Thus some of these skips caused unintentional selections. The MicroTouch screen requires extremely minimal contact with screen surface so one would expect this problem to be more noticeable on a membrane technology touchscreen. Perhaps some sort of filtering is possible that would minimize this effect.

Certainly there are situations where simple strategies are the best choice. An application requiring just a few large items on the screen at one time may not benefit greatly from the take-off strategy. However it is reassuring to know that as the number of items increases and their size decreases, more intricate touchscreen strategies can be designed that have low error rates and high user satisfaction.

Note

The success of the take-off strategy coupled with the positive comments of visitors and experimental participants is encouraging. University officials are seeking to patent the take-off strategy with the multiple refinements that have been developed.

Sparks of Innovation in Human-Computer Interaction,
B. Shneiderman, Ed., Ablex Publ., Norwood, NJ (1993)

4.2 High precision touchscreens: design strategies and comparisons with a mouse

Andrew Sears
Ben Shneiderman

Three studies were conducted comparing speed of performance, error rates and user preference ratings for three selection devices. The devices tested were a touchscreen, a touchscreen with stabilization (stabilization software filters and smooths raw data from hardware), and a mouse. The task was the selection of rectangular targets 1, 4, 16 and 32 pixels per side (0.4x0.6, 1.7x2.2, 6.9x9.0, 13.8x17.9 mm respectively). Touchscreen users were able to point at single pixel targets, thereby countering widespread expectations of poor touchscreen resolution. The results show no difference in performance between the mouse and touchscreen for targets ranging from 32 to 4 pixels per side. In addition, stabilization significantly reduced the error rates for the touchscreen when selecting small targets. These results imply that touchscreens, when properly used, have attractive advantages in selecting targets as small as 4 pixels per size (approximately one-quarter of the size of a single character). A variant of Fitts' Law is proposed to predict touchscreen pointing times. Ideas for future research are also presented.

The sections describing the results of the second and third experiment and the results for an experienced user have been summarized. A brief section describing possible directions for future research has been deleted. For the complete text, please see the original article in the *International Journal of Man-Machine Studies 34, (1991), 593-613.*

Introduction

Overview

Many pointing devices are available for use with computers, but none are as natural to use as the touchscreen. Pointing at an item, or touching it, is one of the most natural ways to select it. Touchscreens allow the software designer to take advantage of this convenient selection method by having the users simply touch the item they are interested in.

Touchscreens are easy to learn to use, require no additional work space, have no moving parts, and are very durable (Pickering, 1986; Shneiderman, 1987; Stone, 1987; Muratore, 1987; Potter, Weldon & Shneiderman, 1988). Durability has made touchscreens popular in many applications, including kiosks at airports, shopping malls, amusement parks and home automation. Even with these positive features, the touchscreen's reputation for a lack of precision, high error rates, arm fatigue, and smudging the screen have resulted in limited use (Pickering, 1986; Shneiderman, 1987). Current touchscreen implementations do not include tasks requiring high resolution or tasks that are performed by frequent or experienced users. An adequate reduction in error rates, combined with the speed of the touchscreen, may help expand this relatively limited use.

Previous experiments

Many studies have compared touchscreens with other selection devices for various tasks. Our summary motivates our experiments. First, studies that compared the touchscreen with other selection devices are reviewed. Then several studies that explored the use of alternative selection strategies, an error reduction method we employ, will also be summarized.

Muratore (1987) did an extensive literature survey, reviewing 14 studies that compared various cursor control devices. Her interpretation of these results implies that the touchscreen was the fastest but least accurate of the devices studied. Hall, Cunningham, Roache and Cox (1908) investigated the effects of various factors on touchscreen performance. The display was an IBM InfoWindow color terminal with a piezo-electric touchscreen using the land-on selection strategy forcing the selection at the location of the initial touch. Feedback was not provided about the accuracy of selections. They reported that accuracy varied from 66.7% for targets 10 mm per side, to 99.2% for targets 26 mm per side, and that accuracy was maximized once targets were approximately 26 mm per side. Ostroff and Shneiderman (1988) compared a touchscreen, mouse, number keys and arrow keys. The touchscreen was a Carroll Touch infra-red touchscreen using the land-on strategy. The study involved selecting words from an interactive encyclopedia (Hyperties™). The results were similar to those of most other studies comparing the touchscreen and the mouse, indicating that the touchscreen was faster. They found no significant difference between error rates for the mouse and the touchscreen. This finding may be due in part to the relatively large size of the targets used and the rapid but awkward form of the jump mouse. (A jump mouse moves the cursor from one target to the next, skipping the space between them.) Ahlstrom and Lenman (1987) compared a conductive touchscreen using the land-on strategy and mouse for the selection of a six-character word from a list of words. This study indicated that the touchscreen was faster, but resulted in much higher error rates. Karat, McDonald and Anderson (1986) compared a touchscreen, mouse and keyboard for selection tasks. The touchscreen used was an Elographics analog membrane touchscreen using the land-on strategy. The task involved selecting items from a menu in a calendar program and a telephone directory. Some tasks also involved a typing sub-task. The results indicated that the touchscreen was the preferred device for the task without the typing sub-task, while the keyboard was preferred when the sub-task was included. The touchscreen was the fastest for both tasks.

These studies have been limited to relatively large targets for selection tasks, but they do give some insight into the potential use of touchscreens. It is clear that a touchscreen can be used for rapidly selecting relatively large targets. Unfortunately, most of these studies also indicate that error rates were significantly higher for touchscreens. There are two explanations that may account for the majority of these errors, the inability of the touchscreens used in these studies to provide precise information about the location of a touch, and inadequate selection strategies for the tasks studied.

The inability of the touchscreen hardware to provide precise information may be due to a lack of resolution or the result of multiple pixel locations, possibly as many as 20 or more, being returned for a touch in a single location. While research by touchscreen manufacturers has dramatically increased the resolution of touchscreens, the problem of returning multiple pixel locations for a single touch remains. The extent to which this is a problem depends on both the touchscreen technology and manufacturer. Carroll Touch has published a Touch Handbook which provides a brief review of current touchscreen technologies including resolution, response time, and environmental resistance (Carroll Touch, 1989). Stabilization of the touchscreen will allow a single touch to result in the selection of a single pixel, possibly resulting in a significant reduction in errors, primarily for small targets. Ideally stabilization would be accomplished at the hardware level, but can also be done in software. Our studies will use software stabilization to filter and smooth raw data from the touchscreen hardware. Stabilization is an important idea that can be applied to many technologies including touchscreens, data gloves and light pens, but has never been tested with touchscreens.

Many alternative selection strategies have been suggested to help reduce errors including take-off, first-contact, land-on, and others requiring a second touch. The land-on strategy uses the location of the initial touch for the selection. If the initial touch corresponds to a selectable region, that region is selected, otherwise no selection is made. The first-contact strategy results in the selection of the first selectable region the finger comes into contact with. With this strategy the users move their fingers on the screen until a selectable region is touched, this region is then selected and the appropriate process is initiated. Once again, all additional contact is ignored until the finger is removed from the screen. The take-off strategy allows users to place their fingers on the screen and move to the desired region on the screen before a selection is made. A cursor is placed slightly above the users' fingers when they touch the screen indicating the exact location of where a selection would be made. Users can then drag the cursor to the desired region, and lift their fingers from the screen to select it. A selection is made only if there is a selectable region under the cursor when users lift their fingers.

Several studies have been conducted to compare alternate selection strategies. The results indicate that some strategies may be promising for a wide range of tasks, and a significant reduction in error rates is possible (Murphy, 1987; Potter et al., 1988; Potter, Berman & Shneiderman, 1989). Murphy (1987) compared seven selection strategies. He conducted an experiment that involved selecting targets that were 19 mm^2 from a matrix of 60 targets. His results indicated few significant differences among the selection strategies, making it difficult to promote any single strategy as the best with respect to either selection time or error rates for this target size.

Researchers at the University of Maryland Human-Computer Interaction Laboratory have performed two experiments comparing the land-on, first-contact and take-off strategies. The first experiment involved the selection of a two character state abbreviation from a 5 x 10 matrix. This study indicated that the first-contact strategy was the fastest, while the take-off strategy produced the fewest errors. The second experiment involved the traversal of a hypertext database by selecting highlighted words. There were no significant differences in the time needed to perform the task, while the first-contact and take-off strategies produced fewer errors than land-on (Potter et al., 1988; Potter et al., 1989).

These experiments indicate that first-contact may be the fastest selection strategy, while the results pertaining to error rates did not consistently favor one strategy over the others. While these studies do provide a comparison of the selection strategies, they do not indicate how well a touchscreen using these strategies will perform compared with other selection devices.

Some researchers have claimed that the current touchscreen technology would not allow high-resolution selection, saying that selection of a single character with a touchscreen would be slow even if it were possible (Sherr, 1988; Greenstein & Arnaut, 1988). Others have blamed the size of the human finger for the lack of precision, claiming that the size of the user's finger limits the size of selectable regions (Beringer, 1985; Sherr, 1988; Greenstein & Arnaut, 1988). Previous studies have made no attempt at evaluating a touchscreen for high resolution tasks, restricting targets to relatively large sizes ranging from a square that is 6.4 mm per side, to targets that were approximately 25.4 x 40.6 mm. In addition, many of these studies have indicated that touchscreens result in significantly higher error rates than many other selection devices, including the mouse. Our experiments studied the selection of small targets with the touchscreen as compared with the mouse. We also studied the effects that stabilization and the use of an alternative selection strategy have on these selections. Error rates and selection speed were measured. User preference data were also collected.

Experiment one:
Stabilized touchscreen, non-stabilized touchscreen, and mouse

Introduction

The main purpose of the first experiment was to provide the comparison of a touchscreen with a mouse, using an improved selection strategy for high resolution tasks. The secondary purpose was to investigate the effect stabilization has on speed of performance, error rates and user preference for selection tasks when using a touchscreen.

Due to the difficulty involved in modifying hardware, stabilization was accomplished using software that filters and smooths raw data from the touchscreen hardware. These results should generalize to stabilization performed by either hardware or software.

The first step was to determine which selection strategy should be tested. To do this, we must understand the requirements of the task being evaluated. A typical high resolution task may be the selection of the start and stop points for a line in a graphics package, or possibly the selection of a character in a word processing program. Since it is difficult to touch a single character accurately, let alone a single pixel on the first attempt, the land-on strategy is not adequate. In addition, many high resolution tasks involve the selection of targets that are not defined before the selection is made, such as the starting point of a line which makes the first-contact strategy inappropriate. On the other hand, the take-off strategy provides continuous feedback about cursor location, allowing the user to position the cursor before a selection is made by lifting the finger. This makes take-off the best candidate for many high resolution tasks.

Subjects

Thirty-six subjects volunteered from the Psychology Department subject pool of the University of Maryland. The amount of computer experience the subjects had was not controlled. Three subjects had used a touchscreen one time, while the remaining subjects had no experience. Experience using a mouse ranged from none to every day, with the majority of the subjects using the mouse very infrequently.

Equipment

All tasks were performed on an IBM PC-AT with an IBM Enhanced Color Display and a MicroTouch touchscreen. The monitor was placed on the desk in the normal monitor position with the keyboard placed in front of it. The monitor measured 27.6 x 19.5 cm and was used in EGA mode (640 x 350 pixels) resulting in pixels that were 0.4 x 0.6 mm. The MicroTouch touchscreen is a capacitive touchscreen that provides continuous information about the location of a touch on a 1024 x 1024 grid. It requires only a light touch to be activated and averages the location of all simultaneous touches and returns a centroid location. The touch-screen was cleaned once before the first subject began the experiment, and was not cleaned again until the last subject had completed the experiment. Software was written to convert the touchscreen coordinates to pixel coordinates and to stabilize the resulting pixel coordinates. A MouseSystems Optical PC-Mouse with three buttons was used with a mouse pad that measured 22.9 x 19.7 cm. The mouse was calibrated so that a single pass horizontally on the pad resulted in the cursor moving the width of the screen, and a single pass vertically on the pad resulted in the cursor moving the height of the screen. Users were free to place the mouse pad anywhere they wanted.

After the experiment was completed it was discovered that the software provided with the mouse only allowed the cursor to be moved in two pixel increments horizontally. This did not impair the selection of targets, however, the resolution of the screen for the mouse tasks was essentially half (320 x 350) that of the screen for tasks using the touchscreen, possibly influencing the results in favor of the mouse. New mouse software was obtained for the second and third experiments to correct these problems.

Stabilization software

Stabilization allowed a touch to result in a single pixel coordinate. The first attempt at stabilizing the touchscreen used running-means of the last 20 x and y coordinates. Although stability was improved dramatically, the selection of a single pixel was still not reliable, and the cursor lagged far behind the user's finger. Several additional steps were necessary to solve these problems.

First, a small region (0.9 x 1.7 mm) around the current cursor location was deactivated, requiring the user's finger to move beyond this region before the cursor moves (Figure 1, Region A). The second step was to define a larger region (8.6 x 16.8 mm) around the cursor that resulted in a movement that was only a fraction of the actual distance between the cursor and finger locations (Figure 1, Region B). For instance, if the user's finger was at point X (Figure 1), the cursor would only move to point Y. In this way, it was possible to perform very precise movements by dragging a finger on the screen.

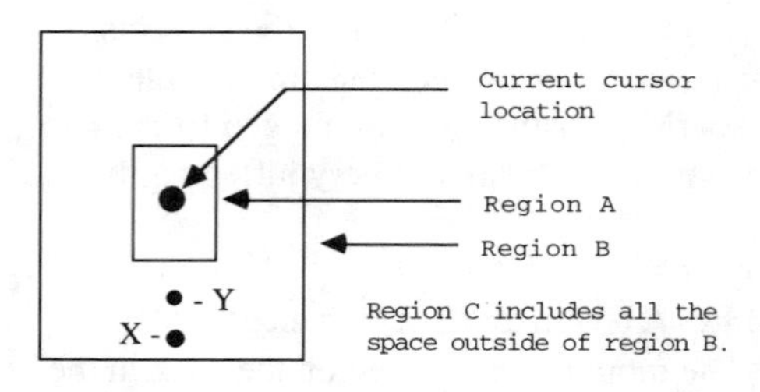

Figure 1. Regions defined for stabilizing the touchscreen. If the current touch is within Region A, the cursor does not move. If the touch is in Region B, then the cursor moves a percentage of the distance between the current touch and the current cursor position. If the current touch is in Region C, then the cursor moves to the location of the current touch.

The steps allowed the selection of a single pixel, but resulted in a significant delay between a movement of the finger and the movement of the cursor. One additional step was necessary to eliminate this delay. Whenever the location of the current touch was far enough from the current cursor location, the cursor moved directly to the location of the touch (Figure 1, Region C). In this way, the cursor could be dragged across the screen very rapidly without a significant distance between the cursor and the user's finger.

Although it may appear that stabilization will lead to a loss of directness between the movement of the finger and the movement of the cursor, careful manipulation of the size of Regions A and B allows stabilization without a loss of directness.

Design and procedure

Selection device and target size were within subject variables. There were three selection devices, a mouse, a non-stabilized touchscreen, and a stabilized touchscreen. There were four rectangular targets: 1, 4, 16 and 32 pixels per side (0.4 x 0.6, 1.7 x 2.2, 6.9 x 9.0, 13.8 x 17.9 mm respectively). The four pixel target was approximately one-quarter of the size of a character which is 9 x 7 pixels. With this range of target sizes the results will be applicable to many practical tasks.

Each subject was tested with all selection devices and target sizes, resulting in three groups of four tasks for each subject. Each task required the selection of a series of six targets that were presented on the screen. Targets appeared in one of four positions, about 2.5 cm from each corner of the screen. Each subject had one practice trial for each task.

Selection device was held constant in each group of tasks, and target size was held constant within a task. Within each group of tasks the target size decreased, in order from 32 pixels per side down to a single pixel. We chose to provide decreasing target sizes to facilitate the subjects' skill acquisition as they moved to smaller and more difficult targets. We recognized the disadvantages of non-random ordering, but we felt the additional experience was important.

The order in which devices were used was randomized among subjects to prevent any possible bias. The order that the six targets within each task were presented was also varied to prevent subjects from anticipating the correct location for the next target.

Instructions were presented on the computer screen. Before each task a short message was presented telling the subject which device would be used. Subjects then pressed ENTER to begin the task. A target was presented and subjects had to select it with the appropriate device. When the target was successfully selected, or five errors were made on the current target, a tone sounded and the next target was presented. An error occurred each time subjects lifted their fingers without making a successful selection. A maximum of five errors was allowed per target to prevent subjects from getting stuck indefinitely on a target if they were not able to select it. Six targets were presented for each task. After the sixth target was selected, a message indicating the number of errors and time taken was presented. Subjects then pressed ENTER to continue to the next task.

When using the mouse, selections were made by moving the mouse until the center of the cursor was on the target and clicking any of the mouse buttons. Selection using both touchscreens involved touching the computer screen, dragging the cursor until the center of the cursor was on the target, and then lifting the finger from the screen. In all cases the cursor was a plus sign (+), made by five pixels vertically and five pixels horizontally, and was presented approximately 6 mm above the subject's finger to allow the subject to view both the cursor and target when selecting small targets. The cursor was blue and targets were red; when the cursor and target overlapped, the intersection became white making it easier to know when the cursor was correctly positioned.

The time to select each group of six targets and the number of errors per group were recorded for each task. In addition, subjects were asked to indicate their preference for each device on a scale from 1 to 9 (1 being strongly disliked, 9 being strongly liked). All data were recorded on the computer.

Results

Selection times

The mean time from the initial presentation of a target until either successful selection or until five errors occurred appear with standard deviations in Table 1 and the means are plotted in Figure 2. An ANOVA with repeated measures for selection device and target size showed significant main effects for selection device, $F(2, 70) = 5.0$, $p = <0.01$, and target size, $F(3, 105) = 232.5$, $p = <0.001$. A significant interaction between selection device and target size, $F(6, 210) = 50.0$, $p = <0.001$, was also found. Tukey's post hoc HSD test showed that both touchscreens are faster than a mouse for targets 16 pixels per side ($p = <0.05$), and the mouse is faster than both touchscreens for a single pixel ($p = <0.05$). There were no other significant differences across the devices.

	Target size (pixels per side)			
	32	16	4	1
Mouse	3.13	3.47*	4.97	6.08*
	(1.28)	(1.60)	(1.98)	(1.87)
Stabilized touchscreen	1.83	1.98	4.27	11.78
	(0.37)	(0.33)	(1.27)	(4.42)
Non-stabilized touchscreen	1.86	1.93	4.57	12.28
	(0.45)	(0.47)	(1.65)	(4.95)

* $p = <0.05$

Table 1. Mean selection time (in seconds) per target (S.D. in parentheses).

Error rates

The mean error rate per target and standard deviations appear in Table 2 and the means are plotted in Figure 3. An ANOVA with repeated measures for selection device and target size showed significant main effects for selection device, F(2,

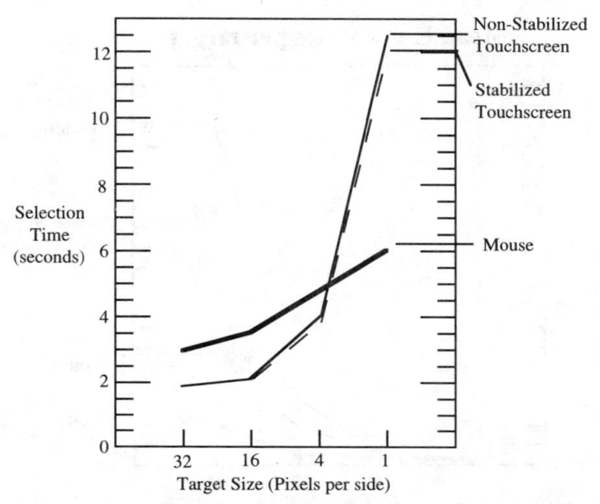

Figure 2. Selection time for four target sizes and three selection devices. key:— , non-stabilized touchscreen; - - . Stabilized touchscreen; ____, Mouse.

70) = 186.4, p = <0.001, and target size, F(3, 105) = 356.6, p = <0 001. A significant interaction between selection device and target size, F(6, 210) = 177.44, p = <0.001, was also found. Tukey's post hoc HSD test showed that the nonstabilized touchscreen resulted in more errors than either of the other devices for the 4 x 4 pixel target (p = <0.05). For the single pixel target, the mouse resulted in fewer errors than either of the other devices, and the stabilized touchscreen resulted in fewer errors than the non-stabilized touchscreen (p = <0.05).

	Target size (pixels per side)			
	32	16	4	1
Mouse	0.08 (0.15)	0.06 (0.12)	0.08 (0.18)	0.50 (0.68)
Stabilized touchscreen	0.03 (0.06)	0.05 (0.10)	0.35 (0.58)	1.53* (1.08)
Non-stabilized touchscreen	0.02 (0.06)	0.06 (0.15)	0.77* (0.60)	4.38* (0.62)

* p = <0.05

Table 2. Mean number of errors per target (S. D. in parentheses).

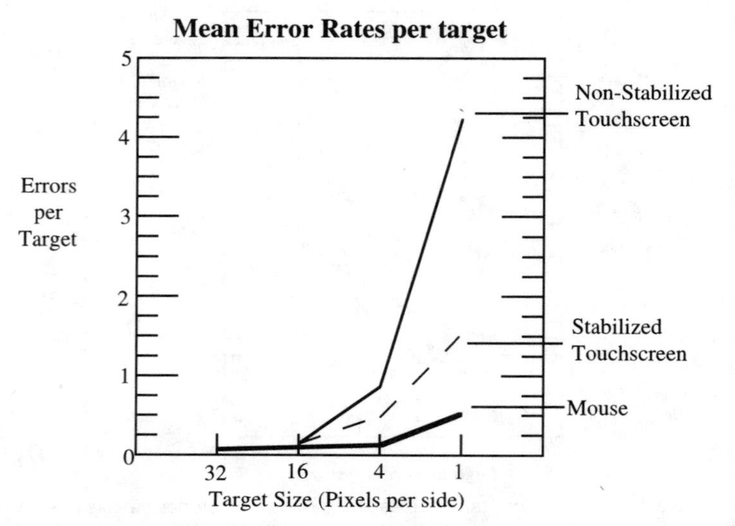

Figure 3. Error rates for four target sizes and three selection devices. key: — , non-stabilized touchscreen; - -, stabilized touchscreen;____, mouse.

	Mouse	Stabilized touchscreen	Non-stabilized touchscreen
Mean user preference rating	7.5 (1.7)	6.7 (1.9)	1.9* (1.5)

*p = <0.05

Table 3. Mean user preference ratings for three selection devices (S.D.in parentheses).

User preference

User preference means and standard deviations appear in Table 3. A one-way repeated measures ANOVA on selection device showed an effect for selection device, $F(2, 70) = 106.9$, $p = <0.001$. Tukey's post hoc HSD test showed that the non-stabilized touchscreen received lower preference ratings than either of the other devices ($p = <0.05$).

Discussion

The stabilized touchscreen was as fast or faster than the mouse while making no more errors for targets as small as four pixels per side. This indicates that a touchscreen can be used for selection of single characters, which are 9 x 7 pixels, in many applications that currently use a mouse. There were no differences in selection times between the two touchscreen implementations, and stabilization resulted in a significant reduction in errors for the two smaller targets.

The results indicate that it was possible to select a single pixel with a touchscreen although the mouse resulted in faster, more accurate selections than either touchscreen. The significant increase in selection time and error rates from the four pixel targets to the single pixel indicates that none of the selection devices, as currently implemented, are appropriate for the selection of the single pixel targets. Additional work must be done to improve the input devices if they are to be used for selecting single pixel targets without a zooming feature.

User preference ratings indicate that the stabilized touchscreen was preferred over the non-stabilized touchscreen. Since subjects are using their fingers to move the cursor on the screen, it seems reasonable to expect the cursor movements to correspond directly to movements of their fingers. When using the non-stabilized touchscreen, the jitter caused by the lack of stability violates this expectation, possibly resulting in lower preference ratings. When stabilization is added, the cursor tracks their fingers accurately, resulting in both higher preference ratings and lower error rates.

The targets explored in this experiment allow predictions to be made about a wide range of practical target sizes. Considering that the majority of high resolution tasks are performed by experienced users, studies that include additional practice, or instructions for selecting small targets, may prove useful. Several subjects devised strategies for selecting the single pixel targets. Two subjects learned that they could position the cursor near the target and then simply roll their fingers up and down or left and right to make fine manipulations. Subjects that were observed using this strategy on the stabilized touchscreen had a mean error rate of only 0.25 when selecting six single pixel targets. When this mean is compared with the overall mean of 1.53, it becomes apparent that this strategy is very successful in reducing errors. If all subjects were exposed to this method of selecting small targets, the error rates might decrease. The second and third experiments incorporated this idea, presenting brief instructions to subjects before the experiment.

Although many people have claimed that smearing will be a significant problem when using touchscreens this problem did not occur in the office-like conditions of this experiment. The touchscreen surface is lightly ground, rather than polished, thereby reducing the glare and impact of fingerprints. The touchscreen used for this study was cleaned once before the experiment began and was not cleaned again. Small amounts of oil and dust accumulated on the screen but the accumulation was similar to that on standard monitors. Actually, less dust appears to collect on the touchscreen used in this experiment than on many standard monitors. No subjects complained that the accumulation affected their performance, and the experimenters did not notice a difference in performance between the early subjects and those at the end of the study.

Experiment two:
Stabilized vs. non-stabilized touchscreen

Summary

The major purpose of the second experiment was to eliminate potential problems with the first experiment. Comparisons were limited to the stabilized and non-stabilized touchscreens. In the first study the targets were presented in one of four locations with decreasing target sizes. In this experiment, the target sizes and locations were randomly determined. In addition, the maximum number of errors allowed per target was increased from five to ten to lessen the ceiling effect. Subjects were also given brief instructions on the selection of small targets with the touchscreen. Stabilization was accomplished using the software from the first experiment and the take-off selection strategy was used. Once again, the cursor was a plus (+) made by five pixels vertically, and five pixels horizontally, and was presented approximately 8 mm above the subject's finger. The cursor was blue, except the center pixel which was black, and targets were yellow. When the cursor and target overlapped, the intersection turned red, except when the center pixel overlapped the intersection turned back to yellow. This allowed subjects to identify when the single pixel targets could be correctly selected.

There were two interesting differences between the results of the first and second experiment. The stabilized touchscreen resulted in an average of 1.53 errors per single pixel target for the first experiment, but only 0.73 errors per target for this experiment. This difference was most likely due to the change in the cursor and the improved instructions. The non-stabilized touchscreen required 12.3 seconds per selection for single pixel targets during the first experiment. This increased to 21.9 seconds per selection for the second experiment. This increase is most likely due to the increased number of errors allowed (maximum was 5 for experiment one and 10 for experiment two).

Experiment three:
Stabilized touchscreen vs. mouse

Summary

Experiment three was the same as experiment two except for the selection devices. Experiment three evaluated the stabilized touchscreen and the mouse. Once again, the results were essentially the same as for experiment one. The only difference was a slight decrease in errors for both the mouse and touchscreen when selecting the two smaller targets. This decrease was likely due to the change in the cursor and the improved instructions.

Case study with an experienced user

Summary

One user (Sears) who was experienced with both the touchscreen and mouse performed the second and third experiments five times each. The results were similar to those of the previous experiments with several important differences. First, selections were much faster for all devices and target sizes, except for the single pixel targets when using the non-stabilized touchscreen. In general, the experienced user required half as long to complete the selections. The second important difference was a large reduction in the number of errors. Errors were reduced to approximately zero for both the stabilized touchscreen and mouse for all target sizes.

Conclusions

Revising Fitts' Law for selection with a touchscreen

Fitts' Law, $T = a + b[\log(2d/w)]$, predicts that the time necessary to select a target (T) is proportional to the distance (d) to the target, the width of the target (w), and two device-dependent parameters a and b. This law has been demonstrated for many situations and devices (Card, English & Burr, 1978). It is not clear that this law, in its original form, applies to all selection methods with all targets.

Cursor positioning with a touchscreen is inherently different than cursor positioning with most other devices. With most devices, there is always a cursor present and movement of the device moves the cursor. With touchscreens, there may not be a cursor present when the user's finger is not touching the screen. Once the user touches the screen, the cursor is placed near the finger and can then be dragged around the screen. In addition, when using most devices, there is some time dedicated to locating the device which moves the cursor.

With the touchscreen there is no time needed to locate the cursor positioning device, but the positioning time must include the time it takes the user to initially place their finger on the screen. Since users typically first touch the screen close to the actual target, the distance they must move the cursor should be relatively small.

For these reasons, Fitts' Law must be modified to predict positioning times for a touchscreen. The modified version of Fitts' Law must have an additional factor that accounts for the time used to initially place a finger on the screen. This time will be relatively small and should be a function of the size of the target and the distance, measured in three dimensions, from the original location of the hand to the target. The second factor in the modified Fitts' Law will account for the time necessary to move the finger to the target once it is placed on the screen. This factor will be a function of the target size; distances will not affect this factor since the user will initially place their finger near the target. Using this information, the following can be offered as a modification of Fitts' Law for touchscreens: $T = a + b[\log(cD/W)] + d[\log(e/W)$, where the first factor, $b[\log(cD/W)]$, measures the time to place the finger on the screen initially. The second factor, $d[\log(e/W)]$, measures the time to position the cursor once the finger has been placed on the screen. The distance, measured in three dimensions, from the original hand location to the location of first contact is D, and W equals some measurement of target size. The constants a, b, c, d and e are determined for each specific case. The distance, D, could be the distance from the previous selection if selections are made in rapid succession, but it may be difficult to measure in many circumstances.

Of course, many other factors influence the time to select a target and therefore the values of the constants in both original and modified Fitts' Law. These include the target background and shape (a long narrow target may be harder to select than a square target of the same area).

Analyzing this revised Fitts' Law using the data from these experiments has proven inconclusive. The limited number of target sizes (four) and the lack of precise distance measurements (from the user's hand to the target) makes analysis difficult, allowing this data to fit many predictive equations including both the original and modified Fitts' Law. Future experiments to investigate this or any other revision to Fitts' Law will need to use additional target sizes and carefully measure the distance between the user's hand and the target.

Impact on practitioners

These results may have a significant impact on the number and type of applications that touchscreens are used for. Knowledge of the effect stabilization has on touchscreen accuracy and speed will allow designers to include touchscreens in applications requiring rapid performance, high precision, and low error rates. The performance achieved with the touchscreen in this experiment should be attainable by any designer, making it a desirable input device for many applications. The results obtained from these experiments indicate that although both the mouse and touchscreen could be used, neither is adequate for selection of single pixel targets. Additional research is necessary for selection tasks involving targets of this small size.

More applications could be designed using touchscreens, taking advantage of their simple operation, ease of learning, rapid performance, and potentially low error rates. Another direction would be to develop software to replace existing mouse drivers, allowing a touchscreen to be used with many applications that currently use a mouse. These results indicate that the touchscreen can easily be used for character selection in word processors, and possibly even for graphics design. Most graphics packages include a zoom option which allows the user to examine a magnified screen image which would make the touchscreen adequate for these applications.

Update

Between the time the software was written for this experiment and the time of publication, touchscreens matured. Several manufacturers have improved the stability of their touchscreens either by hardware improvements, or by smoothing the raw data in software. Single pixel accuracy is now available from several touchscreen manufacturers.

We would like to thank Kent Norman, Linda Weldon, Yoram Kochavy, John Schnizlein, NCR Corporation, the members of the Human-Computer Interaction Laboratory and the User Interface Design class (CMCS 828S, Fall 1988) for their useful suggestions. We appreciate the excellent comments of three anonymous reviewers who led us to make more precise descriptions of our experimental methods. We also thank the volunteers for their assistance.

Sparks of Innovation in Human-Computer Interaction,
B. Shneiderman, Ed., Ablex Publ., Norwood, NJ (1993)

4.3 Touchscreens now offer compelling uses

Ben Shneiderman

If you thought touchscreens were a thing of the past, this essay will bring you up to date on improvements to this input device's user interface. I suspect we will be seeing touchscreens being used for more applications than ever before.

Michelangelo's fresco of God's finger reaching down to touch a person's hand is compelling. The process of touching is immediately recognizable as the gift of life. Inventors of the touchscreen in the 1960s may have been inspired by this image in their cultural unconscious. Touchscreens have an unrivaled immediacy, a rewarding sense of control, and the engaging experience of direct manipulation.

IEEE Software Vol. 8, No. 2, (March 1991) 93-94, 107

First-generation touchscreens have been successfully applied in sales kiosks, public information services, and computer aided instruction — in spite of poor precision, slow and erratic activation, and poorly designed displays. Now, second-generation touchscreens are supporting novel applications that are likely to enormously expand access to computing and information resources as well as enjoyable entertainment, art, and music applications.

Why touchscreens? Touchscreens have several distinct advantages over other pointing devices:

Touching a visual display of choices requires little thinking and is a form of direct manipulation that is easy to learn.
Touchscreens are the fastest pointing device.
Touchscreens have easier hand-eye coordination than mice or keyboards.
No extra workspace is required as with other pointing devices.
Touchscreens are durable in public access and in high volume usage.

These advantages mean that touchscreens are highly effective in public access information systems, cash machines, home automation, museums and libraries, medical instruments, education, and many other domains.

Of course, touchscreens have some problems:

Users' hands may obscure the screen.
Screens need to be installed at a lower position and tilted to reduce arm fatigue
Some reduction in image brightness may occur.
They cost more than alternative devices.

These are real problems, but they can be addressed successfully. Some critics suggest that smudges on the screen may be a problem, but we clean our touchscreens no more frequently than our standard monitors or our mice.

What's new?

The second generation of touchscreens uses several techniques to overcome previous limits. Lift-off strategies were one such technique that offers several advantages in precision of item selection and the movement of elements.

The use of lift-off strategies enables higher precision by showing users a cursor on the screen slightly above their fingers. (My colleagues and I compared three lift-off strategies in "Improving the accuracy of touch screens: An experimental evaluation of three strategies," *Proc. of the Conference on Human Factors in Computing Systems*, ACM SIGCHI, NY, 1988, pp. 27-32). With lift-off, you can drag the cursor smoothly and continuously along the screen's surface. Functions can be activated when users lift their fingers off the surface — something we call the "un-touchscreen."

Our early study showed that, with lift-off, people could easily select targets the size of a pair of letters. However, we had to add stabilization software to allow single pixel selection on a 640 x 480 display (a VGA - resolution display) or less than a square millimeter.) Improved hardware and software supporting this high precision strategy is now available in commercial touchscreens (vendors include MicroTouch Systems Inc., Wilmington, Mass. and Elographics Corp., Oak Ridge, Tenn.).

Dragging a cursor is only one use of the lift-off strategy. The most engaging applications are those that enable users to drag icons, buttons, sliders, words, flags, or clock hands. But why not allow dragging of musical notes, paint brushes, or large sections of the screen image? In our experience, there is a delightful sense of magic about dragging images around the screen.

What's possible?

Designers' imaginations become freer when they enter the world of touching, dragging, and drawing with these improved touchscreens. Our first application was with our Hyperties hypermedia system (available from Cognetics Corp., Princeton Jct., NJ) applied to a Smithsonian Institution installation containing information on 200 archaeological dig sites that accept volunteers. Users could touch words in the text for more information or locations on the 11 world maps.

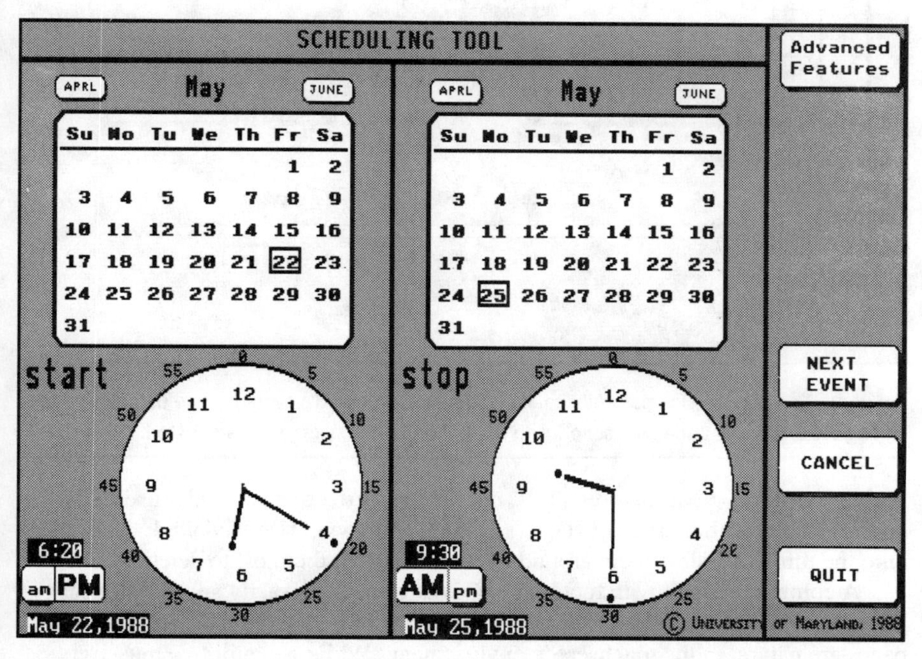

Figure 1. The 12-hour clock scheduler - Each start and stop portion of the screen consists of a Gregorian calendar and a 12-hour analog watch. Users first select the day on the calendar then rotate the hands of the clock to the desired position. An A.M./P.M. toggle is available.The boxes around dates and the hands on the clock may be dragged via touch screen.

Most users succeeded in using the kiosk immediately. About 15% were momentarily confused by the lift-off strategy, but they quickly learned it after one or two touches. We observed and interviewed early users to make improvements and analyzed the log data for the 4461 users in the first four weeks of the 18-month six-city tour.

As we became more comfortable with the idea of high precision touchscreens and lift-off, we developed several versions of home control scheduler tasks such as scheduling VCRs. Pointing at a day on a monthly calendar was very natural when the user could smoothly drag a box-shaped cursor. Then to choose the time, we let the users drag the hands on an analog clock as Figure 1 shows. Participants in our

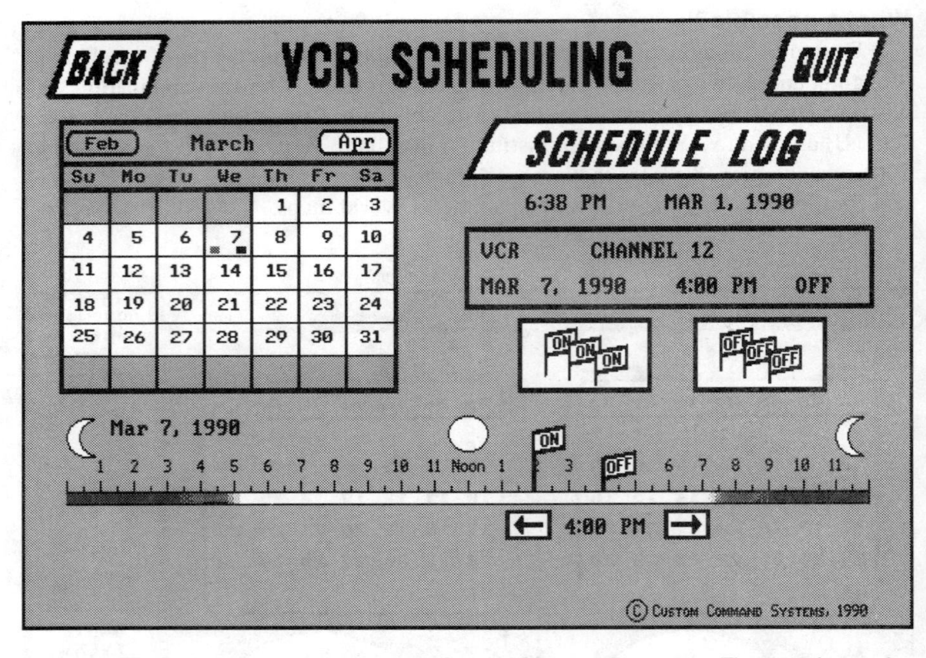

Figure 2. The final version currently used in Custom Command's system. The use of on and off flags was the most effective scheduling metaphor for touchscreen users tested.

usability test had great fun doing this, but the most effective scheduler used a 24-hour time-line with on and off flags (as Figure 2 shows). Users could drag the flags onto the time-line, slide them around to adjust, or drag them off to delete.

A common pursuit with touchscreens is developing visually appealing metaphors that react predictably. Opening a book, touching lettered tabs, and turning pages are natural in the touchscreen environment. While we built two museum versions of books, Cognetics Corporation's artist, Paul Hoffman, made a strikingly realistic ring binder telephone book for a conference messaging system that

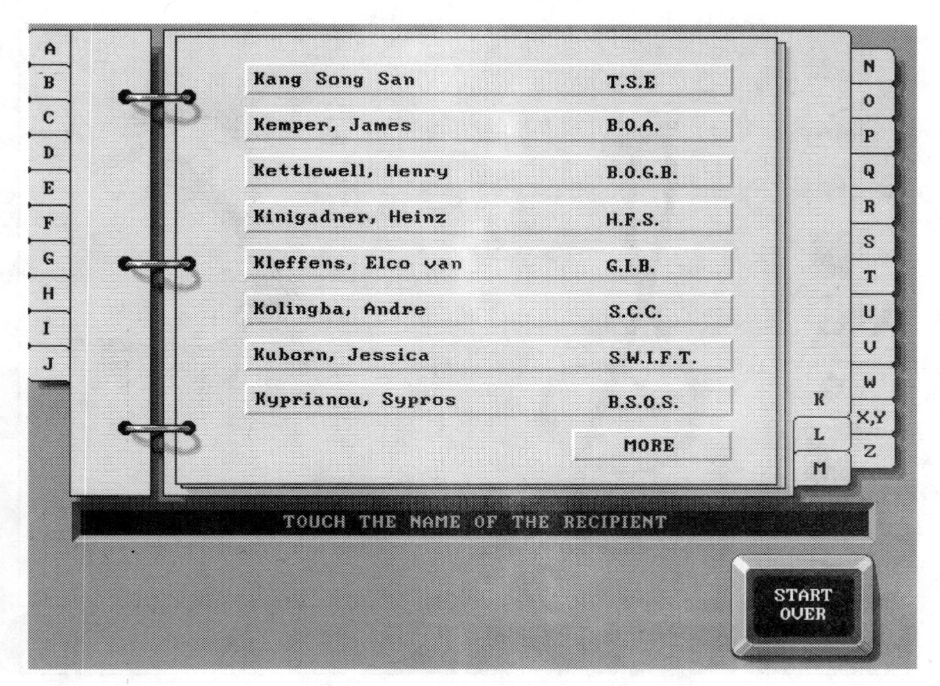

Figure 3. The ring-binder metaphor worked very well as a touchscreen application.

eliminated the keyboard and used touchscreens and scanners only, as Figure 3 shows.

Smiles were common when demonstrating an art and music environment that allowed electronic finger painting. In PlayPen II, created by Andrew Sears, users select colors, textures, sounds, and shapes with their fingers. Figure 4 shows an example. The results depend not only on finger position, but also on the velocity and direction of motion. This additional information can be used in other applications, such as touchscreen versions of musical instruments in which the volume depends on the velocity of touch on a set of strings or piano keys.

Touchscreen keyboard replacements become attractive when only occasional data entry is necessary. Typists achieved 25 word per minute speeds with our near normal-size touchscreen keyboards, compared with 58 words per minute using standard keyboards and 17 words per minute using a mouse to select the keys (Figure 5 shows the touchscreen typing screen). However, the touchscreen keyboard can be adjusted to reduce the size to less than 2.5 inches wide and still preserve reasonable typing speed. A small keyboard is applicable for portable or pocket sized computers, as a pop-up tool to enter data on a medical form or sales receipt, or to enter a search string in an electronic book.

Figure 4. The PenPlay II tool combines traditional touch-and-select technology with velocity and motion sensing. This added information can be used to control volume, pitch, brightness, speed and other such attributes.

What's next?

Further advances with high precision touchscreens seem very likely, in both the hardware technology and the software designs that apply lift-off. While some touchscreens can provide 3-4 levels of touch pressure, improvements are needed to make this notion viable. Another improvement would be to allow multiple simultaneous touches to support the pressing of a SHIFT key while typing, selecting colors while drawing, touch typing, or selecting an object and an action simultaneously.

The most exciting breakthroughs will probably be in innovative applications, like controlling three dimensional artificial realities (let your fingers do the walking), selecting irregular shaped objects (for example, pointing at human body parts and getting lab results), or selecting moving objects (for example, pointing at fish swimming in a pool to find out more about the species, or pointing at a rotating globe to select countries).

We found that the challenge was to break free from the older notion that touchscreens are for buttons, and to explore how we might use sliding, dragging, and other gestures to move objects and invoke actions.

Figure 5. A touchscreen keyboard. Although slower than a traditional keyboard, it works well for note-taking, forms-entry, and other applications that require small amounts of input in a portable or small device.

Who knows what new forms of video games are possible if we let our imaginations go free? Why not a touchscreen Ouija Board or labyrinth? Who will be the first to make a magical Aladdin's lamp with a genie that pops-out when you rub it?

Soon enough we can envision a pocket-sized computer with two folding halves each having at least 80 characters x 25 line high precision touchscreens. Your calendar, address book, current projects, and the morning newspaper could all be a touch or an un-touch away. And why not high-resolution LCD touchscreens next to museum art works to give you the artist's biography, provenance, and description? Every refrigerator door, automobile dashboard, household main entry doorway, or TV is a potential place for un-touchscreens with useful information, assistance, and data entry.

Sparks of Innovation in Human-Computer Interaction,
B. Shneiderman, Ed., Ablex Publ., Norwood, NJ (1993)

4.4 Touchscreen interfaces for alphanumeric data entry

Catherine Plaisant
Andrew Sears

Touchscreens have been demonstrated as useful for many applications. Although a traditional mechanical keyboard is the device of choice when entering alphanumeric data, it may not be optimal when only limited data must be entered, or when the keyboard layout, character set, or size may be changed. A series of experiments has demonstrated the usability of touchscreen keyboards. The first study indicated that users who type 58 wpm on a traditional keyboard can type 25 wpm using a touchscreen and that the traditional monitor position is suboptimal for touchscreen use. A second study reported on typing rates for keyboards of various sizes (from 6.8 to 24.6 cm wide). Novices typed approximately 10 wpm on the smallest and 20 wpm on the largest of the keyboards. Users experienced with touchscreen keyboards typed 21wpm on the smallest and 32 wpm on the largest. We then report on a recent study done with more representative users and more difficult tasks. Thirteen cashiers were recruited for this study and were required to complete ten trials in which they typed names and addresses with punctuation. Results indicate that the users improved rapidly from 9.5 wpm on the first trial to 13.8 wpm on the last trial, reaching their fastest performance after only 25 minutes. Although custom interfaces will be preferred for special types of data (e.g. telephone numbers, times, dates, colors) there will always be situations when limited quantities of text must be entered. In these situations a touchscreen keyboard can be used.

Proc. of the Human Factors Society-36th Annual Meeting , vol. 1 (Atlanta Oct. 12-16,1992) 293-297.

Introduction

There are many situations where typing limited quantities of text is required. For example: cashiers at a department store sometimes enter a customer's name and address, managers of fast food franchises occasionally access information easily available from the cash registers, and users of a portable hypertext system primarily follow links but occasionally enter text for a search. Although the traditional keyboard is well known and allows rapid data entry, its physical presence and inability to adapt to special needs may be a problem. Handwriting recognition has improved (Pittman, 1991) but is still slow and constrained, resulting in less satisfactory and less natural interfaces than expected. For several years we have been investigating the use of touchscreens to provide alternative interfaces for traditional tasks (Sears, Plaisant, & Shneiderman, 1992). A recent series of studies has focused on using touchscreen keyboards for limited data entry.

In most situations, the traditional mechanical keyboard remains the alphanumeric data entry device of choice. However, when users only occasionally enter limited quantities of alphanumeric data, a traditional mechanical keyboard may not be optimal if one of the following is true:

- the system is accessible to the public (durability),
- the layout must be changed (QWERTY vs. Dvorak),
- the character set must be changed (internationalization),
- feedback must be altered (users with special needs), or
- size is a concern (notebook or palmtop computers).

Touchscreen interfaces provide an attractive alternative to a traditional keyboard when these circumstances are considered. Unlike traditional keyboards, touchscreens have consistently been shown to be durable enough for public access systems and the layout, character set, feedback and size can be changed dynamically to fit user demands. In addition, the touchscreen keyboard can be displayed only when needed, increasing the space available for other purposes and possibly decreasing the size of systems.

Previous research

Target selection studies

There has been a great deal of research that focused on target selection. Various strategies have been explored with targets as small as 0.4x0.6 mm (Sears and Shneiderman, 1991). This research has resulted in a relatively consistent set of recommendations. The land-on strategy only allows users to make selections where their fingers first touch the screen. Research indicates that targets 20 mm square or larger can be accurately selected using this strategy (Beringer, 1989; Hall et al., 1988; Weisner, 1988). The lift-off strategy allows users to touch the screen, drag their finger to adjust the selection, and lift it once it is in the correct location to make the selection (Murphy, 1987; Potter et al., 1989). This strategy allows the selection of targets as small as 1.7x2.2 mm (Sears and Shneiderman, 1991).

Summary of first keyboard study

Touchscreen keyboard design and comparisons with a mouse and traditional keyboard

This study investigated many factors that influence the efficiency of touchscreen keyboards, and compared them with the traditional keyboard and a mouse activated keyboard (Sears, 1991). Ten subjects participated in the first phase of the study which demonstrated that the standard monitor position (approximately 75 degrees from horizontal) is sub-optimal, at least when using a touchscreen. Subjects preferred using touchscreens mounted at 30 or 45 degrees from horizontal, with the majority preferring 30 degrees. These results were supported by Ahlström, Lenman and Marmolin (1991) who reported less fatigue and errors for a touchscreen mounted at 30 degrees from horizontal. They also demonstrated that providing an elbow rest is beneficial.

The second phase of this study demonstrated that biases exist when touchscreens are mounted at an angle other than perpendicular to the users line of sight (also see Beringer and Peterson, 1985; Beringer and Bowman, 1989; Hall et al., 1988). Using a monitor mounted at 30 degrees from horizontal, fourteen subjects consistently touched below targets regardless of the location on the screen. This bias can be explained by the small amount of parallax introduced by the touchscreen. Subjects also consistently touched to the left of targets that were on either side of the screen.

The final phase of this study compared a touchscreen keyboard to a standard QWERTY keyboard and a keyboard activated using a mouse with novice users and no practice. The touchscreen and mouse used an abbreviated QWERTY keyboard (alphabetic, done, backspace, and space keys). The touchscreen was mounted at 30 degrees from horizontal and software was written to correct for all biases discovered in the second phase of the study. Nine subjects typed six short strings with a total of 138 characters. A speed of 25 words per minute (wpm) placed the touchscreen keyboard between the standard keyboard (58 wpm) and the mouse (17 wpm). Although the touchscreen was not as fast as the standard keyboard it was demonstrated as a usable input device.

Summary of second keyboard study

Effect of keyboard size on performance

This study investigated the effect of keyboard size on typing rates for touchscreen keyboards (Sears, Revis, et al., 1992). This study explored four touchscreen keyboard sizes which varied from 6.8 to 24.6 cm wide (from Q to P keys) (see Figure 5 in Section 4.3).

Once again, abbreviated QWERTY keyboards were used. Twenty-four novice and four experienced users typed a series of three strings with a total of sixty-nine letters. This study demonstrated the potential speed of touchscreen keyboards which varied from 10 wpm (for the smallest keyboard) to 20 wpm (for the largest keyboard) for novices, and from 21 to 32 wpm for experienced users. There were no significant differences in the number of errors in the final strings users typed. A comparison of the results of the novices and experienced users illustrates the benefits of experience. While experienced users were 60% faster than novices on the largest keyboard, they were 113% faster than novices on the smallest keyboard indicating the increased importance of practice for smaller keyboards.

Measuring user performance with limited practice

The study presented in this paper attempts to measure the typing speed of more representative users after limited practice. There were several goals for this study. First, subjects were selected to provide a representative sample of one set of potential users. Second, we wanted to estimate the typing speed reached after limited practice and determine how long users must work with touchscreen keyboards before they achieve a significant improvement in typing rates. Third we intended to explore the use of a complete QWERTY keyboard (Figure 1) since previous studies had used abbreviated keyboards.

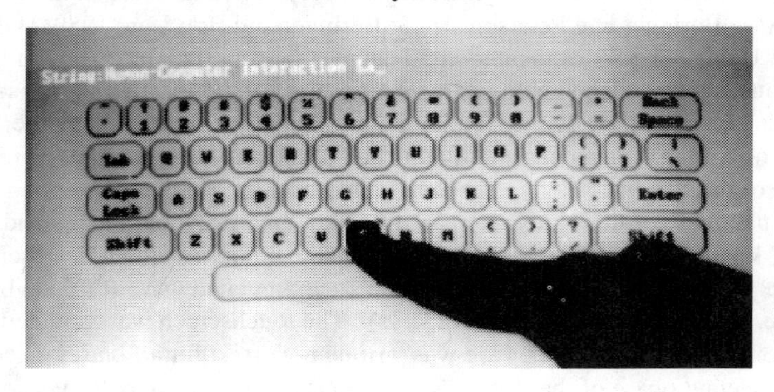

Figure 1. Complete QWERTY keyboard used in this study.

Apparatus

An NEC PowerMate 386/25 PC with a Sony Multi-scan HG monitor and Microtouch capacitive touchscreen was used. A special desk allowed the monitor to be mounted below the desk surface at 30 degrees from horizontal. The keyboard slid into the desk when not in use (Figure 2).

The touchscreen keyboard was a complete QWERTY keyboard. Alphabetic keys measured 1.14 cm per side for a total keyboard size of 13.2 cm between the P and Q keys (this was chosen to be equal to the size of the medium keyboard of the previous study by Sears, Revis, et al., 1992). Other keys were proportional in size. To shift a key (to get a capital letter or symbol) users touched the shift key first, lifted their finger, and then typed the key to be shifted. A shift-lock key was also available for longer strings of capital letters. The lift-off selection strategy was used since keys were too small to be reliably selected using land-on strategy. When a key was touched it highlighted, users could then drag their finger to a different key if desired; when the user lifted their finger, the key returned to its normal colors

Figure 2. Desk used in this study showing the touchscreen mounted at a 30 degree angle with an arm rest.

and a soft clicking noise was heard. The shift key remained highlighted after it was touched until the next key was touched. When the shift-lock key was touched it remained highlighted until it was selected again (deactivated). The space bar was activated by touches that fell anywhere on or below it to allow for easier selection.

Subjects

Thirteen cashiers were recruited for this study. Cashiers were chosen since they represent one set of potential users of systems where touchscreen keyboards may be useful and speed remains important. They were recruited from personnel offices from several stores in the College Park, Maryland area. All subjects were familiar with, but not necessarily experienced using, the standard QWERTY keyboard. Subjects were paid $20 for participating in the experiment which lasted approximately 2 hours. Subjects were instructed that speed and accuracy were both important and that bonuses of $20 and $15 would be given to the two best performances.

Design and procedure

A single trial consisted of typing ten names and two names with addresses including numbers and punctuation (Table 1). Every trial contained exactly the same number of characters and was controlled to eliminate any extremely difficult names or addresses.

Sue Shapiro	Nadine Jacobs
Rebecca Lee	Yonina Slavin
Marica Smith	Martine Ferret
Doron Stadlan	Sophie Atwood
David Griver	Joe Cob
Joseph Garvy	Ronit Romero
586 Burton Rd.	603 Hyde St.
Rockville, MD 20873	Silverville, MO 69043

Table 1. A sample list of names and names with addresses users typed for a single trial.

MONDAY
FIRST WE MUST START
THE QUICK BROWN FOX JUMPED OVER THE LAZY DOG

Table 2. The three reference strings typed at the beginning and end the study.

Subjects were instructed in the use of the shift key, then typed a practice string followed by a set of three reference strings using the touchscreen keyboard. These strings were the same as those used in a previous study (Sears, Revis, et al., 1992) and were used to allow a comparison between this study and the previous study (Table 2). Next, users typed ten trials of names and names with addresses using the touchscreen keyboard. There was a break of about 3 to 4 minutes between each trial. When all ten trials were completed users then retyped the practice string and set of three strings typed earlier to allow a comparison of their initial performance with performance after limited practice.

These tasks were calibrated in a pilot test to provide enough practice to allow an increase in typing speed while keeping each trial reasonably short. We wanted to avoid simulating extended, strenuous use of the touchscreen keyboard since in such cases the standard keyboard would be preferred.

Subjects answered several questions concerning fatigue between each trial. The time to enter each string was automatically recorded. Two types of errors were also recorded. A corrected error was any contiguous string of backspaces, and an uncorrected error was any letter (or sequence of letters) in the final string which was incorrect.

Results and discussion

Ten trials of names and addresses

Time. Mean times, mean+standard deviation, and mean-standard deviation for users to type each of the lists appear in Figure 3. An ANOVA with repeated measures for trial showed a significant effect $F(9,108)=13.2$ ($p < .001$). Tukey's post hoc HSD showed that trials four through ten were faster than trial one, and that

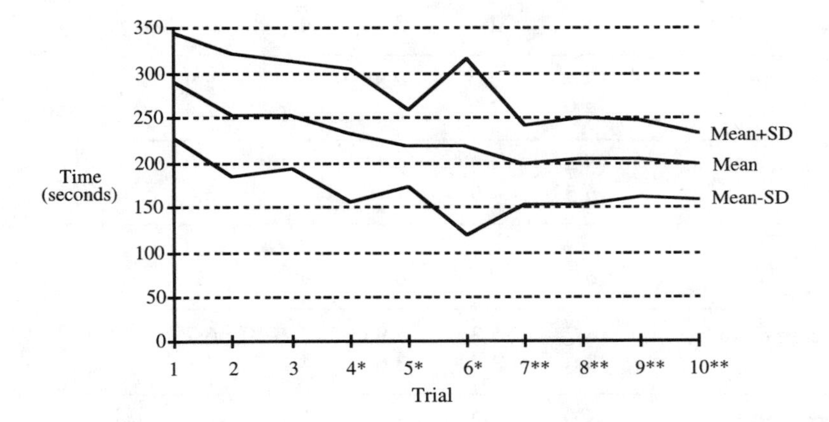

Figure 3. Graph of mean time to complete each trial. Mean+SD and Mean-SD are also plotted.
* Significantly faster than trial 1.
** Significantly faster than trials 1 through 3

trials seven through ten were faster than trials one through three ($p < .005$). These results indicate that subjects improved steadily, reaching their fastest performance at trial seven and then maintained that speed.

Errors. Means and standard deviations for the number of corrected and uncorrected errors appear in Table 3. Any sequence of consecutive backspaces is considered one corrected error. Any incorrect letters (or sequence of letters) in the final string is considered one uncorrected error. Two ANOVAs with repeated measures for trial were performed, one for corrected errors and one for uncorrected errors. The results showed no significant effects of trial on either type of error.

Discussion. The results for the ten trials show that subjects steadily increased in speed. On trial seven, subjects reached their peak speed, 30% faster than their first trial, and maintained that speed for the remainder of the experiment. Overall, these results indicate that subjects reached their peak performance after an average of approximately 25 minutes of touchscreen keyboard use. Subjects quickly learned that it was not possible to "touch-type" on the touchscreen as they might on a traditional keyboard and adopted various strategies using several fingers.

On average subjects improved from 9.5 wpm (assuming 5 characters per word) in the first trial to 13.8 wpm in the last trial. The previous study (Sears, Revis, et al., 1992) found speeds of 16.5 wpm for novice college students with the same size abbreviated keyboard. It is likely that the presence of uppercase characters, numbers, and punctuation resulted in these differences.

Between each trial the subjects rated the fatigue they felt in their eyes, arms, fingers and overall on a scale from 1 to 10. The results show that the ratings grew slowly but never came close to the maximum value, which seems to indicate that

Trial	**1**	**2**	**3**	**4**	**5**
Corrected Errors	8.7	7.0	7.8	5.8	5.9
SD	4.9	2.9	5.4	3.7	2.4
Uncorrected Errors	5.4	4.2	6.1	3.4	4.0
SD	6.5	4.9	10.0	4.4	3.6

Trial	**6**	**7**	**8**	**9**	**10**
Corrected Errors	4.7	5.3	5.9	7.2	6.7
SD	3.6	3.8	3.6	4.2	4.8
Uncorrected Errors	3.6	3.2	3.1	2.6	4.0
SD	4.8	4.3	4.0	4.0	4.5

Table 3. Mean and standard deviation for corrected and uncorrected errors for each trial.

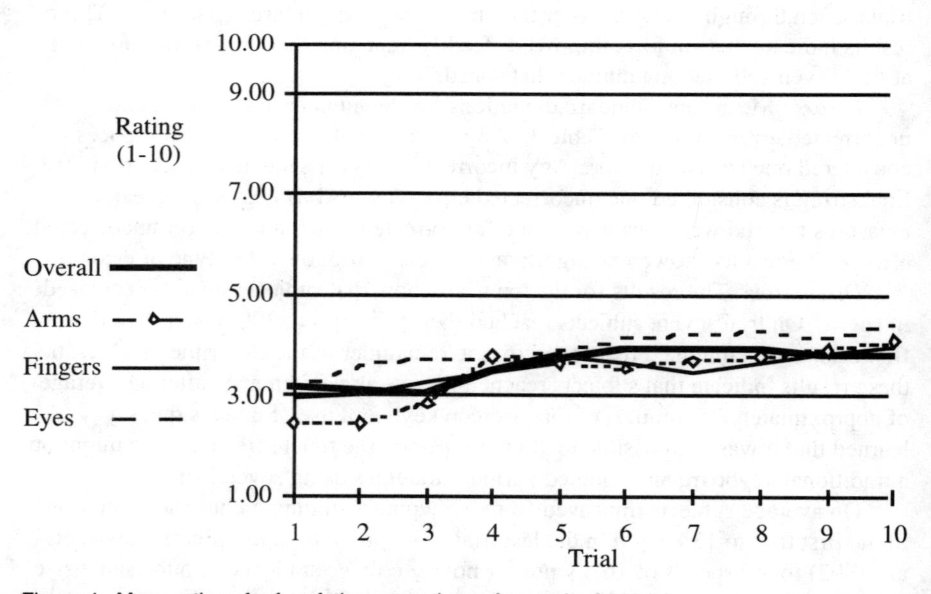

Figure 4. Mean ratings for four fatigue questions after each of 10 trials.

fatigue was not a factor in this study (Figure 4). Several subjects stated that a touchscreen keyboard would be fine to use.

Reference strings

Time and Errors. The three reference strings were used to provide a supplementary measure of speed increase during the test and also to compare the results of this experiment with the previous experiment. Means and standard deviations for time, corrected, and uncorrected errors for this study appear in Table 4. A t-test was performed for time, corrected, and uncorrected errors. Results indicate that performance improved significantly in both time and corrected errors between the first and last time subjects used the touchscreen keyboard ($T=5.374$, $p < .001$ and $T=3.247$, $p < .01$ respectively). There was no significant difference for uncorrected errors.

Discussion. These results also show that users improve significantly given limited practice with a touchscreen keyboard. A comparison of the results with those of Sears, Revis, et al. (1992) indicates that at the beginning of the experiment subjects in the current study performed slightly worse than the novices in the previous study (Tables 4 and 5). By the end of the current study subjects improved to perform better than the novices, but not as well as the experienced subjects in the previous experiment (Tables 4 and 5).

Attempt	Time	Corrected	Uncorrected
First	65.8 (22.9)	3.0 (2.5)	0.3 (0.6)
Last	42.8 (11.2)	1.2 (1.0)	0.2 (0.4)

Table 4. Mean time, corrected errors, and uncorrected errors to enter the two sets of three strings (standard deviations in parentheses).

Users	Time	Corrected	Uncorrected
Novice	55.2 (15.0)	3.4 (2.8)	0.4 (0.6)
Experienced	32.3 (1.4)	1.3 (1.0)	0.0 (0.0)

Table 5. Mean time, corrected errors, and uncorrected errors for novices and experienced users to enter the set of three strings (standard deviations in parentheses) from Sears, Revis, et al. (1992).

Conclusions

The standard mechanical keyboard remains the input device of choice when large quantities of alphanumeric data needs to be entered. However, when data entry is limited, a keyboard is not practical, or flexibility is a requirement (alternative layouts or languages), a touchscreen or stylus keyboard may prove useful. We have provided a benchmark for typing speed that may help designers decide how appropriate this technology is for their application. We have also shown that users reached their fastest performance during this experiment after only 25 minutes of practice. Although performance did not improve between the seventh and tenth trials, additional practice may result in even faster performance. A touchscreen interface provides easy solutions to many problems. Although custom interfaces will be preferred for special types of data (e.g., telephone numbers, times, dates, compass directions, colors) (Sears, Plaisant, and Shneiderman, 1992), there will always be situations when limited quantities of free form text must be entered. In these situations a touchscreen keyboard can be used.

Acknowledgments

We want to thank Miriam Weiss for her many hours preparing and administering the experiment, Daniel Mosse and all the members of the Human-Computer Interaction Lab for their help, and NCR for partial support of this research.

Note: A video showing the touchscreen keyboards, "Open House '91", is available from the Human-Computer Interaction Lab, A.V. Williams Building, University of Maryland, College Park, MD 20742.

Sparks of Innovation in Human-Computer Interaction,
B. Shneiderman, Ed., Ablex Publ., Norwood, NJ (1993)

4.5 Scheduling home control devices: a case study of the transition from the research project to a product

Catherine Plaisant
Ben Shneiderman
Jim Battaglia

Introduction

Many electronically controlled devices are now found in modern homes, e.g., VCR's, heating and cooling systems, or security systems. One of the benefits of home automation systems (Time, 89; Smith, 88) is to provide integrated control of those devices, therefore allowing the use of a single consistent interface to schedule any device to turn ON or OFF or perform a complex function at a later time.

Human Factors in Practice, Computer Systems Technical Group, Human Factors Society (Santa-Monica, CA, Dec. 1990) 7-13.

This case study describes the transition from a research project on scheduling home-control devices to a product integrated in an existing home automation system. First we describe the research that explored several designs to schedule devices over time periods ranging from minutes to days: four designs were compared, three of them prototyped and tested. One of the designs was selected for implementation in the commercial system. We then categorize the actions that were taken in order to improve and mold the prototype design into an integrated product. Finally we report on an additional study that emerged from the first one - the scheduling of periodic events - and on the extensions of the scheduler interface design to other aspects of home automation.

A joint project

In 1987 the Human-Computer Interaction Laboratory was contacted by Custom Command Systems, Inc. (previously American Voice and Robotics Inc.) and with the support of the Maryland Industrial Partnerships program we were able to start a long and beneficial relationship. Custom Command is a growing company and a participant in the University of Maryland's Technology Advancement Program, a state-sponsored initiative designed to support local high-technology companies. Custom Command specializes in the development and marketing of integrated entertainment, security, and automation systems for homes and commercial conference rooms. Their focus is on providing state-of-the-art systems that are easy for the novice homeowner to use. Custom Command's systems incorporate all of the major electronic subsystems typically found in the home, such as audio/video entertainment, security, lighting, heating and cooling, energy management, telephone, information services, and a variety of convenience features. The systems are controlled through the use of touchscreens, hand-held remotes, voice recognition, touch-tone telephones, and programmable wall switches.

After a first review of Custom Command's product, the scheduling interface was identified as one feature that could benefit from improved human factors design. It was decided to explore possible alternatives to the original interface, which required a long and tedious process of incremental specification of dates, times and states through a deep menu structure.

The requirements

The new scheduler has to simply replace the existing one, therefore it must be consistent with the existing environment: The control of the scheduler is through a touchscreen interface. The home owner sees the screen flush mounted into a wall or custom built into furniture or cabinetry. The Microtouch or Elographic touchscreens that are used return a continuous flow of coordinates with a 1024x1024 resolution. (This allows the dragging of objects, the identification of sliding motion and the use of a lift-off strategy for selection. This strategy reduces the error rates (Potter, Shneiderman & Weldon 88) and allows the selection of small targets, as small as one pixel (Sears & Shneiderman, 91)). The color, graphical screen displays are implemented under MS-DOS in EGA mode (640x350 pixels).

The touchscreen and the home devices are controlled by an AT class microcomputer.

The scheduling interface has to be general enough to be used with all the devices controlled by the home automation system. Some examples of the items to be scheduled are:

- VCR
- Lawn-watering system
- Heating and cooling system
- Lights
- Audible reminders/announcement

In Custom Command's current system users first select a device to be scheduled and then are presented with the "standard" scheduling interface labeled with the device's name. It is the redesign of this "standard" interface that we will now discuss.

The research project

Examples of the difficulties encountered by occasional users dealing with scheduling tasks are commonly reported, especially with VCR's which are well known to be frustrating (Nemy, 89; Norman, 88). Nevertheless only a few studies are attempting to understand or solve this problem (Robson, 90; Sebillote, 90).

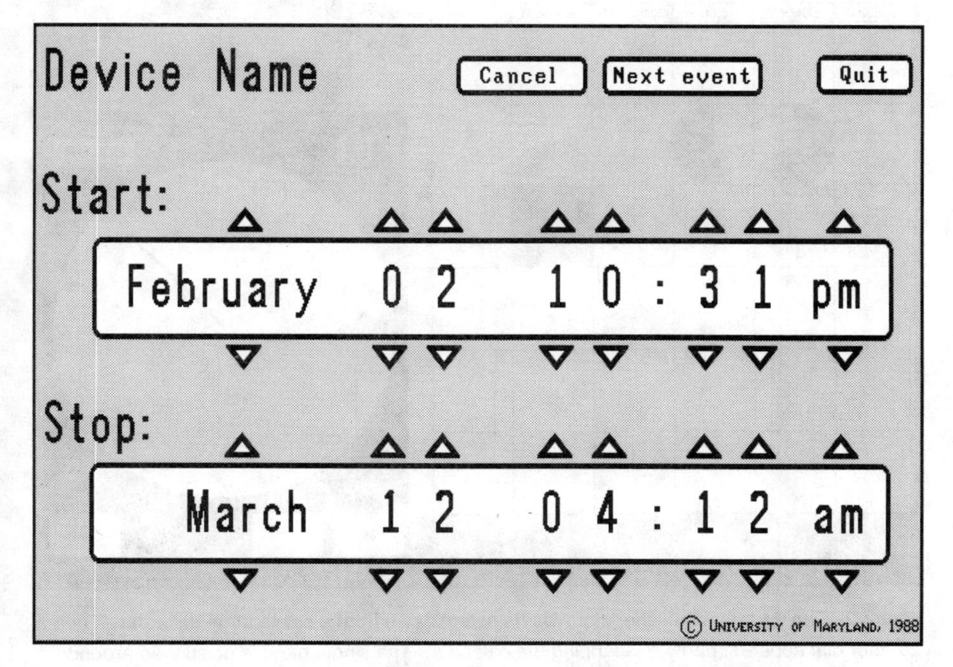

Figure 1. The digital scheduler - Each of the two textual fields indicate date and time for the start and end of the event scheduled. Up and down arrows are located respectively on top and under each digit. The default value of each digit is the median of possible values.

Our initial research goal was to raise the issues involved in designing scheduling interfaces. In our designs we tried to make the best use of direct manipulation techniques and also to take advantage of the common representation of time (calendar, clocks, etc.) We selected four designs including a digital clock scheduler (Figure 1), a dual 12-hour clock scheduler (see Figure 1 of paper 4.3, p 183), a 24-hour dial scheduler (Figure 2) and a 24-hour timeline scheduler (Figure 3).

First the four designs were compared on a feature by feature basis (Plaisant & Shneiderman, 92). For example, we compared the average number of actions required to perform various tasks and found the digital clock at a disadvantage. Because the advantages and disadvantages of the digital clock are well known and we wanted to explore novel ways to do scheduling, we prototyped only the 3 remaining designs and conducted a formative usability study (Plaisant and Shneiderman, 92) with 14 subjects to identify strengths and weaknesses of each design and verify our intuitions about potential problems. Additionally, remarks and problems encountered by about 30 reviewers were collected and taken into account. Subjects were retired volunteers and non-technical employees of the

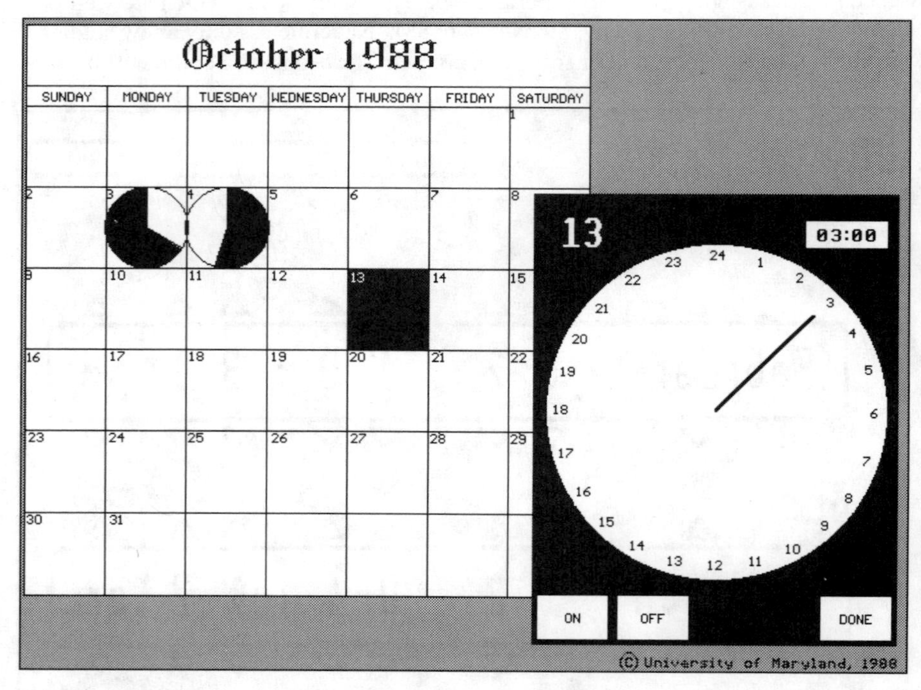

Figure 2. The 24-hour dial scheduler - Users select dates from a single large calendar. Then a 24-hour dial appears, partly overlapping the calendar. The single hand is positioned around the dial and the ON button pressed. The operation is repeated for the OFF time or DONE is pressed if another date is to be selected for the end of the event. Feedback about scheduled events is given by small dials on the calendar.

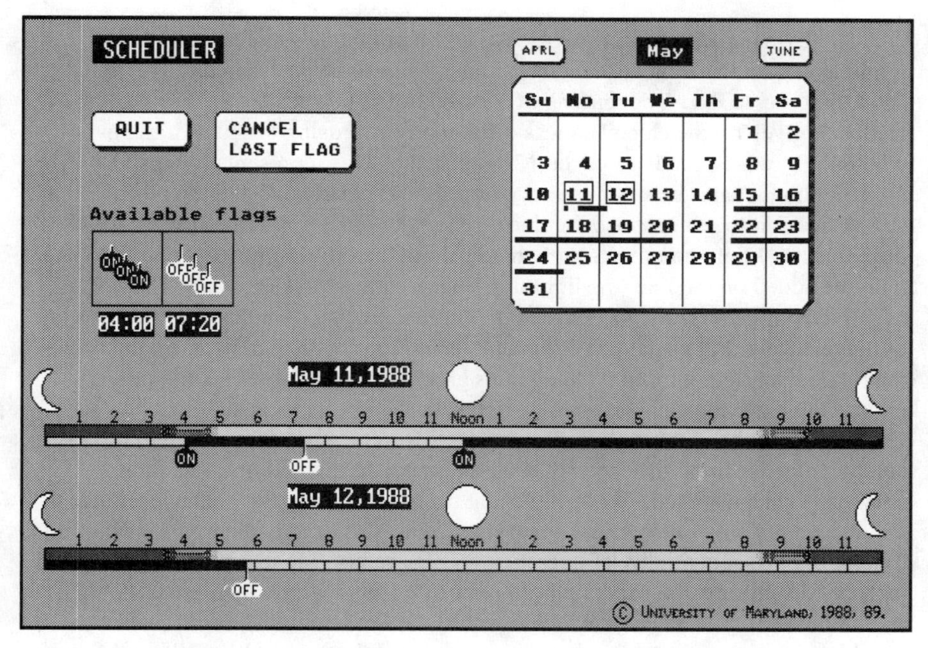

Figure 3. When a date is selected from the calendar the corresponding 24-hour timeline is displayed, along with a group of ON and OFF flags. Users can drag the appropriate flags onto the line to schedule events. The position of the flags can be adjusted or they can even be removed from the line. Red lines show the duration of the event on the line and on the calendar.

University. After a very brief demonstration, subjects were given a set of scheduling tasks to perform and used all three schedulers for a total of about an hour. Subjects were videotaped and they were asked to order the schedulers by preference and ease of use.

Summary of the usability study results

Each of these versions has its strengths and weaknesses, and the usability test showed that all three could be used by novice users. A wide range of personal preferences was observed. Each version had its defendants.

Subjects had no difficulties selecting dates even on the smaller calendar: the lift-off strategy allows a box to be shown surrounding the day currently pointed at and its location can be adjusted if necessary before lifting the finger off the screen.

Contrary to our initial expectation, the 12-hour clock was not the easier to use and was the only one with which errors occurred (when subjects forgot to set the AM/PM properly). The smooth manipulation of the clock's hands is widely appreciated but some difficulties appear when the hands are close together and the selection mechanism has to be mastered.

The 24-hour dial was felt to be easy to use but many subjects had to be reminded about the right sequencing of operations to be performed (e.g. first set the hand then press ON). The reading of a 24-hour dial (especially the pie-shaped feedback given on the calendar) was often found confusing because of the overwhelmingly widespread use of the 12-hour scale. This representation also brought up many hot debates between military time (1-24) defendants and the others.

A little bit to our surprise the linear scheduler did not present any difficulty to the subjects. Many comments were made about the information that could potentially be added on the line (daylight duration, weather forecast, etc.). The only negative comments made were about the limited precision on the line. At the time of the test we didn't use any stabilization technique for the touchscreen, therefore the flag/cursor kept jumping a few pixels around the touched point and only 10 minute intervals could be selected, which is sufficient for most devices.

The presence of the 2 lines allowed users to set events over several days with complete feedback on the screen but the existence of the 2nd line was found annoying when not used. We believe that the advantage of the linear scheduler is that it requires only one concept (operation/principle) to remember — set flags on a timeline. The sequentiality of operations is also reduced to a minimum and it even includes the editing and canceling of previous events with no increase of complexity (unlike the other schedulers which would require additional developments).

Many extensions are possible with the linear scheduler. Other types of flags can be used in addition to the ON and OFF flags (e.g., an ON-for-half-hour flag for a sprinkler, an ON-until-done flag for the pool cleaner, a do-this-everyday flag for the security system, etc., as well as scheduling a sequence of more complex actions). Many more lines could be used to allow multiple device scheduling with synchronization.

Our conclusion was that the usability testing and the number of potential extensions favored the linear scheduler. It was then selected to be included in Custom Command's home automation system, and we will now describe the steps taken to mold the prototype design into a product.

From a research prototype to an integrated product

Once the design was selected, a specification document was prepared by Custom Command in an attempt to describe the piece of software to be included in the complete system. The overall design of the scheduler was respected. Nevertheless, we identified four directions in the modifications made to the original design in order to produce the commercial product (see Figure 2 of paper 4.3, p 184):

1. Incorporation of usability testing suggestions,
2. Style consistency with the other elements of the product,
3. Compensation for minor hardware differences,
4. Adaptation to the available devices to be scheduled.

Incorporation of usability testing suggestions. Only one line was used. The touchscreen position was stabilized in order to allow more precise positioning of the flag. A precise tuning was made available by + and - arrows once the flag was dropped on the line. Other revisions were made to respect aspects forgotten in the prototype: e.g., the calendar - first object to be used - was moved to the top left.

Style consistency with the other elements of the product. Size and shape of the buttons were modified to match the ones used in other parts of the Custom Command product. The always available QUIT and BACK buttons were placed at their usual locations. The use of color and highlighting to show selectable items and their various states was done consistently with the rest of the system's interface.

Compensation for minor hardware differences. The research prototype was implemented in a very close variant of the product equipment (same graphic resolution, same type of CPU, etc.) which avoided the need for a complete redesign as is often the case when sophisticated technologies are used to do the prototyping. Nevertheless, we encountered some differences in speed and touchscreen technology when the transfer to the product environment was made. Unlike the touchscreen used in the prototype (capacitive touchscreen), the product's touchscreen is of resistive technology and requires a slightly greater pressure to be applied for a touch to be identified. Practically it means that a lift-off can be wrongly detected while dragging an object, causing users to "lose" the flag. To compensate for this problem another strategy for positioning the flag was added: it is now possible to touch the flag pile, then the destination on the line. Better touch interaction algorithms were also developed which alleviated this problem.

Adaptation to the available devices. The prototype scheduler gives a very clear feedback about the scheduled state of the device at any time. A colored line is used to mark the ON time of the devices. But practically most of the devices receiving remote commands still have direct controls on them that allow anybody to change their state at anytime without making that information available to the central system handling the scheduling database. Therefore the state shown on the line cannot be guaranteed. A new generation of appliances will soon make this two-way communication possible. Custom Command decided not to show a state that couldn't be guaranteed. Only the commands sent to the device (i.e., the flags) are shown on the line. On the calendar color dots indicate the presence of flags for the day. The research team felt this was a drawback from the original design, but it was a necessary step for the scheduler to match practical hardware limitations.

The scheduler is now installed in homes and is being used successfully. We are now eager to be able to evaluate the daily use of the scheduler in a real home environment.

Reaching out for new extensions

Two types of extensions to the scheduler prototype were made. First the use of the linear scheduler was extended to the scheduling of periodic and non-periodic events. In parallel, Custom Command has used elements of the scheduler design in

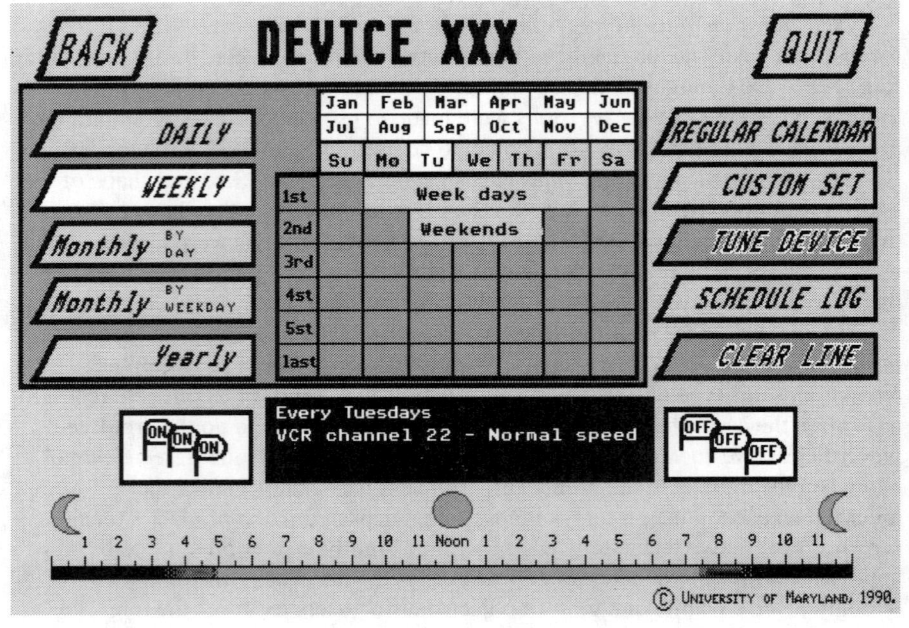

Figure 4. Periodic scheduling - Weekly schedule. The flags can be positioned on the "Every Tuesday" line.

other applications where the placement of items on a line is an effective method of representation.

Repetitive scheduling. We studied the large number of possible cases of repetitive scheduling, including periodic and non-periodic events. To allow the creation of all types of schedules and their editing implies a rather complex interface. Our approach was to select a subset of schedule types including the most common repetitive schedules and allowing a consistent interface with a relatively small menu structure.

Periodic scheduling is fairly straightforward. To be consistent with the interaction style of the original schedule, the desired period is selected first (for example, "weekly" is selected, then "Tuesday" if an event to be repeated every Tuesday is scheduled). Then a line appears, representing the selected period (e.g., every Tuesday) and flags can be moved to the line (Figure 4). Periodic flags are visible on the "Every Tuesday" line as well as on the lines of the corresponding individual days. They are graphically different than regular flags to remind users of their special status. Periodic events can be edited globally by moving them on the corresponding line (e.g., on the "every Tuesday" line), or an occurrence can be moved individually by moving the flag on the individual line (e.g., the "Tuesday October 24th" line), but in this case the periodic flag is "degraded" to a regular flag for that day which is memorized by the scheduler as an exception.

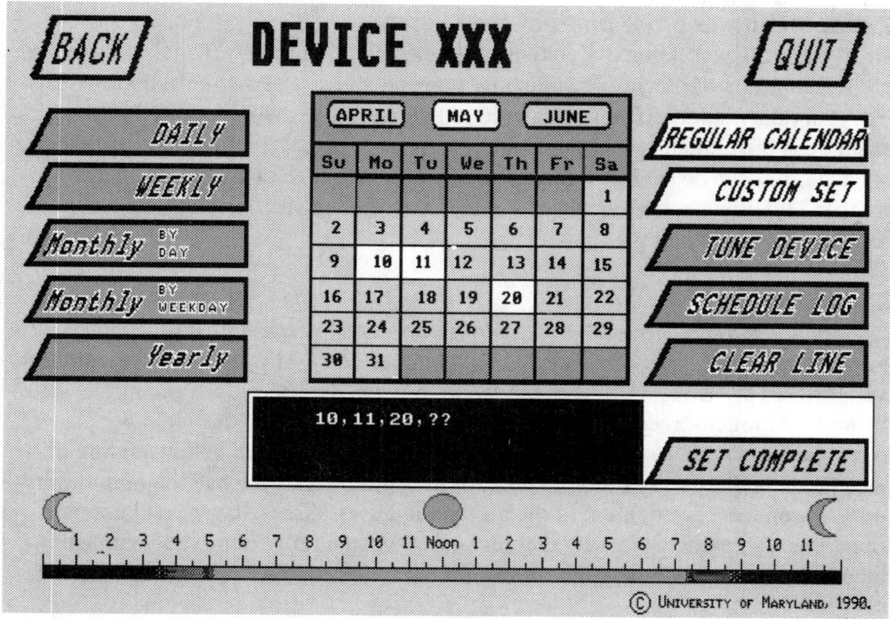

Figure 5. Repetitive scheduling - a custom set of days is being specified.

Non-periodic schedules are more complex if unlimited sets of days and periods are to be allowed for scheduling and editing. For example the scheduling of an event for the 10th, 11th and 22nd of May is done by selecting each day (Figure 5) then touching Set Complete, and placing the flags. The editing of those events requires a way to specify the set of days originally chosen. This has been done by giving a name to the set of days, which can be retrieved from a list at a later time. Even if a touch keyboard could be used without difficulty to enter a name for the set, our quest for overall structure simplicity pushed us to reject this option. Therefore, non-periodic schedules can be created (as a fast way to create multiple copies of regular flags) but they cannot be edited globally as a set.

Despite our effort to describe those functions in simple terms, the previous two paragraphs illustrate the complexity of repetitive schedules. The main difficulty for us was to decide on the level of complexity to be allowed in the user interface versus the level of flexibility offered by the system. A user interaction strategy which may be very flexible, i.e., accommodate virtually any scheduling situation, may end up being more complex and thus less satisfying than one which, say, accommodates only those situations that are most frequently used.

A prototype was made for repetitive event scheduling and Custom Command is currently implementing it in its product.

Extrapolating to other parts of the system

This is the second type of extension to the original project. To take advantage of the simplicity of placing or adjusting items on a line (and also to support consistency) similar user interfaces were used in other parts of the system. The best example is the climate control user interface. As shown in Figure 6 the temperature of each room can be set by selecting the room from a map of the house. Markers are then slid along a thermometer to indicate normal and setback temperatures for both heating and cooling.

Conclusion

About the university/corporate collaboration. We believe that this university/corporate collaboration was beneficial to both partners. The university researchers were offered a serious challenge that led to innovative designs, advancing the state-of-the-art in touchscreen applications and direct manipulation designs. We explored the advantages of multiple metaphors and refined our understanding of perceptual, cognitive, and motor skills for user interfaces. We had the opportunity to follow on the development of the product in all its phases. Custom Command found that the relationship with the university substantially improved its image in the minds of purchasers and investors. The attention to usability issues (e.g., their

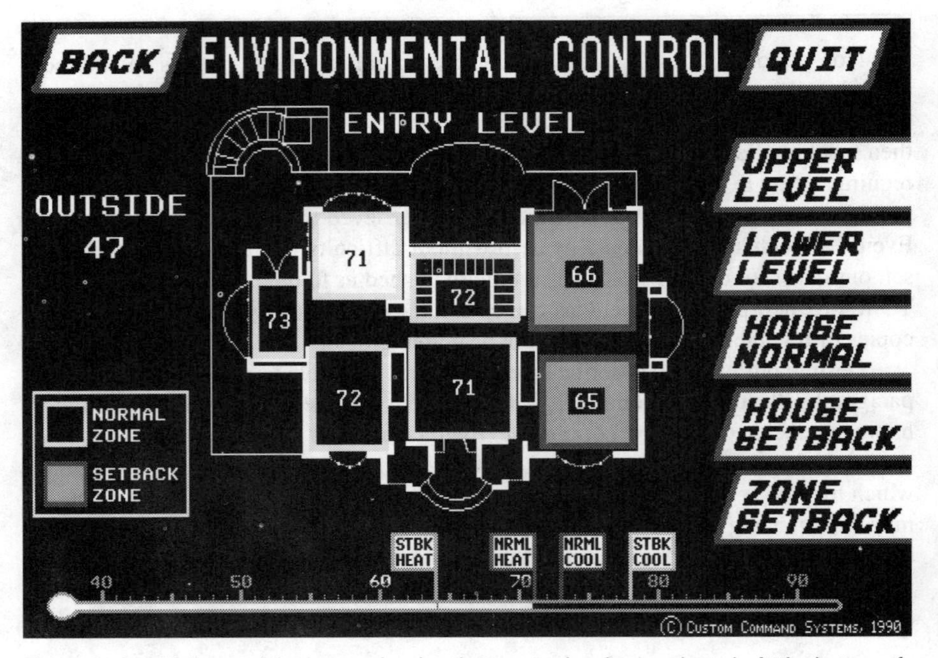

Figure 6. A partial map of the house showing that a room has been selected. At the bottom of the screen, markers can be slid on the thermometer to indicate the chosen temperatures for the room.

presentations could add a phrase such as "usability tested with elderly users") was perceived very positively.

The University of Maryland has filed for a patent on the scheduler. Custom Command's systems, including the scheduler interface, are being featured in several private homes and in home automation demonstrations sponsored by Bell Atlantic Corporation, General Electric, the Electric Power Research Institute, Pacific Gas and Electric, and the National Association of Home Builders.

For the user interface designer. We observed that intuition alone cannot be relied on in designing user interfaces that take advantage of new technologies. Some members of our design team initially believed that the linear representation of time on a "timeline" would be less acceptable to novice users than a more traditional analog clockface. However, their conjecture was not supported because the improved touchscreen interaction dynamics with the timeline approach resulted in a higher user satisfaction.

Our developments were entirely based on our conjectures of the most potentially useful functions. For example, it is interesting to observe that no data is available about the type of repetitive scheduling useful in the home. When home automation systems start to be more widely available, we will be able to better assess the needs of home-owners confronted with large numbers of electronically controlled devices and suggest useful additional features. Home-automation systems are a new challenge for user interface designers because of the diversity of potential users that have to be considered novice users as well as regular users.

As researchers we might have preferred a series of more controlled psychologically-oriented experiments with a small number of independent variables. Such experiments might produce more fundamental results and support perceptual, cognitive, and motoric theories; however, the sense of progress and insight from the usability studies was greatly encouraging. We did not demonstrate that we developed the best possible interface, but we have a great sense of confidence that we made an important step towards a breakthrough in design.

Acknowledgments

We want to thank all the members of the Human-Computer Interaction Laboratory and of Custom Command Systems for their useful suggestions. We appreciate the support of the Maryland Industrial Partnerships program in providing funding for this research.

Note: The HCIL Open House '91 Video includes two segments illustrating this work. A segment on the scheduler is also a part of the ACM CHI '91 Video.

References

Ahlström, B., Lenman, S., Marmolin, T. (1991) Overcoming touchscreen user fatigue by workplace design. Interaction and Presentation Lab., Department of Computer Science, Royal Institute of Technology, S-100 4 Stockholm, Sweden.

Beringer, D., Peterson, J. (1985) Underlying behavioral parameters of the operation of touch-input devices: biases, models, and feedback, *Human Factors* Vol. 27, No. 4, 445-458.

Beringer, D. (1989) Touch panel sampling strategies and keypad performance comparisons, *Proc. of the 33rd Annual Meeting of the Human Factors Society*, Santa Monica, CA.

Beringer, D., Bowman, M. (1989) Operator behavioral biases using high-resolution touch input devices, *Proc. of the 33rd Annual Meeting of the Human Factors Society*, Santa Monica, CA, 320-322.

Card, S., English, W., Burr, B. (1978) Evaluation of mouse, rate-controlled isometric joystick, step keys, and text keys for text selection on a CRT. *Ergonomics*, Vol. 21, 601-613.

Carroll Touch (1989) *Touch Handbook*, Round Rock, TX: Carroll Touch Inc.

Eller, T. S. (1987) Personal communication.

Grant, A. (1987) The computer user syndrome, *Journal of the American Optometric Association*, Vol. 58, 892-901.

Greenstein, J., Arnaut, L. (1988) Input devices, *Handbook of Human-Computer Interaction*, M. Helander, Ed., 495-519.

Hall, A., Cunningham, J., Roache, R., Cox, J. (1988) Factors affecting performance using touch-entry systems: Tactual recognition fields and system accuracy. *Journal of Applied Psychology*, Vol. 73, No. 4, 711-720.

Karat, J., Mcdonald, J., Anderson, M. (1986) A comparison of selection techniques: touch panel. mouse, keyboard, *International Journal of Man-Machine Studies*, Vol. 25, No. 1, 73-92.

Muratore, D. A. (1987) Human Performance Aspects of Cursor Control Devices, *MITRE Corporation Working Paper* 6321, Houston, Texas.

Murphy, R. A (1986) Evaluation of methods of touch screen implementation for interactive computer displays, Westinghouse Electric Corporation, Baltimore, Maryland.

Murphy, R. (Nov. 1987) Evaluation of methods of touch screen implementation for interactive computer displays, *The Second International Conference of Human-Computer Interaction*, Honolulu, HI.

Nemy, E. (Sept. 24, 1989) *New Yorkers, etc., The New York Times* .

Norman, D. A. (1988) *The Psychology of Everyday Things*, Basic Books, New York.

Ostroff, D. Shneiderman, B (1988) Selection devices for users of an electronic encyclopedia: An empirical comparison of four possibilities, *Information Processing and Management*

Vol. 24, No. 6, 665-680.

Pickering, J. A (1986) Touch-sensitive screens: the technologies and their application, *International Journal Man-Machine Studies*, 25 249-269.

Pittman, J. A. (May, 1991) Recognizing handwritten text, *Proc. of Human Factors in Computing Systems*, ACM Press, New York, (New Orleans) 271-273.

Plaisant, C. Shneiderman, B. (1992) Scheduling home control devices: design issues and usability evaluation of four touchscreen interfaces, *International Journal for Man-Machine Studies* 36 375-393.

Plaisant, C., Battaglia, J., Shneiderman, B. (Dec. 1990) Scheduling home-control devices: a case study of the transition from the research project to a product, *Human Factors in Practice*, 7-12. Santa-Monica, CA: Computer Systems Technical Group, Human Factors Society.

Plaisant, C., Wallace, D. (1990) Touchscreen toggle switches: push or slide? Design issues and usability study.

Potter, R.L., Weldon, L.J., Shneiderman, B. (1988) Improving the accuracy of touch screens: an experimental evaluation of three strategies, *Proc. of the Conference on Human Factors in Computing Systems* (CHI 88), 27-32.

Potter, R., Berman, M., Shneiderman, B. (1989) An experimental evaluation of three touch screen strategies within a Hyperties database, *International Journal of Human-Computer Interaction*, 1, 1, 41-52.

Robson, J. (1990) Applying direct manipulation techniques to video cassette recorders (VCR's), Getting good human factors into fashionable boxes, *Contemporary Ergonomics*, E.J. Lovesey, Ed., Taylor and Francis Publ.

Sears, A., Plaisant, C. Shneiderman, B. (1992) A new era for high-precision touchscreens, *Advances in Human-Computer Interaction*, Vol. 3, Hartson, R. & Hix D. Eds., Ablex Publ., NJ, 1-33.

Sears, A., Shneiderman, B. (1991) High precision touchscreens: design strategies and comparisons with a mouse, *International Journal of Man-Machine Interaction* Vol. 34, No. 4, 593-613.

Sears, A., Plaisant, C. (Oct. 1992) Touchscreen interfaces for flexible alphanumeric data entry, *Proc. of the Human Factors Society-36th Annual Meeting,* 293-297.

Sears, A., Revis, D., Swatski, J., Crittenden, R., Shneiderman, B. (1992) Investigating Touchscreen Typing: The effect of keyboard size on typing speed. *Behaviour & Information Technology*. Vol. 12, No. 1, 17-22.

Sears, A. (1991) Improving touchscreen keyboards: design issues and a comparison with other devices, *Interacting with Computers*, Vol. 3, Vol. 3, 253-269.

Sebillote, S. (1990) Action representation for home automation, *Human-Computer Interaction - Interact '90,* Diaper D. et al. Eds., North Holland Publ.

Sherr, S. (1988) *Input Devices*, San Diego, CA: Academic Press.

Shneiderman, B. (1987) *Designing the User Interface: Strategies for Effective Human-Computer Interaction*, Addison-Wesley, Reading, MA.

Shneiderman, B. (March 1991) Touch screens now offer compelling uses, *IEEE Software* Vol. 8, Vol. 2, 93-94, 107.

Smith, R.L. (1988)*Smart House - The Coming Revolution in Housing*, GP Publishing, Inc., Columbia, MD, USA.

Stone, M. D. (Aug. 1987) Touch-Screens for intuitive Input, *PC Magazine*,183.

Time.Magazine, Boosting your home's IQ (Jan. 1989)

Weisner, S. (Oct. 1988) A touch-only interface for a medical monitor, *Proc. of the Human Factors Society — 32nd Annual Meeting*, 435-439.

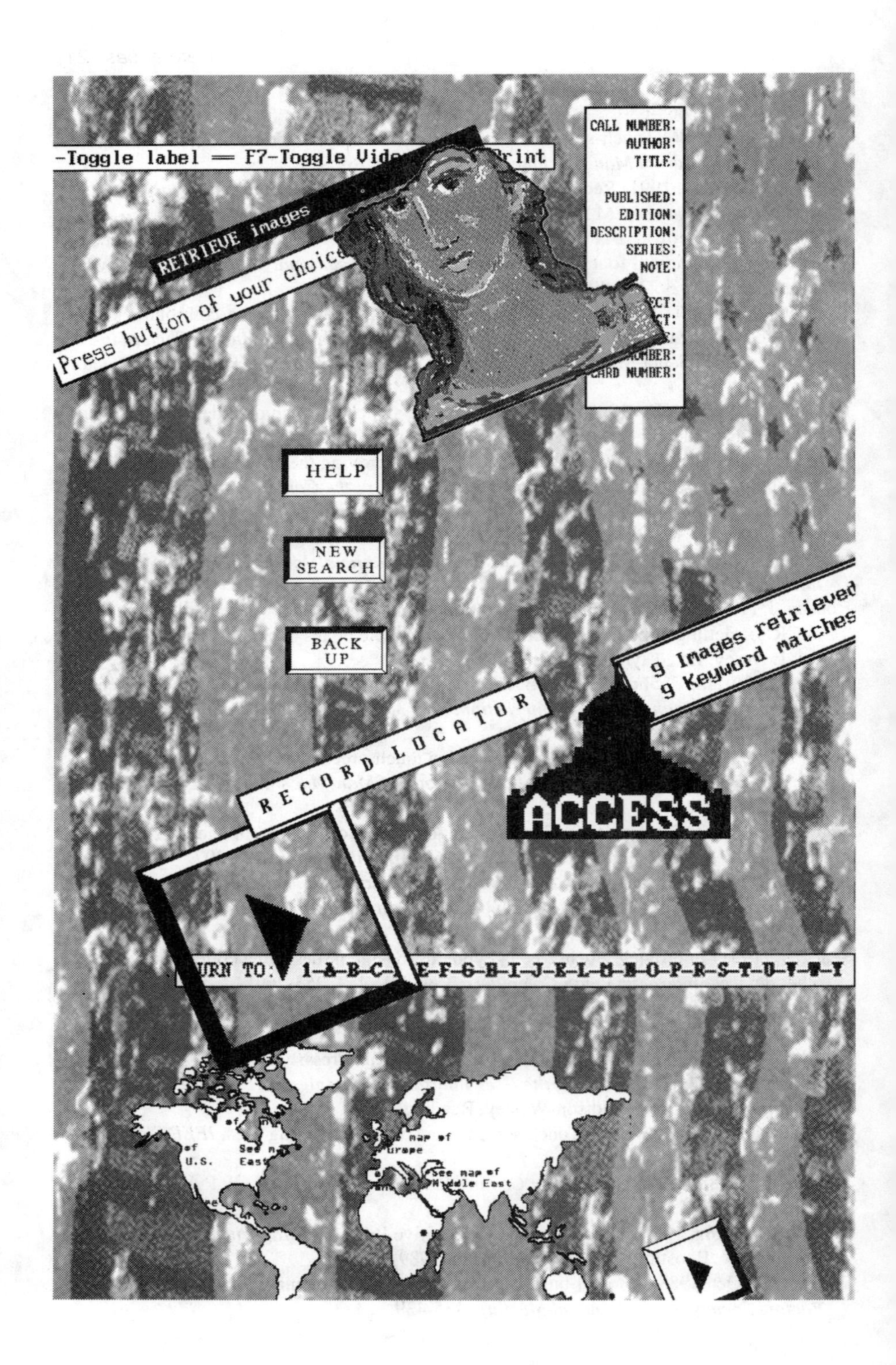

-Toggle label = F7-Toggle Vide Print
RETRIEVE images
Press button of your choice
CALL NUMBER:
AUTHOR:
TITLE:
PUBLISHED:
EDITION:
DESCRIPTION:
SERIES:
NOTE:
CARD NUMBER:
HELP
NEW SEARCH
BACK UP
9 Images retrieved
9 Keyword matches
RECORD LOCATOR
ACCESS
See map of Europe
See map of Middle East

Sparks of Innovation in Human-Computer Interaction,
B. Shneiderman, Ed., Ablex Publ., Norwood, NJ (1993)

HCIL

5. Public access

Introduction

Designing systems for experienced users, such as programmers or air traffic controllers, is demanding because these users know what they want, expect a lot, and complain when they are unsatisfied. By contrast, designing for museum kiosks or other public access situations is demanding because the users have little idea of what to expect, their information needs are poorly formed, and instead of complaining about the system they feel guilty for their inability to use the system. The goal is "zero-trial learning" in which the users walk up and start using the system successfully, without training. This means that the first screen, and every successive screen, must be comprehensible to a variety of users with differing levels of experience with computers, knowledge of the task domain, motivation, command of English, and physical abilities.

There is no single secret, but we have gained some useful experiences about the process and product. Development of a successful public access application requires a clear and simple goal that can be expressed in a few words: Guide to Opportunities in Volunteer Archaeology, Library of Congress Online Catalog, National Library of Medicine Microanatomy Videodisk Database, or Introduction to the Computer Science Department. The first screen is critical and it has to function as an attention-getter plus instruction for getting started. After the users get started, they need recognizable landmarks (such as the traditional Main Menu) that they can always get back to, clear affordances indicating what they can do, consistent design to help speed comprehension, the security that comes when every action is reversible, and the safety of knowing that they cannot break the machine, get stuck, or get lost.

The hypertext database on the Guide to Opportunities in Volunteer Archaeology was installed in March 1988 at the Smithsonian Institution's National Museum of Natural History in connection with the exhibit "King Herod's Dream" (described in the Introduction to section 3; in paper 5.1, Plaisant, 1991; and in paper 5.2, Shneiderman, Brethauer, Plaisant & Potter, 1989).

Our collaboration with the Library of Congress was directed at installing 18 touchscreen computers to support first time user access to the Library of Congress Information System (see paper 5.3, written especially for this book). This ambitious venture took two years but resulted in a successful system that is used daily by hundreds of visitors. This joint effort involved Gary Marchionini, Kent Norman, Ben Shneiderman, and Charles Kreitzberg (of Cognetics Corp.). It gives me great satisfaction to visit the beautiful old Library of Congress Jefferson Building, pass through the high-domed Main Reading Room and enter the Computerized Catalog Center where dozens of patrons are using the products of our work.

Our work for the National Library of Medicine Microanatomy Videodisk Database was a different challenge. We were given an existing system and asked to critique and possibly redesign it. Our analysis showed inconsistent layout, colors, usage of terms, choice of function keys, etc. and we delivered complete screen designs for a revision. To our delight, Daniel Masys of NLM quickly engineered the changes and then returned with a further challenge: could we prove that the changes we suggested would make a difference in performance and subjective satisfaction? It is rare to get such a chance and we went about the job eagerly, but with some doubts too. The results of our study (see paper 5.4, published for the first time in this book) were supportive of our position: consistency does matter in performance and in satisfaction!

One innovative project that we spawned but turned over to Cognetics Corporation was the construction of an electronic message board for use at a large annual international banking conference. Three previous attempts with keyboards had been disasters, but Cognetics' touchscreen design proved to be successful and has been used for three years in a row. Delegates can put their registration badges through the reader and get a list of their messages. A single touch brings up the image of the handwritten message at any of the seven kiosks located in the hotel and conference center. Replies are written on slips of paper, business cards, or maps in any language and then scanned by the TV camera.

Our experiences have been largely with museums, libraries, and universities, but we believe that what we have learned applies in shopping malls, sports stores, banks, doctors' offices, airports, office building lobbies, phone booths, or post offices. The work on menu selection, hypertext, and touchscreens is directly relevant to public access system design. We believe that there will be a large expansion in public access computer facilities because of improved and lower priced hardware, but also because designers are learning how to create effective user interfaces.

Sparks of Innovation in Human-Computer Interaction,
B. Shneiderman, Ed., Ablex Publ., Norwood, NJ (1993)

HCIL

5.1 Guide to Opportunities in Volunteer Archaeology: case study on the use of a hypertext system in a museum exhibit

Catherine Plaisant

Introduction

This case study describes the steps of the birth and traveling life of GOVA, the Guide to Opportunities in Volunteer Archaeology, and demonstrates that such an adventure can be successful without being burdensome. The database was constructed by the professors and students at the University of Maryland History Department. Regular updates of the database were made for each new venue of the exhibit. Finally the database was translated into French for use in Canada. System users were observed in the museum and usage data were collected and analyzed. Helpful features of the hypertext system as well as the difficulties encountered are described here.

Hypertext/Hypermedia Handbook, Berk E. & Devlin, J. Eds., McGraw-Hill Publ. (1991) 498-505

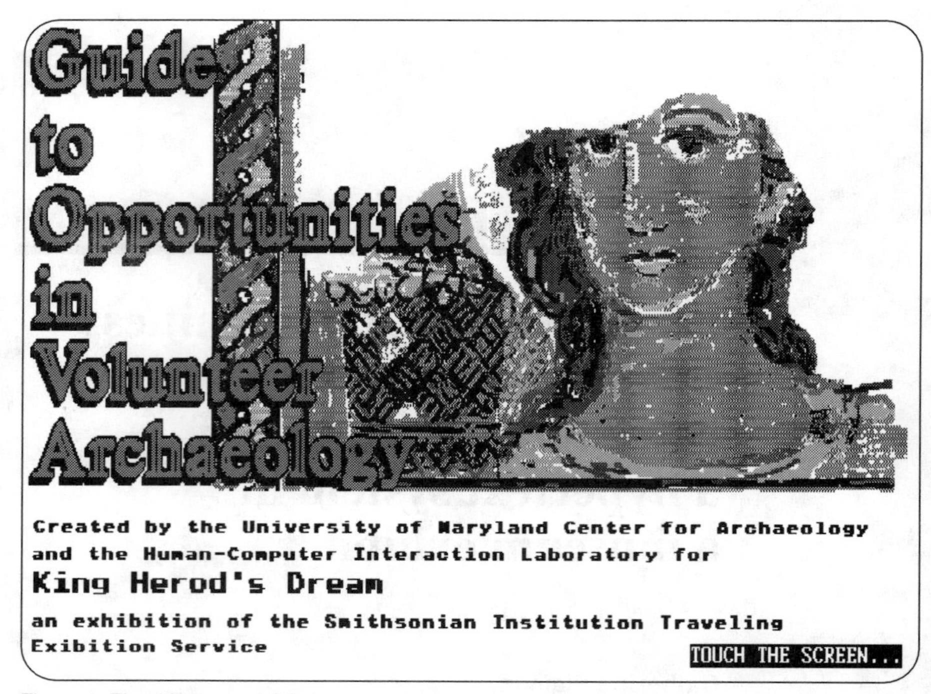

Figure 1. The title page of GOVA.

In the summer of 1987, Professor Ken Holum of the University of Maryland History Department approached the Human-Computer Interaction Laboratory for help in developing a hypertext application for a museum exhibit to open the following spring. Thus began a two-year collaboration between the two groups, which allowed us to test Hyperties (Hypertext Interactive Encyclopedia System) (Shneiderman, et al., 1989) in the "real world".

The exhibit was organized by the Smithsonian Institution Traveling Exhibition Service. It opened in Washington, DC, March, 1988 at the National Museum of Natural History, then traveled to five museums for the next two years (Los Angeles, Denver, Minneapolis-St. Paul, Boston and Ottawa.)

The museum exhibit

Two freestanding podiums were installed in the final chamber of the exhibit on "King Herod's Dream". This exhibit was about the ancient Roman port city of Caesarea located on the shores of what is now modern-day Israel. It focused on the rise of urbanism in ancient times and the archaeological methods used during the past 20 years of excavation (Holum, 1988; Holum, et al., 1988). This last station of the exhibit invited visitors to learn more about the archeological sites around the world that welcome volunteers, and about how to join such a dig.

The two custom made podiums housed IBM PC-AT computers. The EGA monitors, each equipped with a Microtouch touchscreen, were at about waist level and tilted at a 45 degree angle to the horizon. The only permanent instruction on each podium was "Touch the screen" written above the monitor. No keyboards were provided.

The database

The GOVA database was developed under the direction of Ken Holum. It consists of about 200 articles. The contents include information about archaeological digs (Figure 2) taking place around the world, descriptions of historical periods, and practical suggestions about how to join a dig.

A special effort was made to cover the local sites near each current exhibiting museum. The archaeological sites are organized both geographically and by historical periods. The information can also be accessed by direct selection on 11 maps (Figures 3 and 4).

The initial database was constructed in a relatively short period of time. Between two and three person-months were necessary to collect information about the digs, structure the information, write each article following a predetermined style, and mark the links. Each author used whatever text editor he or she was most

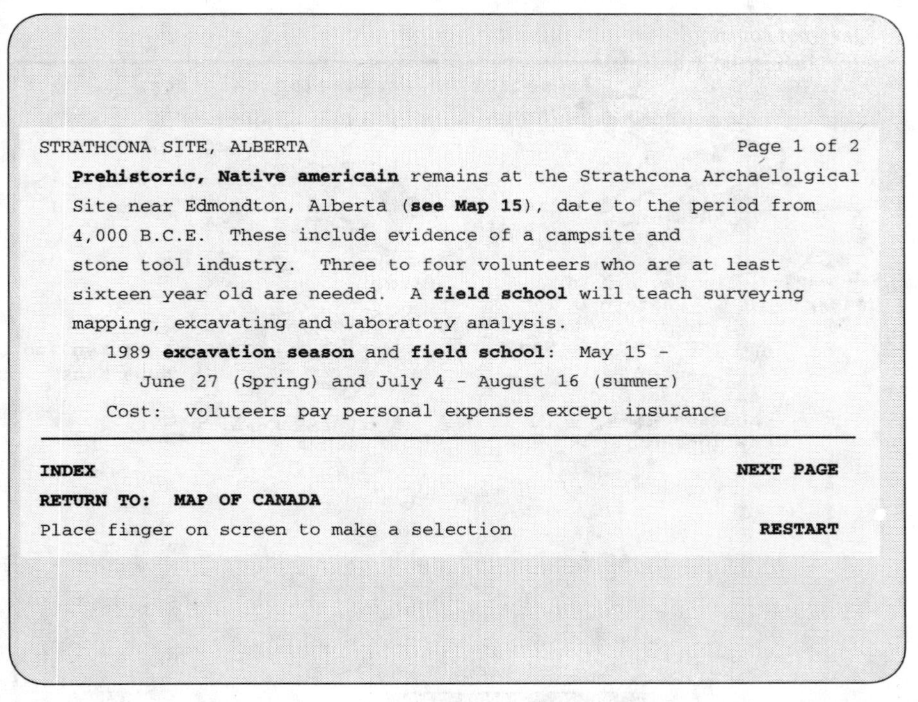

STRATHCONA SITE, ALBERTA
Page 1 of 2
Prehistoric, Native americain remains at the Strathcona Archaelolgical Site near Edmondton, Alberta (**see Map 15**), date to the period from 4,000 B.C.E. These include evidence of a campsite and stone tool industry. Three to four volunteers who are at least sixteen year old are needed. A **field school** will teach surveying mapping, excavating and laboratory analysis.
1989 **excavation season** and **field school**: May 15 - June 27 (Spring) and July 4 - August 16 (summer)
Cost: voluteers pay personal expenses except insurance
INDEX
NEXT PAGE
RETURN TO: MAP OF CANADA
Place finger on screen to make a selection
RESTART

Figure 2. Page 1 of 2 of the article giving information on the archaeological site of Strathcona in Canada. Each blue word (bold in this book) is selectable.

familiar with to accomplish this task. Graphic artist Karen Norman prepared the maps and created three graphic screens (an example of which is seen in Figure 1). Then about two weeks of work was necessary to build the database in the computer (import articles, adjust their formatting, verify the links in the text and create the graphic links). As expected -- as it probably should be -- the initial writing itself was found to be the most important and time consuming task. Most of the help given by the Human-Computer Interaction Laboratory team had to do with the use of DOS and of the package used to create the graphics. Hyperties was easily learned by the History Department team.

The browser

We used a version of Hyperties which supported the use of a touchscreen as our input device, automatic restart after a period of inactivity at the computer, and the automatic logging of usage data. The museum patrons merely touched highlighted words on the screen to see a linked article.

Blue highlighting indicates the selectable items in both text as well as maps. Users receive feedback about the exact touch position by a cursor just above their fingers. When the cursor is on a selectable item, the area is highlighted. The selection is activated when users lift their fingers from the screen. This method produces low error rates and high user satisfaction (Potter, et.al., 1988).

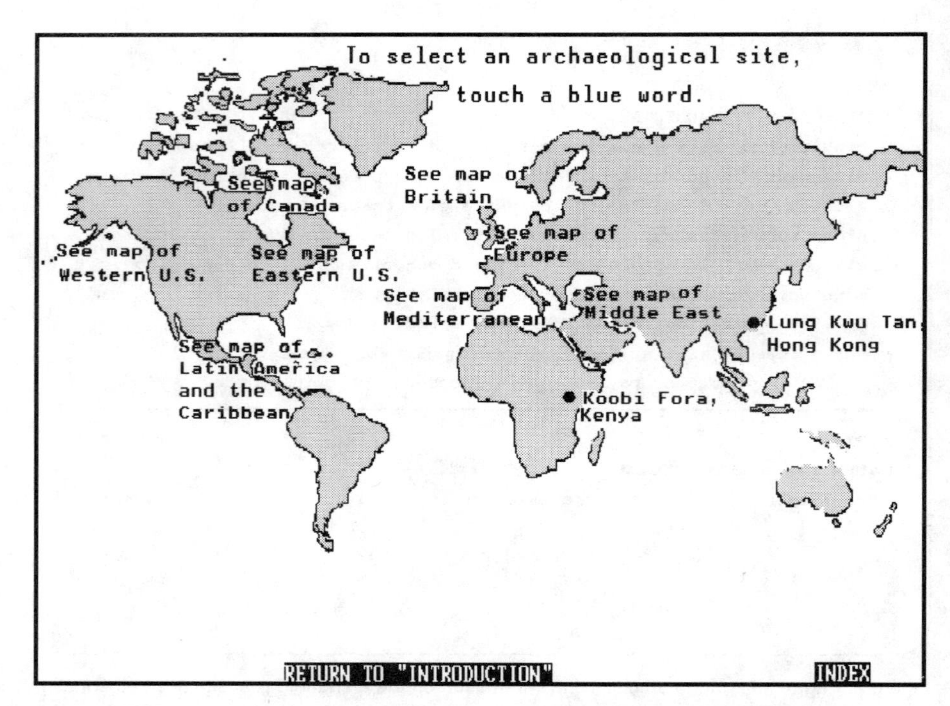

Figure 3. The world map allows patrons to select a geographical area of interest.

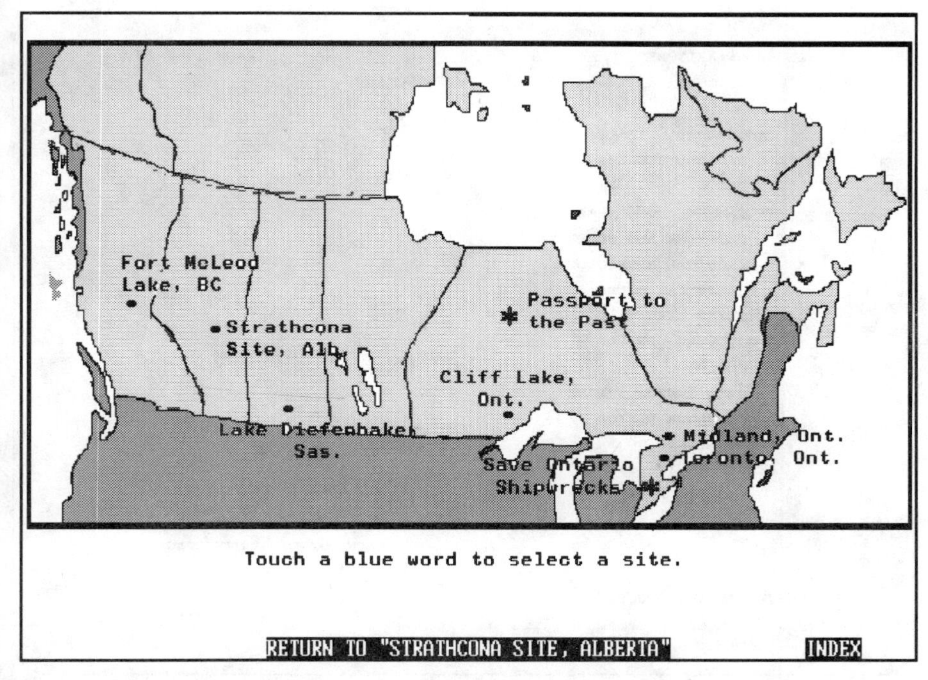

Figure 4. The map of Canada allows users to select an archeological site in Canada by pointing to a spot on the map with their fingers.

Data collection and observations in the museum

Data on the articles accessed, the time spent in each article, the number of times the index was accessed, etc. were collected from a total of about 4500 sessions while the exhibit was in Washington, DC. Results show that visitors used the links embedded within the articles of the hyperdocument more than the traditional index.

Article selection appeared to reflect anticipated interests of patrons suggesting they were able to successfully navigate the database (patrons exhibited a pronounced tendency to ask for information about local sites even though information pertaining to local sites was neither the focus nor the front end of the database) (Shneiderman, et al., 1989).

The data collection was complemented by direct observation and interviews of the museum patrons. Three observers spent 4 sessions of about 2 hours each at the exhibit, observing and discussing three potential problems: the touchscreen interface, the Hyperties mechanism and the database structure. Each session allowed us to pick out the weaknesses of the application and put in place a productive mechanism of criticism and modification between laboratory and museum. This double approach (usage data collection and direct observation) appeared to be appropriate for improving the user interface and database structure and guarantee-

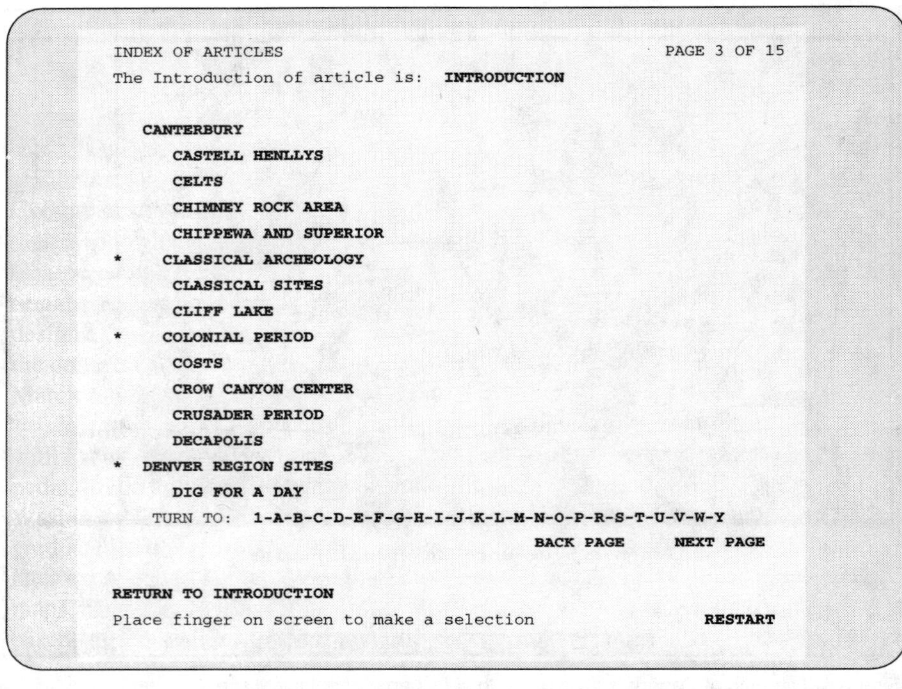

Figure 5. This is page 3 of 15 of the index. It provides direct access to all the articles of the database.

ing the usability of the system (Shneiderman, et al., 1989). Most of the patrons were able to traverse smoothly from article to article and focus on their reading and not on the navigation mechanism.

The process of regular revisions of the database

For each new venue of the exhibit, the database was updated to show the current archeological digs and also to emphasize the sites local to the museum area. The authors of the database found that making these revisions were facilitated by the simple, yet powerful, Hyperties authoring tool. The alphabetical index of articles was highly appreciated when revising an already existing database. Additionally, the browser guarantees that no invalid links (therefore no error messages) are presented to readers, allowing authors to simply remove outdated information without danger.

Updating of maps was the most time-consuming task. The authors of the database expressed the need for a tool for handling lists of topics (e.g., list of sites per area or per period of the past). Some assistance in the maintenance of the overall structure would probably also be useful. For example, using newly developed tools (Botafogo, 1990), we found several structure anomalies in the fifth version of the database revised two years after the original writing (e.g., some articles could not be reached other than by the index).

A language translation

For the last stop of the traveling exhibit, in Ottawa, Canada, the database was translated in French and the browser modified to handle the two languages. The translation was performed from a printed copy of the database by a team in Canada.

Links in Hyperties are embedded in nodes. A Hyperties link is marked by a pair of tildes surrounding a word or group of words to be highlighted. Therefore, translators were instructed to leave the tildes in the French text just as they appeared in the English. Translators also retained the formatting commands (e.g., @p for next paragraph).

The French text was then automatically imported by the author tool. Most of the links were resolved directly by the authoring tool, and a French-speaking person then verified the accuracy of the links. Most of the human intervention involved assigning synonyms to counteract the human translation variations and fixing instances where the authoring tool didn't handle the accentuated vowels in the article titles properly. Changes to graphics had to be handled manually. A few changes were made to the browser: very few messages and command names changed, and an introduction allowed users to choose which language they wanted to use.

Conclusions

This hypertext system was used successfully for two years. Patrons were able to traverse the database and find information related to their own interests. We depended on direct observation in museums to identify problems and successes, and patron-suggested improvements were made in the first two weeks of operation.

The authors of the database were able to easily update the content and the structure of the database over the two-year duration of the exhibit. The translation process was made easier by the textual representation of the links and the automatic reconstruction of the database.

Acknowledgments

Ben Shneiderman, Professor of Computer Science and Richard Potter, graduate student of the laboratory, were major participants in the development and evaluation of GOVA. Professor Ken Holum initiated the project and actively directed the writing of the database, assisted by Diane Everman. Rodrigo Botafogo created the graphic tools used with Hyperties. We greatly appreciate the cooperation of Myriam Springuel of the Smithsonian Institution.

Sparks of Innovation in Human-Computer Interaction,
B. Shneiderman, Ed., Ablex Publ., Norwood, NJ (1993)

5.2 Evaluating three museum installations of a hypertext system

Ben Shneiderman
Dorothy Brethauer
Catherine Plaisant
Richard Potter

This study explores the use of a hypertext system by patrons of three museums. Data on the articles accessed, the time spent in each, the number of times the index was accessed, etc., were collected from a total of more than 5000 sessions. Results show that visitors at all three museums used the embedded menus of the Hyperties hypertext system in moving from one article to another far more than the traditional index. Article selection appears to reflect anticipated interests of patrons at each museum suggesting success in traversing the database. At the third museum, the data collection was complemented by direct observation and interviews of the museum patrons. This approach appears to be more appropriate to analyze the usage data, as well as to improve the user interface and database structure.

Journal of the American Society for Information Science, Vol. 40, No. 3, 172-182.

Introduction

Interactive databases have been widely used in settings such as business offices, airline reservation counters, libraries and supermarkets for the purpose of storing, retrieving, and manipulating data. The use of databases for browsing and educational purposes is less common, and research on the use of interactive databases in museums is nonexistent. This paper describes a study of Hyperties, an interactive encyclopedia system, in three museum settings.

Hyperties was developed at the University of Maryland for use by novices in a museum and other environments. It is a software tool for constructing and reading a database composed of articles containing text and pictures on a given topic (Shneiderman, 1987). Such hypertext systems (Conklin, 1987) have become popular, especially since the recent development of Apple's HyperCard.

Within each Hyperties article certain words and phrases, determined by the author of the database, appear in color or boldface. When selected (by using arrow keys, a mouse, or a touchscreen), a brief definition of the word or phrase appears near the bottom of the screen. The reader can then select a FULL ARTICLE on the topic. The goal of the database author is to create logical links between articles so that readers can progress from one to another in a natural manner and according to personal interests. At all times the user has the option of selecting NEXT PAGE, BACK PAGE, RETURN TO (previous article), or INDEX (See Figure 1).

One aim of designers of systems such as Hyperties is to facilitate browsing and information retrieval by novices. In over twenty experiments at the University of Maryland, student volunteers have generally needed little or no instruction. In a museum setting, however, patrons may have a broader range of backgrounds, abilities, and expectations (Marchionini & Shneiderman, 1988). This study was done to determine how readily museum visitors would use Hyperties and to see whether they would exploit the hypertext feature, as opposed to using the index, in moving from one article to the next. In related studies (Wang et al., 1988), library science students used the index more than 80% of the time and only exploited the embedded menus after gaining familiarity with the system.

At least one study (Young, 1987) has explored how users of an online help facility locate information when given the choice of several methods, such as reading a more general article versus doing a string search for a particular word or phrase or reading a specific article about the topic. It appeared that new users tended to read the more general articles and performed string searches while expert users immediately read specific articles. It is difficult to generalize such results to our study, however, as Hyperties had no "string search" feature at the time of these studies.

This evaluation of Hyperties utilization in three museum settings is divided into two parts. In Part I, a common database was used in two different museums and only quantitative data was logged by the computer. In Part II of the evaluation at a third museum, we used a different database and were able to couple direct observations of patrons with more detailed log data.

```
Chim—an overview                         PAGE 1 OF 2

David Seymour (1911-1956), known to his friends as "Chim", applied
his
skilled hand, warm heart, and perceptive eye to photographing
poignant
and dramatic events of the 20th century. Chim's photographs have
appeared in many magazine articles, books, and exhibits, and a
number
of memorials have been dedicated to his memory. His photographs of
famous personalities of the 20th century are widely known.
  This exhibit "David Seymour 'Chim' The Early Years 1933-1939"
will remain on view at the International Center of Photography
through January 1987.
_______________________________________________
BOOKS WITH DAVID SEYMOUR'S PHOTOS - a description of books
containing photographs taken by David Seymour

FULL ARTICLE ON BOOKS WITH DAVID SEYMOUR'S PHOTOS
NEXT PAGE          RETURN TO CAPA, ROBERT          INDEX
```

Figure 1. This screen shows the first page of the Introduction article used at the International Center of Photography in New York. The bold items were selectable by pressing the left and right arrow keys to move a selector box. The selector box is now resting on the word **books** and the brief definition for the referenced article appears on the lower part of the screen. The user can now select the full article, turn to the next page, return to the previously read article, or choose the index. The back page command appears on the screen only when the reader has gone on to the second page of an article.

Part I - Log data only

The museums:

B'nai B'rith Klutznick Museum (BBK)

The B'nai B'rith Klutznick Museum is a well-established but modest-sized museum in downtown Washington, DC. Typical attendance is 150 people per day. The exhibit "Chim: Photographs by David Seymour" occupied one gallery of the museum from May to November 1986. A specially built painted wood cabinet housing an IBM PC-XT computer was situated across from the entrance to the gallery, behind a freestanding partition that held exhibit materials. The monochrome monitor was at eye level for a seated person, and three chairs were provided. The keyboard was covered by a clear plexiglass plate with holes punched in it to allow users to press the left and right arrow keys and the RETURN key. A silk-screened plexiglass label was attached with brief instructions.

International Center of Photography (ICP)

The International Center of Photography is a 14-year-old museum located on upper Fifth Avenue in New York City. Typical attendance is 400 people per day. The exhibit "David Seymour 'Chim' the Early Years 1933-1939" was on display at the ICP from November 1986 to January 1987. An elegantly fashioned freestanding podium that housed an IBM PC-XT computer was installed near the gallery's center. The monitor was at about waist level at a 45 degree angle for comfortable viewing while standing up. The sturdy podium enabled viewers to rest their arms or elbows while viewing the CGA monitor. A wooden plate completely covered the keyboard. The arrow and RETURN keys were manipulated by pressing wooden pegs that protruded from holes in the plate and rested on the keys below.

The databases

The databases used at both museums were entitled "David Seymour: Chim" by Jeremy Symington, and consisted of 26 and 30 articles at BBK and ICP, respectively. The screen in Figure 2 was displayed on the monitor when the database was not in use. The index (here an alphabetical list of the article titles) is shown in Figure 3. Articles were from 1 to 8 screens long, some single and others double spaced, according to author preferences.

The INTRODUCTION article gave an overview to the topics and included highlighted references to key articles. The contents included information about David Seymour's life, including a time-line of his accomplishments, the exhibit, the host museum, related photographers, and various testimonials.

DAVID SEYMOUR: CHIM
edited by Jeremy Symington

You can learn more about David Seymour by reading
articles on this computer. Move the blue highlight
from yellow word to yellow word by pressing the left
or right arrow keys. Then, to select the word in
blue highlights, press the ENTER key.

Figure 2. The title page seen by visitors at the ICP museum. A silk-screened plexiglass note with instructions for use was pasted to the cabinet at the BBK. The instructions were slightly different because the monitor was monochrome at the BBK.

INDEX OF ARTICLES Starting index entry 1 out of 26
INTRODUCTION: CHIM—AN OVERVIEW

Article	Accesses
1. ARTICLES ABOUT DAVID SEYMOUR	32
2. B'NAI B'RITH KLUTZNICK MUSEUM HISTORY	54
3. B'NAI B'RITH KLUTZNICK MUSEUM OVERVIEW	40
4. BISCHOF, WERNER	9
5. BOOKS WITH DAVID SEYMOUR'S PHOTOS	28
6. CAPA, CORNELL	14
7. CAPA, ROBERT	18
8. CARTIER-BRESSON, HENRI	33
9. CHIM— AN OVERVIEW	490
10. CHIM: PHOTOGRAPHS BY DAVID SEYMOUR (1911-1956)	0
11. CHRONOLOGY OF DAVID SEYMOUR'S LIFE	30
12. EXHIBITS WITH DAVID SEYMOUR'S WORK	20
13. HAAS, ERNST	10
14. INTERNATIONAL CENTER OF PHOTOGRAPHY	31
15. ISRAEL	117

(Second screen of index)

Article	Accesses
16. MAGNUM PHOTOS	32
17. MEMORIALS IN DAVID SEYMOUR'S HONOR	10
18. NEWSWEEK'S TRIBUTE TO CHIM	13
19. PERMANENT COLLECTIONS OF DAVID SEYMOUR'S WORK	1
20. PERSONALITIES PHOTOGRAPHED BY DAVID SEYMOUR	50
21. QUOTATIONS ABOUT DAVID SEYMOUR	38
22. RODGER, GEORGE	2
23. SEYMOUR, DAVID	55
24. SHNEIDERMAN, EILEEN	26
25. SPANISH CIVIL WAR	33
26. VANDIVERT, WILLIAM	12

Figure 3a. Index for BBK database with total number of accesses for each article.

INDEX OF ARTICLES Starting index entry 1 out of 30

INTRODUCTION: CHIM—AN OVERVIEW

1. ARTICLES ABOUT DAVID SEYMOUR	48
2. BISCHOF, WERNER	21
3. BOOKS WITH DAVID SEYMOUR'S PHOTOS	26
4. CAPA, CORNELL	52
5. CAPA, ROBERT	112
6. CARTIER-BRESSON, HENRI	93
7. CHIM, A MAN OF PEACE	74
8. CHIM, A MAN OF PEACE: PART 2	22
9. CHIM— AN OVERVIEW	551
10. CHRONOLOGY OF DAVID SEYMOUR'S LIFE	71
11. DAVID SEYMOUR 'CHIM' THE EARLY YEARS 1933-1939	45
12. EXHIBITS WITH DAVID SEYMOUR'S WORK	12
13. ICP'S BROAD RANGE OF PROGRAMS	48
14. ICP/MIDTOWN	74
15. INTERNATIONAL CENTER OF PHOTOGRAPHY	157

(Second screen of index)

16. ISRAEL	47
17. MAGNUM PHOTOS	72
18. MEMORIALS IN DAVID SEYMOUR'S HONOR	13
19. NEWSWEEK'S TRIBUTE TO CHIM	14
20. PERMANENT COLLECTIONS OF DAVID SEYMOUR'S WORK	11
21. PERSONALITIES PHOTOGRAPHED BY DAVID SEYMOUR	75
22. PHILLIPS, CHRISTOPHER	12
23. QUOTATIONS ABOUT DAVID SEYMOUR	57
24. REGARDS MAGAZINE	18
25. RODGER, GEORGE	15
26. SEYMOUR, DAVID	168
27. SHNEIDERMAN, EILEEN	49
28. SPANISH CIVIL WAR	44
29. TARO, GERDA	39
30. VANDIVERT, WILLIAM	28

Figure 3b. Index for ICP database with total number of accesses for each article.

Data collection

The computer automatically recorded the time at which each session began, the name of each article accessed, and the number of seconds spent in each article.

Index accesses were also recorded, but the time spent in the index was not. If the user did not execute a QUIT command at the end of a session, the screen reverted to the title page after 5 minutes of inactivity, and a "timed out" message was stored in the data for the last article.

Results

Data from 373 sessions at BBK and 361 sessions at ICP were recorded and analyzed. The data included:

Non-Article-Specific Data:

- Articles per session: the number of articles accessed during one session (index accesses were not counted).
- Index accesses per session: the number of times the index was accessed during one session, excluding any access just prior to the end of the session, since such an access was necessary to execute the QUIT command.
- Articles read per index access: Average number of articles read per session divided by average number of index accesses per session.
- Duration of session: the sum of the time spent in each article for which a valid time value had been recorded. In sessions that were "abandoned" the time for the last article was not included.
- Percentage of sessions abandoned: the proportion of sessions not terminated by a QUIT command.
- Average time per article: the sum of all time values recorded divided by the number of articles from which the time values were obtained (last articles of abandoned sessions ignored).
- Corrected duration: the duration of a session plus the average time per article for each article whose time value was not included in duration.

Figures 4-7 show the frequency distribution for key data items at each museum. The average length of a session was slightly more than 2 minutes at BBK and approximately 6 minutes at ICP. The average number of articles accessed per session was 3.2 at BBK and 5.7 at ICP. This difference may reflect the differing interest of the museum patrons or their skill with computers. The average time spent in each article was approximately 41 seconds at BBK and 64 seconds at ICP. We assume that the greater persistence of ICP visitors reflects a different profile of usage. 47% of the sessions at BBK were abandoned, compared to 39% of the sessions at ICP. Articles read per index access was similar for the two museums. NOTE: 8 sessions were not included in the above analysis (7 at BBK and 1 at ICP) because they consisted of one INDEX access (no articles were read).

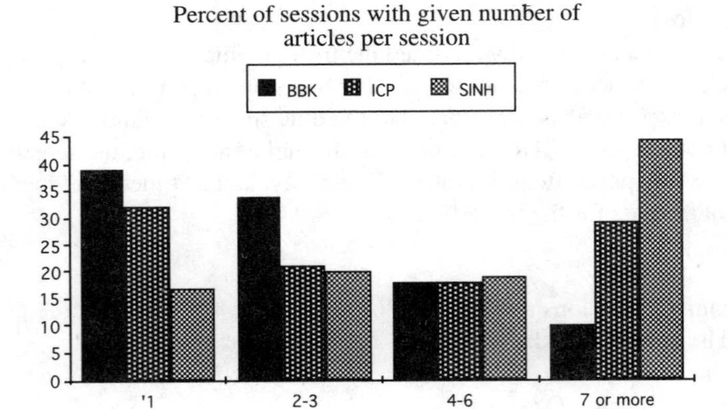

Figure 4. A histogram showing the percent of sessions that accessed the given number of articles in the session at all three museums. Visitors at ICP viewed more articles on the average than visitors at BBK. Visitors at SINH viewed even more articles on the average than the visitors to ICP.

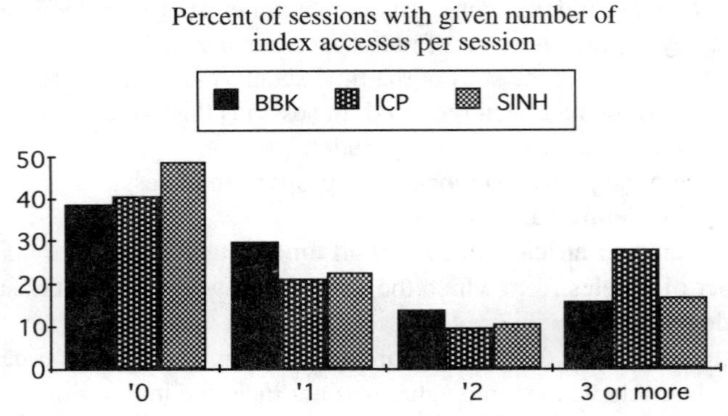

Figure 5. A histogram showing the percent of sessions with the given number of index accesses per session. ICP visitors used the index more per session than BBK visitors, possibly reflecting deeper interest in the photographers or more sophistication with computer usage. SINH visitors used the index less per session, possibly reflecting the difficulty in making good use of the much larger index.

Article-Specific Data:

- First access: The proportion of sessions beginning with the index and the proportion beginning with the introduction.
- Second article in session: The proportion of sessions (of those containing two or more items) that had each item as their second member.
- Second article in sessions beginning with the introduction: The proportion of sessions, of those containing two or more items and beginning with the introduction, that had each item as their second member.

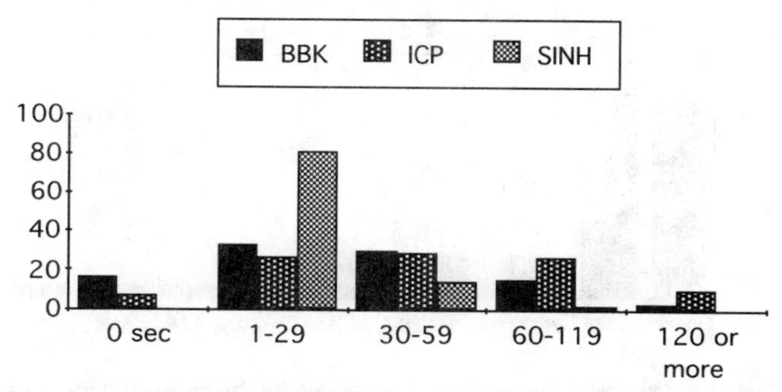

Figure 6. A histogram of the percent of sessions with the average time per article in seconds. Visitors at ICP spent an average of 64 seconds per article versus 41 seconds at BBK. Visitors at SINH spent an average of 16 seconds per article, possibly reflecting the ease of traversal with the touchscreen, the greater connectivity, and the brevity of the articles.

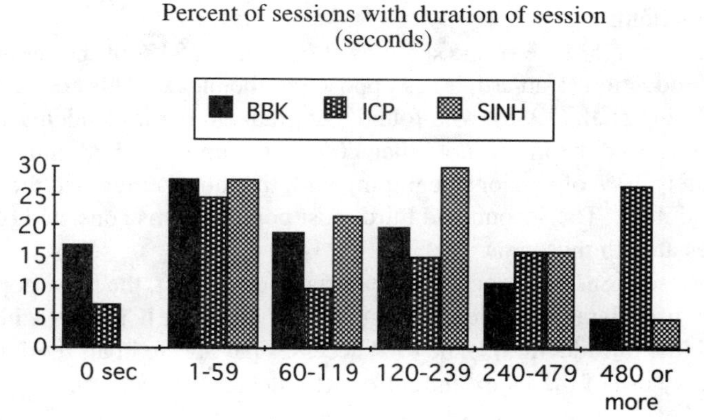

Figure 7. A histogram showing the percent of sessions with the given duration of the session in seconds. Visitors at ICP spent an average of approximately 6 minutes per session versus just over 2 minutes at BBK. Visitors at SINH spent an average of 2.6 minutes per session. We conjecture that this reflects the ease of exploration with the touchscreen that enabled users to quickly explore a few articles (notice the brief times spent per article in Figure 6) and satisfy their information needs or their sense of the system. Also the SINH crowds may have encouraged people to move on quickly.

- Second article in sessions beginning with the index: The proportion of sessions, of those containing two or more items and beginning with the index, that had each item as their second member.
- Third article in all sessions: The proportion of sessions, of those containing three or more items, that had each item as their third member.

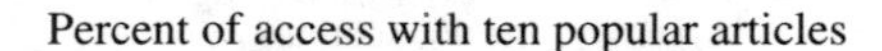

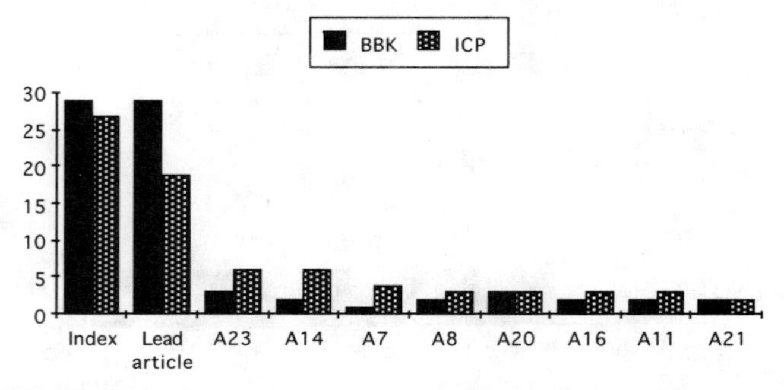

Figure 8. A histogram showing the percent of accesses for the index and the most popular articles that were included in the databases at both BBK and ICP. The numbers refer to the article numbers as shown in the BBK index in Figure 3a. The BBK visitors viewed the lead article often and did not explore as widely as the ICP visitors.

- All articles in all sessions: The proportion of total accesses accounted for by each item.

The first item in 80% of the sessions at ICP and in 84% of the sessions at BBK was the introduction (lead article) as opposed to the index. This contrasts with the results in Wang et al. (1988), who found that graduate library students answering fact questions used the index more than 80% of the time. At both museums, approximately 50% of sessions beginning with the introduction had the index as their second item. The second and third most popular items consisted of the same two articles at both museums.

In those sessions in which the index was selected first, the most popular article at the BBK was "Israel", while the most popular article at ICP was "Chim-an overview" (the introduction). The total accesses per article in all sessions also reflects heavy use of the index and introduction (Figures 3 and 8).

Discussion

Based on the comments of curators at both museums, Hyperties was well-received by visitors. Of course, these comments are biased and interviews with visitors should be used in future studies. As designers of the software, we were interested in suggestions from visitors, curators, and colleagues to improve the system, but the data logging turned out to be insufficient for this purpose. Nevertheless, we identified some ideas that might produce greater involvement and satisfaction. The lack of instructions on the title page of the BBK database, may have contributed to the short duration of many sessions there. In addition, both databases lacked instructions on how to quit. Users had to discover the QUIT commands on the index screen to terminate the session. We conjecture that the longer sessions at the ICP were due to a more knowledgeable and interested user population, both with respect to the subject matter of the database and to computers in general. The ICP users also spent more time reading each article and explored a wider range of topics.

Both user groups utilized the embedded menu feature of Hyperties more frequently than the index, as evidenced by the number of articles read per index access. In addition, the distinctive distribution of articles accessed at the two museums seems to indicate that users selected articles based on their perceived content, rather than at random. Visitors at BBK, for example, were more likely to read the articles on Israel and on the museum itself, while visitors at ICP were more likely to read articles about the various photographers profiled in the database.

The problem of "abandoned" sessions could have been reduced by adding QUIT to the commands that appear at the bottom of each screen when an article is displayed, and by mentioning the quit procedure in the instructions on the title page.

There are a number of pitfalls that must be avoided if one wishes to use the data collected in this study to evaluate a particular database. The average duration of a session, for instance, is not reliable since there is no way of knowing whether one session was the work of one individual or of a series of people. The heavier volume of visitors at ICP may have accounted for part of the longer duration of the sessions.

The proportion of abandoned sessions may only be an indication of the clarity of the instructions. Average time per article is a more important measure of the utility or efficacy of the system, and the proportion of total accesses accounted for by each article should give a good indication of which articles were most attractive to users.

Part II - Direct observation and log data

The museum

The third museum is the well known Smithsonian Institution's National Museum of Natural History. Two IBM Personal Computers are installed in the final room of the exhibit on "King Herod's Dream" — the ancient Roman port city of Caesarea, located in Israel. The exhibit focuses on the rise of urbanism in ancient times and the archaeological methods used during the past 20 years of excavations (Holum, 1988). This last station of the exhibit invites visitors to learn more about the sites that welcome volunteers, and how to join a dig. This exhibit organized by the Smithsonian Institution Traveling Exhibition Service was in Washington, DC from March 22 to June 19, 1988. It is now traveling to five other museums for the next two years (Los Angeles, Denver, St-Paul, Boston and Ottawa). Two freestanding podiums house the IBM PC-AT computers. The EGA monitors, each equipped with a touchscreen, are at about waist level at a 45-degree angle. There is no keyboard. The only permanent instruction is "Touch the screen", written above the monitor.

The database

The GOVA (Guide to Opportunities in Volunteer Archaeology) database was developed under the direction of Ken Holum (Professor of History at the University of Maryland). It consists of about 200 articles. The contents include information about archaeological digs taking place in Israel, the United States and around the world, and practical questions about how to join a dig. A special effort was made to cover the local sites near the current exhibiting museum, and the database will be updated during its travels. The archaeological sites are organized both geographically and by historical periods. The information can also be accessed by direct selection on 11 maps.

The touchscreen interface

In this exhibit a touchscreen interface is used. The museum patrons need only touch highlighted words on the screen to see the related article. A standard strategy indicates the touchable items: in the text as well as the maps only the blue words are selectable. This third study offered an opportunity to test the "touch-mouse" strategy developed at the Human-Computer Interaction Laboratory (Potter, et al., 1988). In this strategy users receive feedback about the exact touch position by a cursor just above their fingers. When the cursor is on a selectable area, the area is highlighted. The selection is activated when users lift their fingers from the screen. This method produces low error rates and high user satisfaction.

Observations in the museum - the effect on the user interface design

In this study we observed museum patrons using our hypertext system and the touchscreen interface in a natural environment. The main goal of this pilot study was to verify the accessibility of the information. Were patrons really able to explore the database with ease and satisfaction? The Hyperties concepts with the touchscreen interface had been thoroughly tested in the laboratory, and it was clear that the system was easy to use with about 15 seconds of demonstration or explanation, but we had less experience with an unattended public access situation.

Three observers spent 4 sessions of about 2 hours each at the exhibit, observing and discussing three potential problems: the touchscreen interface, the Hyperties mechanism and the database structure. Each session allowed us to pick out the weaknesses of the system and put in place a productive mechanism of criticism and modification back and forth between laboratory and museum.

The first observation was that the suppression of our 15 second demonstration was transforming an easy to use system into a frustrating mystery game for some of these totally untutored users. The time spent at the computer shouldn't have been spent guessing and missing. We observed 3 main problems: the mis-selection rate was still very high (the screen is touched but nothing is selected), the few lines of instructions were not clear or accessible enough to get started, and many patrons didn't figure out the 2 steps required to get a new article (first select a word and get a definition, then select its full article).

During the first sessions no usage data were logged by the computer. The data would have been able show the average of the very small number of articles accessed and the high number of mis-selections, but the simple observation of the patrons and some informal interviews was sufficient to give us the hints necessary to understand why the system wasn't working as hoped and how to improve it. In fact, direct observation and interviews worked better to improve the system than the data collection in Part I of this study.

After implementing the changes described below, we saw an obvious and satisfactory improvement. Most of the patrons were able to traverse smoothly from article to article and focus on their reading and not on the mechanism. We were then able to concentrate on improving the structure of the database (contents and links) to make the information more accessible.

About the touchscreen

We observed a surprisingly wide variety of ways to touch a screen! Some users pressed hard or rubbed the screen, some touched with 3 fingers, some swished elegantly with a fingernail, etc. In spite of our efforts to design the screens clearly, there was confusion about where to touch. In this Hyperties application all the touchable areas were words written in blue, an easy concept only if you have read the instructions. To reduce the users' confusion on both of these issues, we provided better instructions and made the touch selection mechanism more forgiving. Our initial selection mechanism was very accurate and easy to use with a few seconds of explanation. For the museum purpose we enlarged the touchable zones as well as the cursor, and installed a help line at the bottom of the screen, continuously updated according to the current step of the selection.

About the instructions

Written paper instructions attached on the side of the screens are not esthetically attractive. To give directions in the introduction article of the database seemed more appropriate. Therefore it has to be accessible to the patron coming to the screen. First we made the RESTART button available at anytime, well separated from the others to avoid accidental hits. The time-out delay was also shorter than during the first installations. Modifying the introduction article and immediately observing the reaction of the patrons allowed us to find a more successful writing style. Patrons were more successful when they were asked to try specific examples than to read about the general hypertext concept. It is better to write "For example, if you touch the blue word "volunteers" on the 3rd line of this page, you will get an article about volunteers", than to explain that the blue words will give you more information by accessing an article about the related subject. Our observations showed the importance of the introduction article. It should give clear instructions, a brief overview of the main database topics, and also easy and clear links to the most attractive parts of the database (maps, for example) (See Figure 9).

GOVA - Introduction PAGE 1 OF 2

Welcome to **GOVA**, the Guide to Opportunities in Volunteer Archaeology. **GOVA** will tell you about **archaeological projects** all over the world (**see Map 9**) that welcomes **volunteers**. You can use **GOVA** to answer **practical questions** like **how to join a dig**, or how much it **costs**.

To Use GOVA, simply touch a blue word with your fingertip— not your fingernail— and release. For example, if you touch the blue word "volunteers" at the third line of this page, you will get an article about volunteers. To turn to the next page touch the blue word NEXT PAGE.

INDEX NEXT PAGE

RETURN TO MAP 9, THE WORLD RESTART

Touch a blue word with your fingertip

Figure 9. This screen shows the first page of the Introduction article used at the Museum of Natural History. The bold items appeared blue on the screen and were the touchable areas. Here, the brief definition space at the bottom of the screen has been removed. The **RESTART** is available at anytime. The style of writing for the introduction article is also different. It gives instructions and examples, and provides the links to the major database topics. In a later version we added a **TABLE OF TOPICS** command at the bottom of the screen.

About the Hyperties mechanism

In the initial system the user had to first select a word, then select the command FULL ARTICLE to jump to a new article. This mechanism had been designed for a keyboard interface with which users simply pressed the Return-Key twice to get an article (thanks to the judicious setting of the default cursor position). In the touchscreen version that mechanism doubles the selection process time and difficulty. The FULL ARTICLE command was also hard to reach in a corner of the screen and our interviews revealed that many patrons were annoyed by it. The solution was to suppress the definition and give direct access to the full article. Each selection now had a very visible and dramatic effect, the trade off being a weaker continuity from screen to screen.

About the contents of the database

After making the software changes, it was possible to check the database structure and accessibility. To find information the user can follow links from article to article, or select an article from an index, which consisted here of an alphabetical list of the 200 articles. We observed that users seemed to be disoriented by the very large index and often left the index without selecting anything. In the previous experiment the index was used often. Our hypothesis is that in the first database the index was small enough (2 pages) to be browsed rapidly, and give the user the possibility of forming a quick idea of the topics covered by the database. With a large number of articles the index was mainly disappointing, except for some people searching for a specific city. We believe that a table of contents will be more useful. We have made the table of contents accessible as an option from any page, but we won't get any feedback from this change until the exhibit is installed in the next museum - Los Angeles. The data analyzed in the next chapter was also recorded before this change.

Different types of use

During our stay at the museum we observed quite diverse behaviors. By making the browsing extremely simple and rapid, we also observed that it can become an attractive game for young children who enjoyed their power over the rapid flashing of the screen. Some other patrons come to the computer driven by their interest in new technology (the touchscreen interface or the software). We saw them study the software, "play" with the selection mechanism, but not always take interest in the information available. A lot of visitors just stop in front of the screen, touch it once or twice and leave. They don't seem to be interested or are exhausted (the computer is the last station of a long exhibit). On the other hand, we observed some patrons spending a long time at the computer (or even coming for a second time!) to explore several sites, take notes of names and addresses.

The data collection and analysis

After improving the usability of the system, usage data was collected during four weeks. Unfortunately, one of the two monitors was out of order at that time and only one of the two computers was used. All selections were recorded, allowing a more precise analysis. The RESTART command being available at all times and the time-out delay being reduced, we saw that most of the patrons started their exploration from the title page. Unlike for the Part I data, we know that each session has most likely been conducted by the same person or group of persons.

In order to collect the most complete information possible for the GOVA exhibit, every selection and the selection's time was logged by the computer. Since all of the user input to the computer was captured, any information about what the museum patron saw on the display could be recreated. We chose to concentrate on the time spent within articles. To get this information the log files were "played through" the museum software, recreating the visitor's experience. At the same time a new condensed log file was generated that contained the pertinent information.

There were 27 days of data collected which contained 4461 sessions. A session in the GOVA exhibit starts when patrons touch the title page. The session ends either after 60 seconds of inactivity (time-out) or when patrons select RESTART. In GOVA, RESTART appears on every screen except the title page. Some sessions could not be included in the analysis. There were 143 sessions that for some reason would not replay through the museum software. The last session for each day was excluded because of the effect of the museum closing and power being cut off from the machine. Because of an oversight, if the user started GOVA by touching the screen in a certain spot, the RESTART on the next page would be selected causing a very short unrepresentative session. This oversight eliminated 730 sessions from analysis. The following results are from the remaining 3561 sessions.

In the average session, patrons looked at 8.5 articles and referenced the index 1.3 times. Thus 6.6 articles were looked at per index reference. The average time per article was 16.4 seconds. The average session lasted 162.2 seconds (2.6 minutes). However, 16 percent of the sessions timed-out, so the time spent looking at the computer during the 60 second timeout period is uncertain. Assuming they spent the 16.4 seconds from the result above, we can include this value into those timed-out sessions and conclude that the average session lasted 165.9 seconds (See Figures 4-7 for histograms).

Of particular interest is the relatively infrequent use of the index. This can be attributed to the effective hypertext writing that encouraged using embedded references. GOVA was written from scratch for the hypertext format. Also the index was long and arranged strictly alphabetically, not by topic. Patrons would have to have a very specific interest to use the index effectively.

Data on the number of accesses for each article was also compiled. Accesses were determined by two criteria: session accesses were the number of sessions that accessed the article. If an article was accessed several times by one session, it counted as only one session access. Total access counted every time the article was visited. In addition, these two criteria were further subdivided according to where the patron was when accessing the article. Three places were identified: any place, an article, and the index.

There were 8 different measures computed for each article. Sorting on each of these measures showed interesting results. The articles embedded in the introduction page topped the list that was sorted by session accesses from any place. One would expect this result since these are pragmatically the most accessible articles. There are two peculiar notes, though. The article PRACTICAL QUESTIONS was by far the least popular article of this group, not even appearing with the others in the top 20. The MAP OF THE WORLD, 9th in overall popularity, was the second least popular of this group, which is surprising since patrons can get an overall view of archaeological digs around the world from this eye pleasing graphic. It appears that it takes a reference with specific information to get the patrons' attention. A user would rather read about ARCHAEOLOGICAL PROJECTS than read about PRACTICAL QUESTIONS (See Figure 10 for table).

Sorting by session access from the index revealed that the index was too long. All the top 20 articles selected by this method started with ‘a’, ‘b’, or ‘c’ except HOW TO JOIN A DIG and a map showing LOCAL SITES. The strong interest in digs in the local area was shown by most of these sorted lists. Counting by total accesses did not generate results much different than by session accesses.

	Number of sessions that accessed article	Accesses from another article	Accesses from index	Average time per visit (seconds)
Introduction	3561	483	259	31
Index of Articles	1802	1802	0	45
Archaeological Projects	1379	1213	310	21
Volunteers	1022	1004	31	24
Costs	773	737	45	28
Age and Health Requirements	658	390	303	26
How to Join a Dig	603	549	68	25
Accommodations	487	388	115	25
MAP 9: The World	447	431	30	27
Periods of the past	369	368	6	15
Local sites	334	327	11	14
Academic credit	329	215	132	13
Excavation season	321	306	18	13
Baltimore	304	148	216	23
Annapolis	293	135	189	24
Mediterranean sites	292	288	6	15
Sites in the U.S. and Canada	290	278	16	15
New World Sites	270	265	11	16
Biblical archaeology	262	220	52	19
Special skills	262	258	5	20

Figure 10. This table shows the top twenty articles sorted by the number of sessions that looked at each article. Underlined articles appear on the introductory page and could be accessed with one selection. A strong interest in the sites local to the Washington D.C. area is shown in this list. All these numbers consider more than one visit during one session as one access.

Sorting by the total time spent in the article revealed that while the maps were not accessed relatively often, time was spent with them once they were found. This may be a distorted result since the time for the map to display itself on the screen was longer than for an article.

The total time spent in each article was determined. In order to better judge which articles caught the patron's attention, the total time for each article was divided by the number of sessions that actually looked at the article. Sorting by this result gave an entirely different view on the articles. Certain articles obviously required in-depth reading. While 5 maps made this top 20 list, the map of THE WORLD did not. Except for two articles that started with 'a' and 'c', embedded references were by far the preferred way to find these articles. For example, the article on the HELLENISTIC PERIOD was accessed 61 times from another article and only 5 times from the index (See Figure 11 for table).

	Number of sessions that accessed article	Accesses from another article	Accesses from index	Average time per visit (seconds)
Nabataean fine ware	1	1	0	62
Index of articles	1802	1802	0	45
Map 1: Northern Israel	180	171	21	43
Tel Dor	18	15	3	41
Caesarea's harbor	32	16	18	37
Map 2: Southern Israel	136	120	19	34
Petra	49	40	10	33
Map 11: Local sites	162	130	46	32
Hellenistic period	64	61	5	32
Introduction	3561	483	259	31
Map 5: Britain and Ireland	157	145	24	31
Map 6: Europe	102	90	22	30
Ashkelon	68	24	58	30
Life on dig	145	127	21	30
Mount Ebal	31	29	2	29
North Straiton	42	40	2	29
Published listings	200	194	10	28
Map 3: Middle East	152	137	28	28
Costs	773	737	45	28
Karnak	86	79	8	28

Figure 11. This table shows the top twenty articles sorted by the average number of seconds for each session that visited the article spent there. We conjecture that these are the articles that the patrons stopped to read. Except for articles that were located at the start of the index, these articles were mostly accessed from other articles. All these numbers consider more than one visit during one session as one access.

Conclusions

For museum exhibit designers

This study demonstrates the feasibility of using interactive databases in conjunction with museum exhibits. Hyperties is not perfect and there is a great deal more to be done to understand how to make successful applications, but the central message is that computers can contribute to an exhibit by offering an engaging, interactive, and personal experience. While only a fraction of the visitors tried the computer, many of those that did succeeded in traversing the articles and index. This study also illustrates the wide differences in database use by different visitor populations in terms of topics selected and willingness to invest time. Exhibit designers can add a computer database to provide detailed information, vary the level of presentation, offer multiple languages, or permit patrons to explore vast databases.

For researchers interested in methodological issues

Although log data was useful in creating some portrait of usage patterns, the direct observation and rapid iterative refinement led to the most dramatic increases in usability of our system in the museum environment. While we were tempted to proceed more slowly and make incremental changes while collecting data, this process would have taken many months. We made dozens of changes in a few weeks and although we do not have statistical data to confirm our conjectures, we feel quite confident that the system was dramatically improved by our efforts at the Smithsonian.

In future studies, we encourage more data collection about who the users were. Age, gender, interests, goals in using the computer, previous interests with the database topic, and previous experience with computers would be worthwhile information to correlate with usage patterns. Converse's recent study of a shopping mall directory (Converse, 1987), found that certain user groups (the elderly) avoided the system, and 20% of users failed to get the information they desired. Such statistics are important in evaluating the effectiveness of a computer system. A second important source of information is post-usage interviews to ascertain whether the users succeeded in retrieving desired information and to determine their subjective satisfaction with the search process. Our observations in the third museum had a great effectiveness on improving the user interface and the structure of the database but were still insufficient to analyze search strategies. We cannot judge whether 2 or 6 minutes with the system is a successful use, only subjective comments can indicate attitudes. However, now we have a baseline of usage data against which to judge future installations.

For user interface designers

The museum environment is very tough to design for since the users are so diverse and even 15 seconds of training may be unrealistic. The initial steps to take should be obvious to the patrons so that they become engaged and experience success. Then the user should be presented with concise information about the database contents, the metaphors for usage, and the syntax for action. The touch-screen appears to be a convenient and reliable device and the take-off strategy is effective if care is taken to provide a comfortable physical installation, visible feedback about the current touch position, and reasonably sized targets. Instructions should be specific and results should be achieved with a small number of steps. The database structure does make a dramatic difference and overviews in the form of a table of contents are necessary to complement a lengthy index. Inspite of your best efforts in design, testing with real users is still necessary. However, testing need not be lengthy or burdensome. Four to six hours should be enough to give an indication of the problems and successes that patrons have, as well as provide ample suggestions for improvement.

Sparks of Innovation in Human-Computer Interaction,
B. Shneiderman, Ed., Ablex Publ., Norwood, NJ (1993)

5.3 ACCESS at the Library of Congress

Gary Marchionini
Maryle Ashley
Lois Korzendorfer

Supporting patron access to library collections requires significant resources in all types of libraries. Card catalogs and reference librarians have traditionally assisted patrons in locating materials related to their information needs and the development of online public access catalogs (OPACs) has begun to affect both of these patron resources (Hildreth, 1982). Many libraries have invested heavily in OPACs in spite of the many problems they present to library patrons. Patrons have difficulty using the computer workstations, formulating queries appropriate to the OPAC command language, and interpreting feedback from the system (Borgman, 1986). In many libraries, reference staff who hoped that OPACs would allow them to assist patrons with challenging information problems have found themselves spending large amounts of time assisting patrons in the mechanics of using the OPAC. This problem is likely to be an ongoing one since patrons in public and academic libraries are what may be termed "casual" rather than "regular" users.

The challenges of OPACs are particularly critical at the Library of Congress (LC), a premier library in the world and host to patrons from all walks of life and experience. The Library was a pioneer in automating bibliographic records and has long provided electronic access to its catalog. Patrons to the library are often visitors to Washington, D.C. who spend a short amount of time using the library and do not want to invest time learning to use the system. The existing systems available to patrons, SCORPIO and MUMS, provide powerful search facilities for the enormous collection of the Library, but require significant skills to use and time to learn. In 1988 Information Technology Services (ITS), the Library's directorate for computer support, began exploring ways to deliver an easy-to-use front-end for the LC OPAC that would allow novice or casual users to quickly conduct searches of the collection without training. Such a system would not only improve patron satisfaction and service, but also relieve some of the training burdens on reference staff.

Recognizing that an essential element of the design problem was the human-computer interface, the Library invited the Human-Computer Interaction Laboratory (HCIL) at the University of Maryland to assist in designing such a system. Over an 18 month period, an HCIL team worked with an LC team first to give background and training in interface development in order to ground the project before it began work, and later to give objective feedback every few months on the interfaces being created. This collaboration took place in three phases.

Phase 1. Human-computer interaction principles orientation and training

A series of planning meetings were held to discuss the goals and directions for the project. A critical early decision was to include both systems staff in ITS and reference librarians from the reading rooms where ACCESS would be available. These meetings culminated in a series of four human-computer interaction training seminars that served to lay theoretical and practical foundations for the design. In addition to the content addressed, these seminars served the valuable purpose of helping systems staff and reference staff to understand each other's requirements and perspectives. The seminars held in late 1988 were half-day sessions and focused on four specific issues. The first seminar was conducted by Ben Shneiderman and provided an introduction and overview of interface design principles. The second seminar was conducted by Gary Marchionini and was focused on mental models for information retrieval. The third seminar was conducted by Kent Norman and addressed design of menus, icons, and interface evaluation. The final seminar was conducted by Charles Kreitzberg (of Cognetics Corp.) and focused on cognitive principles and project management issues. At the conclusion of the seminars, a cohesive team had formed with a common experience base and language for approaching the design process. Based on what they had learned in the seminars, the group was able to focus on a commonly perceived problem as they began imagining their new system. Also important, the team members had developed personal rapport as they participated in the seminars.

Phase 2. Design consultations

After the seminar series was completed, HCIL team members met with the LC team to discuss how to get the project started. Touch panel and keyboard input were recommended for the physical user interface and simple non-Boolean queries and hypertext-like, usage-sensitive help were recommended for the conceptual user interface. HCIL suggested that each team member try to imagine the system installed in the Library's reading room displaying its logo screen; then to imagine a patron walking up to it and touching the opening screen: What happens next? The first design meeting thus began with sharing each team member's image of what the system could be like.

From this imaginary start, the LC team, or subgroups from the team formed around a specific task or area, began creating and discarding many paper versions of how their ideal screens would appear. After enough consistency developed to chart out the opening screens and some search paths, the HCIL team was asked to examine and critique them. By this point, technical processing staff had joined the team to help in determining the most productive search strategies. Their knowledge of the underlying data structures of the bibliographic data and its intent assisted in selecting which "behind-the-scenes" retrieval commands were best to use to answer patrons' search requests.

The selection of a name for the new system also took place during the design phase. The beginning of each team meeting devoted about 10 minutes to brainstorming candidate names, which came and went as quickly as the paper screen designs. When the name ACCESS began to catch on, definitions of what the acronym could stand for resulted in a landmark decision: the acronym ACCESS means what it says—ACCESS.

Once ideas about the opening screen displays began to converge, the system staff converted them into prototype computer displays and met regularly with the reference and technical processing staff to discuss and modify them. The reference staff and technical processing staff soon gained appreciation for the constraints of system implementation and management, and the system staff gained appreciation for the types of problems and concerns patrons had as they used the Library and existing systems. After several iterations, the prototypes were discussed in a meeting of the full LC and HCIL teams. After additional revisions and the addition of a "fail-safe" code to intercept system errors and shield the patron from any awareness of error messages, the ACCESS system was ready for testing with users.

Phase 3. Evaluation and feedback

The system was first tested with reference librarians not involved with the project. Based on their positive response and after incorporation of some 30 suggested improvements, the system was tested with the public in the Adams Building beginning in November of 1990. Feedback from reference librarians and patrons was gathered from observations, interviews, and an optional online questionnaire where patrons recorded their opinions via the touch panel. These reports illustrated that patron acceptance was high and that patrons could quickly and easily learn to conduct searches with ACCESS. Based on these results, the system was ready for implementation in the refurbished Main Reading Room of the Library when it reopened in June of 1991.

The ACCESS system

The ACCESS system was built on an MS-DOS platform using 386SX and 386 machines, a touch panel, and EASEL software. The ACCESS system software was written primarily in EASEL language which is a fourth generation language. The EASEL software provides a graphical user interface for communication with the patron, and then translates the patron's choice into the appropriate command for the LC mainframe database software. When the mainframe returns the result set, the EASEL software again handles the information and reformats it for the patron. EASEL is a hybrid language having some characteristics of object-oriented languages but still retaining some features of procedural code. As such it offered a faster startup for the system staff than undertaking an orientation to object-oriented paradigms. Subsequent design iterations have capitalized on the more modular approach available through EASEL's constructs such as class and hierarchy.

To use ACCESS, patrons make selections via the touch panel by pressing "buttons" that are shadowed to give a three-dimensional effect (see Figure 1). Authors, titles, or subject headings are entered via a keyboard. Results of searches are displayed in a brief record format to facilitate browsing within the retrieved set (see Figure 2). When users select a record, the full bibliographic record is displayed (see Figure 3). All screens are titled and consistent wording is used throughout. Context-sensitive help is always available by touching the Help button which is consistently located at the bottom of all screens (see Figure 4 for an

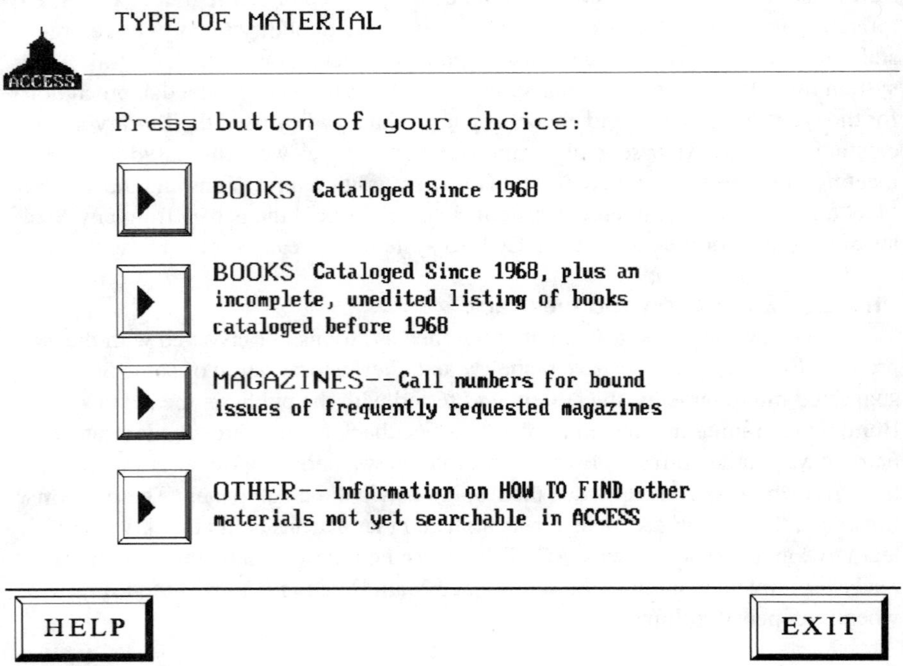

TYPE OF MATERIAL

ACCESS

Press button of your choice:

BOOKS Cataloged Since 1968

BOOKS Cataloged Since 1968, plus an incomplete, unedited listing of books cataloged before 1968

MAGAZINES--Call numbers for bound issues of frequently requested magazines

OTHER--Information on HOW TO FIND other materials not yet searchable in ACCESS

HELP

EXIT

Figure 1. ACCESS search screen

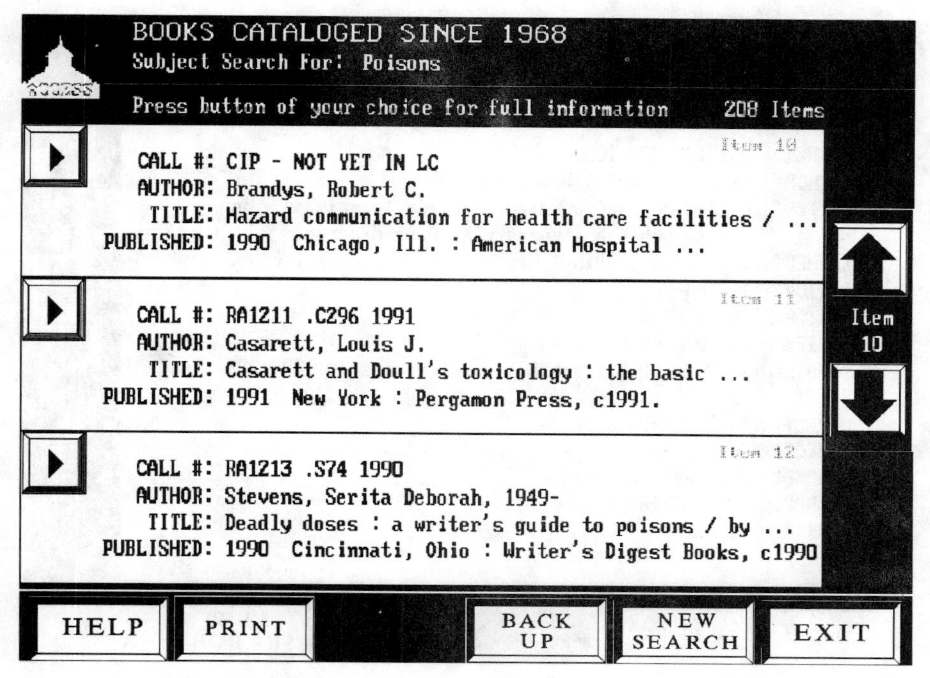

Figure 2. ACCESS brief record screen

example of a help screen). Help screens offer embedded menus (highlighted terms/phrases) that allow users to get additional or related information with a simple touch.

The reopening of the newly renovated and refurbished Main Reading Room and Computer Catalog Center (CCC) in the Library's Jefferson Building coincided with the full production release of ACCESS. Eighteen ACCESS workstations were installed in three bays of the CCC, along with 36 other terminals of varying types. All terminals communicate with the LC mainframe over a token ring connection. The construction of the workspace around the ACCESS workstations had been designed and finalized long before ACCESS was conceived. However, at installation, ergonomic considerations were made that resulted in adjustable chairs at each workspace, recessed incandescent lighting overhead, and table space for books and patron belongings. The touch panel is placed on the system unit and the printer is alongside. Because only six ACCESS workstations are installed per bay, there is a sense of space between them. Also, the placement of the ACCESS workstations closest to the entrance and the continual display of the colorful ACCESS logo were intended to attract patrons who may enter the CCC for the first time, thus allowing them to try using ACCESS on their own before asking a reference librarian for assistance.

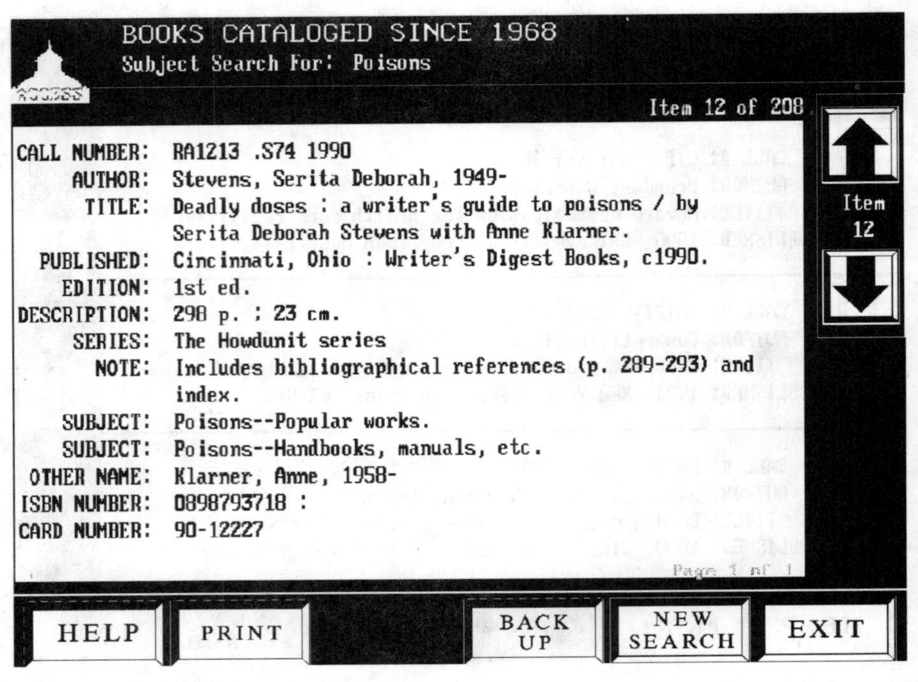

Figure 3. ACCESS full bibliographic record screen

Status and outcomes

Patron response has been very positive. Comments are often made on the "user friendliness" and design of the system. Patrons who struggled with command-driven SCORPIO and MUMS also comment about the ease of using ACCESS.

ACCESS is a front-end for a large, existing system. In order to test the concept and feasibility of ACCESS, the more difficult implementation of Boolean searches was deferred in favor of single concept searches (e.g., a single author, a single subject heading, a single title, etc.). Since between 30% and 50% of all searches with online bibliographic systems (e.g., OPACs, Medline, etc.) result in no hits, and many of these are due to overspecification, the decision to defer Boolean may have unwittingly contributed to the system's success. From an implementation point of view, providing only single concept query support was easier and made query translation to the underlying system more direct, but reduced the searching power of the system. From the user's point of view, however, this approach has increased the user's chance of getting some hits in subject searches because over-specification is avoided. Furthermore, Library of Congress Subject headings were incorporated into the browse list of subject searches so that users see cross references that offer useful alternatives in subject searching. Users are given a button to select specific subject headings or to "Fast Forward" through records. To further assist users in

BOOKS CATALOGED SINCE 1968
Subject Search For: poisons

Press button of your choice: Number of Items

▶	Poisonous substances See Poisons	
▶	Poisonous wastes See Hazardous wastes	
▶	Poisons	208
▶	Other search suggestion(s) for Poisons	
▶	Poisons See also Chemicals--Toxicology	
▶	Poisons--Analysis	29
▶	Other search suggestion(s) for Poisons--Analysis	

Hold For Fast Back

More Subjects

Hold For Fast Forward

HELP | PRINT | BACK UP | NEW SEARCH | EXIT

Figure 4. ACCESS subject headings screen

specifying LC subject headings appropriate to their searches, the system offers alternatives from the LC thesaurus. (see Figure 6).

ACCESS has dramatically changed the work at the LC for the reference staff on duty there. More time is available to develop search strategies for patrons and the mind-numbing days of repeating navigational commands over and over are only a memory. The staff is hoping to implement the ACCESS front end for other files in the library's SCORPIO system in early 1993. Work is progressing on adding other search capabilities for the book files, including the ability to request books directly through ACCESS. Many of the more specialized reading rooms at the library have recognized the success of ACCESS and work is progressing on a Spanish language prototype for the Hispanic Reading Room. The Newspaper and Current Periodical Reading Room is planning to install ACCESS soon.

Summary and discussion

The success of the ACCESS project was based on three principles. First, this was a team effort. Systems staff, reference staff, technical processing staff, and the HCIL team invested time to understand their respective perspectives. This team effort was made possible by strong yet supportive leadership in the LC teams and the shared experience of the seminars and meetings.

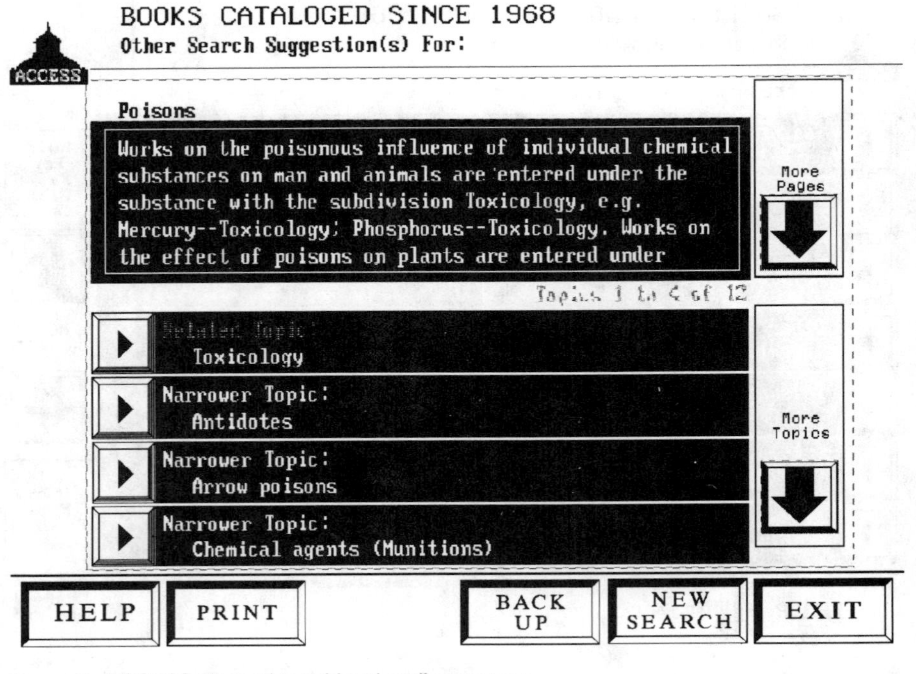

Figure 5. ACCESS alternative subject headings screen

Second, success is due to attention to solid human-computer interaction design principles. Specific to this project were:

1. user needs were considered from the start;
2. a direct manipulation interface was used;
3. consistency was maintained in screen displays, wording, selection mechanisms, and system feedback;
4. help was context-sensitive and under user control; and
5. design proceeded in an iterative fashion with systematic and constructive feedback.

Third, the institution took the risk of implementing an innovative system and providing it as an alternative to the existing system. Providing an easy to use touch-panel interface met the needs of the many novice and casual users who visit the Library. Advanced users are still able to use the SCORPIO and MUMS systems that support Boolean queries, field specifications, and set combinations. This two-system strategy has proven to be a prudent way to meet the needs of various users of the Library and freeing reference staff from many of the system assistance demands of the past.

Sparks of Innovation in Human-Computer Interaction,
B. Shneiderman, Ed., Ablex Publ., Norwood, NJ (1993)

5.4 User interface consistency: an evaluation of original and revised interfaces for a videodisk library

Richard Chimera
Ben Shneiderman

Abstract

Original and revised versions of the National Library of Medicine MicroAnatomy Visual Library system were evaluated with an empirical test of nineteen subjects. The versions of the program's interface differed on issues relating to consistency of wording and screen layout, use of color coding, display of status information, and availability of help information. Each subject used both versions of the program to perform matched sets of tasks. The dependent variables were time to perform tasks correctly and subjective satisfaction as reported via the QUIS questionnaire. The revised version was statistically significantly faster for five of twenty tasks and more satisfying to use on a number of dimensions. The benefits of consistency and guidelines for design of interactive computer systems are discussed.

Introduction

Interactive computer systems are common in professional environments and are becoming more widely used in library and public information settings, such as online catalog systems, local area maps, and museum exhibit information. For these systems to be used effectively by untrained users the user interface must be carefully designed. Important considerations are: the multiple dimensions of consistency, cognitively-sound structuring, close correspondence of functionality to user goals, and small sets of choices provided to users at any one time (Lewis, et al. 90; Reisner 90; Nielsen 89; Kearsley 93).

Initial informal references to consistency have turned into ambitious attempts at formal definitions that get more elusive as they are scrutinized (Reisner 90; Wiecha et al. 90). Kellogg (Kellogg 89) points out that "Consistency has no meaning on its own; it is inherently a relational concept. Therefore to merely say that an interface is consistent or that consistency is a goal of user interface design is also meaningless." The issue of defining consistency has even started a heated community debate (Grudin 92; Wiecha 92). It is now commonly accepted that when a competent user's view of the system differs from the designer's view of the system, then the system is inconsistent (Reisner 90; Grudin 89). The interface design community agrees that the user's tasks and application domain are a major focus for providing consistency. At the same time, the community acknowledges that adhering too much to physical metaphors and the status quo can limit an interface's usefulness by potentially ignoring inherent advantages of the computer medium.

There is also a widely held belief that internal consistency (e.g., layout, terminology, color, etc.) is a crucial issue in the usability of highly interactive computer programs (Shneiderman 92; Reisner 90; Nielsen 89). Nielsen states that consistency leads to "improved user productivity by leading to higher throughput and fewer errors because the user can predict what the system will do in any given situation and can rely on a few rules to govern use of the system." Further, he points out "it is desired to have the system be consistent with users' expectations whether formed by other applications or by non-computer systems." More encouragement for consistent design can be found in various guidelines documents (Brown 88; Smith & Mosier, 86).

The goal of this project was to validate empirically that modest changes to an interface to make it more consistent with respect to the users' domain and task context would increase comprehension, thereby decreasing completion times and increasing subjective satisfaction.

History

The NLM MicroAnatomy Visual Library system is an interactive computer system that allows users to view videodisk images of human cell structures. The images are accessed in a number of ways: via word search, videodisk frame number, and by prepared slideshows. It was created in 1987 by the National Library of Medicine to be used in medical schools and libraries by students and

```
MicroAnatomy Visual Library

FIND and Display Image Records

REVIEW / EDIT  Database Records

REPORTS for Database Records

CLIPBOARD / SHOWFILE functions

VIDEODISC Setup

SYSTEM Utilities

Highlight choice with arrow keys, Enter to select, ESCape to quit  F1-Help
```

Figure 1. Main menu screen in the original interface. Menu items are verbose and use computer-oriented rather than task-oriented language.

professors. These users are knowledgeable of medicine but not necessarily of computers.

NLM submitted the original version of this program to the Human-Computer Interaction Laboratory for an evaluation (i.e., Figures 1-3). Usability studies were performed and the results were the basis for suggestions to improve the user interface (Young & Shneiderman 89). The suggested improvements focus on internal consistency and harmony with users' application domain, expectations, and tasks. NLM revised the interface and challenged us to prove whether the changes would make a difference.

Despite the obvious utility of comparing original and revised versions of an interface to see which is faster, more comprehensible, or leads to fewer errors, this

```
R E C O R D   L O C A T O R

Enter Search words or phrase: (be as specific as possible)

embryo
_____________________________________________________

Search may include organs, tissues, structures and/or cell types

Press [PgDn] for keyword index
or enter search mask (ex.  embry*)
ESCape to return to main menu
```

Figure 2. Dialog box for keyword seach of images in the original interface. Screen title is not consistent with wording of menu item that brings user here. Instructions creep into center of screen and are not well organized. Description of '*' charatcter uses computer language and is not well explained.

```
Nr Frame  Hits          Partial description                 Total retrieved = 58

 1 06509   1 embryo: human, pancreas, duodenum, stomach (cardia)         100x
 2 06558   1 embryo: human, 42 day 22mm, stomach, pancreas (doral and    40x
 3 06600   1 embryo: human, splenic primordium, testis, dorsal pancreas  40x
 4 06250   1 embryo series 43: 169 human, common bile duct, fortal vein  3x
 5 06257   1 embryo seriex 44: 170 human, pancreas, suprarenals, hernia  3x
 6 04727   1 pancreas: secretory acini (red granules), intralobular duc 160x
 7 04734   1 pancreas: secretory acini note secretory granules (red), i 160x
 8 04678   1 pancreas: intralobular ducts, acini (note basophilia of ba 160x
 9 04664   1 pancreas: acinar cells with basal basophilia(rer) and apic 400x
10 04671   1 pancreas: acinar cells with basal basophilia (rer) and api 400x
11 04699   1 pancreas: interlobular duct with simple columnar epitheliu 400x

Currently selected: 06257
embryo series 44: 170 human, pancreas, suprarenals, herniated loop of gut,
inferior vena cava
                              Maginf: 3x             Stain: H & E
  F2-Clipboard, F3-Summary, F4-Edit, F5-Graph, F6-Labels
            F1-Help  F7-Toggle Video  F8-Print  ESCape to quit
```

Figure 3. Retrieved-images screen with a selected item in the original interface. No title at top and the jumble of function key descriptions at the bottom can each lead to confusion. Magnification and stain information is not set apart for clear identification.

type of study is still underutilized in the human-computer interaction community. This study addressed only those aspects of the interface that were different between versions. The tasks the subjects performed were created in a goal-oriented way, and did not take advantage of specific differences in either version. For example, the task descriptions used goal-oriented language, not interface version specific language.

Improvements

Consistent use of colors: The revised interface used seven different color schemes, each one representing a particular function. The uniqueness of the function-color mapping makes it easy to locate the type of information needed by briefly glancing at the screen and focusing attention on the appropriate color. Each screen contains no more than four different colors reducing the distraction effect due to multiple colors. The original interface used an inconsistent color scheme.

- White: as the border for the menu screen.
- Green: to represent an option that can be selected.
- Inverse: to represent an option that is currently selected.
- Light blue: to represent instructions or methods of finding help.
- Yellow: to represent titles and labels.

- Red: to represent deletion and error messages.
- White text on a blue background: to indicate form fill in.

Phrasing menu items for consistency: Menu items satisfy the following conditions (Figure 4):

- Phrases are familiar using task- and domain-oriented terminology.
- Each item starts with a unique letter to allow a single keystroke to select any menu item (mnemonic selection).
- Each item has an accurate one line description which appears at the bottom of the screen when highlighted.

Function key operations (which are performed simply by pressing a function key located at the top of the keyboard) are displayed along the bottom of the screen in numerical order with the format "function key label - operation" (e.g., "F1 - Help").

The original interface used computer-oriented language in some menu items (Figure 1) and was inconsistent in labeling function keys (Figure 3).

Consistent screen layout: The top section of the screen displays information relevant to the orientation of users (see Orientation below). The label "Current

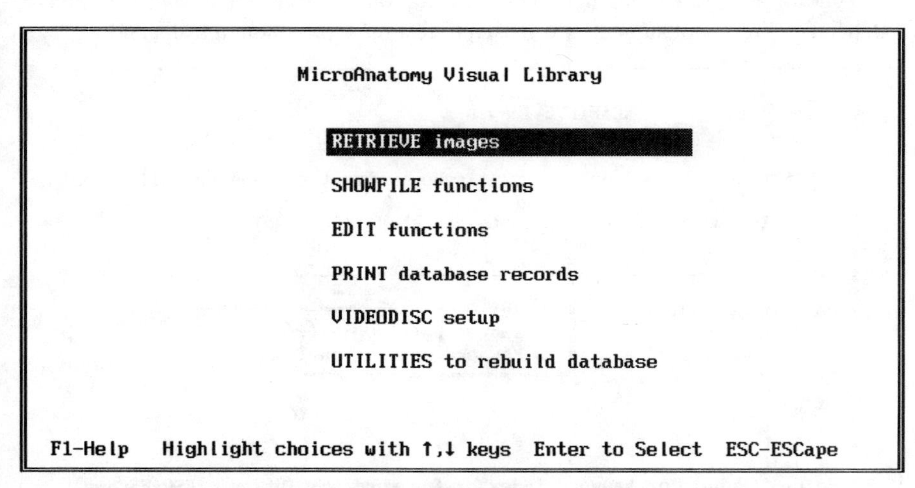

Figure 4. Main menu screen in the revised interface. Improvements include wording consistent with task domain (e.g., "print" instead of "report"), a onetime description of the highlighted menu item is always shown, and a more clear and consistent description of the ESC key.

Record" appears at the top left corner with the record number of the currently selected record. Each screen has a unique title which is displayed at the top center. Menus appear in the center of the screen, menu selection can be made by moving the cursor vertically with arrow keys. The one-line description of each menu item appears below the border of the screen. The bottom section of the screen displays functional information. At the left is "F1 - Help" and at extreme right is "ESC - ESCape" with the other function keys in between numerically sorted (Figure 6). The active window of the screen has a double lined border while the inactive section has a single lined border.

Orientation and information display: The menu structure has no more than five levels. The menu item selected becomes the exact title for the next screen to remind users of their choice (Figures 4-5). The currently selected record number is displayed. If a list of options requires more than a page to display all the options, there is an indication of the page number at the top of the screen, as well as PgUp and PgDn references. Hitting ESCape always returns users to the previous menu so that users can easily back out of selections. Input values are echoed to the screen providing confirmation feedback.

Experimental procedures

We used a within-subject design to test whether the revised interface was more clear and comprehensible than the original interface for first-time users. This would be evidenced through faster task completion times because there were no execution speedups made between versions, only changes to interface organization, color, and word choice as described earlier. The presentation order of versions was counter-balanced. Three pilot subjects were used to test the experimental tasks and

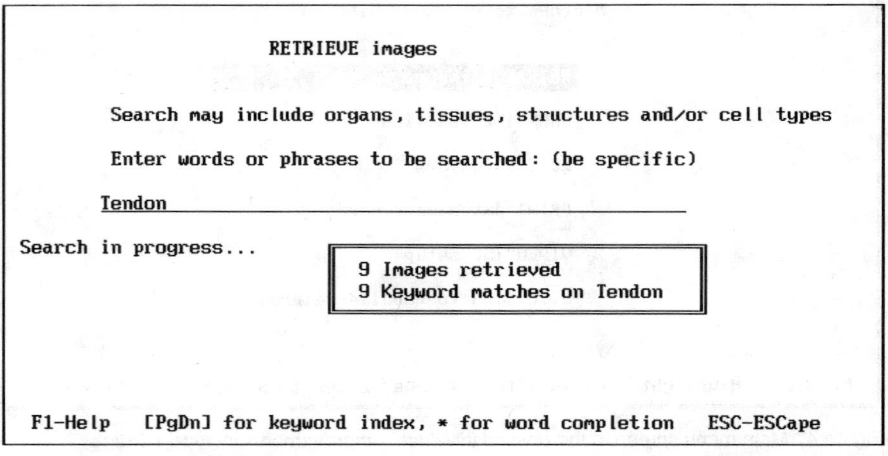

```
RETRIEVE images

Search may include organs, tissues, structures and/or cell types

Enter words or phrases to be searched: (be specific)

Tendon

Search in progress...
                        9 Images retrieved
                        9 Keyword matches on Tendon

F1-Help   [PgDn] for keyword index, * for word completion   ESC-ESCape
```

Figure 5. Dialog box for keyword search of images in the revised interface. Notice screen title is consistent with the menu item that was chosen to bring the user here. The instructions remain confined to bottom line with everday language to explain use of '*' character.

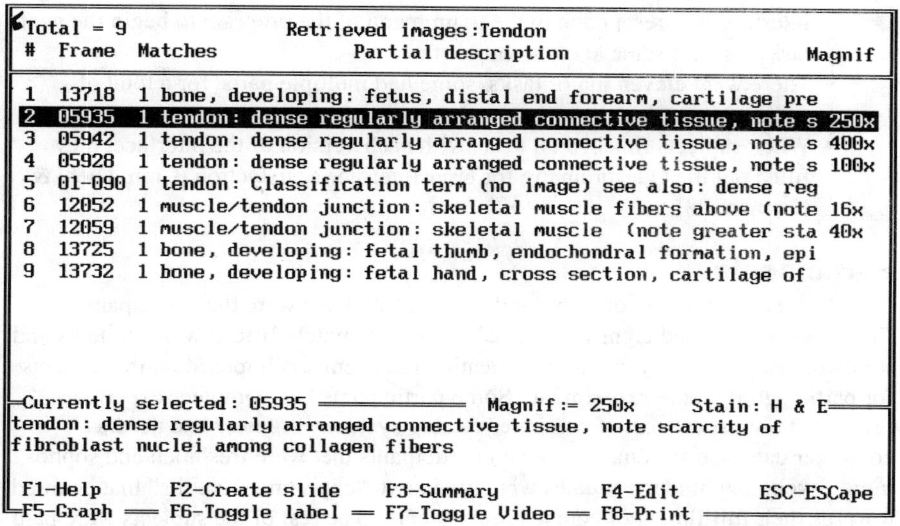

```
Total = 9              Retrieved images:Tendon
 #  Frame  Matches              Partial description                        Magnif

1  13718  1 bone, developing: fetus, distal end forearm, cartilage pre
2  05935  1 tendon: dense regularly arranged connective tissue, note s 250x
3  05942  1 tendon: dense regularly arranged connective tissue, note s 400x
4  05928  1 tendon: dense regularly arranged connective tissue, note s 100x
5  01-090 1 tendon: Classification term (no image) see also: dense reg
6  12052  1 muscle/tendon junction: skeletal muscle fibers above (note 16x
7  12059  1 muscle/tendon junction: skeletal muscle  (note greater sta 40x
8  13725  1 bone, developing: fetal thumb, endochondral formation, epi
9  13732  1 bone, developing: fetal hand, cross section, cartilage of

Currently selected: 05935 ========  Magnif:= 250x    Stain: H & E
tendon: dense regularly arranged connective tissue, note scarcity of
fibroblast nuclei among collagen fibers

F1-Help      F2-Create slide      F3-Summary       F4-Edit       ESC-ESCape
F5-Graph  =  F6-Toggle label  =  F7-Toggle Video  =  F8-Print
```

Figure 6. Retrieved-images screen with a selected item in the revised interface. Title of screen is consistent with menu item, column labels are less violent ("matches" instead of "hits"). At bottom of screen function keys appear in numerical order, and magnification and stain are placed away from the instructions for clarity.

procedure; changes were made to decrease the number of tasks and to use more descriptive text to explain some of the tasks. The procedure for testing each subject was:

- Subjects read a one page instruction sheet about the experiment in which they were told to pretend they were medical students looking in the library for information and images of human cell structures. They were told how they would be timed and that they must continue solving each part of each task until they got it correct or a time limit of five minutes expired. No training or other explanation about the system was given in order to mimic the situation real users in the library would encounter in a walk-up-and-use system.
- A standard consent formed was signed.
- Each task description, which may have several parts, would be given to subjects to read in its entirety. Then for each part of the task, subjects would say, "I'm beginning." For each part of the task subjects would say, "I'm done" and give an answer. If the answer was incorrect, the experimenter would state this and the subject would continue solving the current part of the task. If correct, the subject would go on the next part of the task. The experimenter used a stopwatch to record the time to successfully complete each part of the task. When the entire task was completed, the

interface was reset back to the main menu of the program to begin the next task from the same known, initial state.

- There were eleven major tasks, some had multiple parts, for a total of twenty-two tasks.
- When subjects finished all tasks with each version of the interface, they filled out the Questionnaire for User Interface Satisfaction (Chin, Diehl & Norman, 88).

Participants

Nineteen University of Maryland staff and students were the participants. Eleven were male and eight were female. Approximately fifteen were students and four were staff. There were no qualification requirements imposed on the subjects for participating in the experiment. Some participants had computer experience, fewer had used some sort of computer catalog system, yet fewer had used a computer database system. The seven participants that were freshmen and sophomore psychology undergraduates were given two "experiment credits" that counted towards their fulfillment of course requirements. The rest of the subjects were paid ten dollars for their participation. All data was collected anonymously.

Materials

The experiment was conducted on an IBM PC AT computer with an IBM InfoWindows color display, Pioneer 6000 videodisk player, the NLM videodisk with magnified images of human cells, and a Sony color monitor on which the videodisk images appeared. The experimenters used a stopwatch to time the tasks. When voice commands were not issued by subjects, the experimenter would realize when the task was initiated and start the stopwatch, it was always clear when the task was completed. Times were rounded off to the nearest second. The two sets of task descriptions were nearly identical, only minute details (e.g., record numbers) were changed so that subjects could not rely on memorization of answers from the first task set to apply to the second task set. The tasks were:

Find all the image records that have to do with "heart".

1a) How many records were found?

1b) Is frame #15339 in the set of records?

1c) Is frame #04677 in the set of records?

Now view the detailed textual information about frame #06201 by Selecting it.

1d) What is the magnification?

1e) What is the stain?

2) Find ALL the image records that have “ju” in any form in them.

3) Find and view the image of frame #12345.

Whenever there is a list of image records on the screen, there is a choice as to whether the image will appear automatically on the video monitor simply by using the arrow keys to move the highlight bar to that line on the screen. This is called Autodisplay mode.

4a) Is the Autodisplay mode currently ON or OFF?

4b) Make the Autodisplay mode the opposite of its current value.

Some video images have tissue labels associated with them that will appear overlayed on the image on the video monitor; however, not all images have these tissue labels. Whether the tissue label will appear or not depends on the value of the Video (tissue) Label mode.

5a) Are the Video (tissue) Labels currently being displayed on the video screen with each image?

5b) Make the Video (tissue) Labels mode the opposite of its current value.

6) Make a print-out of frame #14635.

7) Make a print-out of the Slideshow/Showfile “tend.sho”.

8a) How many Slideshows/Showfiles do you have the choice of loading?

8b) View on the video monitor every image in the Slideshow/Showfile “tend.sho”.

9a) View all the images of the Slideshow/Showfile “show1.sho”.

9b) Make it so that there is no current Slideshow/Showfile.

Load the Slideshow/Showfile “long.sho” to be the current Slideshow/Showfile such that its contents are the only contents in the Slideshow/Showfile.

10a) How many images are there in this Slideshow/Showfile?

10b) What is the SORT CODE number of frame #12345 in this Slideshow/ Showfile?

10c) What is the STRUCTURE type of frame #12345 in this Slideshow/ Showfile?

10d) Add frame #06194 to be the second to last image of the Slideshow/ Showfile "long.sho".

11) Create a brand new Slideshow/Showfile with frames #14586 and #16473 in it.

The 72-item Questionnaire for User Interface Satisfaction was used to collect subjective reactions (QUIS is available for license in paper, Macintosh, and MS Windows formats. Contact Carolyn Garrett at Office of Technology Liaison, University of Maryland, 4312 Knox Road, College Park, MD 20742. 301-405-4210, Carolyn_A_Garrett@umail.umd.edu).

Results

A paired samples t-test was run for both the timing data and QUIS data. Mean times were computed individually for each task; there was a statistically significant difference ($p < .01$) favoring the revised interface for five out of twenty tasks (table 1).

One task, task 6, favored the original interface ($p < .01$). Tasks 10d and 11 were not analyzed because less than half of the subjects completed these complex slideshow editing tasks within the time limit.

In the QUIS data, 19 out of the 72 questions favored the revised interface with a statistically significant advantage ($p < .05$) over the original interface (table 2). Five of the six questions inquiring about the system overall showed statistically significant differences favoring the revised interface ($p < .02$). Specifically, the revised interface, when compared to the original interface, received a higher rating on these dimensions:

wonderful (vs. terrible)
satisfying (vs. frustrating)
stimulating (vs. dull)
easy (vs. difficult), and
flexible (vs. rigid).

Task #	Original Interface Mean	Original Interface Stan. Dev.	Revised Interface Mean	Revised Interface Stan. Dev.
1a	39.3	(50.2)	50.6	(88.5)
1b	26.8	(24.4)	38.1	(65.4)
1c	11.8	(11.2)	34.3	(68.2)
1d	44.7	(37.4)	48.6	(40.2)
1e	14.6	(23.4)	16.5	(28.5)
2	63.8	(89.6)	23.5	(16.4)
3	37.2	(67.5)	39.4	(73.9)
4a	78.2	(68.2)	28.6	(33.3)
4b	122.7	(114.6)	51.9	(68.7)
5a	48.7	(38.1)	45.6	(54.7)
5b	50.0	(93.2)	18.4	(20.5)
6	44.9	(43.4)	144.7	(98.9)
7	200.4	(91.4)	48.9	(46.8)
8a	33.9	(16.7)	15.9	(14.9)
8b	95.1	(85.7)	106.8	(104.9)
9a	49.9	(42.0)	58.4	(68.9)
9b	62.9	(86.5)	49.5	(70.6)
10a	137.7	(82.6)	56.8	(64.2)
10b	29.5	(41.6)	33.8	(67.2)
10c	3.3	(3.2)	24.4	(70.1)

Table 1. The mean time to complete each task for each interface is listed with the standard deviation in parentheses. An underlined time denotes that a statistically significant difference ($p < .01$) favored that interface for that task. A time limit of 300 seconds was imposed for completion of each task. There were 19 participants.

Some of the other revealing QUIS questions which favored the revised interface ($p < .05$) were:

- "terms on the screen" are more precise
- "messages to the user" are more clear
- "instructions for commands or choices" are more clear
- "learning to operate the system" is easier
- "getting started" is easier
- "exploration of features by trial and error" is more encouraged
- "operations" are more dependable
- "the needs of both experienced and inexperienced users are taken into consideration" more often.

Discussion

We believe that the revised interface yielded faster performance and higher satisfaction due to how information was displayed with respect to location, wording, and color choices. Consistent location on the screen for key objects allows users to find and attend to them easily. Using consistently-assigned color schemes for conceptually similar objects allows (extra) information to be displayed without cluttering the screen or confusing users (Hoadley, 90; Marcus, 86). Another major difference that allows the revised design to be more usable is word choice; this is especially evident in the slideshow menus. Words consistent with the task domain such as "print," "show," and "create/edit" were comprehended more quickly than "report," "run," and "review/edit," respectively.

Task 6 yielded faster performance with the original interface. In the revised interface, the function key approach to printing had been inadvertently removed (this was not one of our suggestions for improving the interface design!). This made it difficult (task 6 had the longest mean time with the revised interface) to complete the task unless they read the help screen.

Two subjects offered handwritten comments on the QUIS forms. Both stated that the original interface was harder to use and less understandable than the revised interface. The comments were:

- "I hope this is the system to be replaced. Numerous little annoyances, primarily lack of information as to what to do at a given spot."
- "I rate this second version (i.e., original version) as much more difficult than the first. The language was better in the first one."

The revised interface was rated superior by a statistically significant difference for all QUIS items about accessing and content of help because the original interface had no working help component. We do not believe that the inclusion of help in the revised interface made a substantial difference in the outcome. The additional time spent reading the help was included in task time. More than half of the participants attempted to use the help. A further study would need to be conducted to examine this issue independently.

A log of comments was kept on how the participants reacted during the experiment. For the most part, the participants had a hard time with certain aspects of the system. For example, most did not perform well on slideshow editing. We were also surprised that some of the participants who accessed help were not able to complete a task even though they viewed all the information needed. Since there was no training prior to the tasks, it is not surprising that subjects had difficulty. This is similar to performance we have seen on other systems in which users were required to begin work without training.

Conclusions

We were pleased to obtain experimental support showing that a modest number of changes to create a revised interface can produce measurable performance and satisfaction differences. The principal guidelines we followed to suggest improvements can be applied to many interactive computer systems.

- Toned down use of color that is systematically used for similar objects, which allows for display of extra information without cluttering the screen or confusing users.
- Choice of words to be task oriented rather than system oriented. Designers should use words from the task domain and everyday language, not "computerese."
- Consistent wording throughout the user interface simplifies comprehension.
- Consistent location for important objects can focus users' attention and bring confidence to expectations.

Subjective user satisfaction should be given adequate attention as a determinant of interface success. Attention to details, such as status feedback and specific rather than generic prompts, can give users a more confident feeling about interacting with a computer system. Careful attention should be paid to issues of color choice, screen layout, and word choice, the latter using application domain terminology.

Acknowledgements

We thank Degi Young for the original usability evaluation of the MicroAnatomy program and suggestions for its improvement, for help administering the experiment, and for providing good cheer and good deeds.
Dr. Kent Norman provided valuable help with analyzing the statistical data and reviewing a draft of this paper. Leslie Carter helped significantly in designing the experimental method and statistical analysis. Dr. Catherine Plaisant also helped to design the experiment and review drafts of this paper. Andrew Sears provided expert assistance with the computer statistics package and a thoughtful review.
This research was funded by the National Library of Medicine, contract number 467-MZ-000159.

References

Borgman, C.L. (1986) Why are online catalogs hard to use? Lessons learned from information retrieval studies, *Journal of the American Society for Information Science*, Vol. 37, No. 6, 387-400.

Botafogo, R. (1990) Structural Analysis of Hypertexts, Masters Thesis, Department of Computer Science, University of Maryland, College Park, MD 20742.

Brown, C. Marlin (1988). *Human-Computer Interface Design Guidelines*, Ablex, Norwood, NJ.

Chin, J.P., Diehl, V.A., and Norman, K. (1988) Development of an instrument measuring user satisfaction of the human-computer Iinterface," *Proceedings of the Conference on Human Factors in Computing Systems, CHI '90.* Association for Computing Machinery, New York, 213-218.

Conklin, J. (1987) Hypertext: An introduction and survey, *IEEE Computer* Vol. 20, No. 9, 17-41.

Converse, S., et al. (1987) Where can I find ? An evaluation of a computerized directory information system, (Unpublished), Department of Psychology, Old Dominion University, Norfolk, VA 23529.

Grudin, J. (Oct. 1989) "The Case Against User Interface Consistency," *Communications of the ACM*, Vol. 32, No. 10, 1164-1173.

Grudin, J. (Jan. 1992) Consistency, Standards, and Formal Approaches to Interface Development and Evaluation: A Note on Wiecha, Bennett, Boies, Gould, and Greene, *ACM Transactions of Information Systems*, Vol. 10, No. 1, 103-111.

Hildreth, C. (1982) *Online Public Access Catalogs: The User Interface*, Dublin, OH: OCLC.

Hoadley, E. (Feb. 1990) Investigating the Effects of Color, *Communications of the ACM*, Vol. 33, No. 2, 120-125.

Holum, K. (1988) Reliving King's Herod's Dream, *Archaeology*, May/June 88, 44-47.

Holum, K., Hohlfelder, R., Bull, R., Raban, A. (1988) *King Herod's Dream - Caesarea on the sea*, W.W. Norton & Company, New York.

Kearsley, G. (1993). *Public Access Computer Systems*, Ablex, Norwood, NJ.

Kellogg, W. (1989) The Dimensions of Consistency, in Nielsen, Jakob (editor) *Coordinating User Interfaces for Consistency*, Academic Press, San Diego, 9-20.

Lewis, C., Polson, P., Wharton, C., and Rieman, J. (1990) Testing a Walkthrough Methodology for Theory-Based Design of Walk-Up-and-Use Interfaces, *Proc. of the Conference on Human Factors in Computing Systems, CHI '90.* Association for Computing Machinery,

New York 235-242.

Marcus, A. (Nov. 1986) The Ten Commandments of Color: a Tutorial, *Computer Graphics Today*, Vol. 3, No. 11, 7-14.

Marchionini, G. , Shneiderman, B. (1988) Finding facts vs. browsing knowledge in hypertext systems, *IEEE Computer* Vol. 21, No. 1, 70-79.

Nielsen, J. (1989) Executive Summary: Coordinating User Interfaces for Consistency, in Nielsen, Jakob (editor), *Coordinating User Interfaces for Consistency*, Academic Press, San Diego, 1-7.

Plaisant, C. (1991) Guide to Opportunities in Volunteer Archaeology: case study of the use of a hypertext system in a museum exhibit, *Hypertext/Hypermedia Handbook*, Berk, E. & Devlin, J., Eds., McGraw-Hill Publ., New York, NY 498-505.

Potter, R., Shneiderman, B., Weldon, L. (1988) Improving the accuracy of touch-screens: an experimental evaluation of three strategies, *Proc. of the Conference on Human Factors in Computing Systems*, ACM SIGCHI, New York, 27-30.

Reisner, P (1990) "What is Inconsistency?" *Proceedings of the IFIP Third International Conference on Human-Computer Interaction, Interact '90.* Elsevier Science Publishers B.V., North-Holland, 175-181.

Shneiderman, B. (1987) User interface design for the Hyperties electronic encyclopedia, *Proc. Hypertext '87 Workshop*, University of North Carolina, Department of Computer Science, Raleigh, NC, 199-204.

Shneiderman, B., Kearsley, G. (1989) *Hypertext Hands-On!*, Addison-Wesley Publ., Reading, MA, 192 pages + 2 PC disks.

Shneiderman, B., Brethauer, D., Plaisant, C., Potter, R. (May 1989) Evaluating three museum installations of a hypertext, *Journal of the American Society for Information Science*, Vol. 40, No. 3, 172-182.

Shneiderman, B. (1992) *Designing the User Interface: Strategies for Effective Human-Computer Interaction*, second edition, Addison-Wesley, Reading, MA, .

Smith, S., and Mosier, J. (1986). Guidelines for Designing User Interface Software. Report ESD-TR-86-278 Electronic Systems Division, The Mitre Corporation, Bedford, MA.

Wang, X., Liebscher, P., Marchionini, G. (1988) Improving information seeking performance in Hypertext: roles of display format and search strategy. Tech. Report No. CAR-TR-353 CS-TR-2006., Human-Computer Interaction Laboratory: University of Maryland, College Park.

Wiecha, C., Bennett, W., Boies, S., Gould, J., and Greene, S. (July 1990) ITS: A tool for rapidly developing interactive applications, *ACM Transactions of Information Systems*, Vol. 8, No. 3, 204-236.

Wiecha, C. (Jan. 1992) ITS and user interface consistency: A response to Grudin *ACM Transactions of Information Systems*, Vol. 10, No. 1, 112-114.

Young, D., and Shneiderman, B. (July 1989) Guidelines to designing an effective interface for the MicroAnatomy Visual Library System," unpublished research report, Human-Computer Interaction Laboratory, University of Maryland.

Young, E., Walker, J. H. (1987) A case study of using a manual online, unpublished manuscript, Symbolics Corp, Cambridge, MA.

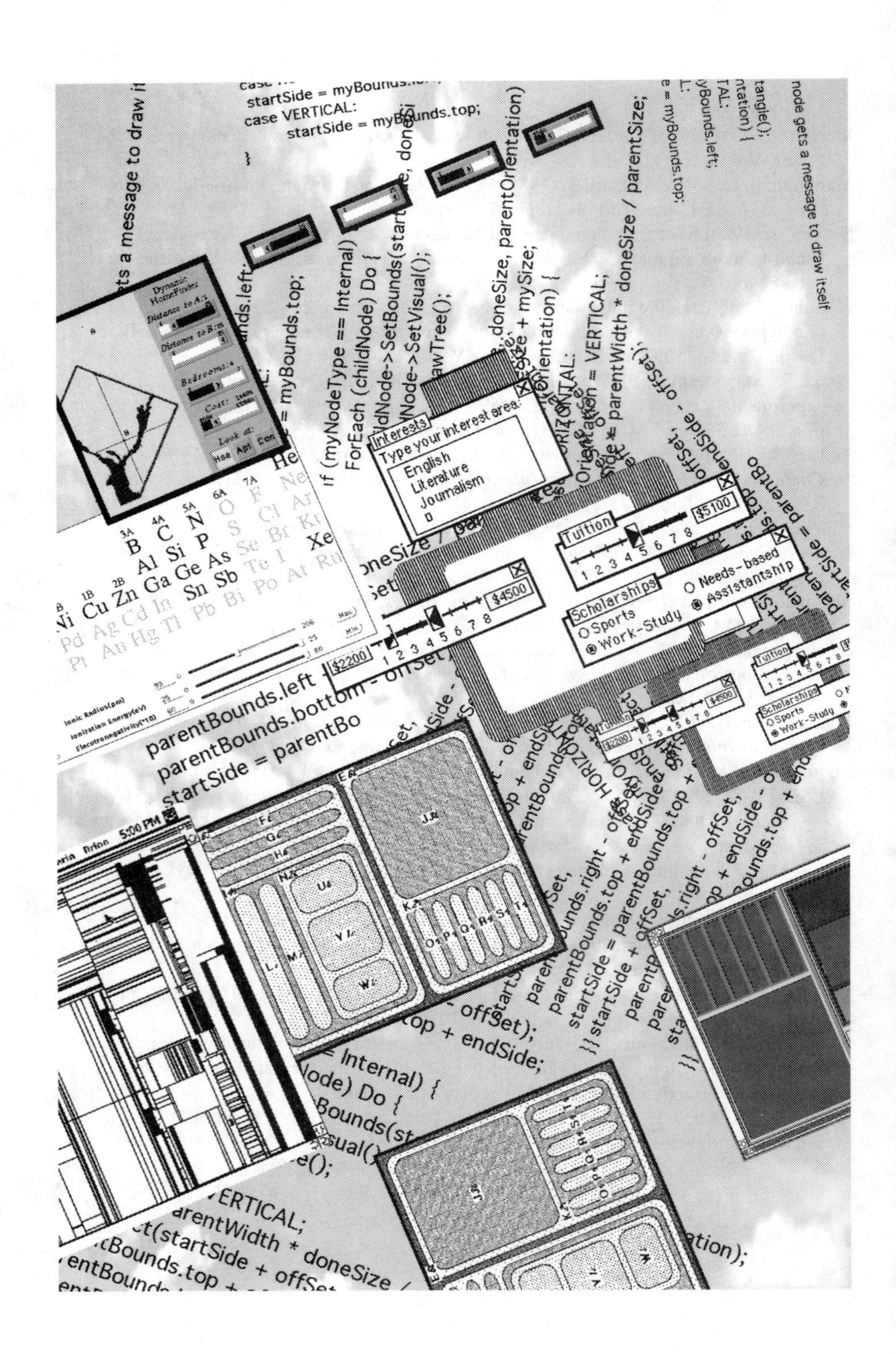

case VERTICAL:
startSide = myBounds.top;
node gets a message to draw itself
If (myNodeType == Internal)
ForEach (childNode) Do {
Interests
Type your interest area:
English
Literature
Journalism
Tuition
$5100
$4500
$2200
Scholarships
Sports
Work-Study
Needs-based
Assistantship
Dynamic HomeFinder
Ionic Radius(pm)
Ionization Energy(eV)
parentBounds.bottom
startSide = parentBo
startSide = parentBounds.top + offSet,
parentBounds.right - offSet,

Sparks of Innovation in Human-Computer Interaction,
B. Shneiderman, Ed., Ablex Publ., Norwood, NJ (1993)

6. Information visualization: dynamic queries, treemaps, and the filter/flow metaphor

Introduction

Carefully designed visual displays can help combat the information anxiety and overload that troubles many people. Our eyes can carry a hundred times more information to the brain than our ears. Adding user-controlled animation can further increase comprehension. The world of the future will be more like driving or flying a plane through colorful three (or four) dimensional information spaces. Users will rapidly select, combine, eliminate and construct new displays. As screens get larger and faster, users will seek them enthusiastically and give up on the older notion of dialog. They will want to fly, drive, explore, steer, direct, operate, bend, push and play. The theme will be Just Do It! and the Turing Test (whether a computer program can deceive users into thinking it is a human) will fade as a meaningful challenge.

As with any powerful technology, there is a danger that users will become overwhelmed with or addicted to these new information spaces. Designers have a responsibility to ensure that users can cope with the flood, recognize the difference between reality and information space, appreciate the needs for privacy, respect interpersonal relationships, and explore the full range of emotional expression (joy, love, anger, guilt, and frustration).

Our recent projects have spawned a new conception of the future of computing. These ideas allow designers to couple the remarkable human ability at visual information processing with the increasing capacity of computers to display high resolution dynamic color images. The result is that users can accomplish superhuman feats, searching vast information spaces with X-ray vision to locate needles in haystacks, uncover trends, discover subtle patterns, and spot exceptional conditions.

The Visual Information Explorer (VIZER) is a multi-year project to develop advanced software and user interfaces that will allow novice and expert users to visually explore very large databases, spreadsheets, geographic information, temporal sales data, financial reports, and medical information.

VIZER is a pun on "visor" which is a simple means to give people a clearer view of their surroundings. Like a pair of sunglasses, a swimmer's face mask, or a motorcyclist's helmet, VIZER will enable users to see clearly and explore new territories. Instead of the EyePhones of virtual reality which block out the world, we hope to provide a clearer view of what might be called "visual reality". While the immersive experience of "being in" is appealing for entertainment and some simulations, we feel that the observing experience of "looking at" is likely to be more widely acceptable.

VIZER's components include the filter/flow representation of boolean operations, dynamic queries that allow small changes in input variables to be shown immediately by changes in a 2- or 3- dimensional display, tree-maps that allow a space filling representation of trees with 3000-5000 nodes on the screen at once, and remote visualization that allows users to browse through telepresence.

Our goals include the construction of an integrated tool to support exploration, retrieval, gathering, traversal and capture with goal-directed task-level actions for saving, printing and sending text, numeric data, images, sound and other structured information through high-speed distributed networks.

Our approach is to build, refine, test, and revise software components and user interface strategies in an evolutionary framework that culminates in an integrated system called VIZER. Multiple high resolution displays, parallel processors with specialized hardware, and terabit networks will be necessary for the ultimate systems, but during the process of development, subsystems that function on commercial workstations and personal computers will be spawned.

Graphical boolean queries using a filter/flow metaphor

In many database management and information retrieval applications, users must specify complex boolean queries. Studies indicate that most users experience great difficulty composing complex queries, using SQL-like query languages or even visual approaches such as Query-by-Example. We implemented a novel visual presentation based on water filter/flow metaphors that reveals the effect of selectors and operators (OR, AND, and NOT) on query outcome (Young & Shneiderman, 1992). Figure 1 shows how it might be applied to help students choose colleges. Users can select from the set of attributes and get an appropriate filter widget (type-in for interest areas, sliders for cost, and buttons for scholarships)

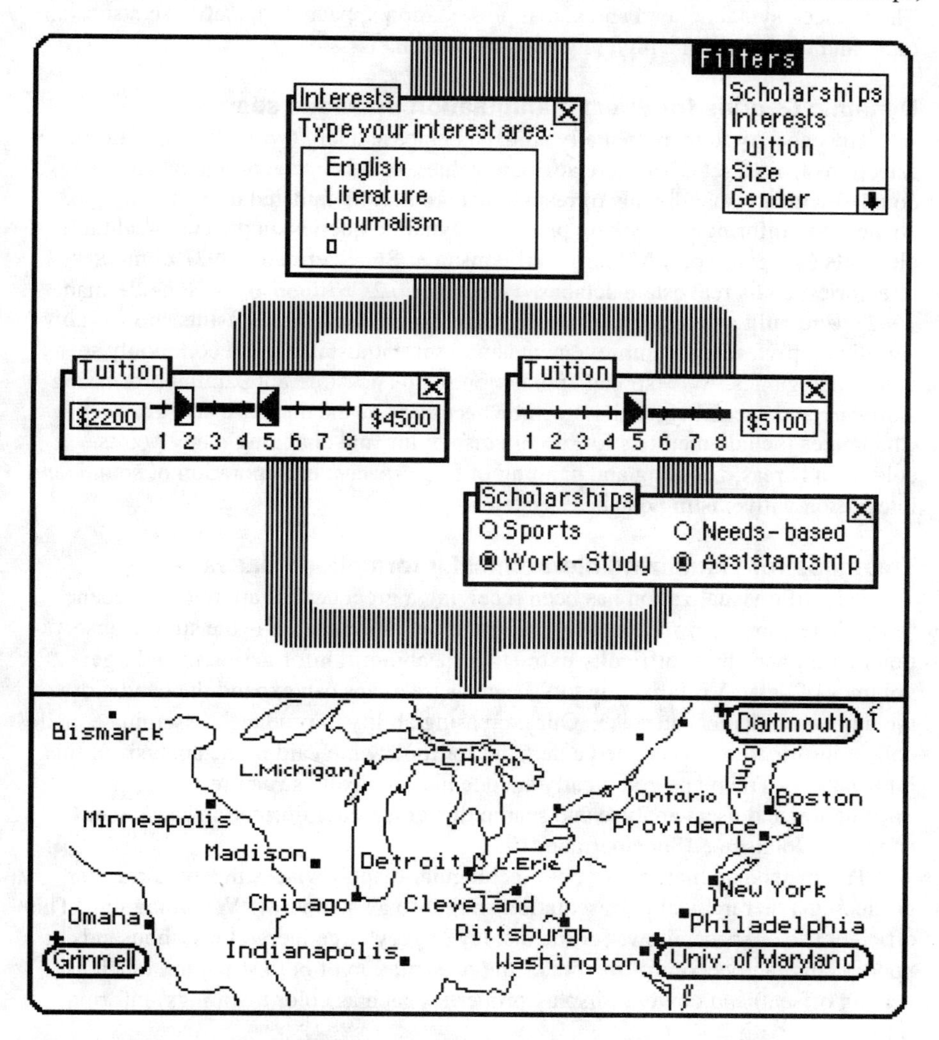

Figure 1. A mockup of a filter/flow boolean query ((Interests = English or Literature or Journalism) AND ((Tuition greater than or equal to $2200 and less than or equal to $4500) OR ((Tuition greater than or equal to $5100) AND (Scholarships are available by Work-Study or Assistantship)))) combined with map output to show the result (Dartmouth, Grinnell, and the Univ. of Maryland).

which is placed on the screen with flow lines showing ANDs (sequential flow) and ORs (parallel flows). The X in each filter widget could be selected to negate the filter values. Clustering of one-in-one-out segments to form a new and saveable filter is possible.

Our prototype implementation, using ToolBook, allowed 20 experimental subjects to comprehend and compose queries far more effectively than with SQL. The reduced syntactic load and visual presentation appears to benefit users substantially and to give them a high level of satisfaction.

Dynamic Queries for direct manipulation database search

The capacity to incrementally adjust a database query (with sliders, buttons, selections from a set of discrete attribute values, or other selection mechanisms) coupled with a visual display of results that are rapidly updated dramatically changes the information seeking process. Dynamic queries on the chemical table of elements (see paper 6.1, Ahlberg, Williamson & Shneiderman, 1992), computer directories, and a real estate database (see paper 6.2, Williamson & Shneiderman, 1992) were built and tested in three separate experiments. The results show highly significant performance improvements and user enthusiasm more commonly seen with video games. Widespread application seems possible but parallel processing hardware and special algorithms will be necessary as the database size grows. Challenges include methods for rapidly displaying and changing many points, colors, and areas; zooming and panning of large spaces; incorporation of sound; and integration with existing database systems.

Treemaps for visualizing hierarchical information spaces

Scientific visualization has been receiving a great deal of attention in recent years. There are many reasons for this but chief among them is the simple observation that humans have difficulty extracting meaningful information from large volumes of data. Visualization tools such as treemaps can expand the bandwidth of the human-computer interface. Our increasing ability to produce, disseminate, and collect information has created a demand for tools which aid in the analysis of this information. Treemaps graphically encode hierarchically structured information,and users analyze and search this graphical information space (see paper 6.3, Johnson & Shneiderman, 1991).

Treemaps map hierarchies onto rectangular display spaces in a tiled manner, producing a hierarchical representation similar to a squared-off Venn diagram. This efficient use of space allows for the display of very large hierarchies (thousands of nodes). Interactive control facilitates the presentation of both structural (such as nesting offsets) and content (display properties such as color mappings) information.

The utility of treemaps was tested during the past year in two experiments designed to reflect "real-world" situations and needs. The experiments dealt with hierarchical file structures and the finances of a corporate product hierarchy.

Results so far are very encouraging: feedback from users has been positive and performance on global tasks was significantly improved.

Hierarchical information structures have long been natural ways of organization and space-filling approaches to their visualization have great potential. The treemap algorithms are general and the possibilities for mapping information about individual nodes to the display are appealing. Treemaps can aid decision making processes by helping users create accurate mental models of the content and structure of hierarchical information spaces.

Sparks of Innovation in Human-Computer Interaction,
B. Shneiderman, Ed., Ablex Publ., Norwood, NJ (1993)

6.1 Dynamic Queries for information exploration: an implementation and evaluation

Christopher Ahlberg
Christopher Williamson
Ben Shneiderman

Abstract

We designed, implemented and evaluated a new concept for direct manipulation of databases, called dynamic queries, that allows users to formulate queries with graphical widgets, such as sliders. By providing a graphical visualization of the database and search results, users can find trends and exceptions easily. Eighteen undergraduate chemistry students performed statistically significantly faster using a dynamic queries interface compared to two interfaces, both providing form fill-in as input method, one with graphical visualization output and one with all-textual output. The interfaces were used to expore the periodic table of elements and search on their properties.

ACM CHI '92 Conference Proc. (Monterey, CA, May 3-7, 1992) 619-626.

Introduction

Most database systems require the user to create and formulate a complex query, which presumes that the user is familiar with the logical structure of the database (Larson, 1986). The queries on a database are usually expressed in high-level query languages (such as SQL, QUEL). This works well for many applications, but it is not a fully satisfying way of finding data. For naïve users these systems are difficult to use and understand, and they require a long training period (Kim, Korth, & Silberschatz, 1988).

Clearly there is a need for easy to use, quick and powerful query methods for database retrieval. Direct manipulation has proved to be successful for other applications such as display editors, spreadsheets, computer aided design/manufacturing systems, computer games and graphical environments for operating systems such as the Apple Macintosh (Shneiderman, 1983). Direct manipulation interfaces support:

- Continuous visual representation of objects and actions of interest
- Physical actions or labelled button presses instead of complex syntax
- Rapid, incremental, reversible operations whose impact on the object of interest is immediately visible
- Layered or spiral approach to learning that permits usage with minimal knowledge.

One of the great advantages of direct manipulation is that it places the task in the center of what users have to do. Rutkowski (1982) describes it as "The user is able to apply intellect directly to the task; the tool itself seems to disappear." The success of direct manipulation can be understood in the context of the syntactic/semantic model which describes the different levels of understanding users have (Shneiderman, 1983). Objects of interest are displayed so that actions are directly in the high level semantic domain. Users do not need to decompose tasks into syntactically complex sequences. Thus each command is a comprehensible action in the problem domain whose effect is immediately visible. The closeness of the command action to the problem domain reduces user problem-solving load and stress.

For databases, there have been few attempts to use direct manipulation. Zloof describes a method of data manipulation based on the direct representations of the relations on the screen, Query-by-Example (Zloof, 1975). Zloof writes "a user dealing with 'simple' queries needs to study the system only to that point of complexity which is compatible with the level of sophistication required within the domain of those queries." Query-by-Example succeeds because novices can begin working with just a little training, yet there is ample power for the expert.

Another attempt to create a more user friendly query language is the PICASSO query language (Kim, Korth, & Silberschatz, 1988). The authors state that the major contribution of PICASSO and graphical interface ROGUE is that users can pose complex queries using a mouse without knowing the details of the underlying database schema nor the details of first-order predicate calculus or algebra.

The power of direct manipulation can be applied even further. Neither Query-by-Example nor PICASSO provide any visual display of actions. Query-by-Example relies on users entering values with a keyboard. Even though PICASSO supports input through mouse and menus, it requires users to perform a number of operations in each step. The combination of graphical input/output is not applied in either system.

A more desirable database interface:

- represents the query graphically,
- provides a visible limit on the query range,
- provides a graphical representation of the database and the query result,
- gives immediate feedback of the result after every query adjustment, and
- allows novice users to begin working with little training but still provides expert users with powerful features.

An interface utilizing dynamic queries possesses the above-mentioned properties (Williamson & Shneiderman, 1992).

In dynamic queries the query is represented by a number of widgets such as sliders (Open Look, 1989) (Figure 1). A slider consists of a label, a field indicating its current value, a slider bar with a drag box, and a value at each end of the slider bar indicating minimum and maximum values. Sliding the drag box with the mouse changes the slider value. Clicking on the slider bar increases or decreases the value one step at a time.

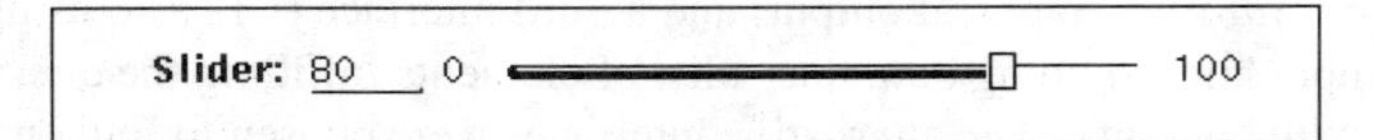

Figure 1. Slider from Open Look

The database is represented on the screen in graphical form. This paper describes a program dealing with the chemical elements and accordingly the periodic table of elements was chosen as the representation. The result of the query can be highlighted by coloring, changing points of light, marking of regions, or blinking.

The combination of a graphical query and graphical output matches well the ideas of direct manipulation. The slider serves as a metaphor for the operation of entering a value for a field in the query - it provides a mental model (Norman, 1988) of the range. Changing the value is done by a physical action - sliding the drag box with a mouse - instead of entering the value by keyboard. By being able to slide the drag box back and forth and getting immediate updates of the query results, it is possible to do tens of queries in just a few seconds, i.e, the operation is rapid. The operation is incremental and if the query result is not what users expected the operation is reversible by just sliding the drag box in the opposite direction. Error messages are not needed - there is no such thing as an ‘illegal’ operation.

The interaction between the database visualization and the query mechanism is important. The sliders have to be placed close to the visualization to reduce eye movement. The highlighting of elements should be in harmony with the coloring scheme of the slider. For example the color of the area to the left of the drag box on the slider bar is the same as the highlighted elements in the visualization, because the values to the left of the drag box are the values that satisfy the query.

The dynamic queries program used for the experiment is an educational program for the periodic table of elements. It allows users to set properties such as atomic number, atomic mass, electronegativity, etc., to highlight elements that satisfy the query displayed on the periodic table. This lets users explore how these properties interact with each other. Other interesting discoveries can be made regarding trends of properties in the periodic table - such as how electronegativity increases from the lower left corner to the upper right corner of the periodic table. Exceptions to trends can also be found easily, such as the two places in the periodic table where the atomic mass does not increase with atomic number.

Experiment

Introduction

This experiment compared three different interfaces for database query and visualization: a dynamic queries interface, a second interface (FG) providing graphical visualization output but using form fill-in as the input method (Rowe, 1985) (Form fill-in - Graphical output) and a third interface (FT) also using a forms fill-in as input but providing output as a list of elements fulfilling the query (Form fill-in - Textual output). The alternative interfaces were chosen to find out which aspect of dynamic queries makes the major difference, the input by sliders allowing users to quickly browse through the database, or the output visualization providing an overview of the database. These were compared using three sets of matched questions.

The primary hypothesis was that because of the visualization of the periodic table in the dynamic queries and the FG interfaces, there would be a major difference compared to the FT interface. Performance results were measured as the time used for each question and the number of correct answers.

For questions asking subjects to find trends in the periodic table, the hypothesis was that the visualization of the periodic table in the dynamic queries and FG interfaces would make the major difference compared to the FT interface. But the ability to perform a large number of queries during a small period of time with the dynamic queries interface would make a difference favoring dynamic queries over FG.

Interfaces

...terfaces were built using the Developer's Guide user interface develop-
...n the OpenWindows environment on a Sun Microsystems
...+ workstation with a 17-inch color monitor and optical three button

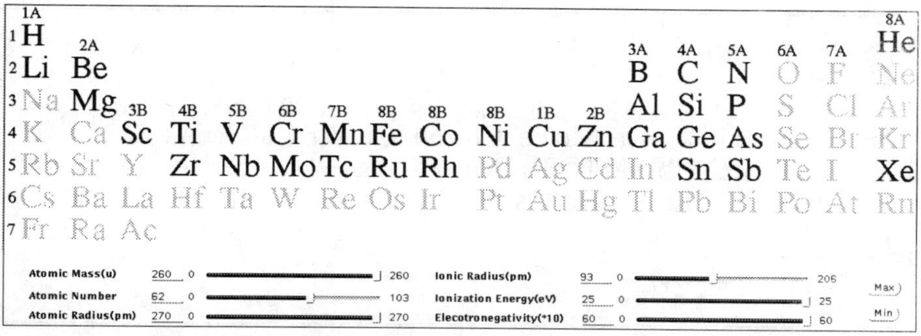

1A 8A
1 H He
2A 3A 4A 5A 6A 7A
2 Li Be B C N O F Ne
3 Na Mg 3B 4B 5B 6B 7B 8B 8B 8B 1B 2B Al Si P S Cl Ar
4 K Ca Sc Ti V Cr Mn Fe Co Ni Cu Zn Ga Ge As Se Br Kr
5 Rb Sr Y Zr Nb Mo Tc Ru Rh Pd Ag Cd In Sn Sb Te I Xe
6 Cs Ba La Hf Ta W Re Os Ir Pt Au Hg Tl Pb Bi Po At Rn
7 Fr Ra Ac

Atomic Mass(u) 260 0 260
Atomic Number 62 0 103
Atomic Radius(pm) 270 0 270
Ionic Radius(pm) 93 0 206
Ionization Energy(eV) 25 0 25
Elecotronegativity(*10) 60 0 60
Max
Min

Figure 2. Dynamic Queries interface for the periodic table of elements

Dynamic Queries interface

The dynamic queries interface (Figure 2) provides a visualization of the query result. A periodic table showing the elements is displayed in 40-point Roman font. The elements that fulfill the criteria set by the user's latest query are highlighted by being displayed in red. The rest of the elements are displayed in light grey. Users perform queries by setting the values of six properties using sliders (Figure 1). All interfaces included two other buttons, 'Max' and 'Min,' that set the values of all input fields to the minimum or maximum value.

The query result is determined by ANDing all six sliders, so all the elements that have an atomic mass less than or equal to X AND an atomic number less than or equal to Y, etc. , fulfill the criteria. The area to the left of the slider drag box is painted in red, corresponding to the red color of the highlighted elements in the visualization and thereby providing feedback about how elements are selected. The sliders are positioned under the periodic table, close to the visualization to minimize the distance users have to move their eyes. One direct manipulation feature in the dynamic queries interface was left out for experimental purposes. It allows users to click on any element and thereby set the sliders to the values of the properties of that element.

FG interface

The FG interface (Figure 3) provides users with the same visualization as the dynamic queries interface, but the query is composed by form fill-in. Instead of a slider, a numeric field allowing users to enter a value for that property by keyboard is provided. To the left of the numeric field the range of the criterion is given. If a value bigger than the upper bound is entered, the field is set to the upper bound.

The search is performed when users press the return key. The cursor indicating which numeric field is active stays in the same numeric field. Entering new values is done by either modifying the old one or deleting it and entering a new one. This is to provide an easy way to do the fine-tuning often needed when completing tasks. Users change the active field by using the up/down arrow keys. The left and right

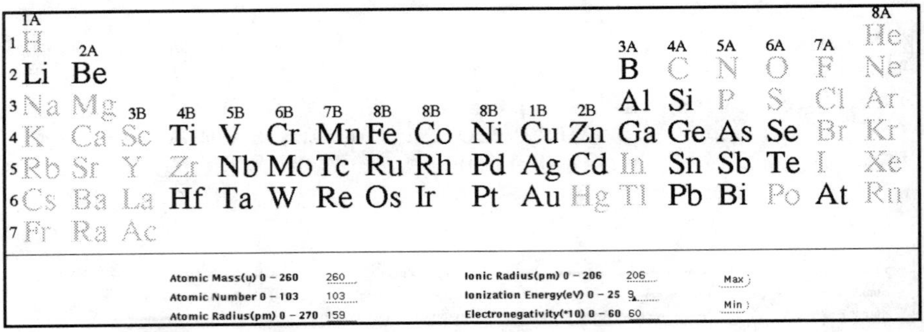

	1A	2A	3B	4B	5B	6B	7B	8B	8B	8B	1B	2B	3A	4A	5A	6A	7A	8A
1	H																	He
2	Li	Be											B	C	N	O	F	Ne
3	Na	Mg											Al	Si	P	S	Cl	Ar
4	K	Ca	Sc	Ti	V	Cr	Mn	Fe	Co	Ni	Cu	Zn	Ga	Ge	As	Se	Br	Kr
5	Rb	Sr	Y	Zr	Nb	Mo	Tc	Ru	Rh	Pd	Ag	Cd	In	Sn	Sb	Te	I	Xe
6	Cs	Ba	La	Hf	Ta	W	Re	Os	Ir	Pt	Au	Hg	Tl	Pb	Bi	Po	At	Rn
7	Fr	Ra	Ac															

Atomic Mass(u) 0 – 260 260
Atomic Number 0 – 103 103
Atomic Radius(pm) 0 – 270 159
Ionic Radius(pm) 0 – 206 206
Ionization Energy(eV) 0 – 25 9
Electronegativity(*10) 0 – 60 60
Max
Min

Figure 3. FG interface for periodic table

keys move the cursor inside the numeric field. The graphical output is exactly the same as in the dynamic queries interface.

FT interface

The all textual interface (Figure 4) provides exactly the same style of input as the FG interface but the output is given in an all textual manner. The elements that fulfill the criteria are listed in order of atomic number in a text window above the input fields. To be able to answer the questions, subjects were provided with a printed periodic table when using this interface.

Experimental variables

The independent variable in the experiment was the type of interface, with three treatments:

i. Dynamic Queries
ii. FG
iii. FT

The dependent variables were:

i. Time to find answers
ii. Number of correct answers
iii. Subjective satisfaction

Tasks

Subjects were presented with a set of five matched questions for each interface. The questions, chosen in cooperation with a chemistry professor at the University of Maryland, were divided into five categories:

1. Out of a certain set in the database, find a certain element fulfilling a simple criteria. This task required subjects to concentrate on a part of the database such as a group or period and find the element that, for example, had the highest ionization energy.

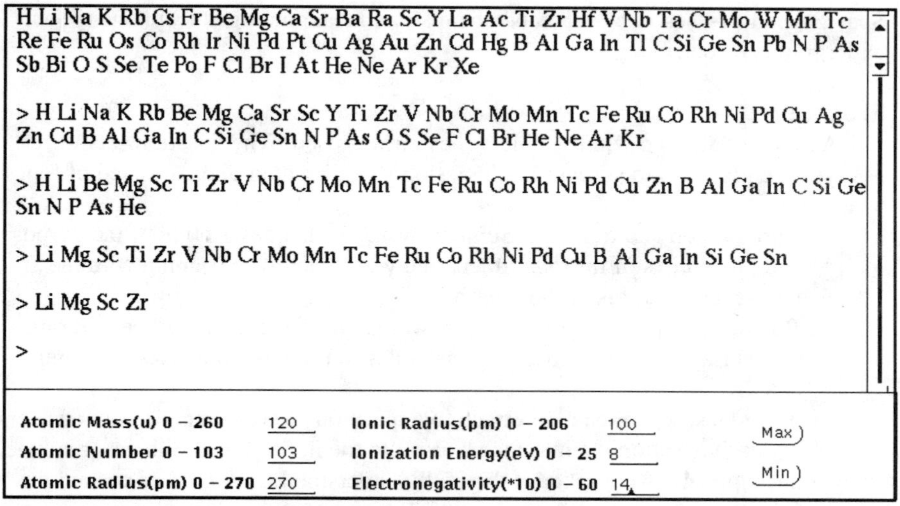

H Li Na K Rb Cs Fr Be Mg Ca Sr Ba Ra Sc Y La Ac Ti Zr Hf V Nb Ta Cr Mo W Mn Tc Re Fe Ru Os Co Rh Ir Ni Pd Pt Cu Ag Au Zn Cd Hg B Al Ga In Tl C Si Ge Sn Pb N P As Sb Bi O S Se Te Po F Cl Br I At He Ne Ar Kr Xe

> H Li Na K Rb Be Mg Ca Sr Sc Y Ti Zr V Nb Cr Mo Mn Tc Fe Ru Co Rh Ni Pd Cu Ag Zn Cd B Al Ga In C Si Ge Sn N P As O S Se F Cl Br He Ne Ar Kr

> H Li Be Mg Sc Ti Zr V Nb Cr Mo Mn Tc Fe Ru Co Rh Ni Pd Cu Zn B Al Ga In C Si Ge Sn N P As He

> Li Mg Sc Ti Zr V Nb Cr Mo Mn Tc Fe Ru Co Rh Ni Pd Cu B Al Ga In Si Ge Sn

> Li Mg Sc Zr

>

Atomic Mass(u) 0 – 260	120	Ionic Radius(pm) 0 – 206	100	Max
Atomic Number 0 – 103	103	Ionization Energy(eV) 0 – 25	8	
Atomic Radius(pm) 0 – 270	270	Electronegativity(*10) 0 – 60	14	Min

Figure 4. FT interface for periodic table

2. This more complex task required subjects to make at least two queries to complete the task; comparing the characteristics of one element to that of another.
3. Combine sliders/fields to get a subset of elements and find the element fulfilling a certain criteria in this set. This task required the set to examine to be formed by combining several criteria.
4. Find a trend for a property. The task requires subjects to create a mental picture of how a property changes through the database. This might be how atomic mass increases with atomic number.
5. Find an exception to a trend. This task asked subjects to find, from a given number of elements, the element that didn't follow 'normal behavior'.

Pilot study results

A pilot study of four subjects was conducted. It led to several changes in the experiment design. The initial manual timing procedure was changed to a computerized procedure. The instrument used for measuring subjective satisfaction was the Questionaire for User Interface Satisfaction (QUIS) [Chin, Diehl, & Norman, 1988], but shortened to 30 of the 72 original questions.

Participants

Eighteen undergraduate students, 9 females and 9 males, from summer session chemistry classes at the University of Maryland participated voluntarily in the experiment. Only two participants had used the Sun SparcStation 1+ used as the platform for the experiment. All but three subjects had used a mouse before, generally Macintosh or some IBM PC mouse, but not the optical mouse that the Sun

SparcStation 1+ uses. The subjects' chemistry education ranged from one to four undergraduate courses.

Procedures

A counterbalanced within-subjects design was used. The question sets were always given in the same order. Each session lasted an hour and consisted of four phases:

1. Introduction and training: Subjects were given a description of the purpose and procedures of the experiment and were also given training with the mouse and controls of the interfaces.
2. Practice tasks: Two practice tasks were given for each interface. During these tasks subjects were free to ask questions about both tasks and interfaces.
3. Timed tasks: For each interface five questions were given. Before answering each question the interface was set to the initial state. Subjects read the question, and were asked if they fully understood it. If so they pushed the Start button and started the query. This was to eliminate variations in subjects' comprehension speed. When subjects found the answer they wrote it down and pushed the Done button.
4. Subjective evaluation: Subjects were asked to fill out a shortened QUIS-form after having completed each interface and to provide open commentary while answering questions.

Phases 2, 3 and 4 were repeated for each interface.

Administration

The experiment was run over a period of 12 days. Subjects were asked to work as quickly and accurately as possible. The experimenter sat next to the subject, presented questions and ensured that the subject initialized the query and followed the proper timing procedures.

Results

Analysis of the timed tasks was done using an ANOVA with repeated measures for interface type. Observing the mean times to complete all tasks 1-5, shows a significant main effect, $F(2,34)=36.1$ ($p<0.001$). Similarly, a significant main effect was found for individual tasks 1, 2, 4 and 5, $F(2,34)=19.0$, 16.4, 21.4, 20.2 respectively ($p<0.001$) and for task 3 $F(2,34)= 7.1$ ($p<0.005$).

Tukey's post-hoc HSD analysis was used to determine which interface(s) was significantly faster. The dynamic queries interface had a significantly faster mean time for completing all tasks than both FG and FT interfaces, ($p<0.005$) and ($p<0.001$) respectively.

The time to complete each task is shown in Table 1. Figure 5 gives a bar chart of the same data.

For task 1 the dynamic queries interface was significantly faster than the FG interface, ($p<0.05$) and the FG interface was significantly faster than the FT interface, ($p<0.001$). For task 2, no difference between dynamic queries and the FG interface was found, but both were significantly faster than the FT interface, ($p<0.001$).

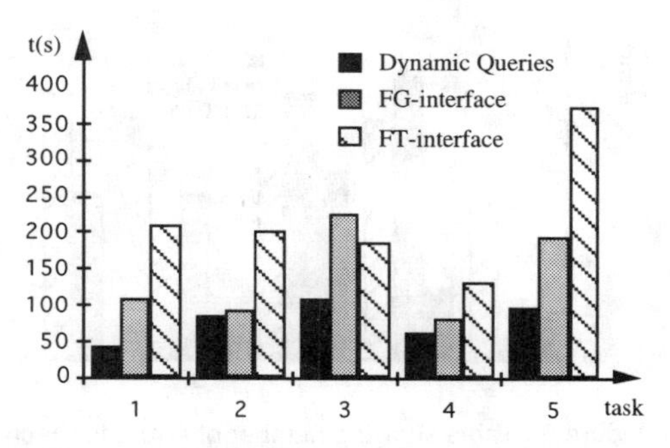

Figure 5. Mean time to complete each task

For task 3 the dynamic queries interface was significantly faster than both FG and FT interfaces, ($p<0.005$) and ($p<0.05$) respectively; no significant difference between the FG and FT interfaces was found. Actually, the mean time for the FT interface was 37.4 seconds faster than the FG interface.

For task 4 both the dynamic queries and FG interfaces were faster than the FT interface, ($p<0.001$). Task 5 showed significantly faster mean time for the dynamic queries interface compared to the FG interface, ($p<0.05$) and the FG interface was significantly faster than the FT interface, ($p<0.001$).

Figure 6 shows the number of errors subjects made for each task and interface, out of a total of 18 questions.

For the QUIS, there was a statistically significant difference between the dynamic queries and FT interfaces for all questions. There was also a statistically

Timing Data For Each Task

	Dynamic Queries		FG		FT
1	40.6 (21.5)	← .05	108.8 (62.3)	← .001	210.2 (129.3)
2	87.3 (92.3)		91.5 (44.8)	← .001	200.8 (79.1)
3	111.0 (55.8)	← .005	225.2 (105.1)		187.8 (114.5)
4	60.4 (41.4)		81.4 (30.9)	← .001	126.8 (32.0)
5	95.9 (51.4)	← .05	202.5 (101.6)	← .001	367.9 (180.1)
Σ	412.0 (216.1)	← .005	709.5 (182.9)	← .001	1093.6 (336.3)

Table1. Table showing mean time to complete each task. Variance is shown in parantheses. An arrow from one cell to another indicates significantly smaller time for the cell being pointed at. Significance level is given above arrow.

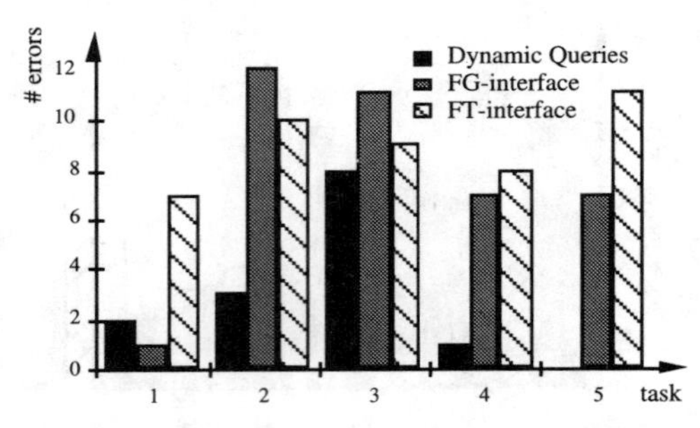

Figure 6. Table showing number of errors for each interface and task.

significant difference between the FG and FT interfaces for all questions, but no significant differences between the dynamic queries and FG interfaces.

Discussion

The hypothesis that the dynamic queries interface would perform better than both the FG interface and the FT interface was confirmed. Similarly, the FG interface produced faster performance times than the FT interface. The major difference in mean performance times was between the dynamic queries and FG interfaces compared to the FT interface. This was also confirmed in participants' comments which indicated that the visualization is the most important part.

The lack of difference in performance between the dynamic queries and FG interfaces in tasks 2 and 4 was surprising. The results for task 2 can possibly be explained by the fact that it was similar to task 1, and therefore subjects learned how to apply a good strategy. For task 4 subjects already had an idea of what the answer should be from their coursework. The range of the properties was limited and not too many values had to be checked to get a picture of the trend, therefore the slider did not make a big difference.

Timed tasks

Task 1: The dynamic queries interface performed significantly better than both the FG and FT interfaces. The correct answer could be found by adjusting the correct slider until either the first or the last element in the subset changed color. Using the FG interface or the FT interface required subjects to use some kind of binary search method to find the correct element since each query had to be typed in, which accounts for the slower performance. Using the FT interface required users to locate the subset of the periodic table in question in the larger set retrieved from the database with the query, which accounts for the longer performance time using that interface.

Task 2: Surprisingly no difference in performance time was found between the dynamic queries interface and the FG interface. This can probably be explained by the fact that the task was similar to task 1, and subjects figured out a good strategy while solving task 1. Similarly to task 1, the FT interface performed poorly as participants had to locate the relevant subset of elements to be analyzed in the larger set.

Task 3: The dynamic queries interface performed significantly better than both the FG interface and the FT interface. No significant difference between the FG interface and the FT interface was found, but the mean time for the FT interface was actually shorter than the mean time for the FG interface. The task required subjects to set two input fields to find a subset of elements, and in this subset find one element that fulfilled a criteria. As the subsets were rather big the visualization of the dynamic queries and FG interfaces caused some problems. To see one element shifting color when moving the slider or entering values was found to be hard. The dynamic queries interface compensated for this by making it possible to quickly change the value. The FT interface performed better than the FG interface as it was possible to see the result of the latest queries on the screen. By comparing the line length of the current and the previous result subjects could easily find the correct element. The FG interface posed an interesting problem for subjects that were novice computer users. Trying to find which element was the first to change from red to gray required them to enter values repeatedly. In doing this, novices had to look down at the keyboard, press <return> and before they had moved their eyes to the screen, the change had already taken place.

Trying to see which element changed color, subjects were found leaning backwards to get an overview. This problem is probably a result of two factors, the colors used and the width of the window. The colors were found to be good in the QUIS results, ~8 on the 1-9 scale, but maybe some better combination can be found.

Task 4: This task required subjects to find an overall trend in the database. The hypothesis that the visualization would make the major difference was confirmed. Finding a trend is greatly simplified by getting an overview of the database, which was reflected in the experiment results. But comparing the dynamic queries interface with the FG interface showed no difference, which was not in line with our hypothesis. The reason for this is twofold; a lot of the students already had a general idea of the answer and only had to confirm it, and even if they did not know the answer they only had to type in a few values to find the solution using the FG interface.

Task 5: The dynamic queries interface performed significantly better than both the FG interface and the FT interface, this stemming from the two advantages of the dynamic queries interface: the visualization and the sliders. The visualization allowed subjects to see exceptions easily when they showed up on the screen and the sliders allowed subjects to quickly change the values to find the correct answer. This task was very hard to solve with the FT interface, as subjects didn't have any visualization and had to use the keyboard to enter the values.

Interface characteristics

Dynamic Queries interface

Studying slider use revealed several interesting possibilities for improvements. Most subjects had never used the optical mouse before and had problems pointing accurately enough with it. This caused problems with the slider as the drag box was small. Similarly, several subjects found it hard to click on the slider bar to "fine tune" the setting. Also the fine tuning feature caused problems as the mouse arrow moved to the end of the slider bar when users clicked on it. For experimental purposes, subjects were unable to type in a value for the slider setting, which several subjects did request. Moving the slider can cause confusion if you move it too fast, and several subjects were found clicking at the sides of the slider bar, to adjust the slider up/down one step at a time, when making big changes.

The interface was wide, ~14 inches, which many subjects found to be a problem. They were observed leaning backwards to get an overview of what was changing on the screen. This was in sharp contrast to the FT interface where subjects were observed to lean forward, put fingers on both screen and the provided periodic table to create some sort of mental model of what they saw. Although the colors used were found to be good by participants, question 3 asking for the largest element in a fairly large set of elements caused problems because it was difficult to see when one single change occurs in the graphical query result. This problem can be overcome by either highlighting elements that changed last or introducing a short "click" sound every time the graphical output changes.

FG interface

Using the keyboard proved to give participants several problems. Subjects invariably failed to remember that they had to delete the last number and forgot to move the cursor to reach another field. It should be noted that three subjects, having somewhat extreme problems with the mouse, stated their definite preference of the FG interface and felt they had more control using it.

Participants found it hard to know the range of the property they were manipulating, even though the range was given to the left of the field. Analogously participants found it hard to know when they reached the upper bound. With the slider it was easy to grasp both the range and the current value. The slider provides an intuition about which set is selected by painting the area to the left of the drag box red and vice-versa for the area to the right. This cannot be done metaphorically with textual input, and accordingly subjects were found having trouble grasping which elements were selected.

FT interface

The FT interface performed very poorly compared to both the dynamic queries interface and the FG interface. This was also reflected in the user subjective evaluation (see section 4.3). This was to be expected but it was interesting to see how subjects reacted when the model of the periodic table was taken away, and they had to create one of their own. Using the FT interface, participants were found holding one hand pointing at the screen and the other on the provided printed periodic table, trying to interpret the query result.

Subjective evaluation

The superior performance using dynamic queries compared to the FG interface was not reflected in the QUIS results. This is surprising as several QUIS questions addressed commands and ways of solving tasks.

Although it was not reflected in the QUIS results, subjects' delight was most obvious using the dynamic queries interface. They offered comments such as "The sliders are more fun than the key punch," "With the sliders you can watch the periodic table and see what changes color right before your eyes," "Dynamic queries presented a more direct method of entering data for trial and error attempt," "You can play around more without worrying about messing it up".

Subjects having problems with the mouse stated for the FG interface: "You have more control over the numbers and you can read better what changes you have made." Some subjects using the dynamic queries interface asked: "Can I set the value directly instead of this guessing?" Participants were very critical of the FT interface, which also was reflected in the users' subjective evaluation, the QUIS. But some positive responses were found; one subject stated, "You can see what you have done before."

Future research

Further research about dynamic queries is needed. The sliders must be examined further:

- construct sliders giving ranges not bound to the minimum or maximum values by providing two drag boxes, and the issues of displaying such a range.
- select a set of sliders from a large set of properties, and
- select boolean combinations of sliders.

The visualization is equally important to examine. For example how to:

- find good visualizations for databases that do not have natural representations as a map.
- solve the problem of visualizations too large to fit into one screen, and
- find the best highlighting methods, such as colors, points of light, blinking, etc.

The last and maybe most important issue to examine is other applications of dynamic queries. How can direct manipulation of databases not consisting of well-formed ordinal data be implemented?

Conclusions

Results of this experiment suggest that direct manipulation can be applied to database queries with success. Results showed that visualization of the database and query result is the most important part of the dynamic queries, but that sliders' direct manipulation of the query are also important.

For dynamic queries to be successfully implemented, several issues must be addressed. A good visualization must be found, such as a map, an organization manipulating the query must be placed in a logical way to reduce eye and mouse movement. Sliders must be implemented so they are easy for novice users to use, i.e., the drag box must be big enough and the slider must provide enough information without being cluttered. The search time must be immediate so that users feel in control and have a sense of causation.

Acknowledgements

We appreciate the support of Sun Microsystems, Inc. and NCR Corporation, as well as the comments from Rick Chimera, Holmes Liao and other members of the HCIL. Thanks also to Staffan Truvé and Dr Samuel O. Grim for help in constructing the tasks.

Sparks of Innovation in Human-Computer Interaction,
B. Shneiderman, Ed., Ablex Publ., Norwood, NJ (1993)

6.2 The Dynamic HomeFinder: evaluating Dynamic Queries in a real-estate information exploration system

Christopher Williamson
Ben Shneiderman

Abstract

We designed, implemented, and evaluated a new concept for visualizing and searching databases utilizing direct manipulation called dynamic queries. Dynamic queries allow users to formulate queries by adjusting graphical widgets, such as sliders, and see the results immediately. By providing a graphical visualization of the database and search results, users can find trends and exceptions easily. User testing was done with eighteen undergraduate students who performed significantly faster using a dynamic queries interface compared to both a natural language system and paper printouts. The interfaces were used to explore a real-estate database and find homes meeting specific search criteria.

Proc. ACM SIGIR '92 (Copenhagen June 21-24, 1992) 338-346.

Dynamic Queries interface to real-estate

The program used for the experiment applied dynamic queries to real-estate. Finding a home is a laborious task for those that have experienced it. The two most common methods currently used are paper and SQL-like database systems. Newspaper and printed listings have survived to still be the most common means for finding a home. These provide little organization, short of being sorted by one field, but are easy-to-use for the novice. In the last few decades, SQL-like systems have appeared to support more complex queries.

Unfortunately, SQL-like systems require training and/or an intermediary; almost none allow the actual home buyer to perform the search. Further, these systems suffer the problems of most command-line query systems: slow, difficult to use, little feedback, nonreversible, and too many boolean logic errors. In addition, these systems offer no easy way to specify locations. The home buyer must know neighborhood names, and attempt to figure out if a given neighborhood is near where they wish to live. Finally, these systems suffer from the classic all-or-nothing phenomenon. This commonly occurs when the searcher does not know the contents of the database (as is usually the case in real-estate) and therefore attempts a query that is too general or too restrictive. As a result, the home buyer alternates

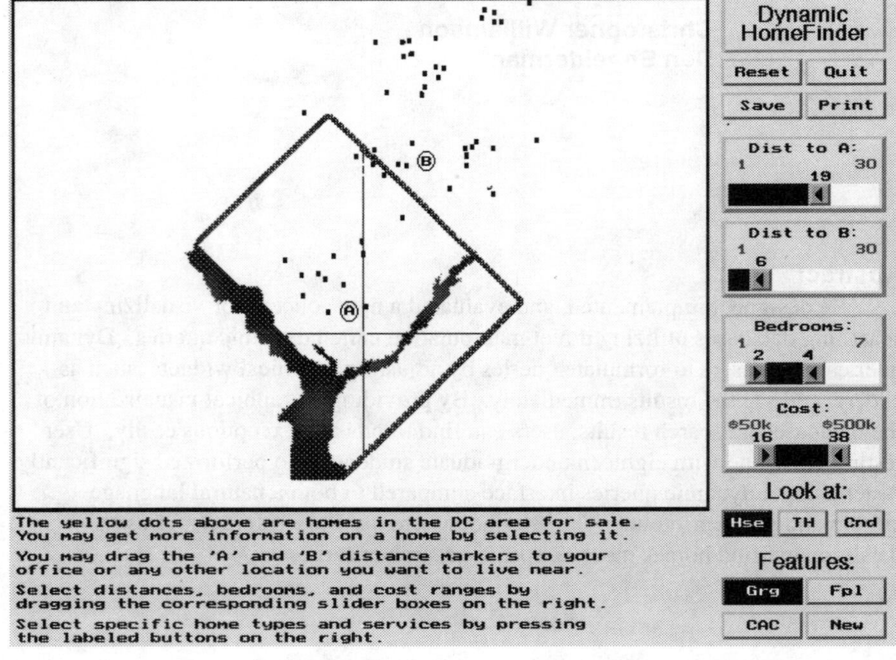

Figure 1. Dynamic HomeFinder (DQ interface) with all homes displayed and A&B markers set. In order to make these snapshots more readable in print, the pallette has been altered; the actual color scheme used was considerably more readable and pleasing than these snapshots depict.

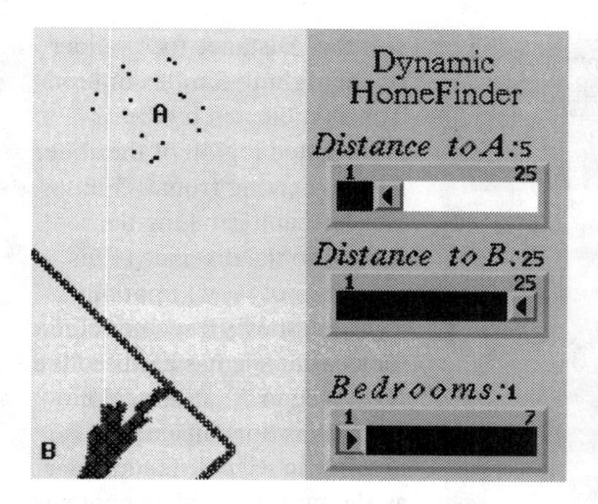

Figure 2. HomeFinder with all homes within a 5-mile radius of the 'A' marker displayed.

between too many and too few results - frantically and laboriously guessing towards the middle to produce a reasonable set of homes. Recently, good natural-language query systems, such as Q&A by Symantec, have been developed in response to complaints about SQL that instead allow queries to be stated in English. This should reduce training with syntax and help novice users, but it does little to correct the other faults of previous query systems.

The dynamic queries interface (Figure 1) provides a visualization of both the query formulation and corresponding results. This application was built using the C programming language. A map of the District of Columbia area is displayed on the left. The homes that fulfill the criteria set by the user's current query are shown as yellow dots on the map. Users perform queries, using the mouse, by setting the values of the sliders and buttons in the control panel to the right. The query result is determined by ANDing all sliders and buttons.

The dynamic homefinder interface is best explained through an example. Take a hypothetical situation where a new professor, Dr. Jones, has just been hired by the University of Maryland. She might encounter this tool in a touchscreen kiosk at a real-estate office or at the student union. She selects the location where she will be working by dragging the 'A' on the map. Next, she selects where her husband will be working, downtown, near the capitol, by dragging the 'B'. Figure 1 shows the interface after Dr. Jones has dragged the 'A' and 'B' indicators to her desired locations (the indicators are more visible in Figure 4).

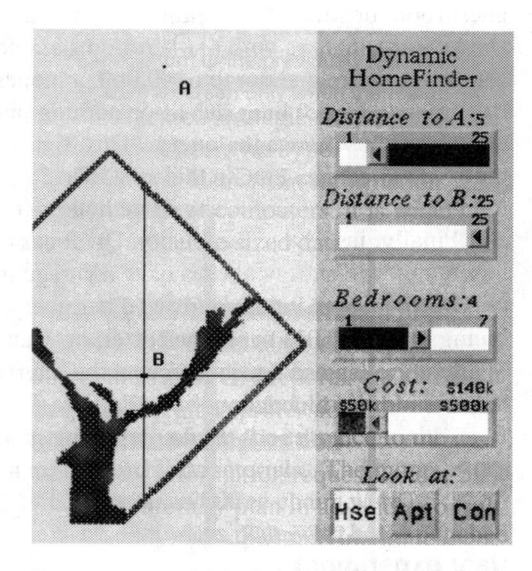

Figure 3. HomeFinder with all houses within a 5-mile radius of the 'A' marker AND have 4 or more bedrooms AND cost less than or equal to $140,000.

Dr. Jones would like to ride her bicycle to work, if possible, so she

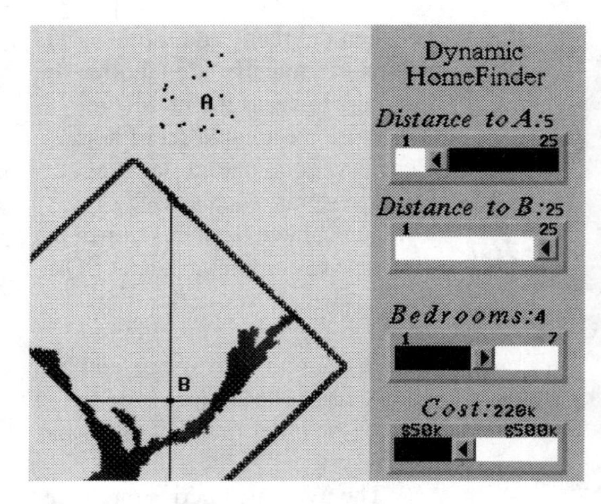

Figure 4. Close-up of Dynamic HomeFinder with all houses within a 5-mile radius of the 'A' marker AND have 4 or more bedrooms and cost less than or equal to $220,000.

sets the 'Distance to A' slider on the right to 5 miles or less. This is indicated by the highlighted region of the slider now indicating from 0-5 miles. Her husband is taking the Metro, so the distance to his office is not very important. Figure 3 shows how the screen looks after she has adjusted the 'Distance to A' slider. Note that this is done instantaneously in a fluid-like manner as she moves which cannot be captured with snapshots, but which enables her to quickly see how homes are eliminated as she narrows the distance requirement.

Dr. Jones is only interested in houses, not in apartments or condominiums, so she toggles those buttons off. Finally, she drags the bedrooms slider down to 4, since she needs at least four bedrooms, she could have more (for a guest room or study, for example), again indicated by the highlighting in Figure 4 showing that houses with 4-7 bedrooms are now being displayed. In Figure 4, she also drags the cost slider to $140,000, a modestly-priced home where she used to live. Here we encounter the all-or-nothing phenomena as Dr. Jones has eliminated too many houses with her query. This is easily solved as she realizes that houses must be more expensive in this area. Dr. Jones drags the cost slider up to $220,000 in Figure 4, a price that many more houses in the area fulfill.

Finally, just out of curiousity, Dr. Jones clicks on the 'Garage' button in Figure 5 only to find that few houses have a garage in the price range and area she is looking at. Once she has narrowed her query, it is easy for Dr. Jones to experiment, seeing what services the homes offer, or what is available if she was willing to pay a little more, and so on. In this way the interface encourages exploration and bolsters user confidence.

Although there is no figure depicting it, a mouse click on any of the homes (represented by the yellow dots) brought up a pop-up window with detailed information on that specific home.

User experiment

This experiment compared three different interfaces for database query and visualization: a dynamic queries interface, a natural language query system known as 'Q&A', and a traditional paper listing sorted by several fields. The alternative interfaces were chosen to find out how dynamic queries would fare against the two most common methods currently used to search real-estate databases. Using a within-subjects counter-balanced design, subjects answered a series of five types of questions for each of the three interfaces, which were presented in random order. The independent variable in the experiment was the type of interface with three different treatments: dynamic queries (DQ), natural language retrieval (QA), and paper listings (Paper). The observed dependent variables were time to find correct answer for each of five questions and the subjective satisfaction with each interface.

The primary hypothesis was that the dynamic queries interface, providing both a graphical query input and a graphical visualization of the search result, would give the best user performance results and would be rated highest in user satisfaction. Performance results were measured as the time until correct answer for each question.

Eighteen undergraduate psychology students, 9 females and 9 males from the University of Maryland subject pool, participated voluntarily in the experiment. Only one subject had previous knowledge of real-estate in the area. Both computer interfaces were run on an IBM PS/2 model 70 (16 MHz 80386) with a 12-inch VGA color monitor and mechanical two-button mouse. All interfaces involved querying information on 944 imaginary homes with varying criteria from real-estate in the Washington D.C., Metropolitan area. Although using real home-seekers would be ideal, a reasonable compromise was made by using novices with varying backgrounds.

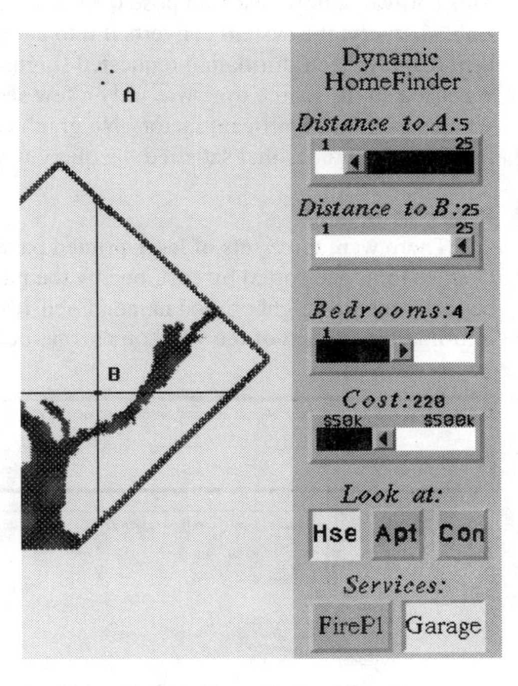

Figure 5. Dynamic HomeFinder with all houses within a 5-mile radius of the 'A' marker AND have 4 or more bedrooms AND cost less than or equal to $220,000 AND have a garage.

Dynamic Queries interface (DQ)

This interface was already described in detail on pages 286-288. As shown previously in Figure 3, it is possible to drag the 'A' icon to a certain location where the home buyer might work, for example. When the distance slider is moved to 5, all houses within 5 miles of that location are then highlighted. However, these distance sliders and the 'A' and 'B' icons on the map were not used in the experiment, since the other two interfaces could not provide this service.

Natural language query interface (QA)

The natural language query interface (Figure 6) used was the 'Intelligent Assistant' of a popular commercial package from Symantec, Inc. known as 'Q&A'. This software allows users to pose queries using English. The user types the English query, the system converts it into a logical database query (Figure 6), and then displays the information requested (Figure 7). A 386 machine with hard disk was used so the search time was only a few seconds, fast enough that computation speed was not a significant factor. No graphical output was provided, a textual listing of the homes that satisfied the query were displayed as shown in Figure 7.

Paper interface

There were three sets of laser-printed paper listings in approximately 11-point Courier font, one sorted by cost, one by the number of bedrooms, and one alphabetically by the neighborhood name. Each 10-page listing contained all the information on each of the 944 homes, one-per-line, as shown in Figure 8.

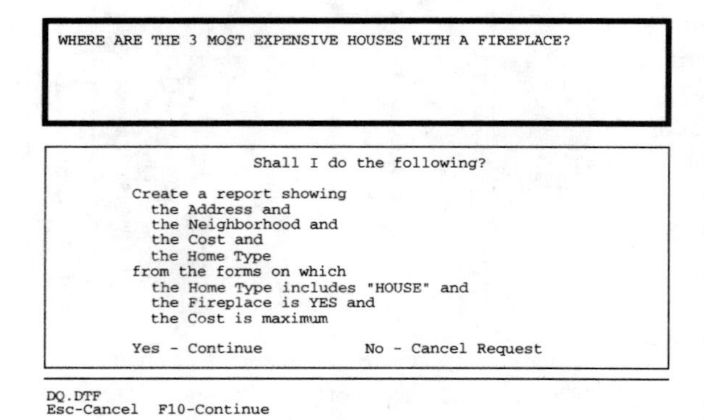

Figure 6. Natural language system (QA interface) processing and converting English query.

Experiment procedure and tasks

A counter-balanced within-subjects design was used. The question sets were always given in the same order, and the interface order was random. The subjects were given a brief description of the tasks and were asked to sign a consent form. Each session lasted an hour and consisted of four phases for each interface condition:

1. *Introduction and training*: The experimenter set up the appropriate interface and briefly explained the interface to the subject. The subject was invited to try-out the system and get comfortable with it. Subjects were permitted unlimited time to try-out using the system and were free to ask any questions to the experimenter about the interface. Actual training time varied from two to ten minutes for each subject. The QA interface required significantly more training due to its less obvious querying mechanism. Subjects were informed on the more complex sorting and set operations available in the QA interface.

```
WHERE ARE THE 3 MOST EXPENSIVE HOUSES WITH A FIREPLACE?
```

Address	Neighborhood	Cost	Home Type
7924 Jones Street	Chevy Chase, MD	$411,950	House
4719 Dorset Ave.	Chevy Chase, MD	$678,235	House
1287 Highland Ct.	Potomac, MD	$782,125	House

```
DQ.DTF
Esc-Cancel  F10-Continue
```

Figure 7. Q&A displaying results of converted English query.

[Key: Bed=bedrooms, Fp=fireplace, Gr=garage, Ac=central air, Nw=new]

ID	Type	Address	Neighborhood	Cost	Bed	Fp	Gr	Ac	Nw
39	Apt	3792 Campus Drive	Beltsville, MD	$80,950	3	N	N	N	N
54	Apt	4634 Baltimore Blvd.	College Park, MD	$90,250	2	N	Y	N	N
230	House	2352 Glass Road	Bladensburg, MD	$100,230	3	Y	Y	N	N

Figure 8. Sample lines from paper listing.

2. *Practice task*: A practice task (similar to the complex query question used) was given. During this task, subjects were free to ask questions about both the task and the interface.
3. *Timed tasks*: Five questions were given on paper. Subjects read each question and were asked if they fully understood it. This was done so as to eliminate variations in subject comprehension speed. When the subject was ready, the experimenter started timing. When subjects found the answer, they verbally expressed it. If it was correct, the experimenter recorded the elapsed time; if not, the experimenter asked the subject to try again. The interface was returned to its initial state between each question.

In deciding the tasks, an informal task analysis was done by asking a local realtor and a few clients what types of questions they would ask a database. The first two are very general, while the final three are probably more representative of 'typical' home-searches:

- *Simple fact*: Find a certain element fulfilling a simple criteria. An actual question of this type is "What is the cost of the cheapest apartment in the database?"

- *Simple neighborhood fact search*: Find the neighborhood (city) fulfilling a simple criteria. An actual question of this type is "What neighborhood has the most expensive houses?"
- *Complex search*: Find one or more elements meeting several criteria. This is the typical type of question a prospective home buyer would likely ask. An actual question of this type is "What is the address of the cheapest house that has 5 or more bedrooms AND has both a garage and central air conditioning?"
- *Find a trend*: Find the trend for some field. This task requires subjects to create a mental picture of how a field changes through the database. An actual question of this type is "Is there a general trend (and if so what is it) of house prices from cheapest to most expensive? (i.e., where are the more expensive houses, and where are the cheapest houses, do they seem to follow any general pattern?) Don't guess, you must find some examples to support your answer."
- *Find exception to trend/Complex search:* Find the exception to a trend in the database. This is, in fact, often what home buyers are looking for. An actual question of this type is "There is a trend of houses to increase in cost with the number of bedrooms. Find the two bargain homes with the most bedrooms but are still inexpensive."
- *Subjective evaluation*: Subjects were asked to fill-out a shortened QUIS (Chin, Diehl, & Norman, 1988) after having completed each interface. Although results for each of the 20 questions (scored on a 7-point scale) were computed, the sum score for each interface (out of a maximum possible of 140) is what is presented in the results section.

Experiment results

The results show a statistically significant difference for the dynamic queries interface over both the other two for all but one task. Analysis of the timed tasks was done using a factorial analysis of variance. An ANOVA showed no significant order or questionnaire difficulty effect (these two were compounded to one factor) with $F(2,51) = 1.17$ ($p > .05$). This, therefore, also shows that there was no significant difference between the three question sets used. Observing the mean times to complete each task shows a significant effect. The mean and standard deviations (in seconds) for each question and interface are shown in Table 1 along with the ANOVA and post-hoc analysis. The results for the QUIS are ratings out of a maximum possible of 140. The performance means, along with 95% error bars, are graphed for comparison in Figure 9.

Discussion and conclusions

The primary hypothesis that the dynamic queries interface would give the best user performance results is supported in the results with a significant difference ($p < .005$) in speed, favoring dynamic queries, for all but one task. The dynamic queries interface also scored significantly higher on the satisfaction questionnaire. Surpris-

	QA		DQ		Paper	ANOVA
1	93.0 (76.0)	→	46.3 (46.2)		30.6 (17.8)	F(2,51) = 9.72 (p < .005)
2	92.8 (83.2)		72.5 (78.0)		98.4 (75.3)	F(2,51) = 0.66 (p > .005)
3	144.8 (71.1)	→	57.6 (28.4)	←	125.1 (72.4)	F(2,51) = 11.6 (p < .005)
4	227.9 (27.0)	→	125.3 (72.4)	←	193.4 (68.5)	F(2,51) = 17.4 (p < .005)
5	189.9 (67.2)	→	58.8 (16.3)	←	135.8 (77.0)	F(2,51) = 29.4 (p < .005)
QUIS	68 (42.3)	→	110 (21.5)	←	84 (12.5)	F(2,51) = 19.6 (p < .005)

→ Scheffe .005 post-hoc showed significant difference favoring indicated interface

Table 1. Means and standard deviations in seconds for each interface and condition for five tasks and subjective satisfaction (out of a maximum of 140)

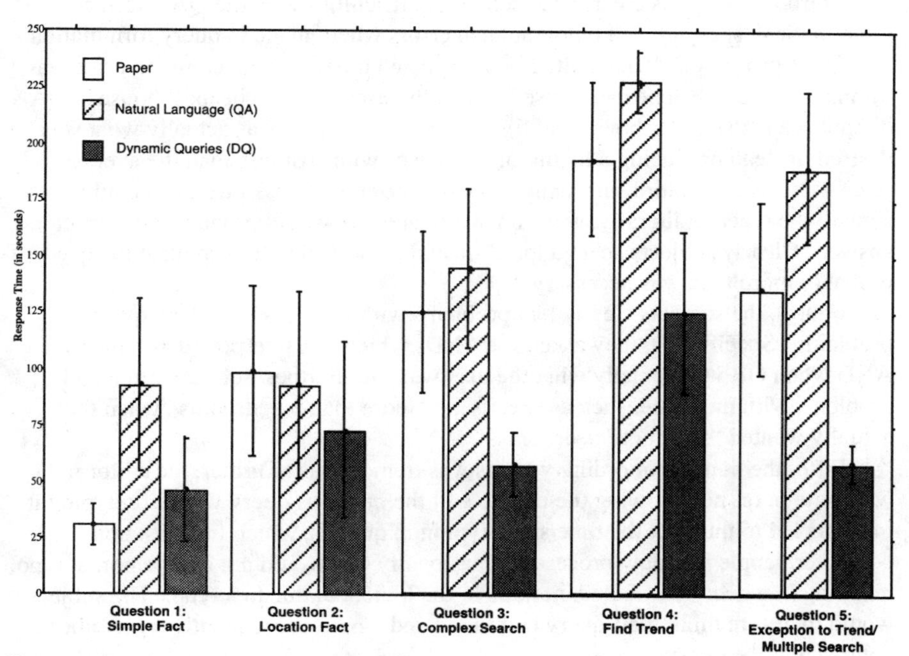

Figure 9. Performance means and standard deviations.

ingly, for all but one task, paper was also better than the QA interface, although often not by a significant amount. The remarks given by the subjects and comments noted by the experimenter suggest several reasons why the dynamic queries interface faired better.

First, the dynamic queries interface was clearly the most 'fun', most likely due to its animated graphical nature, and this may have produced a motivational factor. The QUIS clearly indicated a preference for DQ (110) over QA (68) and Paper (84), with subjects rating DQ an average of 6.1 on a range from 1 to 7. Many subjects became very frustrated with the QA interface, attempting to figure out how to form a query (this is discussed more later). One subject remarked: "What the hell does this thing want, anyway?" Subjects seemed very comfortable with paper and usually attacked the question in a logical fashion, utilizing the sorted paper listings to their maximum benefit. The DQ interface was clearly preferred by the sighs of relief and the relaxed manner with which they formed queries. One subject said "I don't want to stop, this is fun!"

Second, the well-known issue of text readability may partially explain the success of both the DQ and paper interfaces. Although a VGA monitor was used, several subjects noted that it was easier to search the laser-printed listings than a listing on-screen using the QA interface. Subjects using the DQ interface rarely actually looked at the textual information on a specific home. One subject noted on their evaluation of QA that it "takes a while for your eyes to adjust to the small print."

Third, the subjects clearly had semantic difficulties with the QA interface. Grammatical, spelling, and typographical errors where made in query formulation. The QA's processor often resulted in unexpected queries. One common error was asking: "What is the cheaper house?" when the user meant "cheapest house." QA did not see the singular house and figure out that cheapest was actually what was desired, instead producing a listing of all houses with cost less than the average price. This is even more surprising since 9 out of the 15 task questions could actually be typed in literally, word for word, and QA would produce the correct answer. Clearly subjects spent a lot of mental effort trying to formulate the query, probably more than was necessary.

Fourth, the subjects clearly had problems with the classic boolean query problems. Specifically, they asked for ANDs which QA interpreted as a literal AND when OR was actually what the user wanted. Further, subjects often had problems with inclusion, such as specifying "more than 5 bedrooms" when they actually wanted "5 or more bedrooms."

Fifth, the number of ordinary typos was tremendous. Further, the editor in QA was quite poor, not allowing the user to edit the previous query without retyping it in. This led to much of the time spent typing in queries, which for most non-computer people is a slow process. Occasionally QA would not even report a typo, resulting in a query that failed, not due to the logic, but due to a typo. The subject would therefore think their query had failed and would consequently try another approach to the question.

Sixth, the QA interface often produced the correct answer but the subject missed it. Subjects expressed they were unsure if they had asked the right query to get the result and were unsure if it was therefore the correct answer. A few subjects tried multiple approaches and only answered when they got the same answer using each approach. A possible explanation may be that the subjects get so caught up in the query formulation they forget exactly what they were originally looking for. This frustrating feeling of being lost and unsure was not expressed with either of the other two interfaces.

Finally, the DQ interface's use of highlighting and display on one single screen was clearly a benefit for users. They were able to easily input the query with the sliders. Not one of the subjects showed any difficulty in using the sliders effectively. One subject explained the feeling well: "You can see them right up front...they're right there." The display of the results on a map made task 4 (finding a trend) clearly easier since the relative location could be viewed directly on the map, instead of having to refer to it from the city, state information.

The clear benefit of dynamic queries, particularly for trend and exception to trend questions, is clear. The significant differences (F=29.4 and 19.5 respectively) for tasks 4 and 5 are dramatic. The fact that a time limit was placed at four minutes probably reduced the effect somewhat, since over half the subjects could not answer task 4 using the QA interface in the time allotted. With the DQ interface, however, all but one subject was able to discern the trend in the time allotted.

The scores for task 5 showed dramatic differences, with the DQ interface averaging 58.8 seconds with a standard deviation of only 16.3 seconds, while the QA interface averaged 189.9 seconds, with a standard deviation of 67.2 seconds. In fact, all but one subject answered the question in less than a minute using the DQ interface. The exception to the trend (or multiple search) question required combining the results of two or more searches or finding the outlying point in a set. In this case, the exception was a home that was cheap for what it offered. These types of questions are often what people are searching for in a database. They often wish to find the most stressed part of an airplane, the cheapest car which provides all the options desired, or the deaths that seem to occur not due to cancer or other common environmental factors. Since dynamic queries excel in searching for these outliers, other applications involving this type of search could clearly benefit from its use.

In all fairness, it is difficult to honestly compare the QA, DQ, and paper interfaces since the ways users use each are so different. QA requires typing with little guidance, while the DQ interface must be 'custom-made' for the fields the user will search on. Therefore, it is difficult to specifically identify the advantages or disadvantages; however, from a usability standpoint, it does seem that the DQ interface does perform better, overall, than QA for some types of questions.

This study and others (Ahlberg, Williamson, & Shneiderman, 1992) have shown dynamic queries to have several benefits over current systems:

- Queries can be made much faster by sliding the sliders and seeing rapid feedback directly on the display.

- Novices can learn to use the system quickly with both query-formulation and result displayed in task domain.

- Intermittent users do not have to remember any syntax. Repeat users quickly remember how to form a query.

- No error messages are needed since sliders restrict ranges. Also encourages user to explore.

- Users can fine-tune their search easily. Simply restricting one field allows tuning until desired number of hits.

- Actions are incremental and reversible.

- Trends and content of the database are easily inferred.

- Well-suited for geographical information systems and public access using a touchscreen.

- Display in task-domain is more useful, less intimidating, and speeds training time.

Although dynamic queries show promise, they are far from perfect. Many drawbacks limit the range of its applicability or pose other problems:

- Data must be ordered in some way, in particular textual fields don't benefit from the dynamic nature of sliders.

- Limited screen real-estate makes it difficult to keep both tools and display on-screen.

- Difficult to use when a large number of fields are searchable due to limited screen space and computational issues.

- Data structures to permit more rapid querying (especially for large databases) are clearly necessary.

- Work best with data which can be displayed in some graphical fashion.

- Difficult for dynamic queries to offer more complex boolean queries such as unions and negations.

- Recently we have devloped a range slider with draggable ends, partially solving some of these limitations.

- Smarter ways to utilize the limited screen space without sacrificing simplicity are clearly needed.

- Perhaps the most major drawback, as of now, they require custom programming to create an interface. Even adding additional criteria (such as crime rate or some such) for querying requires significant adjustment. We are currently designing a DQ toolkit to minimize this difficulty.

This initial study needs to be replicated with other subjects, database domains, queries, and with more experienced users to assess the full range of strengths and weaknesses of dynamic queries. Despite the drawbacks, dynamic queries clearly have application in a range of areas. For geographic information systems they show clear promise. For textual purposes, however, the problems outweigh the benefits. Since the results of this study suggest users find dynamic queries more enjoyable to work with and can complete typical tasks in equal or less time than a traditional natural-language query system, it seems clear these principles have a place in the design of future information retrieval systems.

Acknowledgements

We appreciate the support of NCR Corporation and Johnson Controls, as well as the comments from Ben Harper, Christopher Ahlberg, Donna Harman, Kent Norman and other members of the Human-Computer Interaction Laboratory at the University of Maryland.

Sparks of Innovation in Human-Computer Interaction,
B. Shneiderman, Ed., Ablex Publ., Norwood, NJ (1993)

6.3 Treemaps: a space-filling approach to the visualization of hierarchical information structures

Brian Johnson
Ben Shneiderman

Abstract

This paper describes a novel method for the visualization of hierarchically structured information. The treemap visualization technique makes 100% use of the available display space, mapping the full hierarchy onto a rectangular region in a space-filling manner. This efficient use of space allows very large hierarchies to be displayed in their entirety and facilitates the presentation of semantic information.

Proc. of the 2nd International IEEE Visualization Conference (San Diego, Oct. 1991) 284-291.

Introduction

A large quantity of the world's information is hierarchically structured:manuals, outlines, corporate organizations, family trees, directory structures, internet addressing, library cataloging, computer programs... and the list goes on. Most people come to understand the content and organization of these structures easily if they are small, but have great difficulty if the structures are large.

We propose an interactive visualization method for presenting hierarchical information called treemaps. We hope that the treemap approach is a step forward in the visualization of hierarchical information, and that it will produce benefits similar to those achieved by visualization techniques in other areas.

As humans we have the ability to recognize the spatial configuration of elements in a picture and notice the relationships between elements quickly. This highly developed visual ability allows people to grasp the content of a picture much faster than they can scan and understand text (Kamada, 1988).

The treemap visualization method maps hierarchical information to a rectangular 2-D display in a space-filling manner; 100% of the designated display space is utilized. Interactive control allows users to specify the presentation of both structural (depth bounds, etc.) and content (display properties such as color mappings) information. This is in contrast to traditional static methods of displaying hierarchically structured information, which generally make either poor use of display space or hide vast quantities of information from users. With the treemap method, sections of the hierarchy containing more important information can be allocated more display space while portions of the hierarchy which are less important to the specific task at hand can be allocated less space (Furnas 1986; Henry & Hudson, 1990).

Treemaps partition the display space into a collection of rectangular bounding boxes representing the tree structure (Shneiderman, 1990). The drawing of nodes within their bounding boxes is entirely dependent on the content of the nodes, and can be interactively controlled. Since the display size is user controlled, the drawing size of each node varies inversely with the size of the tree (i.e., number of nodes). Trees with many nodes (1000 or more) can be displayed and manipulated in a fixed display space.

The main objectives of our design are:

Efficient space utilization

Efficient use of space is essential for the presentation of large information structures.

Interactivity

Interactive control over the presentation of information and real time feedback are essential.

Comprehension

The presentation method and its interactive feedback must facilitate the rapid extraction of information with low perceptual and cognitive loads.

Esthetics

Drawing and feedback must be esthetically pleasing.

Hierarchical information structures contain two kinds of information: structural (organization) information associated with the hierarchy, and content information associated with each node. Treemaps are able to depict both the structure and content of the hierarchy. However, our approach is best suited to hierarchies in which the content of the leaf nodes and the structure of the hierarchy are of primary importance, and the content information associated with internal nodes is largely derived from their children.

Motivation: current methods and problems

This work was initially motivated by the lack of adequate tools for the visualization of the large directory structures on hard disk drives.

Traditional methods for the presentation of hierarchically structured information can be roughly classified into three categories: listings, outlines, and tree diagrams. It is difficult for people to extract information from large hierarchical information structures using these methods, as the navigation of the structure is a great burden and content information is often hidden within individual nodes (Vincente, Hayes, & Williges, 1987).

Listings are capable of providing detailed content information, but are generally very poor at presenting structural information. Listings of the entire structure with explicit paths can provide structural information, but require users to parse path information to arrive at a mental model of the structure. Alternatively, users may list each internal node of the hierarchy independently, but this requires users to manually traverse the hierarchy to determine its structure. Outline methods can explicitly provide both structural and content information, but since the structural indentation can only be viewed a few lines at a time, it is often inadequate (Chimera, Wolman, Mark, & Shneiderman, 1991).

The number of display lines required to present a hierarchy with both the listing and outline methods is linearly proportional to the number of nodes in the hierarchy. These methods are inadequate for structures containing more than a few hundred nodes. A great deal of effort is required to achieve a mental model of the structure in large hierarchies using these methods.

Tree drawing algorithms have traditionally sought efficient and esthetically pleasing methods for the layout of node and link diagrams. These layouts are based on static presentations and are common in texts dealing with graph theory and data structures. They are excellent visualization tools for small trees (Bruggemann-Klein & Wood, 1989; Henry & Hudson, 1990; Kamada, 1988; Knuth, 1973; Robertson, Mackinlay & Card, 1991). However, these traditional node and link tree diagrams make poor use of the available display space. In a typical tree drawing more than 50% of the pixels are used as background. For small tree diagrams this poor use of space is acceptable, and traditional layout methods produce excellent results. But for large trees, traditional node and link diagrams can not be drawn adequately in a limited display space. Attempts to provide zooming and panning have only been only partially successful (Henry & Hudson, 1990).

Another problem with tree diagrams is the lack of content information; typically each node has only a simple text label. This problem exists because presenting additional information with each node quickly overwhelms the display space for trees with more than just a few nodes.

The presentation of content information in all of these traditional methods has usually been text-based, although tree diagrams are a graphically based method capable of making use of many of the visualization techniques presented in this paper. Unfortunately, global views of large tree diagrams require the nodes to be so small that there is virtually no space in which to provide visual cues as to node content.

Treemaps efficiently utilize the designated display area and are capable of providing structural information implicitly, thereby eliminating the need to explicitly draw internal nodes. Thus, much more space is available for the rendering of individual leaf nodes, and for providing visual cues related to content information.

Treemaps provide an overall view of the entire hierarchy, making the navigation of large hierarchies much easier. Displaying the entire information structure at once allows users to move rapidly to any location in the space. As Beard states in his paper on navigating large two-dimensional spaces (Beard & Walker, 1990), "If the two-dimensional information space fits completely onto a display screen, there is no navigation problem .... Users are never lost because they can see the complete information space."

A directory tree example

Obtaining information about directory trees was the initial motivation for this research and provides a familiar example domain. For illustrative reasons, the hierarchy in this example is small and nodes have only an associated name and size. While reading through this example, think about how the techniques described would scale up to a directory tree containing 1000 files. An Apple Macintosh screen snapshot showing a treemap of 1000 files from one of our laboratory's hard disk drives follows this example.

Presenting directory structures is a very practical problem. The following are the methods widely available today:

- Command Line Listing (e.g., UNIX "ls", DOS "dir");
- Outlines (e.g., UNIX "du", Microsoft Windows);
- Windowing (e.g., Macintosh Finder);
- Tree Drawings (e.g., OpenWindows File Manager).

We are not aware of approaches that provide a visual representation of the relative sizes of files or directories.

Even moderately sized directory trees are difficult to visualize using standard operating system interfaces. With command line interfaces such as UNIX "ls" or DOS "dir", only the immediate children of any directory are listed. An overall view of the directory tree must be pieced together by traversing the various paths and listing the immediate children of the currently active directory.

Desktop metaphors and their windowing strategies are another alternative. One of the problems with windows is that they often obscure each other, and users may spend much of their time arranging windows. Also, the tree structure is not apparent unless windows have been carefully placed. Desktop icons generally show only the type of the file. Much richer visual mappings are possible but are currently not available, for instance, the depth of an icon's shadow could be used to indicate file size.

We will use a small directory tree hierarchy as an example. Tree A depicted in Figures 1 through 7 contains 23 nodes; of these, 6 are directories (internal nodes) and 17 are files (leaf nodes). This tree is structured such that among siblings, file nodes always precede directory nodes.

In Figure 1 we see an outline view similar to the presentations provided by PCShell under DOS, the UNIX command "du", or Microsoft Windows 3.0. This presentation requires 23 lines; a structure with 1000 files would require a minimum of 1000 lines in order to present both directories and files.

```
A 160
├ B 10
├ C 30
├ D 60
│ ├ F 6
│ ├ G 6
│ ├ H 6
│ └ I 42
│   ├ L 7
│   ├ M 7
│   └ N 28
│     ├ U 8
│     ├ V 12
│     └ W 8
└ E 60
  ├ J 36
  └ K 24
    ├ O 4
    ├ P 4
    ├ Q 4
    ├ R 4
    ├ S 4
    └ T 4
```

Figure 1. Outline

Figure 2 presents a typical tree diagram; such drawings can be found in graph theory textbooks. This tree drawing approach is similar to the presentation method used by the OpenWindows File Manager. Directory trees with 1000 files cannot be drawn all at once on a typical screen (if all files are at the same level, each file node will have less than one pixel in which to draw itself). The problem becomes even more severe when real file names are used as node labels.

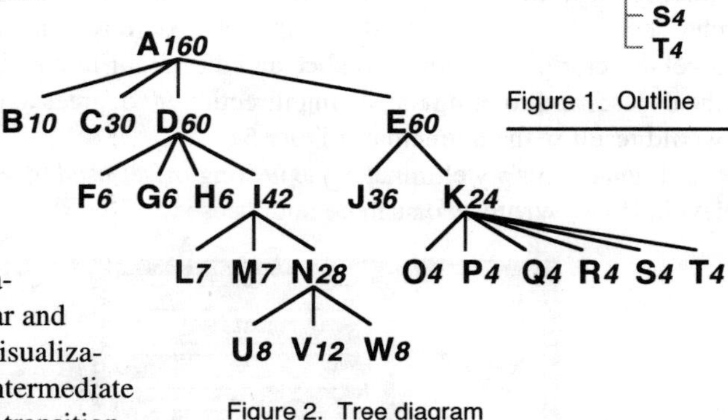

Figure 2. Tree diagram

Figure 3 presents the same information in yet another manner, as a Venn diagram. We use this figure for illustrative purposes as a familiar and often used set theoretic visualization technique. It is an intermediate step which facilitates the transition from traditional presentations to treemaps. This is an odd use of Venn diagrams, as one does not usually think of files and directories as sets. However, simple directory structures can be thought of as set theoretic collections of files, using only the containment (subset) property. Note that each node has been drawn proportionate to its size.

The space required between regions would certainly preclude this Venn diagram representation from serious consideration for larger structures. Note that this "waste" of space is also present in traditional tree diagrams. Using boxes

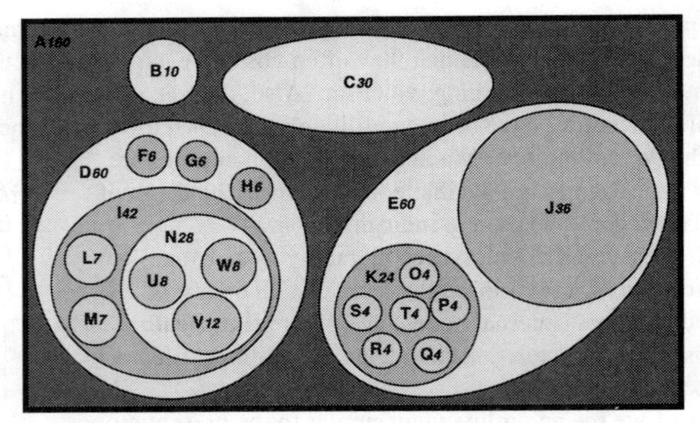

Figure 3. Venn diagram

instead of ovals and a bin-packing algorithm could partially solve this space problem. But bin-packing is an NP-complete problem and does not preserve order.

Figure 4 is a box-based Venn diagram which illustrates a more efficient use of space and is an excellent tool for the visualization of small hierarchies. But even the small degree of nesting present in this technique renders it unsuitable for the presentation of large hierarchies. Fortunately space efficient results can be achieved without bin-packing, using our "slice and dice" treemap approach, a simple linear method in which the algorithm works top-down. An analogy should quickly illustrate this concept. If the hard disk drive were a large, flat, rectangular cheese, one could certainly slice it into chunks representing the size of each top level directory. Applying this slice and dice algorithm recursively to each piece of the cheese, and rotating the slicing direction 90 degrees at each recursive step, would result in the treemap of Figure 5.

Figure 5 simply eliminates the nesting offset used to seperate objects at each level. If we wanted to distribute our cheese to 17 people based on their weights,

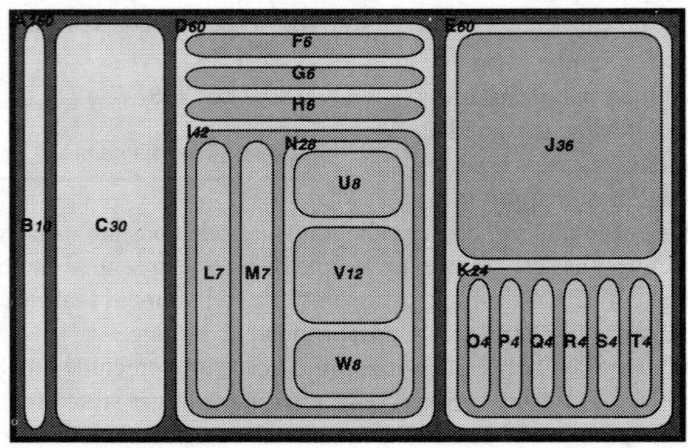

Figure 4. Nested treemap

Figure 5 would give us a slicing diagram. This weight-proportionate distribution is one of the important features of treemaps. The treemap snapshots of Figures 6 and 7 (see color plates) are the full color, machine generated screen snapshots of Figures 4 and 5. All screen snapshots in this paper have been made while using our TreeViz application on an Apple Macintosh II.

Figure 8 (see color plates) is a screen snapshot showing a treemap of 1000 files. A simple color mapping has been used to code some of the various Macintosh file types: treemap applications are red; all other applications are purple; system files are green; picture files are magenta; text files are yellow; archive files are cyan; and all other file types not currently of primary interest are gray. This treemap shows 21 root level files on the left, followed by 19 root level directories moving across to the right. Detailed file information is displayed in a pop-up dialog window as the mouse is dragged over files in the display.

In this directory structure it can be observed that purple application files are generally the largest files on this disk, and take up relatively the same percentage of overall disk space as system related (green) files. A duplicate set of files exists just

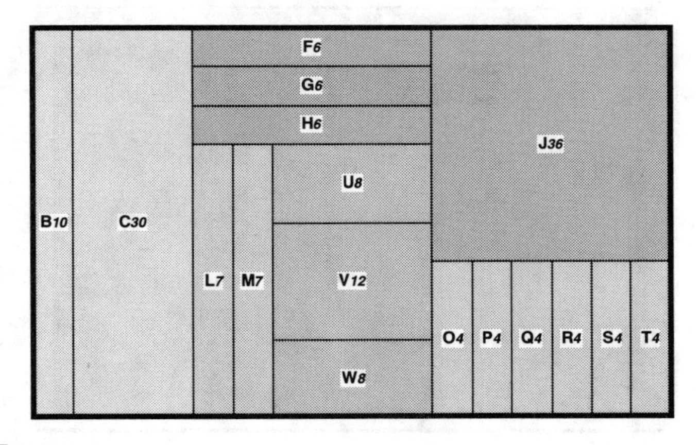

Figure 5. Treemap

to the right of the vertical green bar. The files in this root level folder can be seen duplicated one level down in subfolders, as repeating geometric patterns offset 900 from their parent.

Since this treemap portrays the overall allocation of disk space, the largest files can be located quite easily. Sorting a large directory listing by size would also make finding the largest files easy, but these files would not be presented in their original context. In addition, sorting a list on two or more properties (i.e., size and type) makes presentation of the results difficult. Treemaps make finding the largest system, application, and picture files on the disk as easy as finding the largest green, purple, and magenta rectangles in Figure 8. This is one simple example of the visual display properties possible; further discussion is contained in section 4.2.

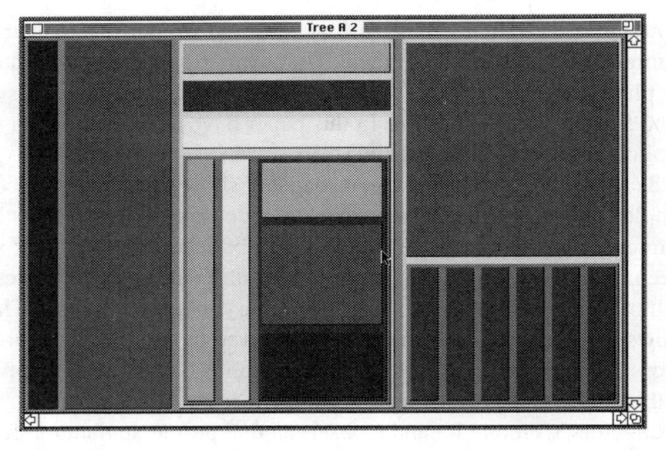

Figure 6. Nested treemap

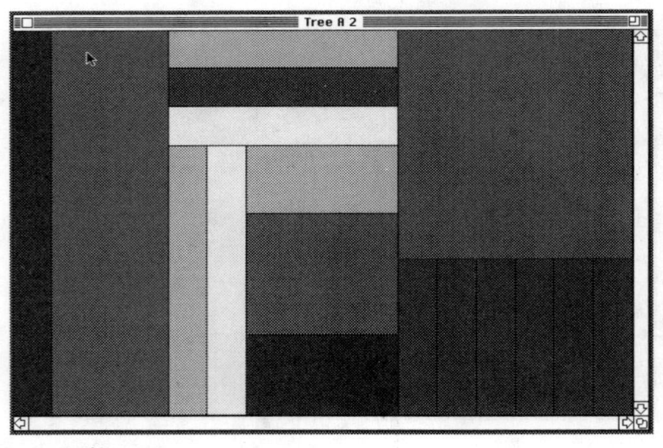

Figure 7. Non-nested treemap

The treemap method

Displaying a directory tree while fully utilizing space and conveying structural information in a visually appealing and low cognitive load manner is a difficult task, as these are often opposing goals. Our interactive approach to drawing directory trees allows users to determine how the tree is displayed. This control is essential, as it allows users to set display properties (colors, borders, etc.) maximizing the utility of the drawing based on their particular task.

Structural information: partitioning the display space

Treemap displays look similar to the partition diagrams of quad-trees and k-D trees. The key difference is the direction of the transformation. Quad-trees create hierarchical structures to store 2-D images efficiently (Samet, 1989), while

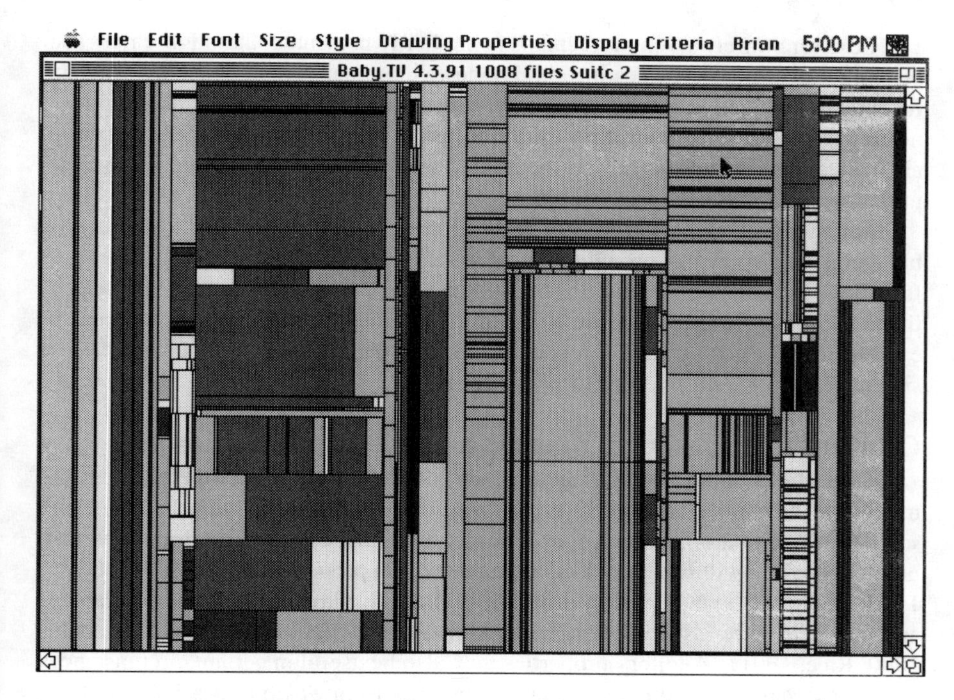

Figure 8. Treemap with 1000 Files

treemaps present hierarchical information structures efficiently on 2-D display surfaces.

Treemaps require that a weight be assigned to each node; this weight is used to determine the size of a nodes bounding box. The weight may represent a single domain property (such as disk usage or file age for a directory tree), or a combination of domain properties (subject to Property 4 below). A node's weight (bounding box) determines its display size and can be thought of as a measure of importance or degree of interest (Furnas, 1986).

The following relationships between the structure of the hierarchy and the structure of its treemap drawing always hold:

Properties

1) If Node 1 is an ancestor of Node 2, then the bounding box of Node 1 completely encloses, or is equal to, the bounding box of Node 2.
2) The bounding boxes of two nodes intersect if one node is an ancestor of the other.
3) Nodes occupy a display area strictly proportional to their weight.
4) The weight of a node is greater than or equal to the sum of the weights of its children.

Structural information in treemaps is implicitly presented, although it may also be explicitly indicated by nesting child nodes within their parent. Nesting provides for the direct selection of all nodes, both internal and leaf. The space required for nesting reduces the number of nodes which can be drawn in a given display space and hence reduces the size of the trees that can be adequately displayed compared to non-nested drawings (Travers, 1989).

A non-nested display explicitly provides direct selection only for leaf nodes, but a pop-up display can provide path information as well as further selection facilities. Non-nested presentations cannot depict internal nodes in degenerate linear sub-paths, as the bounding boxes of the internal nodes in the sub-path may be exactly equal. Such paths seldom occur and tasks dependent on long chains of single child nodes will require special treatments.

Content information: mapping content to the display

Once the bounding box of a node is set, a variety of display properties determine how the node is drawn within it. Visual display properties such as color (hue, saturation, brightness), texture, shape, border, blinking, etc., are of primary interest, but the interface will not limit users to purely visual properties (Ding & Mateti, 1990). Color is the most important of these visual display properties, and it can be an important aid to fast and accurate decision making (Hoadley, 1990; MacDonald, 1990; Rice, 1991). Auditory properties may also be useful in certain circumstances. Nodes may have many domain dependent properties, in which case a rich set of mappings exists between content information and display properties.

The drawing of individual nodes within their bounding boxes determines the content information statically presented in a treemap. The number and variety of domain properties that can be statically coded in the drawing of the tree is limited. As Kuhn states, "Since human perception imposes an upper bound on the complexity of graphic representations, only a small number of relations can be shown." (Ellson, 1990; Kuhn, 1990) Interactive control of the drawing is therefore critical because the mapping of content information to the display will vary depending on the information users require. Dynamic feedback is provided by a pop-up window which displays information about the node currently under the cursor.

For example, files could have weights (display size) proportional to their creation date, color saturation dependent on their last modification date, and pitch (tone heard while crossing border) based on size. Using this scheme it is easy to locate old files which have changed recently, and as the cursor crosses into their bounding box a deep tone tells users that the file is large even before they read the information about that file.

Algorithms

Algorithms are given to draw a treemap and to track cursor movement in the tree. The algorithms may be applied to any tree, regardless of its branching degree. Both algorithms appear on the following page as Figures 9 and 10.

```
DrawTree() The node gets a message to draw itself          The Root node is set up prior to the
                                                              original recursive call
{  doneSize = 0;                                           The percent of this node's subtree
                                                              drawn thus far
   PaintDisplayRectangle();                                The node sends itself a Paint
                                                              Message
   switch (myOrientation) {                                Decide whether to slice this node
                                                              horizontally or vertically
      case HORIZONTAL:
         startSide = myBounds.left;                        Set start for horizontal slices
      case VERTICAL:
         startSide = myBounds.top;                         Set start for vertical slices
   }
   if (myNodeType == Internal) {                           Set up each child and have it draw
                                                              itself
      ForEach (childNode) Do {
         childNode->SetBounds(startSide, doneSize, myOrientation); Set childs bounds
                                                              based on the parent partition
                                                              taken by previous children of
                                                              parent
         childNode->SetVisual();                           Set visual display properties (color,
                                                              etc.)
         childNode->DrawTree();                            Send child a draw command
}}}

SetBounds(startSide, doneSize, parentOrientation)
{  doneSize = doneSize + mySize;                           How much of the parent will have
                                                              been allocated after this node
   switch (parentOrientation) {                            Decide which direction parent is
                                                              being sliced
      case HORIZONTAL:
         myOrientation = VERTICAL;                         Set direction to slice this node for its
                                                              children
         endSide = parentWidth * doneSize / parentSize;    How much of the parent will have
                                                              been sliced after this node
         SetMyRect(startSide + offSet,                     Left side, Offset controls the nesting
                                                              indentation
            parentBounds.top + offSet,                     Top
            parentBounds.left + endSide - offSet,          Right
            parentBounds.bottom - offSet);                 Bottom
         startSide = parentBounds.left + endSide;          Set start side for next child
      case VERTICAL:
         myOrientation = HORIZONTAL;                       Set direction to slice this node for its
                                                              children
         endSide = parentHeight * doneSize / parentSize;
         SetThisRect(parentBounds.left + offSet,           Left side
            startSide + offSet,                            Top
            parentBounds.right - offSet,                   Right
            parentBounds.top + endSide - offSet);          bottom
         startSide = parentBounds.top + endSide;           Set start side for next child
}}
```

Figure 9. Drawing AlgorithmThe basic drawing algorithm produces a series of nested boxes representing the structure of the tree.

```
FindPath(point the Point)
{  if node encloses thePoint then
   for each child of thisNode do {
   path = findPath(thePoint);
     if (path != NULL) then
        return(InserInList(this Node, path));          Add child to path
}
return (NULL);                                          Start path, the Point is in this node,
                                                           but not in any of its children
}
```

Figure 10. Tracking algorithm

The cursor tracking algorithm facilitates interactive feedback about the tree. Every point in the drawing corresponds to a node in the tree. While the current tracking point (from a mouse or touchscreen input device) is in a node, the node is selected and information about it is displayed.

Drawing algorithm

The treemap can be drawn during one pre-order pass through the tree in O(n) time, assuming that node properties (weight, name, etc.) have previously been computed or assigned. The current algorithm has been implemented in object-oriented Think C on a Macintosh II. The drawing algorithm proceeds as follows:

1) The node draws itself within its rectangular bounds according to its display properties (weight, color, borders, etc.).

2) The node sets new bounds and drawing properties for each of its children, and recursively sends each child a drawing command. The bounds of a node's children form either a vertical or horizontal partitioning of the display space allocated to the node.

Tracking algorithm

The path from the root of the tree to the node associated with a given point in the display can be found in time proportional to the depth of the node.

In our implementation, when a node draws itself it stores its bounding box in an instance variable. Every point in the treemap corresponds to a node in the hierarchy; in addition, every node is contained in the bounding box of the root node. Recall that each node's bounding box completely encloses the bounding boxes of its children, and that the bounding boxes of sibling nodes never overlap. Finding the path to a node containing a given point thus involves only a simple descent through one path in the tree, until the smallest enclosing bounding box is found.

Coping with size

A typical 13-inch display has a resolution of 640 x 480, or roughly 300,000 pixels. Drawing an 80mb directory tree (weight = disk usage) on such a display requires that each pixel represent 260 bytes, i.e., there are roughly 4 pixels per

Kilobyte. Assuming that such a directory structure may contain roughly 3,000 files (as on one of our lab's hard disks) implies that there are approximately 100 pixels per file on average. A box with 10 pixels per side (roughly $4mm^2$) is easily selectable using a standard mouse or touchscreen device (Sears & Shneiderman, 1990). This average case analysis is only part of the story since file sizes may vary widely.

The range of file sizes on our hard disk varied from a few hundred bytes to well over one million bytes. In the treemap of Figure 8, groups of very small files often become completely black regions as there is only enough space to draw their borders. Magnification over these regions or zooming can provide access to these files. But since the assignment of node weights can be user controlled, presumably the nodes with the greatest weights are of greatest interest and the nodes with the smallest weights are of least interest.

Future research directions

Further research includes the exploration of alternate structural partitioning schemes, appropriate visual display of both numeric and non-numeric content information, dynamic views such as animated time slices, and operations on elements of the hierarchy. Standard operations such as zooming, marking, selecting and searching also invite designers to explore variations on the treemap strategy.

Dr. Ram Naresh-Singh, a visiting research scientist in our lab, is working on an alternate directory only approach to partitioning the display which we have termed "top-down". His implementation on a Sun Sparcstation preserves the traditional notion of having the root node at the top and the leaves at the bottom.

Animation, or time-sliced displays, could provide insight into evolving structures. For example, the hierarchical organization of a university could be mapped from the university level (root), to the college level, to the department level, to the research lab level. If weights were assigned based on personnel resources, it would be easy to see the structure of the university based on the distribution of employees, and hence understand its strengths and weaknesses. Furthermore, if the saturation of red was proportionate to the funds spent at each node, and the saturation of cyan (the inverse of red) was proportionate to the funds allocated, nodes (labs, departments, colleges) which were on budget would be shades of gray (equal amounts of red and cyan), nodes over budget would become increasingly red, and nodes under budget would become increasingly cyan. The magnitude of the nodes funding would range from black (small budgets and expenditures) to white (large budgets and expenditures). If a series of these displays are generated based on data over the last ten years, it would be possible to see how funding and personnel resources have evolved and been distributed within the university.

The range and variety of potential applications of this technology is vast. For instance, stock market portfolios are often hierarchically structured. Animations over time of financial portfolios could be a valuable application of this technology.

Conclusion

We believe that space-filling approaches to the visualization of hierarchical information structures have great potential. The drawing algorithm we have given is quite general, and the numerous possibilities for mapping information about individual nodes to the display are appealing. The treemap approach to visualizing hierarchical structures enables meaningful drawings of large hierarchies in a limited space.

Acknowledgments

We would like to acknowledge the support of the members of the Human-Computer Interaction Lab, whose suggestions and criticisms have been greatly appreciated. They have forced us to prove the value of treemaps and allowed us to hone our presentations of the idea.

References

Ahlberg, C., Williamson, C., Shneiderman, B. (1992) Dynamic Queries for information exploration: an implementation and evaluation. *Proc. CHI'92: Human Factors in Comp. Systems*, ACM, New York, 619-626.

Beard, D. V., Walker II, J. Q. (1990) Navigational techniques to improve the display of large two-dimensional spaces. *Behaviour & Information Technology*, Vol. 9, No. 6, 451-466.

Brüggemann-Klein, A., Wood.D. (July 1989) Drawing trees nicely with tex, *Electronic Publishing*, Vol. 2, No. 2, 101-115.

Card, S. K., Robertson, G. G., Mackinlay, J. D. The information visualizer, an information workspace, *Proc of ACM CHI'91,* Conference on Human Factors in Computing Systems, Information Visualization, 181-188.

Chimera, R., Wolman, K., Mark S., Shneiderman, B. (Feb. 1991) Evaluation of three interfaces for browsing hierarchical tables of contents, Technical Report CAR-TR-539, CS-TR-2620, University of Maryland, College ParK.

Chin, J., Diehl, V., Norman, K. (1988) Development of an instrument measuring user satisfaction of the human-computer interface, *Proc. CHI'88* Human Factors in Comp. Systems Conf., ACM Press, 213-218.

Cox, D. J., The art of scientific visualization,(March 1990) *Academic Computing*, 20.

Ding, C., Mateti, P. (May 1990) A framework for the automated drawing of data structure diagrams, *IEEE Transactions on Software Engineering*, Vol. 16, No. 5, 543-557.

Ellson, R., Visualization at work (March 1990) *Academic Computing*, 26.

Feiner, S. (March 1988) Seeing the forest for the trees: hierarchical display of hypertext structures, *ACM Proc. COIS'88* , Conf. on Office Information Systems (Palo Alto, CA), 205-212.

Fowler, R., Fowler, W., Wilson, B. (1991) Integrating query, thesaurus, and documents through a common visual representation, *Proc. SIGIR '91*, ACM Press, 142-151.

Furnas, G. W. (1986) Generalized fisheye views, *Proc. of ACM CHI'86* , Conference on Human Factors in Computing Systems, Visualizing Complex Information Spaces, 16-23.

Harman, D., Candela, G. (1990) Bringing natural language information retrieval out of the closet, *SIGCHI Bulletin* Vol. 22, 42-48.

Helander, M. (1988) *Handbook of Human-Computer Interaction*, Chapter 13, North-Holland, New York.

Henry, T. R., Hudson, S. E. (May 1990) Viewing large graphs, Technical Report 90-13, University of Arizona.

Hoadley, E. D. (February 1990) Investigating the effects of color. *Communications of the ACM*, Vol. 33, No. 2, 120-139.

Johnson, B., Shneiderman, B. (April 1991) Tree maps: a space-filling approach to the visualization of hierarchical information structures, *Proc. of the 2nd International IEEE Visualization Conference* (San Diego, Oct. 1991) 284-291.

Kamada, T. (Dec. 1988) On visualization of abstract objects and relations, Ph.D. thesis, University of Tokyo, Department of Information Science, 7-3-1 Hongo, Bunkyo-ku, Tokyo, 113 JAPAN.

Kim, H., Korth, H, Silberschatz, A. (1988) PICASSO: a graphical query language, *Software -Practice and Experience*. Vol. 18, 169-203.

Knuth, D. E. (1973) *Fundamental Algorithms, Art of Computer Programming,* vol. 1, Addison-Wesley, Reading, MA, 2nd edition.

Korfhage, R. R. (1991) To see, or not to see - is that the query? *Proc. SIGIR '91*, ACM Press, 134-141.

Kuhn, W. (1990) Editing spatial relations, *Proc. of the 4th International Symposium on Spatial Data Handling*, (Zurich, Switzerland) 423-432.

Larsson, J. A. (1986) A visual approach to browsing in a database environment, *IEEE Computer*, Vol. 19, 62-71.

MacDonald, L. W. (July 1990) Using colour effectively in displays for computer-human interface, *DISPLAYS*, 129-142.

Norman, D. A. (1988) *The Psychology of Everyday Things*, Basic Books, Inc., New York.

OPEN LOOK - GUI Functional Specification. Sun Microsystems, Inc. Reading, MA, 1989.

Rice, J. R. (March 1991) Ten rules for color coding, *Information Display*, Vol. 7. No. 3, 12-14.

Robertson, G.G., Mackinlay, J. D., Card, S. K. (1991) Cone trees: animated 3d visualizations of hierarchical information, *Proc. of ACM CHI'91,* Conference on Human Factors in Computing Systems, Information Visualization, 189-194.

Rowe, L.A. (1985) Fill-in-the-form programming, *Proc. 11th International on Very Large Databases*, ACM Press, 394-403.

Rutkowski, C. (1982) An introduction to the human applications standard computer interface, *Byte*, Vol. 7, 291-310.

Salton, G. (1983) *Introduction to Modern Information Retrieval*, McGraw-Hill, New York.

Samet, H. (1989) *Design and Analysis of Spatial Data Structures*, Addison-Wesley Publishing Co., Reading, MA.

Sears, A., Shneiderman, B. (April 1991) High precision touchscreens: design strategies and comparisons with a mouse. *International Journal of Man-Machine Studies*, Vol. 34, NO. 4, 593-613.

Shneiderman, B. (1983) Direct manipulation: a step beyond programming languages, *IEEE Computer*, Vol. 16, 57-69.

Shneiderman, B. (Sept. 1990.) Tree visualization with tree-maps: a 2-d space-filling appoach, *ACM Transactions on Graphics,* Vol. 11, No. 1, 92-99.

Travers, M. (1989) A visual representation for knowledge structures, *ACM Hypertext'89 Proc.*, Implementations and Interfaces, 147-158.

Tufte, E.R. (1983) *The Visual Display of Quantitative Information*, Graphics Press, Cheshire, CT.

Vincente, K. J., Hayes, B. C., Williges, R. C. (1987) Assaying and isolating individual differences in searching a hierarchical file system, *Human Factors*, Vol. 29, No. 3,:349-359.

Weiland, W.J., Shneiderman, B. (1991) A graphical query interface based on aggregation/

generalization hierarchies, *Information Systems* (to appear 1993).

Williams, M. (1984), What makes RABBIT run?, *International Journal of Man-Machine Studies*, Vol. 21, 333-352.

Williamson, C., Shneiderman, B. (1992) The Dynamic HomeFinder: evaluating dynamic queries in a real-estate information exploration system, *Proc. ACM SIGIR Conference*, ACM, New York, 338-346

Young, D., Shneiderman, B. (May 1992) A graphical filter/flow representation of boolean queries: a prototype implementation, *Journal of the American Society for Information Science* (to appear, 1993).

Zloof, M. (1975) Query-by-example, *National Computer Conference*, AFIPS Press, 431-437.

Sparks of Innovation in Human-Computer Interaction,
B. Shneiderman, Ed., Ablex Publ., Norwood, NJ (1993)

7. Essays and explorations

Introduction

Science can never be isolated from social concerns. I believe that reflection on social issues can lead to bolder science and that we have a responsibility to participate in the major issues of our time. Many of our greatest scientists from Galileo to Einstein have had to deal with social, ethical, and moral issues raised by their science. If scientific work has no social impact then it can't be important.

I have often felt strongly about social, ethical, and philosophical issues, but I was aware as a junior faculty member that dealing with such issues was risky. During one evaluation I was explicitly discouraged from aspiring to write about social issues in the popular press. I ignored this warning, but recognized that I would have to be careful in addressing contemporary issues until I achieved promotion and tenure. I do feel more comfortable speaking out now, but I am aware that there can be disapproval of non-technical involvements by some traditional academics.

My major concern has been to promote the importance of user interface issues. I have sometimes taken provocative positions to evoke responses and engage people in discussion. This is great fun through electronic mail where debates and responses sprout rapidly during the day with comments flowing in from around the world. But the email community is mainly computer-philic; we must also reach the computer-phobic population and those who are still excluded because of the economics. I believe we have a responsibility to build a better world through use of the amazing technology of user interfaces.

The first essay goes back to a basic quest to distinguish between people and computers (see paper 7.1, Shneiderman, 1989). I have persevered on this theme in "Beyond Intelligent Machines: Just Do It!" (Shneiderman, 1993) by pointing out how anthropomorphic scenarios limit designer imagination, and offering a new vision of predictable and controllable interfaces. I propose a Declaration of Responsibility (see paper 7.2, Shneiderman, 1990) to encourage development of truly beneficial technology. It sometimes seems like an unrealizable goal, but I had to write it. A new direction for education in the computer age is proposed in the third essay (see paper 7.3, Shneiderman, 1992).

The issue of responsibility also influenced my participation in one of the great legal conflicts of the past decade - the Apple vs. Microsoft/Hewlett-Packard case. In March 1988 Apple brought suit to stop distribution of Microsoft's Windows 2.03 and Hewlett-Packard's NewWave. In 1985 Apple had licensed its copyrighted audiovisual works from the Macintosh Finder and other programs in the Windows 1.0 product. This agreement seemed like a fair way to settle a disagreement and promote sharing of technology. But when the Windows 1.0 tiled window manager was replaced with an overlapped window manager in Windows 2.03, Apple protested that Microsoft was taking more than was specified in the 1985 agreement. Both sides contacted me to participate as an expert witness, but I didn't want to get involved. However, after much reflection I came to believe that it was important to be able to protect user interfaces and when Apple called again in June 1988 I agreed to take a look at their videotapes. I understood that it was a tough case for Apple to win, and also that it was risky for me professionally to stick my neck out for Apple. The majority of my colleagues felt that sharing new ideas would promote the evolution of user interfaces, and that Apple had taken ideas from the Xerox STAR. Ideas are not protected by copyright, only specific expressions are protectable. No company or individual can protect the idea of a desktop, window, icon, or scroll bar, but they can protect their expression of that idea. Anyway, the Xerox STAR did not have overlapping windows, allowed icons only in fixed grid positions, and had a confusing variety of pop-up menus, keyboard buttons, and property sheets. As an early user of the STAR I recognized its strengths and weaknesses, and when the Macintosh arrived in January 1984 I appreciated its elegant integration. I felt that to promote user interface design as a profession and to encourage others to innovate rather than rip off (see paper 7.4, Shneiderman, 1990), I had to speak up on Apple's behalf (see paper 7.4, this paper is the declaration filed with the United States District Court in the Northern District of California).

My first encounter around a large wood conference table on August 22, 1989 at Apple's lawyer's (Brown & Bain in Palo Alto) office was breathtaking. Six of Brown & Bain's lawyers plus Apple's Vice President and General Counsel Ed Stead focused on me and I felt that I should somehow be able to instantaneously turn around their case. My powers were not so strong and for the next three years I was intermittently called on to review the literature about window management, comment on documents, offer my declarations (see paper 7.5) and help form the case. My toughest days were clearly during depositions when the opposing five lawyers questioned me intensely while the court reporter tapped away and the videotape cameras captured my smiles and sweat.

The judge has chosen to base his decision on precedents which focus on the specific elements of the interface, not the overall look and feel. By my understanding, this reasoning would mean that anyone who wanted to rip off an interface would need to make only superficial changes, equivalent to stealing a poem by merely changing fonts and capitalization. This is not a happy resolution, but there will be appeals and other cases. As for my legal career, I have not signed up for law school as predicted by some and I have turned down a half dozen invitations to participate in other cases. I'd rather spend my time working with my colleagues and students, making sparks of user interface innovations.

Sparks of Innovation in Human-Computer Interaction,
B. Shneiderman, Ed., Ablex Publ., Norwood, NJ (1993)

HCIL

7.1 A nonanthropomorphic style guide: overcoming the Humpty Dumpty syndrome

Ben Shneiderman

A savvy 16-year-old informed his naive friend that "the computer knows about the AUTOEXEC file." Unimpressed, the naive friend asked, "Can it solve my math homework problems?"

Computer talk

There is a great temptation to talk about computers as if they were people. It is a primitive urge that children and many adults follow without hesitation. Children will readily accept human-like references and qualities for almost any object, from Humpty Dumpty to Tootle the Train. Adults reserve anthropomorphic references for objects of special attraction such as cars, ships, and computers.

Unfortunately, the words and phrases used when talking about computers can make important differences in people's perceptions, emotional reactions, and motivation to learn. Attributing intelligence, independent activity, free will, or knowledge to computers can mislead the reader or listener.

The Computing Teacher, 16 (7) (1989) 5.
Reprinted with permission of The Computing Teacher, Intern'l. Society for Technology in Ed., Eugene, OR 1988.

The suggestion that computers can think, know, or understand may give children an erroneous model of how computers work and what their capacities are. For example, bank terminals that ask, "How can I help you?" suggest more flexibility than they deliver. Ultimately the deception becomes apparent, and the user may feel poorly treated. A more realistic description of computers' capabilities may help children grasp the potential uses of computers and increase trust in their teachers, possibly increasing their motivation to learn.

A second reason for nonanthropomorphic phrasing is that it is important for children to have a clear sense of their own humanity. They need to know that they are different from computers, and that relationships with people are different from relationships with computers. They may learn to control computers, but they must respect the unique desires of individuals. The dual images of computer as executor of instructions and anthropomorphized machine may lead children to believe that they are automatons themselves. This undercuts their responsibility for mistakes and for poor treatment of friends, teachers, or parents. It is important to remind children that they have control over their lives (even if there are limitations). Blurring the boundary between computers and people may undermine a child's emerging sense of self (Turkle, 1984).

Third, because children can benefit from using computers, designers should make them accessible. An anthropomorphic machine may be attractive to some children but anxiety producing or confusing for others. Instead of suggesting that computers are like people, presenting computers through the powers that they offer may be the strongest stimulus to learning. As children become engaged, excited, and empowered, the computer becomes transparent and they can concentrate on their writing, problem solving, or exploration. They recognize that the product is a result of their own effort, not that of some magical machine.

Although children, and some adults, may be seduced by the anthropomorphized computer, eventually they seem to prefer the sense of mastery, internal locus of control, competence, and accomplishment that can come from understanding the computer's real abilities.

These arguments are largely subjective and express my personal view about value laden issues in discussing computer systems, but empirical data is beginning to emerge. In an experiment with 26 college students, the anthropomorphic design ("HI THERE, JOHN! IT'S NICE TO MEET YOU," "I SEE YOU ARE READY NOW.") was seen as less honest than a mechanistic dialog ("PRESS THE ENTER KEY TO BEGIN SESSION.") (Quintanar, Crowell, & Pryor, 1982). In this CAI task, subjects took longer with the anthropomorphic design--possibly contributing to the improved scores on a quiz--but they felt less responsible for their performances.

In a study of 36 junior high school students, conducted under my direction, the style of interaction was varied (Gay & Lindwarm, 1985). Students worked on a CAI session in one of three forms: I ("HI! I AM THE COMPUTER. I AM GOING TO ASK YOU SOME QUESTIONS."); you ("YOU WILL BE ANSWERING SOME QUESTIONS. YOU SHOULD...."); or neutral ("THIS IS A

MULTIPLE CHOICE EXERCISE.''). Before and after each session at the computer, subjects were asked to describe whether using a computer was easy or hard. Most subjects thought using a computer was hard and did not change their opinion, but of the seven who did change their minds, the five who moved toward hard-to-use were all in the I or neutral groups. Both of the subjects that moved toward easy-to-use were in the you group. Performance measures on the tasks were not significantly different, but anecdotal evidence and the positive shift for you group members warrant further study.

I used these ideas when I wrote a book for my third-grade daughter and her friends (Shneiderman, 1985). I wanted them to learn problem solving skills and some aspects of BASIC programming while experiencing how programming applies to playful and practical problems. In the text I was careful to present the computer in a mechanical way and to emphasize the task the reader was doing.

The artwork carries this same theme; there are no dancing robots or computers with faces. The computer is portrayed as a tool to help children reach their goals in examples such as recipe portion computations, counting minutes of piano practice, learning arithmetic, or writing a story. The artwork shows the computer as a tool or a fantasy machine: The computer becomes a piano, abacus, car, or spaceship.

The following examples illustrate how authors and teachers might present computers in a nonanthropomorphic style.

In discussing computers, avoid verbs such as:

know, think, understand, have memory (POOR).

In their place use more mechanical terms such as:

process, print, compute, sort, store, search, retrieve (BETTER).

When describing what a child does with a computer, avoid verbs such as:

ask, tell, speak to, communicate with (POOR).

In their place use terms such as:

use, direct, operate, program, control (BETTER).

Still better is to eliminate the reference to the computer and concentrate on what the child is doing, such as writing, solving a problem, finding an answer, learning a concept, or adding a list of numbers.

Here are some examples of poor (but commonly used) phrases and their better counterparts.

POOR: The computer can teach you some Spanish words.
BETTER: You can use the computer to learn some Spanish words.

Make the user the subject of the sentence.

POOR: The computer will give you a printed list of animals.
POOR: Ask the computer to print a list of animals.
BETTER: You can get the computer to print a list of animals.
EVEN BETTER: You can print a list of animals.

The last sentence puts the focus on the user and eliminates the computer.

POOR: The computer needs to have the disk in the disk drive to boot the system.
BETTER: Put the disk labeled A2 in the disk drive before starting the computer.
EVEN BETTER: To begin writing, put the Word Processor disk in the drive.

The last form emphasizes the function or activity that the user is going to perform.

POOR: The computer knows how to do arithmetic.
BETTER: You can use the computer to do arithmetic.

Focus on the child's initiative, process, goals, and accomplishments. Remember, computers have no more intelligence than a wooden pencil.

Software suggestions

The same principles apply to computer software (Shneiderman, 1987): Software designers and evaluators should be alert to phrasing and choice of words. The anthropomorphic computer that uses first person pronouns may be counterproductive because it deceives, misleads, and confuses. It may seem cute on first encounter to be greeted by "I AM SOPHIE, THE SOPHISTICATED TEACHER, AND I WILL TEACH YOU TO SPELL CORRECTLY", but by the second session this approach feels uselessly repetitive. By the third session it is an annoying distraction from the task.

The alternative for the software designer is to focus on the user and use second person singular pronouns or to avoid pronouns altogether.

POOR: I will begin the lesson when you press RETURN.
BETTER: You can begin the lesson by pressing RETURN.
BETTER: To begin the lesson, press RETURN.

I prefer the you form for introductory screens because it is more personal and engaging and it emphasizes the user as initiator. But once the session is underway I reduce the number of pronouns to avoid distracting from the material. For young children a fantasy character such as a teddy bear or a busy beaver can be a useful guide through the material. A cartoon character can be drawn and possibly animated on the screen to add visual appeal.

Well-chosen words and phrases make a difference in dozens of places, for example, in menu choices, instructions, prompts to remind users of available commands, on-line assistance screens, and on-line tutorials. Successful designers carefully test alternatives and continually refine their decisions.

I strongly believe that software designers should put their names on a title or credits page, just as authors do in a book. The credits are an acknowledgment for the work done, and they identify those responsible for the contents. In software there is the additional motivation of making it clear that people created the software and the computer is merely the media. Software design is a complex, highly creative process, and designers may try a little bit harder to create a good product if they know their names will appear.

Educational computer software is a new domain. The criteria here are meant to promote high quality software that serves the user's needs. As with any initial set of suggestions or guidelines, these need to be validated through empirical studies, refined for different situations, and extended to cover more situations.

As computers and software become more powerful, they become more empowering. We can help our students gain a sense of control by attributing the power to the user.

Sparks of Innovation in Human-Computer Interaction,
B. Shneiderman, Ed., Ablex Publ., Norwood, NJ (1993)

7.2 Human values and the future of technology: a declaration of responsibility

Ben Shneiderman

Abstract

"We must learn to balance the material wonders of technology with the spiritual demands of our human nature."
John Naisbitt (1982)

We can make a difference in shaping the future by ensuring that computers "serve human needs (Mumford, 1934)." By making explicit the enduring values that we hold dear we can guide computer system designers and developers for the next decade, century, and thereafter. After setting our high-level goals we can pursue the components and seek the process for fulfilling them.

Revised version (11/90) of Keynote address, originally published in the *Proc. of ACM SIGCAS Conference: Computers and the Quality of Life '90*, 1-6, as reprinted in *ACM SIGCHI Bulletin 23* (1), (Jan. 1991) 11-16.

High-level goals might include peace, excellent health care, adequate nutrition, accessible education, communication, freedom of expression, support for creative exploration, safety, and socially constructive entertainment. Computer technology can help attain these high-level goals if we clearly state measurable objectives, obtain participation of professionals, and design effective human-computer interfaces. Design considerations include adequate attention to individual differences among users, support of social and organizational structures, design for reliability and safety, provision of access by the elderly, handicapped, or illiterate, and appropriate user controlled adaptation. With suitable theories and empirical research we can achieve ease of learning, rapid performance, low error rates, and good retention over time, while preserving high subjective satisfaction.

To raise the consciousness of designers and achieve these goals, we must generate an international debate, stimulate discussions within organizations, and interact with other intellectual communities. This paper calls for a focus on the "you" and "I" in developing improved user interface (UI) research and systems, offers a Declaration of Empowerment, and proposes a Social Impact Statement for major computing projects.

Introduction

> "The machine itself makes no demands and holds out no promises: it is the human spirit that makes demands and keeps promises. In order to reconquer the machine and subdue it to human purposes, one must first understand it and assimilate it. So far we have embraced the machine without fully understanding it."
>
> *Mumford (1934) p.6*

Those who believe that they can change the future will change the future. This optimistic view is an extreme statement, but it does contain an important, useful, and action-oriented message. If commentators give up cursing the darkness of fatalism and light a candle of hope, they can guide us to a positive image of the future. However, even with a positive attitude, inventing the future is not easy.

As scientists and technologists we must begin with a belief that we can influence the future of technology (Florman, 1976). This seems a realistic goal since each day corporations and government agencies choose which technologies to support and thereby shape the future. The lively debates about space exploration, the strategic defense initiative ("star wars plan"), heart transplants, high-definition television, recombinant DNA, birth control, etc. are powerful testimony that social forces are at work to shape the future of technology.

In fact the philosophical drift is towards still more profound changes in perceptions of our powers. The editors of *Scientific American* dared to call their September 1989 Special Issue "Managing Planet Earth," suggesting that we have the power and responsibility to shape our ecological future. At the same time John McPhee dealt with these issues in his book "The Control of Nature" while Brian McKibben wrote on "The End of Nature." These sources emphasize that decision makers must grapple with the issue of responsibility for the ecological future of our planet.

Similarly, I argue that decision makers in government, corporations, universities, etc., can and must take responsibility for our technological future. Specifically, I focus on shaping the future for people who use computers. My concern is on how users are empowered by new technologies, how they apply their growing power, and the choices that researchers and developers can make to influence user interfaces. I believe that we can choose to build a future in which computer users experience competence, clarity, control, and comfort and feelings of mastery and accomplishment. At the end of the day these users can take pride in a job done well, and appreciate the designers who created the technology.

Philosophical foundation and goals

> "I firmly believe that any organization, in order to survive and achieve success, must have a sound set of beliefs on which it premises all its policies and actions...the basic philosophy, spirit, and drive of an organization have far more to do with its relative achievements than do technological or economic resources...."
> *Tom Watson, Jr. (1962), cited by Jin (1990)*

A sound philosophical foundation will help us to deal with specific issues. The challenge is to produce a set of goals that would be widely accepted, yet still specific enough to be useful. A starting point would be fundamental concerns such as:

- world peace
- medical and psychological health care
- adequate nutrition and housing
- safe transportation
- protection of the environment
- effective education
- access to communication and information resources
- freedom of expression
- support for creative exploration
- privacy protection
- socially constructive entertainment and sports

Presumably these societal concerns could be translated into personal experiences of freedom, challenge, engagement, pleasure, accomplishment, and self-actualization. Responding to these grand concerns and enduring values may seem to be beyond the scope of computing researchers and designers, but I believe that we can define them by specific and measurable goals such as 10% (or more) changes to:

- reduce nuclear and conventional forces
- increase life expectancy
- slow population growth
- reduce homelessness
- reduce automobile accident deaths

- increase air quality in major cities
- reduce illiteracy worldwide
- reduce costs of long-distance telephone and air travel

In some cases, it is clear that information and computer technology can make an impact, e.g., by educational applications in literacy training or by computer control of automobile engines to reduce pollution. In other situations, the linkage with improved human-computer interaction may be less clear initially. In fact, some goals may be more difficult to attain by only redesigning computer technology, but the example of our profession taking up the cause may prove to be an inspiration to others. Therefore, even though we may not know the path, a clear statement of the destination will benefit us and inspire participation as we ask others for assistance.

Earlier in this century physicists recognized their responsibility in dealing with atomic energy and vigorously debated the issues. I believe that we in the computing professions must also recognize our responsibilities, set an example of moral leadership by inspiring discussion and influencing colleagues in other fields of science or in engineering, social sciences, medicine, law, etc. I believe that computer technology is pivotal in shaping the future since it influences daily life in every office, store, farm, school, factory, and home (Zuboff, 1988). We have a unique responsibility to consider the impact of our technology and to guide it to produce the maximum benefits with the minimum harm.

Therefore, I propose a Declaration of Empowerment:

1. We, the researchers, designers, managers, implementers, testers, and trainers of user interfaces and information systems, recognize the powerful influence of our science and technology. Therefore we commit ourselves to studying ways to enable users to accomplish their personal and organizational goals while pursuing higher societal goals and serving human needs.
2. We agree to preparing a Social Impact Statement (patterned on the Environmental Impact Statement) at the start of every human-computer interaction project. The Social Impact Statement will identify user communities, establish training requirements, specify potential negative side-effects (health, safety, privacy, financial, etc.), and indicate monitoring procedures for the project's lifetime.
3. We recommend that professional societies prepare an agenda of vital, specific, and realizable goals for the next decade (with some thought to the next century and thereafter). These goals should be ambitious and inspirational for our profession and for others.

Philosophers and ethicists can help refine the higher level goals, while the entrepreneurs and marketeers can inform us of the practical realities. Managers and regulators can help shape the Social Impact Statement so that it helps designers meet their goals while reducing costs, saving time, and increasing quality. For those directly involved in creating the scientific theories and designing working systems, the following sections are a starting point for new ways of thinking.

Questions for designers

> "The real question before us lies here: do these instruments further life and enhance its values, or not?"
> *Mumford (1934) p. 318*

In an earlier work (1987), I described "Ten Plagues of the Information Age" and cautioned designers. However, each one of these potential plagues is also a challenge to be overcome; can contemporary designers build a better world by preventing these plagues?

1. Anxiety: Can we build improved user interfaces and systems that will reduce or eliminate the current high level of anxiety experienced by many users? In fact, can we not set our goal to make use of computers appealing, engaging, relaxing, and satisfying?
2. Alienation: Can we build user interfaces that encourage constructive human social interaction?
3. Information-poor minority: Can we build systems that empower low-skilled workers to perform at the level of experts? Can we arrange training and education for every able member of society?
4. Impotence of the individual: While large complex systems may overwhelm individual initiative, it seems clear that computers have the potential of dramatically empowering individuals. How best to ensure that this happens?
5. Bewildering complexity and counterproductive speed: This is a serious challenge to designers because the normal social and economic pressure is for more power, complexity, and speed. Stern adherence to basic values may be the only path to a safer, saner, simpler, and slower world where human concerns predominate.
6. Organizational fragility: The complexity of technological systems sometimes leads to their breakdown, but disaster can be avoided by effective design, proper training, and wise management. Can developers anticipate the dangers and produce robust designs?
7. Invasion of privacy: Can managers seek policies and systems that increase rather than reduce the protection of privacy?
8. Unemployment and displacement: Improved systems should lead to economic expansion but individual job displacement is a serious issue. Can employers develop labor policies that ensure retraining and guarantee jobs?
9. Lack of professional responsibility: Complex and confusing systems enable users and designers to blame the machine, but with improved designs responsibility and credit will be properly given and accepted by the users and designers.
10. Deteriorating image of ourselves: Rather than be impressed by smart machines, accept the misguided pursuit of the Turing test, or focus on computational skills in people, I believe that designs that empower users will increase their appreciation of the richness and diversity of unique human abilities.

These ten challenges are a useful checklist for designers, but I find that there are four fundamental questions that can act as useful guides:

Have I considered individual differences among users in the design of my system?

Have I considered the social context of users?

Have I arranged for adequate participation of users in the design process?

Have I considered how my design empowers users?

I'm sure that there are other important questions, philosophies, guidelines, rules, or maxims that can aid designers. I look forward to lively debates about how best to build the happier, wiser, and safer world of the future.

Kindling the fires

> "Before large-scale action can be taken, however, there must be public awareness, public debate, and a decision to take action as a society. We are not naive enough to think that this can take place overnight, but we do know that major transformations have already come about rapidly."
> *Ornstein and Ehrlich (1989)*

Hard-core computing professionals often have little patience with grand social visions. To capture their hearts and minds requires practical and realizable steps. This expectation is legitimate and even helpful. I think the excitement of creating new products and theories will be sufficiently engaging for many people, but courageous leaders must encourage the shift in attention.

First steps would be to produce discussions within professional societies, corporations, government agencies, and international organizations. Professional societies, such as the Association for Computing Machinery (ACM), Computer Professionals for Social Responsibility (CPSR), or IEEE Computer Society, can respond to the Declaration of Empowerment by educating their members, issuing public position papers, stimulating discussions in their journals and conferences, and guiding corporations and governments. They can begin by refining the proposal for the Social Impact Statement.

Corporations stand to gain the most and are likely to carry the vision forward if their officers can understand how profits can be increased, stockholders pleased, and employees satisfied. Any vision of expanded use of computers is likely to lead to increased production of hardware and software, with attendant increases in service, training, maintenance, etc. Although proof is hard to come by and there are certainly negative side-effects, I believe that expanded use of computers increases productivity, improves quality, and stimulates economic growth. In short, corporations are likely to support a suitable plan. Directors of research and corporate officers might be invited to national and international planning sessions to coordinate activity (Jin, 1990).

Government officials and agencies in the United States and other countries can often become leaders in these novel directions. For example, the U. S. Office of

Technology Assessment convenes working groups addressing novel technologies which might recommend ways to apply the Declaration of Empowerment. Financial support from the National Science Foundation can steer research directions, and initiatives from the National Institute for Standards and Technology are often influential. A set of principles espoused by the Office of Personnel Management or the Government Accounting Office can direct developments within other government agencies. I hope the members of Congress and other government officials will recognize the opportunities before they are challenged for their abdication of responsibility. Similar agencies exist in governments in many countries.

International scientific organizations can also play a role by raising these concerns at conferences such as the triennial IFIP World Conference on Computers. United Nations agencies or the International Commission on Human Aspects of Computing can disseminate the ideas and reach key parties in corporations, governments, and scholarly institutions around the world.

There is an opportunity for professional, academic, corporate, and governmental leaders to take the initiative in shaping the future before the ozone hole of irresponsibility grows too large. Positive visions are important, but practical plans and innovative theories are also necessary. Then, as steps are taken, there is a need for a feedback and evaluation process to make mid-course corrections.

While inspiring leadership is essential, ultimately every step is taken by an individual designer who makes one decision at a time. Each decision may be an opportunity to make the world a better place by enabling a doctor to make a more effective treatment plan, a teacher to be more successful in helping a student learn, an airline reservationist to find a shorter and cheaper routing, or an arms-control negotiator to more easily revise a treaty. Ultimately, quality, cooperation, and compassion emerge from solitary decisions made by committed and concerned individuals.

Acknowledgments

I am grateful to the SIGCAS Conference Committee for inviting me to present this keynote address. Parts of the presentation were developed at the invitation of Louis Berlinguet to speak on these issues at the Work With Display Units Conference in Montreal, Canada in September 1989. I am grateful also for constructive and supportive comments from Christine Borgman, Richard Chimera, Lance Hoffman, Reinhard Keil-Slawik, John Kohl, Gary Marchionini, Anthony Norcio, Catherine Plaisant, Phyllis Reisner, and Terry Winograd.

Sparks of Innovation in Human-Computer Interaction,
B. Shneiderman, Ed., Ablex Publ., Norwood, NJ (1993)

7.3 Engagement and construction: educational strategies for the post-TV era

Ben Shneiderman

Introduction

We all remember the empty faces of students seated in rows, intermittently taking notes, and trying to retain disjointed facts. This old lecture style seems as antiquated as a 19th century clockwork mechanism; familiar and charming, but erratic and no longer adequate. The orderly structure of industrial age mechanisms and the repetitiveness of the assembly line are giving way to the all-at-once immediacy of McLuhan's non-linear electrified global village (McLuhan, 1964). The early electronic media such as radio, stereos, and television have created a snap-crackle-and-popular culture that is enjoyable, but passive. The post-TV era will be different. Computing and communication technologies offer opportunities for engagement with other people and the power tools to construct remarkable artifacts and experiences.

Educators can now create engaging processes for their students that will motivate them to work together and explore the frontiers of knowledge. Students

*Computer Assisted Learning: Proc. of 4th International Conference ,I*CCAL '92, I. Tomek, Ed. (Wolfville, Nova Scotia, Canada, June 1992) Springer-Verlag, NY, 39-45.

from elementary schools through college can apply computing technology (word processors, spreadsheets, databases, drawing programs, design tools, music composition software, etc.) to construct high quality products that they can proudly share with others. Advanced communications tools (electronic mail, network access, bulletin board systems, videotape recorders, TV broadcasts) support engagement among students, connection to the external world, information gathering, and dissemination of results.

Defining Engagement

My definition of engagement focuses on interaction with people; students working together, as they must in the workplace, community, and family. Paired collaborations, team projects, and class presentations can teach valuable skills that are now left to sports teams and after school clubs. Secondly, students can interact with people outside the classroom; by visiting adults in the workplace, interviewing community leaders, and communicating with students in other schools, cities, states, and countries. Instead of requiring conjugation of French verbs, teachers might set the goal for students to make a videotape about their community in French to send to students in Canada or Togo. The students would have to learn conjugation, but they would work as a team to create a product of which they could all be proud. Instead of memorizing the sequence of British monarchs, students might create a hypermedia document with a timeline, photos, music, and biographies that could be stored in the library for future students to access or expand. Instead of merely reading about the disease patterns in urban areas, students might collect data from local hospitals on patterns of flu outbreaks and build a simulation model of disease epidemics in communities as a function of age, gender, and sociological factors, with the goal of reporting results at community meetings, to medical groups, in local newspapers, or in electronic bulletin boards.

In support of these projects students would have to work together and also reach out to others to collect information from librarians, city officials, physicians, scientists, bankers, business leaders, etc. Imagine how a report on World War II would be enriched by an interview with a D-Day participant in a retirement home. Imagine how an ecology report would be enlivened after a discussion with a local park naturalist, a political science project would become livelier after an interview with a local or state politician, and biology would become more meaningful after a visit with a hospital lab technician. The experience of speaking to adults at work would be educational, the process could improve social and communication skills, and the discussions are potentially illuminating for everyone involved.

The second aspect of engagement is the cooperation among students needed to complete projects. When working in teams students can take on more ambitious projects, can learn from each other, and must make their plans explicit to coordinate. Engagement with fellow students can help make learning more lively and effective as a model for the future world of work, family, and community.

The rich environment of computers and networks is already being used to support engagement across cities and countries. For example, approximately

10,000 elementary school children at 150 sites collected and exchanged acid rain data. In another project, high school students in the U.S. were paired with Russian students for email exchanges. A science project involved hundreds of sixth graders simultaneously measuring the length of a shadow and exchanging data to measure the earth's diameter.

Electronic mail opens up new possibilities for cooperation among students, guidance from teachers, and communication with national or international leaders. For example, students in my graduate seminar on user interface design undertook the common task of reading research journal papers and critiquing them, but interest in the task increased when they were required to send their critiques to the authors by email. The discussions were deeper, the usual off-hand attacks were softer in tone, but sharper in insight. The replies and contact with leading professionals gave my students a sense of importance and maturity.

Defining construction

The second part of my theme is construction, by which I mean that students create a product from their collaboration. This may not seem so different from current expectations of writing a computer program or a term paper. But when coupled with the engagement theme, I mean constructing something of importance to someone else. Instead of having database management students write the same safe class project, my students have implemented database management programs for the University's bus service, generated a scheduling program for a local TV station, prepared an online information retrieval program for a suicide prevention clinic, and developed record keeping software for a student scuba club.

Instead of writing a term paper on computer applications for the elderly, two of my students in a Computers and Society course offered computing lessons for elderly residents of a local apartment complex. Then the students prepared a report for the director of the complex, with a copy for me to grade. Several teams of students worked with their former high schools or elementary schools to suggest ways to improve the use of computers. One student wrote computer programs to manage lists of volunteers and contributors for a local soup kitchen. One student challenged the University's legal policy about student access and privacy rights with respect to their accounts. Another student wrote a handbook about educational software for parents of deaf children, while another pair of students prepared a hypertext guide to coping with computer software viruses. Computer tools enable construction of ambitious projects; there is a special sense of pride when students produce an animated hypertext, laser-printed report, or collect/disseminate data through networks.

In addition to these semester-long projects, there are many opportunities for short-term construction projects ranging from the traditional programming exercise done as a team project to class presentations by students on normal lecture material. Requiring a team of two students to present a topic to the entire class can make the topic appealing for the whole class, and the designated students will be likely to take their responsibility seriously. Turning work into a communal experience is made practical by the presence of word processors/text editors because making suggested revisions has become easy.

Cooperative groups in general studies

College level computer science has been my academic domain, so it might seem that these notions are only suitable for that age group and subject. However, I feel that engagement and construction are appropriate at most ages and in most fields. In fact, related ideas have been proposed by many reports on education during the past decade. The Final Report of the Study Group on the Conditions of Excellence in American Higher Education, National Institute of Education, wrote that "Active modes of teaching require that students be inquirers - creators, as well as receivers, of knowledge." That report also stressed projects, internships, discussion groups, collaborations, simulations, and presentations (Figure 1). Similarly, the Principles for Good Practice in Undergraduate Education presented by the American Association for Higher Education (Figure 2) pushed for cooperation among students and active learning projects.

1) Student Involvement
- involving students in faculty research projects
- encouraging internships
- organizing small discussion groups
- requiring in-class presentations and debates
- developing simulations
- creating opportunities for individual learning projects

2) High Expectations
3) Assessment and Feedback

Figure 1. Conditions for Excellence in Undergraduate Education, Involvement in Learning: Realizing the Potential of American Higher Education, Final Report of the Study Group on the Conditions of Excellence in American Higher Education (National Institute of Education, 1984).

Exploration and creation

The spirit of engagement is to enable students to experience the challenge of exploratory research and the satisfaction of creative accomplishment. I believe that imaginative teachers can find ways in every discipline and at every grade to create an atmosphere of exploration, novelty, and challenge. Whether collecting scientific data or studying Greek theater, there are provocative open questions that students can attempt to answer. My undergraduate students regularly conduct empirical studies related to my research in user interface design (Shneiderman, 1992b) and their work is published in scientific journals. Only one in ten projects leads to a publishable result, but the atmosphere of exploration at the frontier of research produces a high level of engagement even for introverted and blase

Encourage Student-Faculty Contact
Encourage Cooperation Among Students
Encourage Active Learning
Give Prompt Feedback
Emphasize Time on Task
Communicate High Expectations
Respect Diverse Talents and Ways of Learning

Figure 2. Principles for Good Practice in Undergraduate Education (American Association for Higher Ed., 1987).

computer science students at my state university. Similarly, my 12-year old daughter did her 7th-grade science project on spaced vs. massed practice with 3rd-graders in her school learning to type.

The concepts of exploration and creation are well-established in the education literature from John Dewey to Seymour Papert. Piaget wrote that "Knowledge is not a copy of reality. To know an object, to know an event is not simply to look at it and make a mental copy, or image, of it. To know an object is to act on it. To know is to modify, to transform the object, and to understand the process of transformation, and as a consequence to understand the way the object is constructed" (Piaget, 1964). The phrase "discovery learning" conveys the key notion that "whatever knowledge children gain they create themselves; whatever character they develop they create themselves," as Wees wrote in his aptly titled book *Nobody Can Teach Anybody Anything* (Wees, 1971).

Summary

The post-TV media of computers and communications enables teachers, students, and parents to creatively develop education by engagement and construction (Figure 3). Students should be given the chance to engage with each other in team projects, possibly situated in the world outside the classroom, with the goal of constructing a product that is useful or interesting to someone other than the teacher. Challenges remain such as scaling up from small class projects to lecture sections with hundreds of students, covering the curriculum that is currently required by many school districts, evaluating performance, and assigning grades. However, there seems to be no turning back and, anyway, the children of the Nintendo and Video Age are eager to press fast forward.

Students want to engage with people to:

Create	Communicate	Plan	Help	Initiate
Explore	Build	Discover	Participate	Collaborate

Students will be engaged by constructing products:

Writing	(poems, plays, essays, novels, newspapers, diaries)
Drawing	(pictures, logos, portraits, maps, birthday cards)
Composing	(music, songs, operas, hypermedias, videos)
Designing	(buildings, furniture, games, animations, family trees)
Planning	(class trips, charity events, vacations, parties, elections)

Teachers should promote:

Engaging in the world	(lobby a Senator, raise environmental awareness, call City Hall to report a problem)
Helping where needed	(teach computing to the elderly, improve recycling, increase awareness of drug abuse or AIDS)
Caring for others	(raise funds for the homeless, improve medical care)
Communicating ideas	(write to a newspaper editor, make a class speech, produce a cable TV show)
Organizing events	(prepare a bake sale or lecture series)

Multimedia technologies can empower students:

Enable students to create multimedia reports
Encourage media-supported class presentations
Develop communication through electronic mail
Provide experience in searching databases
Explore information networks and bulletin board systems
Promote use of word processing, drawing, spreadsheets

Project orientation enhances engagement:

Help an elementary school to improve computer use
Teach elderly users word processing
Find or develop aids for a handicapped person
Revise university policy on information protection and privacy
Improve university administration, registration
Evaluate and suggest improvement to bank machines, library systems, public access terminals, voicemail
Write guide for parents about kids' software
Review workplace practices for computer users

Figure 3. Strategies for increasing engagement and construction

Sparks of Innovation in Human-Computer Interaction,
B. Shneiderman, Ed., Ablex Publ., Norwood, NJ (1993)

7.4 Protecting rights in user interface designs

Ben Shneiderman

Sacrificing individual rights in the hopes of benefiting the public good is a tempting but often misguided pursuit. I believe that protecting individual rights (civil, voting, privacy, intellectual property, etc.) is usually the best way to benefit and advance the public good.

The current policy debate rages over the merits of offering intellectual property protection to user interface designs. While most commentators agree that copyright is appropriate for books, songs, or artwork, some are reluctant to offer such protection for user interfaces. These critics argue strenuously that intellectual protection for user interfaces is "monopolistic" and that it would have a destructive effect on the public good by limiting dissemination of useful innovations and inhibiting standardization. These critics claim that the traditional individual and corporate rights to creative works should be denied to user interface designers.

ACM SIGCHI Bulletin, Oct. 1990. Excerpt of this paper also appeared as: Intellectual protection for user interfaces? *Communication of the ACM*, 34, 4, (April 1991) 13-14.

This position deserves some respect on its merits and because it is quite widely held, but I strongly disagree. I am now ready to speak out in favor of protecting individual rights as the more effective and durable path to increasing the public good. My insight to these issues has been enriched by participation as an expert witness for the plaintiff in a major case now before the courts. I had initially rejected invitations to participate by lawyers from both sides of the case. Then during 1989, I more clearly realized the importance of fighting for user interface designers as creative people who should have the right to protect their creative work.

Background

Advocates of public domain software and shareware have benefited the computing community and I hope they will continue to do their work. However, I am a strong believer in recognizing, rewarding, respecting, and protecting individual creative activity in music, film, poetry, writing, drawing, and user interface design. Similarly, I support protection of functional devices (mechanical, optical, electrical, etc.) by patent. Creative works are extensions of ourselves and, like our children, deserve protection.

I believe that participants in this debate are all in favor of increasing the public good, but the issue is whether individual rights must be given up. Advocates of state-controlled economies, communal utopias, restrictive zoning, and stop-and-search laws also have argued that individual rights must be given up to increase the public good, but often these arguments are short-sighted. Although there are compelling examples on both sides of the issue, I think that the benefit to the public good is usually maximized by allowing individuals and corporations to protect their efforts.

The case for protection

If individuals or corporations have invested time and resources to produce a creative work, they should be able to secure legal protection. This encourages innovation in at least two ways.

First, it offers the promise of honor and financial reward plus the knowledge that they can influence who uses their work and how it is used. If I write a book or design a user interface, I want to know that my name will remain connected with the work, that I will be asked permission for its use, that I can influence the context of its proposed use, and that I can ask compensation if I so wish. I regularly grant permission to use my works for free, but in other situations I feel entitled to ask for payment. Financial remuneration is often necessary to continue development, refine the creative work, and adequately market a product.

Second, new user interface designers are compelled to push forward the state of the art to gain similar recognition and reward. If user interfaces are unprotectable, then designers can rip-off the currently fashionable design. This can lead to acceptance of the lowest common denominator while marketeers pat themselves on the back in the belief that they are promoting standardization. But this lazy approach undermines the public good in that there is little pressure or incentive to push the technology forward with innovative solutions.

Challenging the fear-mongers

Critics of protection paint a fearsome portrait of vicious corporations and monopolistic individuals, but these scare tactics seem exaggerated and naive. Individuals and companies that produce creative works want to see their creations put to work and are usually eager to negotiate licenses that permit access for a fee. This is quite well accepted even in the gentle world of folk music, but also in the competitive worlds of film making and book publishing.

It does seem ironic that critics of protection publish their articles in copyrighted journals. Also the professional societies (ACM, IEEE, etc.) have moved vigorously to assert their copyright over written materials and more recently for electronically published sources.

Allowing individuals or companies to assert ownership stimulates them to disseminate their works, rather than keep them secret for as long as possible. Without protection, innovators might be reluctant to share their developments until products were distributed. With protection an innovator can show a novel design and openly seek partnerships.

Of course there will be extreme anecdotes told by both sides and strong claims made in legal briefs, but overall I vote to pursue the market-oriented policies that have more often than not been generative of innovation. The user interface industry is growing up fast and like the rock music superstars, we must also learn to live with the lawyers and the legal system.

The lawyers, courts, and judges are not malicious or poorly informed, but they do have a different set of rules that have been established over decades. The sooner we learn the rules, the more effective will be our use of them to guide and promote innovation.

Are user interfaces different from other expressive works?

Copyrights are traditionally applied to creative works such as books, poems, songs, or movies that have expressive aspects. Copyrights are secured easily and last for the author's lifetime plus fifty years. Infringement is established as "substantial similarity as judged by ordinary observers." Patents are traditionally applied to inventions such as staple guns, telescopes, motors, and radios that are functional. Patents take several years to obtain and last 17 years, but protection is strong. Neither protection applies to principles of nature or generic ideas.

Even critics recognize that the user interfaces for video games, children's entertainment software, and educational software are expressive and that they are copyrightable. Designers of business computer applications such as word processors, spreadsheets, database managers, etc. have become more attentive to the expressive aspects of their user interfaces. These interfaces now have eye-catching visual images, engaging animations, colorful decorations, appealing sound effects, and playful aspects (cute icons, 3-D, texture, shading, etc.) forming a harmonious ensemble.

While the line between videogames and business applications is not clear and the line between expressive and functional is not always clear, I believe that the expressive aspects of user interfaces should be protectable by copyright or possibly some new form of intellectual property protection.

Increasingly, I find it possible to separate the user interface from the functional components of an application. We will have to rely on the progress of our technology of specification and on legal precedents to help chart a course. This is a complex issue and clean solutions are not to be expected, but that does not discourage me from pursuing this path. I will stand up to protect individual rights.

In some cases it is clear that infringement has occurred (exact copying), and in other cases the jury or judge will listen to the opposing parties and then make their judgment, just as they do for songs or movie scripts. Cooperation by licensing and mediation when there is conflict seem preferable, but when an adversarial situation arises we have traditionally relied on the courts for resolution and precedents. I prefer the courtroom, with all its burdens and expenses, to the Wild West environment of Rip-off City.

Is a new form of intellectual protection needed?

Where there is an expressive component to a user interface, copyright seems appropriate. Where the boundary between expression and function is fuzzier we may need a new form of protection. I propose that researchers, developers, lawyers, and legislators explore the need for new forms of protection that would:

- permit rapid filing and dissemination of novel works (more difficult than copyright, but easier and quicker than patent)
- contain a clear statement of what is protected
- offer a limited time of protection (maybe 8-10 years)
- encourage licensing for reasonable royalties
- support a reasonable standardization process

Conclusion

Members of the user interface community should be aware that important issues are at stake in these debates and court cases. It will be helpful to be informed so that they can sort out the rhetoric and participate intelligently and constructively.

A cooperative world in which partnership naturally leads to respect for individual accomplishments is a great dream, but my experience leads me to believe in the benefit of proper legal protection. I recommend support for intellectual property protection for user interfaces in the belief that individual rights are the foundation for a more progressive society. At the same time, let's honor user interface designers with our own form of Emmys, Oscars, and Pulitzer Prizes.

Sparks of Innovation in Human-Computer Interaction,
B. Shneiderman, Ed., Ablex Publ., Norwood, NJ (1993)

7.5 Declaration in Apple vs. Microsoft/Hewlett-Packard

Ben Shneiderman

I, Ben Shneiderman, declare as follows:

1. I am a Professor in the Department of Computer Science and Head of the Human-Computer Interaction Laboratory at the University of Maryland at College Park. My background and qualifications are detailed in my declaration of March 30, 1990 that previously was filed in this action.

2. I am making this supplemental declaration to provide further examples of design alternatives referred to in my prior declarations and to further identify the arrangement that is unique to Apple and that makes the overall appearance of the Lisa/Macintosh interface widely recognizable.

3. *The Macintosh "Look and Feel."* To understand the distinctive appearance of the Macintosh interface, known as the Macintosh "look and feel" or "the Macintosh look", one needs to consider not only the individual elements that make up the appearance of the interface but also the way those elements are arranged and interact with one another to create the consistent and distinctive Macintosh inter-

---

United States District Court, Northern District of Calif., Jack E. Brown, Lois W. Abraham, Chris R. Ottenweller, Martin L. Lagod, Brown & Bain; Bernard Petrie, Attorneys for Plaintiff, Apple Computer, Inc.; APPLE COMPUTER, INC., Plaintiff, vs. MCROSOFT CORP. & HEWLETT-PACKARD CO. , Defendants, April 1992.

face. One way to describe that look and feel is by reference to the following main features of the Macintosh interface. The alphanumeric designations appearing in brackets correspond to items from Apple's list of similarities.

3a. *The ""desktop.*" The desktop in Macintosh provides a home base from which users can enter, exit, and manage their computer environment [Supplemental List, A.1.a, A.1.b, items in square brackets refer to the list of user interface elements in the case.] Each time a user enters the Macintosh environment he or she is immediately presented with a muted grey desktop and a collection of icons lying on that desktop (these icons may represent applications, folder directories, or documents and are identified by titles centered beneath each icon) (G1, G5, G6). To interact with the Macintosh a user opens one or more of these icons into its corresponding window. The resulting screen appearance (a representative screen is shown in Figure 1) contains many displays that are characteristic of the Macintosh:

3a(1) Unlike any earlier system, the Macintosh uses and displays icons in such a way that the typical user will not only see icons lying on the desktop [G5] but will also see icons inside of open windows [I4], and can open those icons into new windows [Al, A.l.a]. Macintosh and Lisa were the first user interfaces to

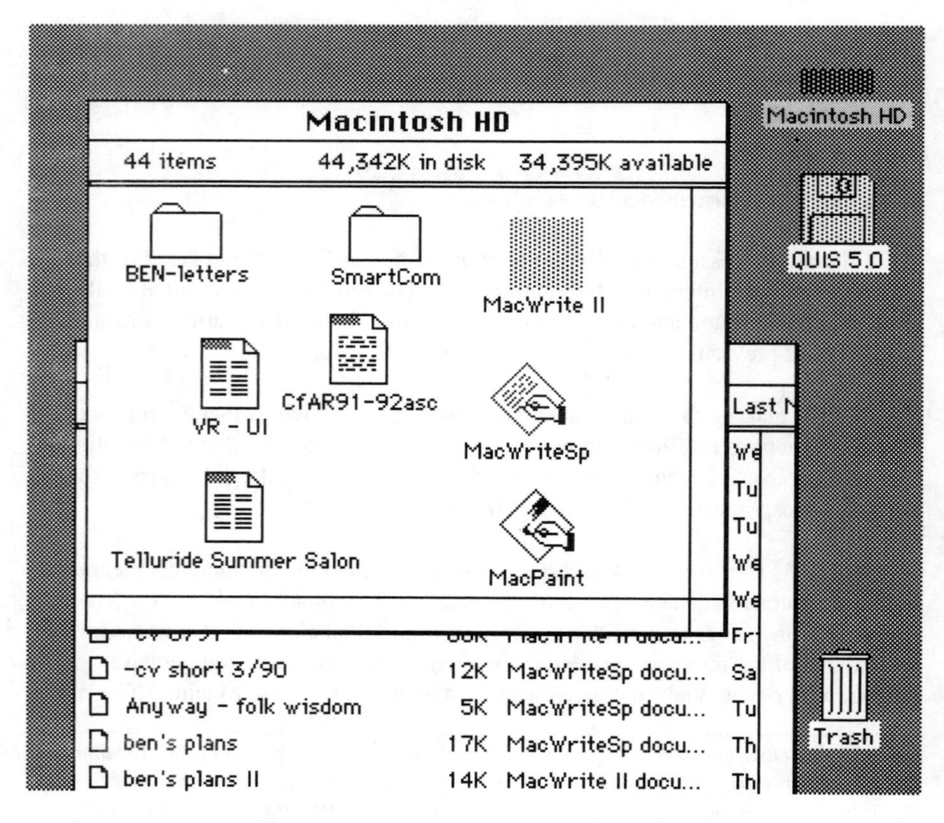

Figure 1.

combine the appearance of overlapping windows with the appearance of graphical icons lying on a desktop. The sequence of displays (opening an icon into a window that contains more icons, and then opening one or more of those icons into windows that overlap on the screen) and the resulting appearance shown in Figure 1 was not possible on any other interface that existed at the time the Lisa and Macintosh were introduced.

3a(2) Opening a window on the Macintosh results in "zooming rectangles," an effect conceived by Larry Tesler for the Lisa that was unique to Apple and produces a distinctive and identifiable Apple look [G28, G29].

3a(3) The top-most window on the desktop is designated as the active window and displays a filled in title bar and scroll bars [B1]. Macintosh users quickly learn that filling-in or decorating a feature is associated with changing that item from inactive to active. The Macintosh reinforces this impression by displaying an inactive window with the details of its title bar and scroll bars "whited out."

3a(4) Apple's designers chose to always place the active window on top of all other open windows before the user can interact with that window [B2]. Although in some respects this Macintosh design diverges from a desktop metaphor, Windows 2.03 and 3.0 mimic the top-most active style of the Macintosh.

3b. *Display of borders*. The Macintosh design displays the controls needed to manage overlapping windows in each window's border. Users can move, scroll, size and close a window by a combination of clicking or clicking and dragging in designated parts of each window's frame. For example, windows are moved using the title bar located at the top of each window [Dl], windows are closed with a close box that is always found in the upper left corner [A5], windows are sized by dragging from the grow box located in the lower right corner [C1], and windows are scrolled using either one of the scroll bars positioned on the right and bottom of each window [E2 - E5].

3c. *Moving animation*. The Macintosh provides a consistent and recognizable set of visual displays associated with moving any object in the environment. To show movement, Macintosh uses an outline of the object and the appearance of that outline being dragged by the mouse cursor. This series of images is applied to all moving actions in the Macintosh and is reinforced every time a user moves a window [D1], moves an icon [G4 , G20 , G21], moves the elevator box located in each scroll bar [E8], or moves the edge of a window to resize it [Cl]. Repeated and consistent use of these displays contributes to the cohesive look and feel of the Macintosh user interface.

3c(1) In the appearance of window moving, Macintosh again displays some arbitrary design choices. First, to move a window the mouse cursor must be positioned in the window's title bar [Dl]. Several alternatives could have been implemented including a move button located on the window or, as in any other system, allowing the user to click and drag anywhere in the window. Second, windows in the Macintosh may be moved anywhere on the desktop and even partially off of the desktop [A8]. The ability to move windows partly off screen was not part of Smalltalk-76, the Xerox Star or Windows 1.0. Some systems permit windows to be moved partially off screen in all directions. Some systems permit windows to be moved completely off screen (Star, SunView, Interslip D, Viewpoint, Metaphor). However, Macintosh Windows may not be moved off the top of the screen. There is no reason why Apple's designers could not have provided such a facility, but they did not. (With respect to both of these aspects of window moving, Windows 2.03 was designed with the same capabilities and limitations as the Macintosh).

3d. *The menu bar*. Macintosh presents menu choices in a dedicated horizontal band above the desktop [Fl]. The arrangement of menu choices always begins with the system menu followed by File and Edit. The first letter of each word is capitalized. Macintosh users quickly become familiar and comfortable with this display and arrangement of menu items.

3e. *Text*. Macintosh uses a proportionally spaced ont for all text that appears in the environment [A.l.d]. The use of proportionally-spaced text in all menu items, title bars, icon names and text directories gives the Macintosh a consistent and distinctive appearance.

Of the numerous aspects of the appearance of the Macintosh described above, no single one fully defines the look and feel of the Macintosh. However, each represents an attribute of the Macintosh environment that Apple's designers portrayed in an imaginative and distinctive fashion. Through exposure to the particular displays selected for the Macintosh, users develop expectations about how the interface should look and act under different circumstances. Those expectations come to characterize the look and feel of the Macintosh to its users.

4. Some of the many alternatives that Microsoft and Hewlett-Packard might have chosen in refining Windows 1.0 to generate Windows 2.03, Windows 3.0, and NewWave.

In my judgment the substantial similarity of Windows 2.03 and Windows 3.0 to the Macintosh is a result of the designer's choices and not because of necessity. Many design alternatives exist that would provide equivalent function. Also there are many ways to have improved on the function of the Macintosh and to have created a visually distinct appearance. Illustratively:

4a. *Window movement.* Movement can be displayed in a wide variety of ways. Where it is possible to move the entire window (Apollo Domain, DesqView, NeXT) this seems preferable, but when not possible a grid (X-Windows), a window corner (Smalltalk), or an XOR'd gray shadow (Tektronix Smalltalk) are just a few of the possibilities open to developers. Movement by dragging on the title bar is also a distinctive feature of the Macintosh that was copied by designers of later systems.

4b. *Opening/closing animation.* There are many ways to show the animation of opening and closing an icon besides the zooming rectangles of the Macintosh, including shooting lines, zooming grids, and an expanding gray or black shadow.

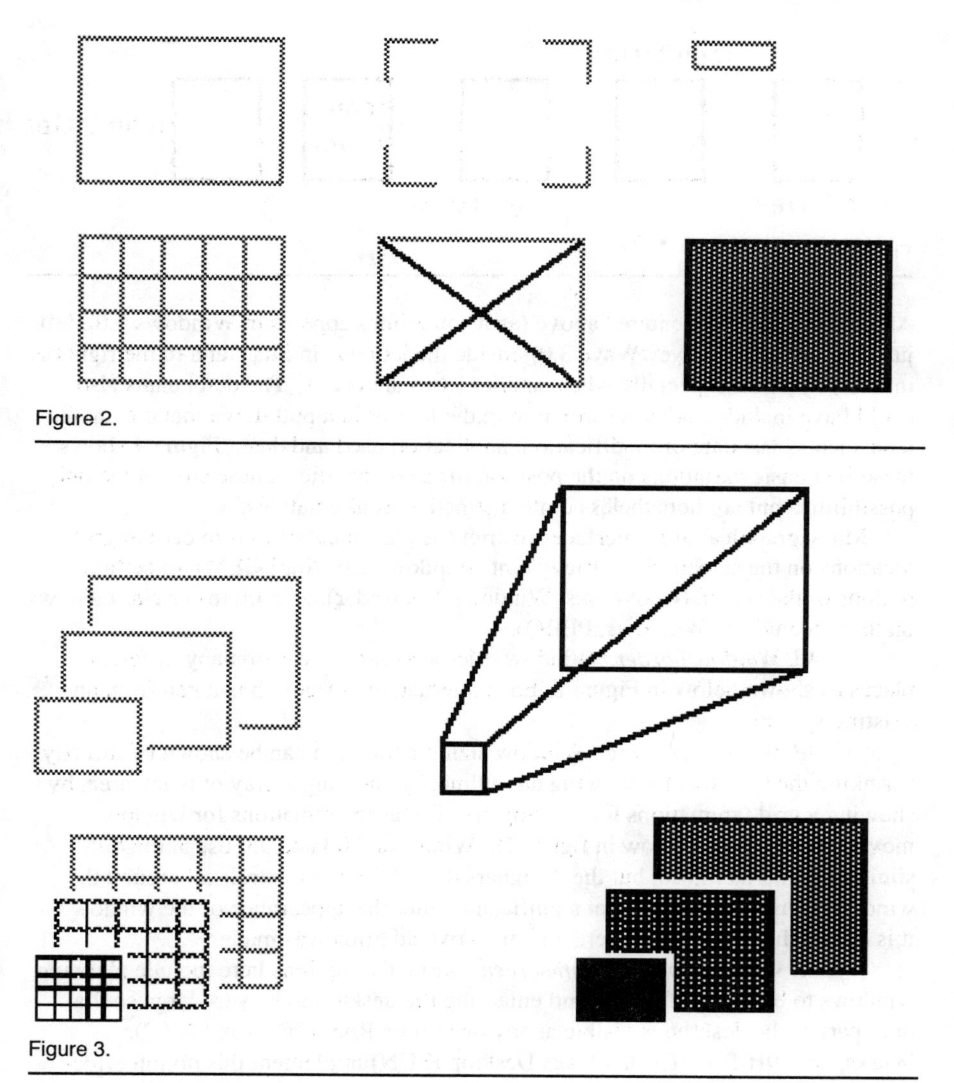

Figure 2.

Figure 3.

Figure 3 shows variations on the theme originated by Apple. Beyond this theme there is a vast number of possible ways to portray the relationship between an icon and its window. The icon could dissolve in place and the window appear in the new location; the icon could dissolve into small dots with the window emerging up from the dots; or the window could be a larger representation of the icon itself (for example, the icon of a binder or folder becomes larger and flips open).

4c. *Icon title placement and labelling* [G6]. Icon titles can be placed in a variety of places, and labelling done in a variety of ways other than the way chosen by Apple as part of the primary Macintosh style (title centered under the icon).

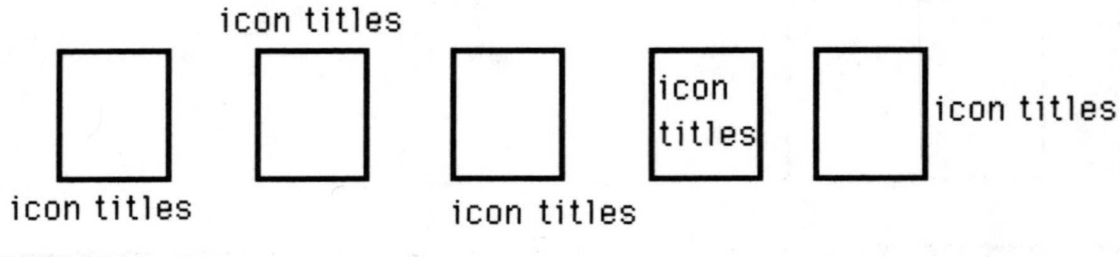

Figure 4.

Alternatives include centered above (as it sometimes appears in Windows 1.0), left justified under (as in NewWave 3.0), inside the icon (as in Star), and to the right (as in many systems, especially when smaller icons are used). The defendants also could have included other information in the title or in a pull down menu from the icon such as last date of modification, application used and date. Figure 4 shows these five basic variations on the position for an icons title. These are not the only possibilities but are nonetheless quite distinctive as alternatives.

Many graphical user interfaces restrict the placement of ions to certain grid locations on the screen (Star, Viewpoint, Windows 1.0, Atari GEM), to certain regions of the screen (GeoWorks, Windows 1.0, Cedar), or even to certain windows on the screen (DECWindows, PERQ).

4d. *Window border.* Window titles also can appear in many different places as shown below in Figure 5. Each alternative in figure 5 is taken from an existing system.

4e. *Window resizing.* Window sizing animation can be shown by directly shrinking the window, by showing an outline, by showing a gray or black area, by showing a grid (animations for resizing are similar to animations for window movement, as shown below in figure 2). Windows 2.03 and 3.0 use animation similar to the Macintosh, but the designers did add sizing controls all around the window. This change does not significantly alter the appearance of the window but it is one of the few places where an innovative addition was made.

4f. *Windows partially off screen.* Attractive options here include allowing windows to be fully off screen and enlarging the desktop to be very large so that only part of the desktop is visible at any one time. Rooms (Xerox PARC), Workspaces 9H-P VUE), and Oaks Desktop (SUN) implement this notion effectively, allowing users to move among collections of open windows. Layers of windows as in Piles-of-Tiles (GO PenPoint) also allow greater flexibility in managing multiple windows, or windows could automatically resize to a smaller window when they hit the side of the screen. Finally, defendants did not need to have windows that could appear partially off the screen at all (Star, SunView, Interslip D, Metaphor, Viewpoint, Smalltalk-76).

4g. *Top window active.* There are a variety of ways to show a window being made active, such as selecting from a menu or clicking on a control point on the window border. Some systems allow a non-top window to be active (SunView, OpenLook). Some systems allow every window to be active with keyboard input

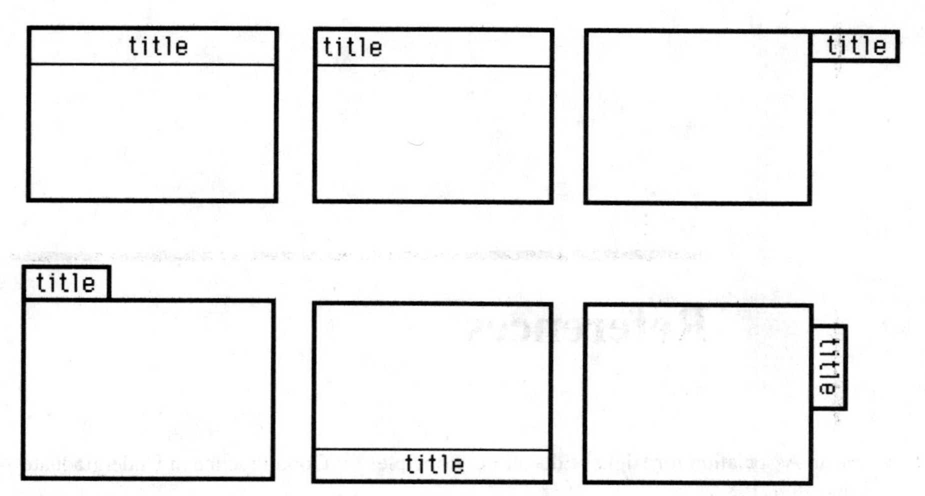

Figure 5.

being sent to the window which contains the mouse cursor. Some systems activate windows by selecting a command such as TOP or FRONT from a pop-up menu.

5. *Refinements of the "Macintosh Look and Feel"*. There are many other refinements that Microsoft and Hewlett-Packard could have made to the Macintosh look and feel that would have represented distinctive innovations and mitigated the mimicking of the Macintosh. For example, synchronized scrolling in which the scroll bar of one window might be linked to another scroll bar so that movement of one scroll bar would cause the other window to also scroll its contents as well. Another option for window closing would be the ability to close all the dependent windows at once. This could be applied to closing dialog, message, and help windows with a single action. Lines, shading, or decoration on the border might indicate families of windows with special marks for parents and children. Other possibilities are shown my recently published *Designing the User Interface: Strategies for Effective Human-Computer Interaction,* Second Edition (Addison-Wesley, 1992).

References

American Association for Higher Education. Principles for Good Practice in Undergraduate Education, 1987.

Eisler, R. (1987) *The Chalice and the Blade: Our History, Our Future*, Harper and Row, Publishers, San Francisco, CA.

Florman, S. (1976) *The Existential Pleasures of Engineering*, St. Martin's Press, New York.

Gay, L., Lindwarm, D. (1985) Unpublished student project, University of Maryland.

Jin, Gregory, K. (1990) An ideological foundation for the MIS profession, *Human Factors in Information Systems*, Vol. 2, Carey, J., Ed., Ablex Publishers, Norwood, NJ.

Kling, R. (March 1980) Social analyses of computing: Theoretical perspectives in recent empirical research, *ACM Computing Surveys* Vol. 12, No. 1, 61-110.

McLuhan, M. (1964) *Understanding Media: The Extensions of Man*, McGraw-Hill Book Company, New York, NY.

Mumford, L. (1934) *Technics and Civilization*, Harcourt Brace and World, Inc., New York, NY.

Naisbitt, J. (1982) *Megatrends: Ten New Directions Transforming Our Lives*, Warner Books, New York, NY.

National Institute of Education (1984) *Involvement in Learning: Realizing the Potential of American Higher Education*, Final Report of the Study Group on the Conditions of Excellence in American Higher Education.

Norman, D. (1988) *The Psychology of Everyday Things*, Basic Books, New York, NY.

Ornstein, R., Ehrlich, P. (1989) *New World New Mind: Moving Towards Conscious Evolution*: A Touchstone Book, Simon & Schuster, New York, NY.

Penzias, A. (1989) *Ideas and Information*, Simon and Schuster, New York, NY.

Piaget, J. (1964) Cognitive development in children: the Piaget papers, *Piaget rediscovered: a report of the conference on cognitive studies and curriculum development*, R. E. Ripple, V. N. Rockcastle Ed., Ithaca School of Education, Cornell University, 6-48.

Quintanar, L. R., Crowell, C. R., Pryor, J. B., Adamopoulous, J. (1982) Human-computer interaction: A preliminary social psychological analysis, *Behavior Research Methods & Instrumentation*, Vol. 14, No. 2, 210-220.

Shneiderman, B. (1980) *Software Psychology: Human Factors in Computer and Information Systems*, Little, Brown and Co., Boston, MA.

Shneiderman, B. (1985) When children learn programming: Antecedents, concepts, and outcomes, *The Computing Teacher*, Vol. 5,14-17.

Shneiderman, B. (1986) Seven plus or minus two central issues in human-computer interaction, *ACM CHI' 86 Proc.*, ACM, New York, NY, 343-349.

Shneiderman, B. (1987) *Designing the User Interface: Strategies for Effective Human-Computer Interaction*, Addison-Wesley, Reading, MA.

Shneiderman, B. (1989) A nonanthropomorphic style guide: overcoming the humpty dumpty syndrome, *The Computing Teacher*, Vol. 16, Vol. 7, 5.

Shneiderman, B. (Sept. 1989) Future directions for human-computer interaction, *Proc. Human-Computer Interaction '89 , Designing and Using Human-Computer Interfaces and Knowledge Based Systems*, Salvendy, G., Smith, M. J. Eds., (1990) Elsevier Science Publishers B.V., Amsterdam, Netherlands. Also *International Journal of Human-Computer Interaction* Vol. 2, No. 1, 73-90.

Shneiderman B. (Jan. 1991), Human values and the future of technology: a declaration of responsibility, Keynote address for the *ACM SIGCAS 90 Conference*: Computers and the Quality of Life. Also *SIGCHI Bulletin* , ACM New York.

Shneiderman, B. (1992) Engagement and Construction: Educational strategies for the post-TV era, Keynote address, *Proc. International Conference on Computer Assisted Learning* 4, Tomek, I., Ed., Springer-Verlag.

Shneiderman, B. (Oct. 1990) Protecting rights in user interface designs, *ACM SIGCHI Bulletin*, Excerpt of this paper also appeared as: Intellectual protection for user interfaces? *Communication of the ACM* Vol. 34, No. 4.(April 1991) 13-14.

Shneiderman, B. (Jan. 1993) Beyond intelligent machines: Just Do It!, *IEEE Software* Vol. 10, No. 1, 100-103.

Shneiderman, B. (1992) Education by Engagement and Construction: A Strategic Education Initiative for a multimedia renewal of American education, *Sociomedia: Multimedia, Hypermedia and the Social Creation of Knowledge*, Barrett, Ed., MIT Press, Cambridge, MA, 13-26.

Turkle, S. (1984) *The Second Self,* Simon and Schuster, New York.

Wees, W. R. (1971) *Nobody Can Teach Anyone Anything*, Doubleday Canada, Toronto, Ontario.

Weizenbaum, J. (1976) *Computer Power and Human Reason: From Judgment to Calculation*, W. H. Freeman and Co., San Francisco, CA.

Winograd, T., Flores, F. (1986) *Understanding Computers and Cognition: A New Foundation for Design*, Ablex Publishing Corp., Norwood, NJ.

Zuboff, S. (1988) *In the Age of the Smart Machine: The Future of Work and Power*, Basic Books, New York.

Appendix-HCIL publications

93-04 Sears, A. (Mar. 1993) Layout appropriateness: guiding user interface design with simple task descriptions.

93-03 Shneiderman, B. (Jan. 1993) Beyond Intelligent Machines: Just Do It! *IEEE Software, Vol 10,* #1 (Jan 1993) 100-103.

93-02 Potter, R. (Jan. 1993) Triggers: guiding automation with pixels to achieve data access, to appear in "*Watch What I DO: programming by demonstration*", Allen Cypher, Ed. MIT Press, Cambridge, MA. May 1993, 360-380. Technical report CAR-TR-658, CS-TR-3027.

93-01 Shneiderman, B. (Jan. 1993) Dynamic Queries: a step beyond database languages, to appear in *IEEE Computer*. Technical report CAR-TR-655, CS-TR-3022, SRC-TR-93-3.

92-16 Kuah, B.-T., Shneiderman, B. (Nov. 1992) Providing advisory notices for UNIX command users: design, implementation, and empirical evaluations. Technical report CAR-TR-651, CS-TR-3007.

92-15 Sears, A., Shneiderman, B. (Nov. 1992) Split menus: effectively using selection frequency to organize menus. Technical report CAR-TR-649, CS-TR-2997

92-14 Jungmeister, W.-A., Turo, D. (Nov. 1992) Adapting Treemaps to stock portfolio visualization. Technical report CAR-TR-648, CS-TR-2996, SRC-TR-92-120.

92-13 Plaisant, C., Carr, D., Hasegawa, H. (Oct.1992) When an intermediate view matters: a 2D browser experiment. Technical report CAR-TR-645, CS-TR-2980, SRC-TR-92-119.

92-12 Plaisant, C. (May 1992) Touchscreen toggle design. Abstract that accompanies a video appears in *ACM CHI '92 Conference Proc.* (Monterey, CA, May 3-7, 1992) 667-668, video available through ACM.

92-11 Chimera, R. (May 1992) Value bars: an information visualization and navigation tool for multi-attribute listings, abstract that accompanies a video appears in *ACM CHI '92 Conference Proc.* (Monterey, CA, May 3-7, 1992) 293-294, video available through ACM.

92-10 Johnson, B. (May 1992) TreeViz: treemap visualization of hierarchically structured information, abstract that accompanied demonstration appears in *ACM CHI '92 Conference Proc.* (Monterey, CA, May 3-7, 1992) 369-370.

92-09 Karl, L., Pettey, M., Shneiderman, B. (July 1992) Speech-activated versus mouse-activated commands for word processing applications: an empirical evaluation. To appear in the *International Journal of Man-*

Machine Studies. Technical report CAR-TR-630 SRC-TR-92-86, CS-TR-2925

92-08 Norman, K. L., Carter, L. E. (May 1992) A preliminary evaluation of the electronic classroom: The AT&T Teaching Theater at the University of Maryland. Technical report CAR-TR-621, CS-TR-2892

92-07 Young, D., Shneiderman, B. (May 1992) A graphical filter/flow representation of boolean queries: a prototype implementation. Technical report CAR-TR-627, CS-TR-2905.

92-06 Turo, D., Johnson, B. (May 1992) Improving the visualization of hierarchies with treemaps: design issues and experimentation, *Proc. Visualization '92*, Kaufman & Nielson, Eds. (Boston, MA, Oct. 19-23,1992) 124-131. Technical report CAR-TR-626, CS-TR-2901, SRC-TR-92-62.

92-05 Carr, D., Hasegawa, H., Lemmon, D., Plaisant, C. (March 1992) The effects of time delays on a telepathology user interface, *The Proc. of the 16th Annual Symposium on Computer Applications in Medical Care* , Frisse, M.E., Ed. (SCAMC, Baltimore, MD, Nov. 7-11, 1992) 256-260. Technical report CAR-TR-616, CS-TR-2874, SRC-TR-92-49.

92-04 Rivlin, E., Botafogo, R., Shneiderman, B. (March 1992) Navigating in hyperspace: designing a structure based toolbox, to appear in the *Communications of the ACM.* Technical report CAR-TR-606, CS-TR-2861.

92-03 Liao, H. S., Osada, M., Shneiderman, B. (Feb. 1992) A formative evaluation of three interfaces for browsing directories using dynamic queries. Technical report CAR-TR-605, CS-TR-2841.

92-02 Sears, A. (Jan. 1992) Layout appropriateness: a metric for user interface evaluation. To appear in *IEEE Transactions on Software Engineering.* Technical report CAR-TR-603, CS-TR-2823.

92-01 Williamson, C., Shneiderman, B. (Jan. 1992) The dynamic HomeFinder: evaluating dynamic queries in a real-estate information exploration system. *Proc ACM SIGIR '92* (Copenhagen June 21-24, 1992) 338-346. Technical report CAR-TR-602, CS-TR-2819.

91-15 Shneiderman, B. (1991) Education by engagement and construction: a strategic education initiative for a multimedia renewal of american education, *Sociomedia: Multimedia, Hypermedia, and the Social Construction of Knowledge*, Barrett, E., Ed., The MIT Press, Cambridge, MA 1992, 13-26.

91-14 Chimera, R., (Oct. 1991) Value bars: an information visualization and navigation tool for multi-attribute listings and tables. Technical report CAR-TR-589, CS-TR-2773.

91-13 Shneiderman, B.,Williamson, C., Ahlberg, C. (Nov. 1991) Dynamic queries: database searching by direct manipulation, video and abstract paper. *ACM CHI '92 Conference Proc.* (Monterey, CA, May 3-7, 1992) 669-670.

91-12 Plaisant, C., Sears, A. (Sept. 1991) Touchscreen interfaces for flexible alphanumeric data entry. To appear in *Proc. of the Human Factors Society - 36th Annual Meeting* (Atlanta Oct. 12-16, 1992). Technical report CAR-TR-585, CS-TR-2764.

91-11 Ahlberg, C., Williamson, C., Shneiderman, B. (Sept. 1991) Dynamic queries for information exploration: an implementation and evaluation, *ACM CHI '92 Conference Proc.* (Monterey, CA, May 3-7, 1992) 619-626. Technical report CAR-TR-584, CS-TR-2763.

91-10 Shneiderman, B. (July 1991) Visual user interfaces for information exploration, *1991 ASIS Proc.*, 379-384. Technical report CAR-TR-577, CS-TR-2748.

91-09 Weiland, W., Shneiderman, B. (July 1991) A graphical query interface based on aggregation/generalization hierarchies. To appear in *Info Systems*, Vol. 18 #4. Technical report CAR-TR-562, CS-TR-2702.

91-08 Norman, K. (1991) Models of mind and machines, information flow and control between humans and computers. *Advances in Computers*, Vol. 32 , M. Yovits, Ed., Academic Press Inc., NY, NY (1991)201-254.

91-07 Sears, A., Revis, D., Swatski, J., Crittenden, R., Shneiderman B. (April 1991) Investigating touchscreen typing: the effect of keyboard size on typing speed *Behavior & Information Technology*, Vol 12, #1, (Jan-Feb 1993)17-22. Technical report CAR-TR-553, CS-TR-2662.

91-06 Johnson, B., Shneiderman, B. (April 1991) Tree maps: a space-filling approach to the visualization of hierarchical information structures, *Proc. of the 2nd International IEEE Visualization Conference* (San Diego, Oct. 1991) 284-291. Technical report CAR-TR-552, CS-TR-2657, SRC-92-62.

91-05 Keil-Slawik, R., Plaisant, C., Shneiderman, B. (April 1991) Remote direct manipulation: a case study of a telemedicine workstation, *Human Aspects in Computing: Design and Use of Interactive Systems and Information Management*, Bullinger, H.-J, Ed., Elsevier, Amsterdam (*Proc. of the 4th Int. Conf. on HCI*, Stuttgart, Sept. 91) 1006-1011. Technical report CAR-TR-551, CS-TR-2655.

91-04 Botafogo, R., Shneiderman, B. (April 1991) Identifying aggregates in hypertext structures *ACM Proc.of Hypertext '91*, (San Anotnio, TX, Dec. 15-18) 63-74. Technical report CAR-TR-550, CS-TR-2650.

91-03 Shneiderman, B. (March 1991) Tree visualization with Tree Maps: a 2-d space-filling approach, *ACM Transactions on Graphics*. Technical report CAR-TR-548, CS-TR-2645.

91-02 Shneiderman, B., (March 1991) Touch screens now offer compelling uses, *IEEE Software 8*, 2, (March 1991), 93-94,107.

91-01 Chimera, R., Wolman, K., Mark, S., Shneiderman, B. (Feb. 1991) Evaluation of three interfaces for browsing hierarchical tables of contents. Technical report CAR-TR-539, CS-TR-2620.

90-13 Norman, K., (Summer 1990) The electronic teaching theater: interactive hypermedia and mental models of the classroom, *Current Psychology: Research & Reviews*, Summer 90, Vol. 9, No. 2, 141-161.

90-12 Shneiderman, B. (Oct. 1990) Protecting rights in user interface designs, *ACM SIGCHI Bulletin*, Oct. 1990. Excerpt of this paper also appeared as: Intellectual protection for user interfaces? *Communication of the ACM*, 34, 4, (April 1991) 13-14.

90-11 Botafogo, R., Rivlin, E., Shneiderman, B. (Dec. 1990) Structural analysis of hypertexts: identifying hierarchies and useful metrics, *ACM Transactions on Information Systems*, Vol. 10, No. 2, April 1992, 142-180. Technical report CAR-TR-526, CS-TR-2574.

90-10 Plaisant, C., Shneiderman, B., Battaglia, J. (1990) Scheduling home-control devices: a case study of the transition from the research project to a product, *Human Factors in Practice*, Computer Systems Technical Group, Human Factors Society (Santa-Monica, CA, Dec. 7-12, 1990).

90-09 Plaisant, C. (Nov. 1990) Guide to Opportunities in Volunteer Archaeology - case study of the use of a hypertext system in a museum exhibit, *Hypertext/Hypermedia Handbook*, Berk E. & Devlin, J., Eds., McGraw-Hill Publ. (1991) 498-505. Technical report CAR-TR-523, CS-TR-2559.

90-08 Plaisant, C., Wallace, D. (Nov. 1990) Touchscreen toggle switches: push or slide? Design issues and usability study. Technical report CAR-TR-521, CS-TR-2557.

90-07 Shneiderman, B. (Sept. 1990) Human values and the future of technology: a declaration of responsibility, keynote address for the ACM SIGCAS 90 Conference: Computers and the Quality of Life. Also in the *SIGCHI Bulletin* (Jan. 1991), ACM New York.

90-06 Sears, A. (revised March 1991) Improving touchscreen keyboards: design issues and a comparison with other devices, *Interacting with Computers,* vol. 3, no. 3 (1991) 253-269. Technical report CAR-TR-515, CS-TR-2536.

90-05 Jones, T., Shneiderman, B. (July 1990) Examining usability for a training oriented hypertext: can hyper-activity be good? *Electronic Publishing* ,Vol. 3(4) (Nov. 1990) 207-225. Technical report CAR-TR-509, CS-TR-2499.

90-04 Butler, S. (June 1990) The effect of method of instruction and spatial visualization ability on the subsequent navigation of a hierarchical database. Technical report CAR-TR-488, CS-TR-2398.

90-03 Lifshitz, J., Shneiderman, B. (March 1990) Window control strategies for hypertext traversal: an empirical study, *Proc. 29th Annual ACM DC Technical Symposium* (June 1991). Technical report CAR-TR-475, CS-TR-2356.

90-02 Shneiderman, B., Plaisant, C., Botafogo, R., Hopkins, D., Weiland, W. (revised May 1991) Designing to facilitate browsing: a look back at the Hyperties work station browser, *Hypermedia*, Vol. 3, #2, 1991, 101-117. Based on Visual engagement and low cognitive load in browsing hypertext. Technical report CAR-TR-494, CS-TR-2433.

90-01 Sears, A., Plaisant, C., Shneiderman, B. (June 1990) A new era for high-precision touchscreens, *Advances in Human-Computer Interaction*, Vol. 3, Hartson, R. & Hix, D., Eds., Ablex Publ., NJ, 1-33. Technical report CAR-TR-506, CS-TR-2487.

89-20 Furuta, R., Plaisant, C., Shneiderman, B. (Dec. 1989) Automatically transforming regularly structured linear documents into hypertext, *Electronic Publishing - Origination, Dissemination and Design* 2, 4 (1990), 211-229.

89-19 Koivunen, M. (Sept. 1989) WSE: an environment for exploring window strategies, *Proc. of Eurographics'90* (North-Holland, 1990) 495-506. Technical report CAR-TR-473, CS-TR-2353.

89-18 Plaisant, C., Shneiderman, B. (revised Feb. 1991) Scheduling home control devices: design issues and usability evaluation of four touchscreen interfaces, *International Journal of Man-Machine Studies* (1992) 36,375-393. Technical report CAR-TR-472, CS-TR-2352.

89-17 Sears, A., Shneiderman, B. (June 1989) High precision touchscreens: design strategies and comparisons with a mouse, *International Journal of Man-Machine Studies*, (1991) 34, 4, 593-613. Technical report CAR-TR-450, CS-TR-2268.

89-16 Faloutsos, C., Lee, R., Plaisant, C., Shneiderman, B. (June 1989) Incorporating string search in a hypertext system: user interface and signature file design issues, *Hypermedia*, Vol. 2, #3 1991. Technical report CAR-TR-448, CS-TR-2266.

89-15 Furuta, R., Plaisant, C., Shneiderman, B. (May 1989) A spectrum of automatic hypertext constructions, *Hypermedia*, (1) 2, (1989), 179-195. Technical report CAR-TR-443, CS-TR-2253.

89-14 Plaisant, C. (May 1989) Semi-automatic conversion to a hypertext database, The case study of the NCR management college course catalog.

89-13 Shneiderman, B. (Sept. 1989) Future directions for human-computer interaction, *Proc. Human-Computer Interaction '89* (Boston, Sept. 18-22, 1989). Also *Designing and Using Human-Computer Interfaces and Knowledge Based Systems*, Salvendy, G. & Smith, M. J., Eds., Elsevier Science Publishers B.V., Amsterdam, Netherlands. Also *International Journal of Human-Computer Interaction* (1990) 2 (1) 73-90. Technical report CAR-TR-436, CS-TR-2235.

89-12 Weiland, W. J., Shneiderman, B. (Aug. 1989) Interactive graphics interfaces in hypertext systems, *Proc. 28th Annual ACM DC Technical Symposium*, 23-28. Technical report CAR-TR-449, CS-TR-2267.

89-11 Shneiderman, B. (1989) Intelligent interfaces: from fantasy to fact, *Proc. IFIP 11th World Computer Congress*, (San Francisco, CA, Aug. 28-Sept. 1, 1989).

89-10 Hobbs, D. J., Shneiderman, B. (1989) Design, implementation, and evaluation of automatic spelling correction for UNIX commands. Technical report CAR-TR-440, CS-TR-2243.

89-09 Jones, T. (May 1989) Incidental learning during information retrieval: a hypertext experiment, *Proc. International Conference on Computer-Assisted Learning*, H. Mauser, Ed., Dallas, TX, Springer Verlag, Berlin, 235-253.

89-08 Shneiderman, B., Brethauer, D., Plaisant, C., Potter, R. (May 1989) Evaluating three museum installations of a hypertext, *Journal of the American Society for Information Science*, 40(3) 172-182.

89-07 Mitchell, J., Shneiderman, B. (April 1989) Dynamic versus static menus: an exploratory comparison, *ACM SIGCHI Bulletin*, 20(4) (1989), 33-37.

89-06 Shneiderman, B., Kearsley, G. (1989) *Hypertext Hands-On!* Available through Addison-Wesley Publ., Reading, MA, 192 pages + 2 PC disks.

89-05 Shneiderman, B. (April 1989) A nonanthropomorphic style guide: overcoming the humpty dumpty syndrome, *The Computing Teacher*, 16(7), (1989), 5.

89-04 Seabrook, R., Shneiderman, B. (April 1989) The user interface in a hypertext, multi-window program browser, *Interacting with Computers*, 1(3) (1989), 299-337. Technical report CAR-TR-437, CS-TR-2237.

89-03 Sears, A., Kochavy, Y., Shneiderman, B. (1989) Touchscreen field specification for public access database queries: let your fingers do the walking, *Proc. of the ACM*

Computer Science Conference '90 (Feb. 1990), 1-7.

89-02 Norman, K. L., Butler, S. A. (Jan. 1989) Search by uncertainty: menu selection by target probability. Technical report CAR-TR-432, CS-TR-2230.

89-01 Shneiderman, B. (1989) Reflections on authoring, editing, and managing hypertext, *The Society of Text*, Barrett, Ed., MIT Press, Cambridge, MA, (1989) 115-131. Technical report CAR-TR-410, CS-TR-2160.

88-10 Wallace, W. F., Norman, K. L., Plaisant, C. (Sept. 1988) The american voice and robotics "guardian" system: a case study in user interface usability evaluation. Technical report CAR-TR-392, CS-TR-2113.

88-09 Potter, R., Berman, M., Shneiderman, B. (Nov. 1988) An experimental evaluation of three touchscreen strategies within a hypertext database, *International Journal of Human-Computer Interaction*, 1(1) (1989), 41-52. Technical report CAR-TR-405, CS-TR-2141.

88-08 Chin, J. P. (Oct. 1988) A dynamic user adaptable menu system: linking it all together. Technical report CAR-TR-396, CS-TR-2120.

88-07 Norman, K. L., Mantel, W., Wallace, D. F. (Oct. 1988) User's guide to the menu selection prototyping system. Technical report CAR-TR-393, CS-TR-2114.

88-06 Shneiderman, B. (1988) We can design better user interfaces: a review of human-computer interaction styles, *Proc. International Ergonomics Association 10th Congress* 31,5 (Sydney, Australia, Aug. 1-5, 1988) 699-710.

88-05 Kreitzberg, C., Shneiderman, B. (1988) Restructuring knowledge for an electronic encyclopedia, *Proc. International Ergonomics Association 10th Congress* (Sydney, Australia, Aug. 1-5, 1988).

88-04 Potter, R.L., Weldon, L.J., Shneiderman, B. (May 1988) Improving the accuracy of touch screens: an experimental evaluation of three strategies, *Proc. of the Conference on Human Factors in Computing Systems*, (CHI '88) (Washington, DC, 1988) 27-32.

88-03 Chin, J. P., Norman, K. L. (June 1988) Declarative and procedural knowledge in menu systems: diagramming cognitive maps of phone and ATM commands. Technical report CAR-TR-366, CS-TR-2053.

88-02 Wang, X., Liebscher, P., Marchionini, G. (Jan. 1988) Improving information seeking performance in hypertext: roles of display format and search strategy. Technical report CAR-TR-353, CS-TR-2006.

88-01 Marchionini, G., Shneiderman, B. (Jan. 1988) Finding facts vs. browsing knowledge in hypertext systems, *IEEE Computer*, 21,#1, 70-80.

87-14 Norman, K., Schwartz, J. (1987) Memory for hierarchical menus: effects of study mode, *Bulletin of the Psychonomic Society* , 25, 163-166.

87-13 Wallace, D., Anderson, N., Shneiderman, B. (Oct. 1987) Time stress effects on two menu selection systems, *Proc. of the 31st Annual Meeting - Human Factors Society*, NY, NY.727-731

87-12 Norman, K., Chin, J. P. (Oct. 1987) The menu metaphor: food for thought *Behavior and Information Technology*, 8, 125-134. Technical report CAR-TR-334, CS-TR-1944.

87-11 Chin, J. P., Diehl, V. A, Norman, K. (Sept. 1987) Development of an instrument measuring user satisfaction of the human-computer interface, *Proc. ACM CHI '88*, 213-218. Technical report CAR-TR-328, CS-TR-1926.

87-10 Callahan, J., Hopkins, D., Weiser, M., Shneiderman, B. (Sept. 1987) An empirical comparison of pie vs. linear menus, *CHI '88 Conference*.. Technical report CS-TR-1919.

87-08 Shneiderman, B. (Aug. 1987) User interface design and evaluation for an electronic encyclopedia, *Proc. of the 2nd International Conference on Human-Computer Interaction*, Honolulu, HI, August 1987. In G. Salvendy, Ed., *Cognitive Engineering in the Design of Human-Computer Interaction and Expert Systems*, Elsevier, (1987) 207-223. Technical report CAR-TR-280, CS-TR-1819.

87-07 Lifshitz, K., Shneiderman, B. (July 1987) Window control strategies for on-line text traversal (unpublished), Computer Science Internal Report.

87-06 Chin, J., Norman, K., Shneiderman, B. (July 1987) Subjective user evaluation of CF Pascal programming tools. Technical report CAR-TR-304, CS-TR-1880.

87-05 Chin, J. (July 1987) Top-down and bottom-up processes in sorting computer menu system commands. Technical report CAR-TR-303, CS-TR-1879.

87-04 Margono, S., Shneiderman, B. (June 1987) A study of file manipulation by novices using commands vs. direct manipulation, *26th Annual Technical Symposium*, Washington, DC Chapter of the ACM, 154-159. Technical report CAR-TR-264, CS-TR-1775.

87-03 Shneiderman, B. (Feb. 1987) A taxonomy and rule-base for the selection of interaction styles Human Factors for Informatics Usability, Shackel, B. & Richardson, S., Eds., Cambridge University Press, Great Britain, 325-342. Technical report CAR-TR-265, CS-TR-1776.

87-02 Mills, C.B., Weldon, L.J. (1987) Reading text from computer screens, *ACM Computing Surveys*, 19(4), 329-358.

87-01 Ostroff, D., Shneiderman, B. (Sept. 1987) Selection devices for users of an electronic encyclopedia: an empirical comparison of four possibilities, *Information Processing & Management*, Vol. 24, No. 6, 665-680. Technical report CAR-TR-321, CS-TR-1910.

87-01 Shneiderman, B. (1987) User interface design for the hyperties electronic encyclopedia, *Proc. Hypertext '87*, 199-205.

86-11 Laverson, A., Norman, K., Shneiderman, B. (1986) An evaluation of jump-ahead techniques for frequent menu users, *Behaviour and Information Technology*, 6, 2, 1987, 97-108. Technical report CAR-TR-168, CS-TR-1591.

86-10 Baroff, J., Simon, R., Gilman, F., Shneiderman, B. (Dec. 1986) Direct manipulation user interfaces for expert systems, *Expert Systems: The User Interface*, J. Hendler, Ed., Ablex Pub., Norwood, NJ, 1987, 101-127. Technical report CAR-TR-244, CS-TR-1745.

86-09 Morariu, J., Shneiderman, B. (Nov. 1986) Design and research on The Interactive Encyclopedia System (TIES), *Proc. 29th Conference of the Association for the Development of Computer Based Instructional Systems*, 19-21.

86-08 Reisel, J., Shneiderman, B. (Oct. 1986) Is bigger better? *Ergonomic and*

Stress Aspects of Work with Computers, G. Salvendy, S. L. Sauter, & J. J. Hurrell, Jr., Eds., Elsevier, Aug. 1987, 113-122. Technical report CAR-TR-231, CS-TR-1722.

86-07 Norman, K., Weldon, L., Shneiderman, B. (Aug. 1986) Cognitive layouts of windows and multiple screens for user interfaces, *International Journal of Man-Machine Studies*, 25, 229-248. Technical report CAR-TR-123, CS-TR-1498.

86-06 Shneiderman, B., Shafer, P., Simon, R., Weldon, L. (May 1986) Display strategies for program browsing: concepts and an experiment, *IEEE Software* 3, 3, 7-15, March 1986. Technical report CAR-TR-192, CS-TR-1635.

86-05 Ostroff, D. M. (May 1986) Selection systems: interactive devices and strategies, Unpublished Masters Thesis, Department of Computer Science, University of Maryland, College Park, MD, 161 pages (see 87-09 condensed published version).

86-04 Koved, L., Shneiderman, B. (April 1986) Embedded menus: selecting items in context, *Communications of the ACM*, 29, 4, 312-318, also appeared as (August 13, 1985), IBM Research Report RC 11310. Reprinted in Hebrew in Maaseh-Hoshev.

86-03 Shneiderman, B. (March 1986) Designing menu selection systems, *Journal of the American Society for Information Science*, 37, 2, 57-70.

86-02 Shneiderman, B. (Feb. 1986) Empirical studies of programmers: the territory, paths, and destinations, keynote address for workshop. E. Soloway & R. Iyengar, Eds., *Empirical Studies of Programmers*, Ablex Publishers, Norwood, NJ, June 1986, 1-12. Technical report CAR-TR-187, CS-TR-1623.

86-01 Ewing, J., Mehrabanzad, S., Sheck, S., Ostroff, D., Shneiderman, B. (Jan. 1986) An experimental comparison of a mouse and arrow-jump keys for an interactive encyclopedia, *International Journal of Man-Machine Studies*, 24, 1, 29-45.

85-04 Koved, L. (July 1985) Restructuring textual information for online retrieval, unpublished masters thesis, Department of Computer Science. Technical report CAR-TR-133, University of Maryland 1529.

85-03 Schwartz, J., Norman, K., Shneiderman, B. (March 1985) Performance on content free menus as a function of study method (Submitted for publication). Technical report CAR-TR-110, CS-TR-1477.

85-02 Parton, D., Huffman, K., Pridgen, P., Norman, K., Shneiderman, B. (1985) Learning a menu selection tree: training methods compared, *Behaviour and Information Technology*, 4, 2, 81-91.

85-01 Weldon, L.J., Mills, C.B., Koved, L., Shneiderman, B. (1985) The structure of information in online and paper technical manuals, *Proc. Human Factors Society - 29th Annual Conference* (Santa Monica, CA) 1110-1113.

84-01 Norman, K., Schwartz, J., Shneiderman, B. (May 1984) Memory for menus: effects of study mode. Technical report CAR-TR-69, CS-TR-1412.

Appendix-videos

Open House '93 Video

- Introduction
- TreeViz: file directory browsing
- Hierarchical visualization with Treemaps: making sense of pro basketball data
- Layout appropriateness
- Improving access to medical abstracts: Grateful Med interface prototype
- HyperCourseware: computer integrated classroom tools
- Dynamic queries on a health statistic atlas

Open House '92 Video

- Introduction
- Dynamic Queries: database searching by direct manipulation
- Tree-maps for visualizing hierarchical information
- Three strategies for directory browsing
- Filter/Flow metaphor for boolean queries
- The AT&T Teaching Theater: active learning through computer supported collaborative courseware
- ACCESS: an online public access catalog at the Library of Congress
- Remote Direct Manipulation: a telepathology workstation
- Guiding automation with pixels: a technique for programming in the user interface

Open House '91 Video

- Introduction
- Scheduling home control devices
- Touchscreen toggles
- A home automation system
- PlayPen II: a novel fingerpainting program
- Touchscreen keyboards
- Pie menus
- Three interfaces for browsing tables of contents

For information about the contents of the videos:

Catherine Plaisant (301) 405-2768
email plaisant@cs.umd.edu

Name index

A

B

C

D

E

F

G

H

J

K

L

U

V

W

Y

Z

Subject index

L

M

N

O

P

The text for this book was assembled by Lian Arrow who imported existing electronic versions of these papers into Pagemaker 4.2 (donated to the lab by Aldus) from various word processing programs. For the older reports that only existed in print form, she scanned them using OmniPage Professional 2.1. Thanks to her willingness to work with programs and machines she never used before and her diligent hammering away at glitches and inconsistencies a monsterous section of work that is usually handled by a team of typesetters and paste-up artists was successfully managed by a single typist.

Teresa Casey directed and designed all aspects of production from searching for the most up-to-date version of each paper, instructing team members on programs they had never used before, styling the layout, placing the figures in the text, to designing the cover and section illustrations (except section 7), and traffic control. The cover background was made in Photoshop 2 and the type was made in Illustrator 3 (both programs were donated by Adobe).

The task of gathering the figures was similar to the text in that some already existed in a variety of electronic forms and were ready to import into Pagemaker. Older papers' figures were either redrawn or scanned to keep the original feel of the old computer look. Ara Kotchian worked non-stop to transfer figures to formats that are compatible with Pagemaker. Some of the programs were so old that the procedures and steps he had to take could qualify him as a brain surgeon.

Next, I asked him to assemble the section illustrations that I designed using a Savin 7640 copier. The backgrounds were scanned in on a HP ScanJet IIc color scanner and assembled along with the figure foregrounds in Photoshop 2. Section 7 was designed by Ara using a ray tracer on an 486 PC and combined with a scanned image in Photoshop. Even though he isn't an artist, the combination of his natural curiosity and expertise in file transferring got him through this monumental and laborous job.

I would like to thank several people who helped handle the overflow at a time when Ara, Lian, and I were doing as much as we could and production was at full throttle. Ruth Golembiewski came with an understanding of the automatic indexing and table of contents features and created the templates for those sections. Dave Turo availled himself of me to use him in whatever way neccessary to expedite the production; first he redrew a number of problem figures and next he wrestled the index into submission with the assistance of Steve Rogers.